PARIS
EVERY DAY

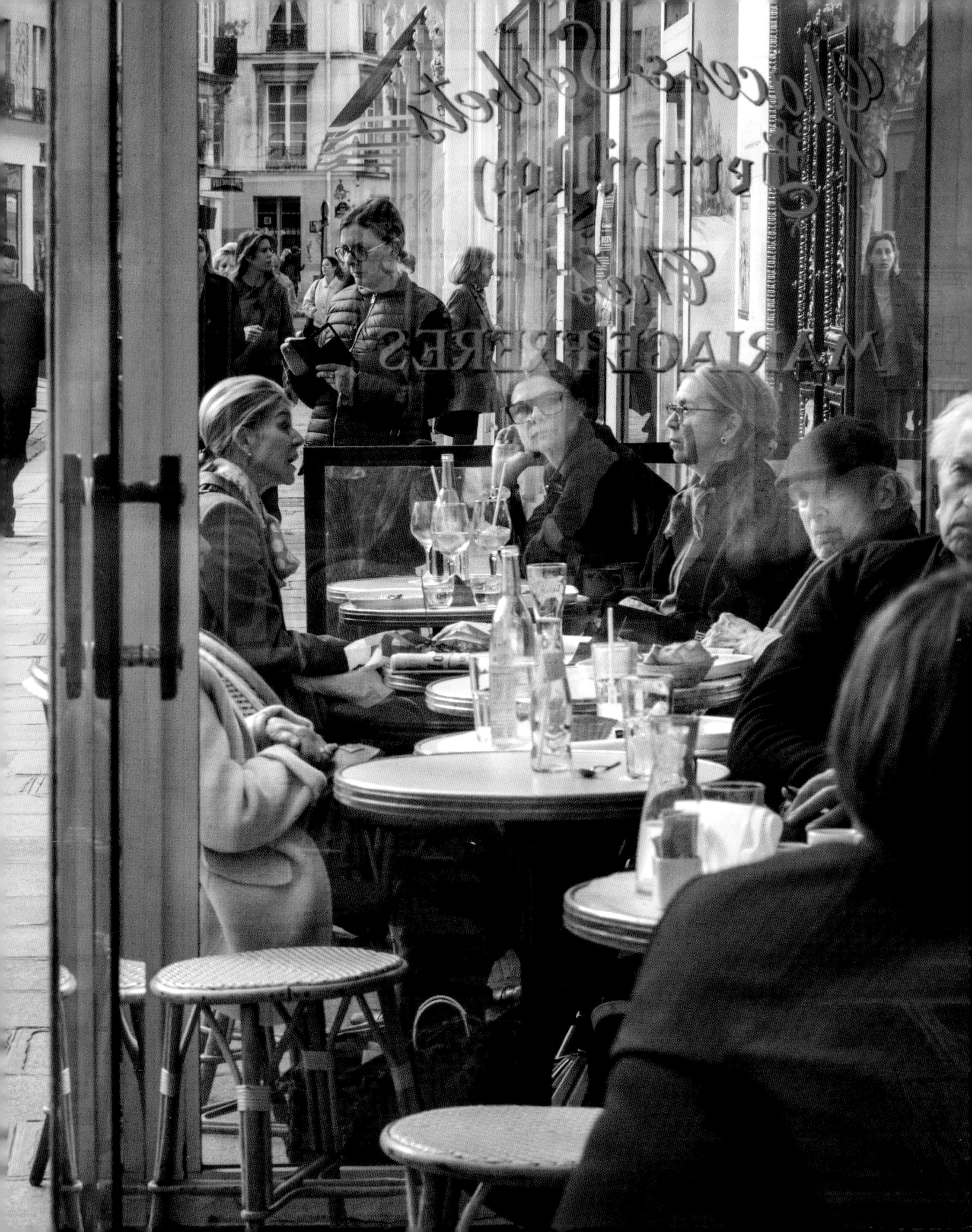

PARIS
EVERY DAY

REBECCA PLOTNICK

83 Press
2323 2nd Avenue North
Birmingham, AL 35203
hoffmanmedia.com

ISBN: 979-8-9913469-6-2
Printed in China

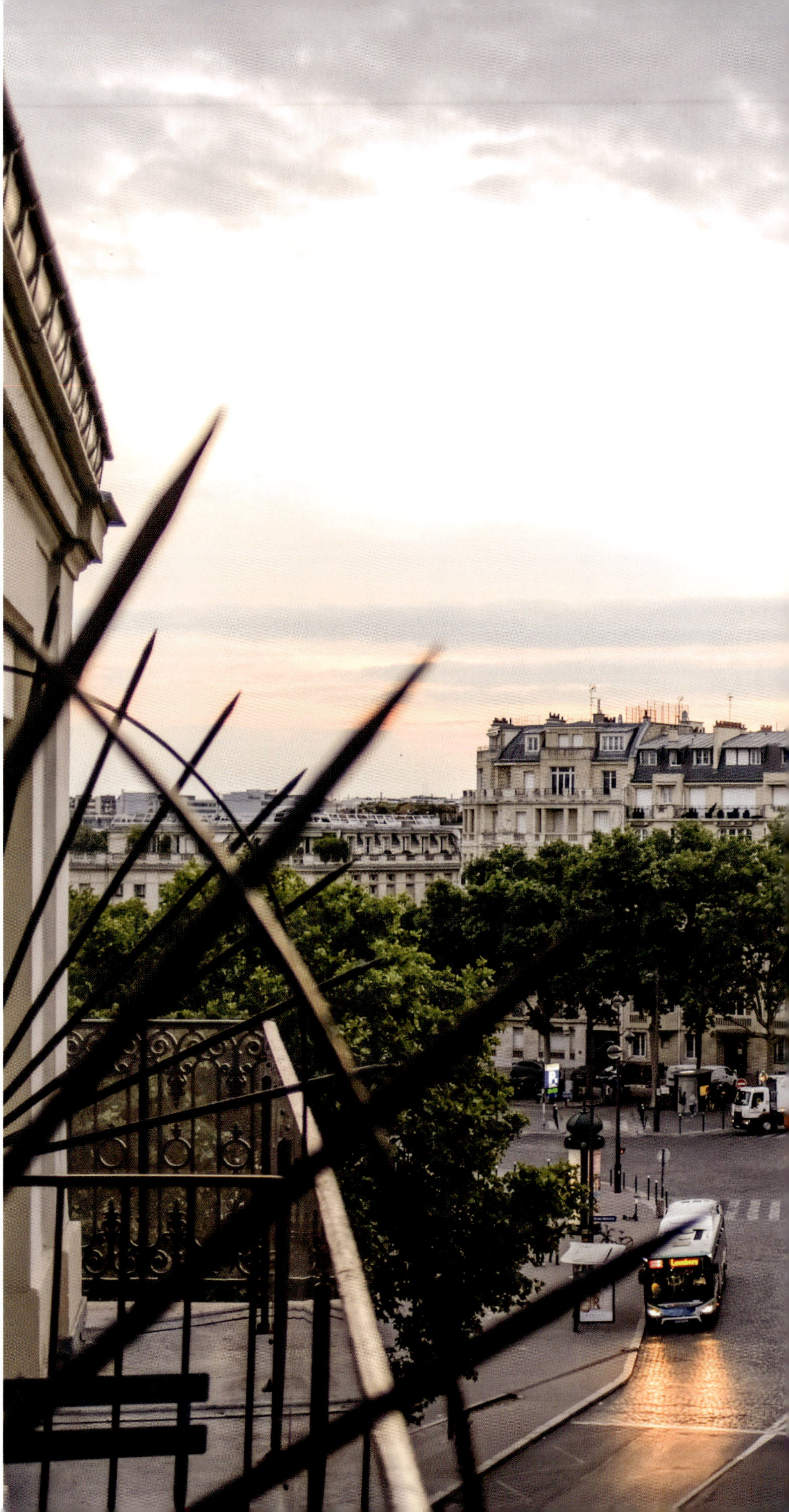

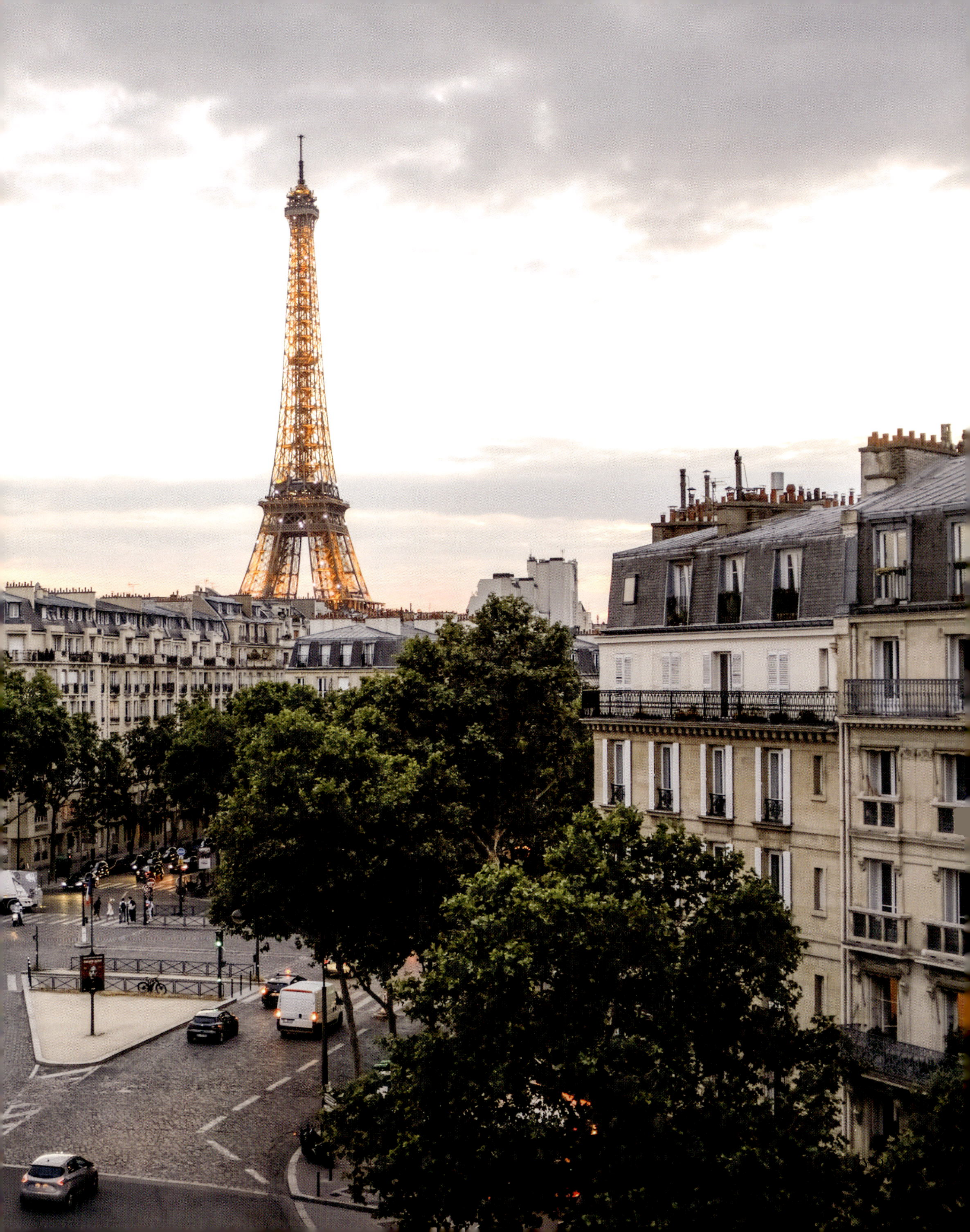

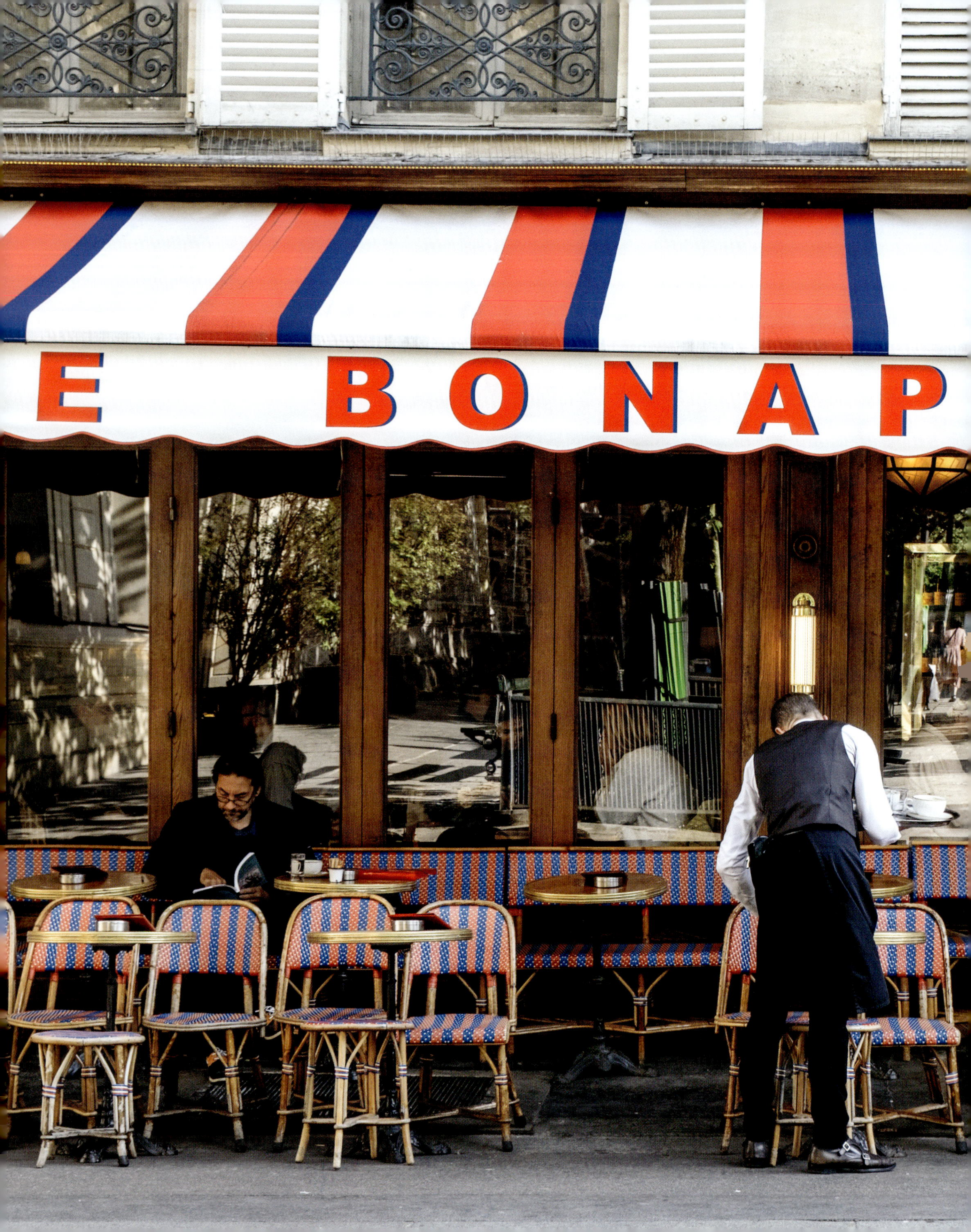
E BONAP

Contents

foreword

BY JANET SKESLIEN CHARLES

When Rebecca and I met, we immediately bonded over our love of reading and writing about France. She confided that my novel *The Paris Library* helped her during a tough time. I feel the same about her friendship, essays, and artwork. Whether we are thumbing through pages in The Red Wheelbarrow Bookstore on Rue de Médicis or enjoying a *chocolat chaud* at nearby pâtisserie Angelina, conversations about the written word flow. So, I am especially thrilled to hold Rebecca's book in my hands. For most authors, books begin with a dream and culminate because of hours of writing, revision after revision, and the key ingredient—relentlessness.

Though she makes it look effortless, Rebecca's friends know how many hours go into researching the city. We know the effort she puts into finding just the perfect place for her readers. Although I've lived in Paris for over 20 years, Rebecca constantly introduces me to new spots here. I adore Rebecca's photography and recommendations. She shines a light on beauty and community. Her artwork is a balm that reminds us of the beauty of everyday life—no matter where we are.

Rebecca's personal story is one of resilience and hope. After losing her job in 2008, she worked as a nanny day and night and started saving in order to make her Paris dream come true. In 2010, she planned her first solo trip to photograph the city. Once back home in Chicago, she sold her artwork on Etsy, and sales took off quickly. By 2011, she was working full-time as a photographer and had started her own business. Rebecca had a vision and made her dream come true. This is a beautiful book. This is your book, whether you are planning a trip to the City of Light, or simply perusing the possibilities from your armchair. In *Paris Every Day*, Rebecca shares her wisdom and unique point of view with those of us who always longed to have our own Parisian chapter.

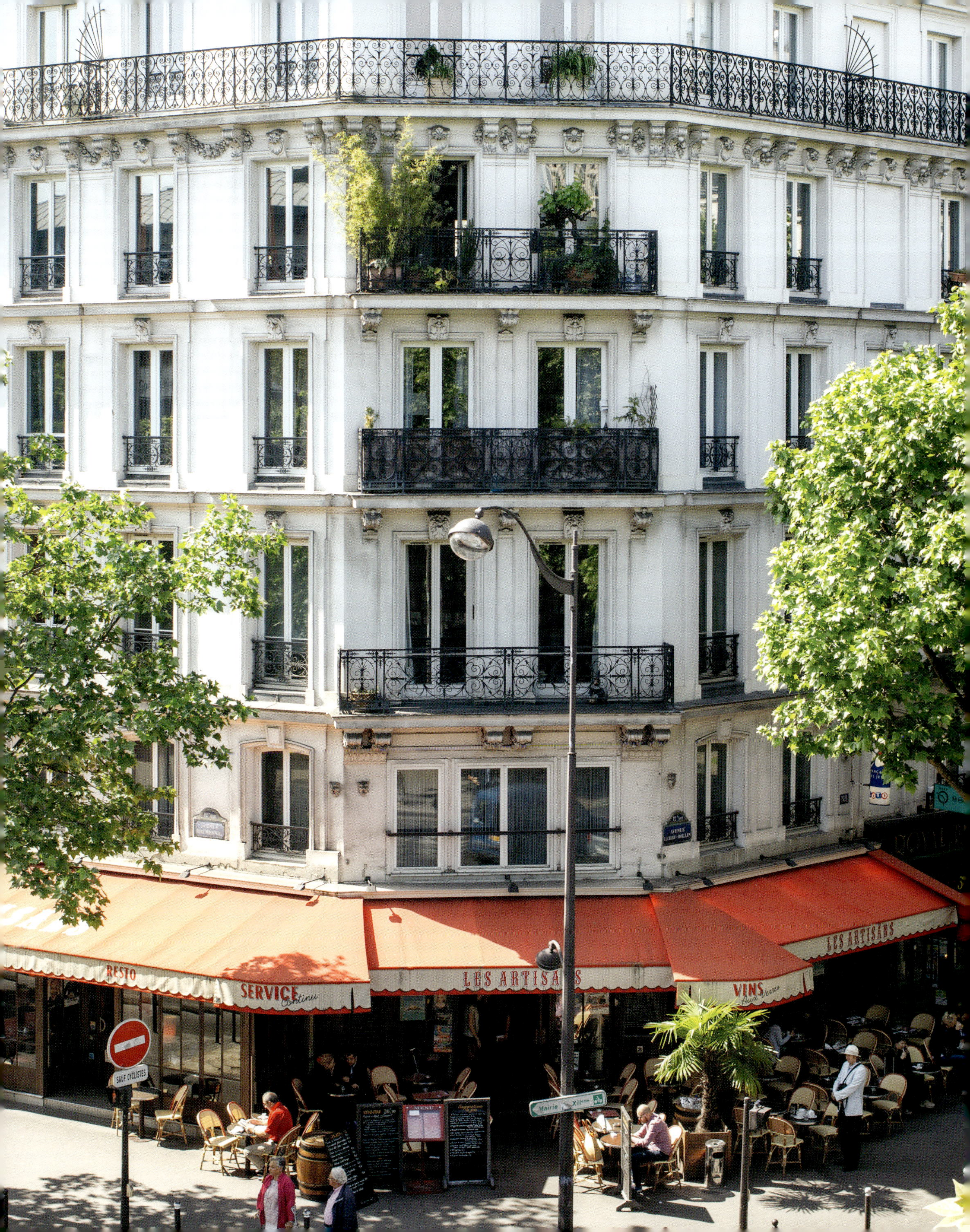
RESTO
SERVICE
Continu
VINS
LES ARTISANS
SAUF CYCLISTES

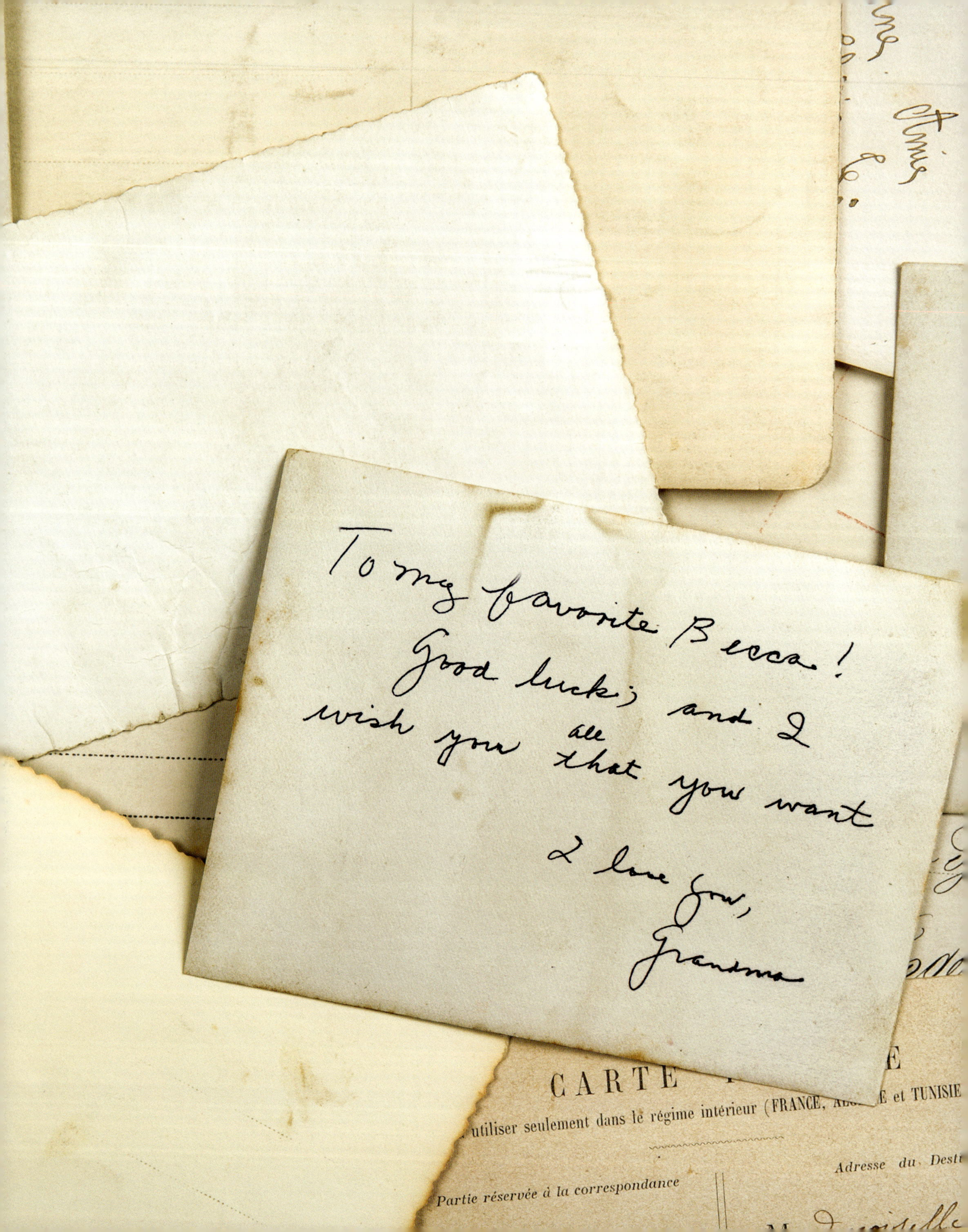

To my favorite Becca!
Good luck; and I
wish you all that you want

I love you,
Grandma

CARTE

utiliser seulement dans le régime intérieur (FRANCE, E et TUNISIE

Adresse du Dest

Partie réservée à la correspondance

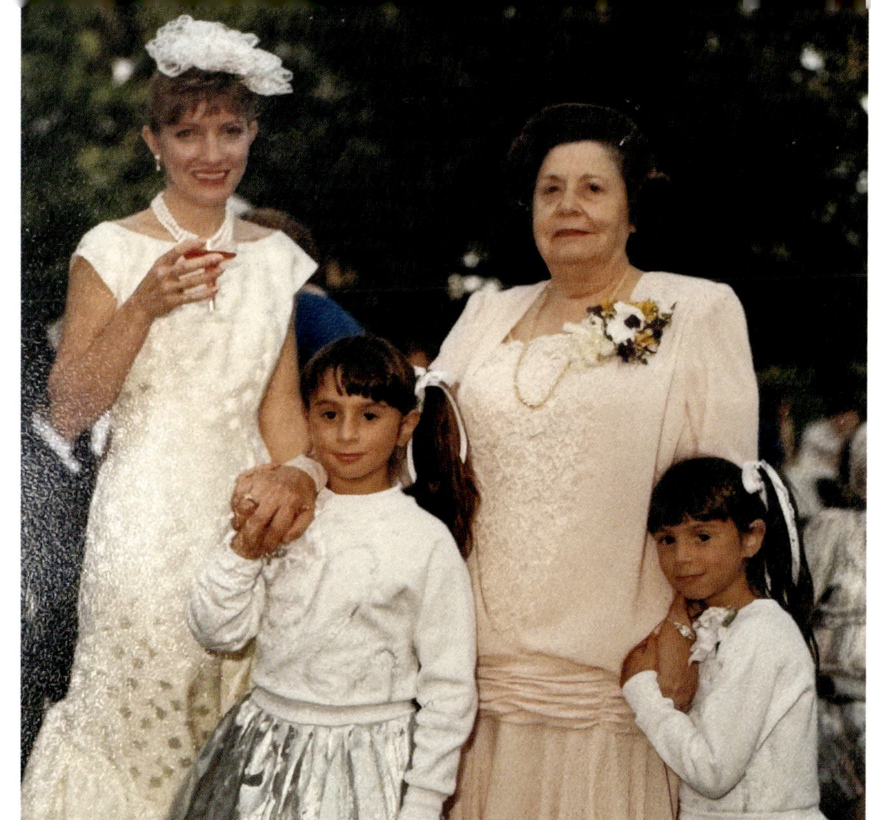

dedication

To my Grandma Plotnick, I miss you every day
and I know you are with me wherever I go.

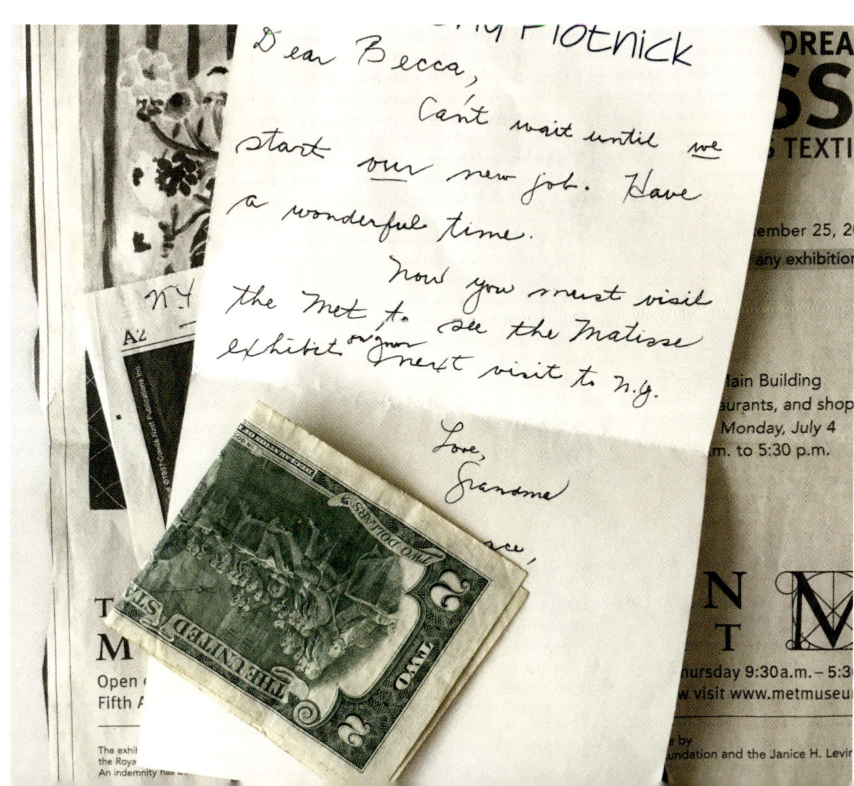

Dear Becca,

Can't wait until we start our new job. Have a wonderful time.

Now you must visit the Met to see the Matisse exhibit on your next visit to N.Y.

Love,
Grandma

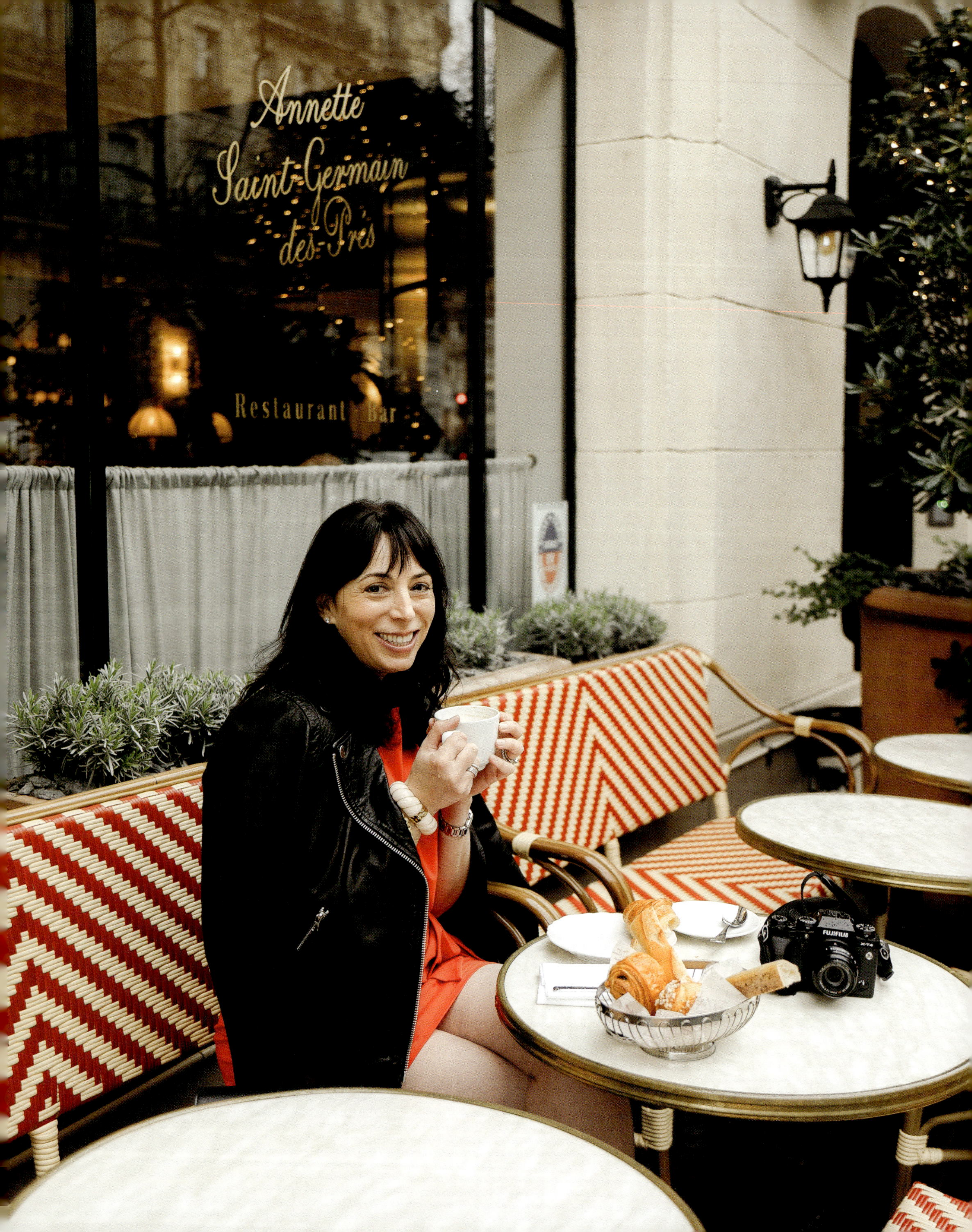
Annette
Saint-Germain
des-Prés
Restaurant Bar
FUJIFILM

introduction

Coffee-table books are beautiful! We collect, stack, and let them sit pretty on display. We flip through the pages quickly, admire the photos, and return them to the coffee table or the shelf where we found them. My intention with this coffee-table book is that you pick it up at least four times a year.

This is a collection of 15 years of photographs taken in Paris. It was not one trip, but years spent capturing the city one frame at a time. The book is broken up by season, taking you through Paris during the cold months of winter, the blooms of spring, the heat of summer, the fall transition, and the year-end with Christmas.

Each chapter should feel like a trip to Paris. Jump into the photographs. Imagine your time in Paris with memories from past trips. If you haven't been to Paris, I hope this book inspires you to take your first trip. Don't wait for the exact right moment or person to travel with you. Traveling solo is one of my favorite ways to experience Paris.

I have been fortunate to experience Paris in every season. I had the idea to publish a book, so I have been photographing and collecting images every trip. Paris has been with me through many chapters of my life—from my first solo trip, where I launched my photography business, to the loss of my grandma, a broken heart, an engagement, and now a special place for my husband and me. The city has changed with me over the past 15 years. Every twist, turn, and roadblock has led me to exactly where I am right now.

This is my love letter to the city of Paris. *Paris Every Day* is a collection of tiny moments combined to tell a larger story of Paris through my lens, season by season.

Rebecca

my story

A Passion Turns into a Successful Business

In 2008, a year of global economic turmoil, I found myself laid off and out of a job. To get back on my feet, I worked as a nanny while I turned to my passion for photography, developing my skills and creating an online Etsy shop to feature my work. I coupled this visual venture with my love for Paris and quickly found that my photographs of the French capital were the most popular with my customers. With this in mind, I headed to Paris, camera in hand, many times over the last two decades. I learned the French language and fell deeply in love with the culture. I eventually opened my own photography shop, The Print Shop, that offers captivating pictures of Parisian streets, landmarks, and day-to-day details of life in the city. I started my blog, *Everyday Parisian*, in 2016 as a result of my desire to meld the French lifestyle with American surroundings and to create a community that shares a love for Paris. This book tells my story and is a culmination of my work over the years.

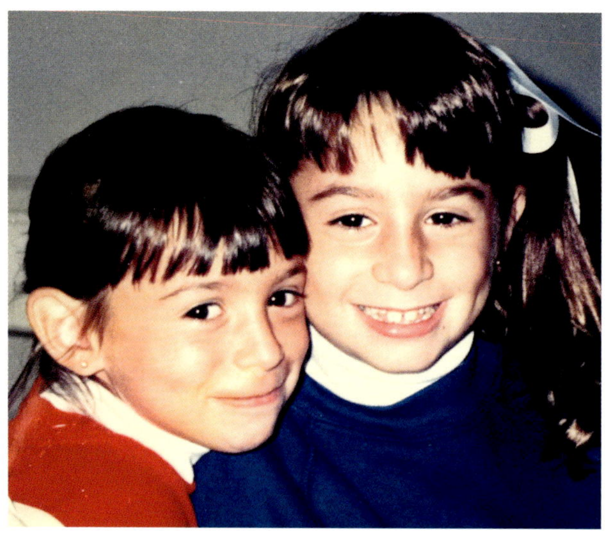

Why I Chose Paris

I don't remember at what age I fell in love with Paris as a kid, but my childhood heavily influenced me. I grew up in Cincinnati, Ohio, with an amusement park, Kings Island, nearby. The park had an Eiffel Tower replica that was about a third the size of the real one in Paris. (I have no idea why or the significance.) Visiting Kings Island was one of our favorite family activities. My sister and I would fight over which ride we would go on first, so my parents devised a game. On the drive to the park, whoever spotted the Eiffel Tower first could pick the first ride.

My sister and I were very competitive so this was a great distraction to keep us busy. My sister is two years older than me and won the game most every time. But on the occasion that I found the Eiffel Tower first, I was thrilled. I always selected going to the top of the Eiffel Tower as the first ride! My fascination with Paris continued to grow. At my middle school, students were allowed to choose a language—French, Spanish, or Latin. After hearing each teacher speak to our class, I immediately chose French. I distinctly remember learning about Parisian culture from Madame Marsh. I couldn't wait for my first trip.

The Lure of Photography

In high school, photography piqued my interest. It was offered as an elective. We learned to use manual cameras and develop our film into prints in the darkroom. The first time I put a piece of photo paper in the developer, I was hooked as I watched the image slowly appear like magic. I filled my high school schedule with courses: Photo 1 and 2, Advanced Photography, and then Independent Study. But when I graduated in 2000, photography wasn't a career path I could see working.

However, my passion for photography remained. Later, my move to digital photography and online platforms like Etsy and Shopify allowed me to make it a career. Like the magic in the darkroom, I love uploading my camera's digital storage card to my computer and opening each image. After each trip, I lengthen the editing process as long as possible. It is my way of extending my time in Paris a little longer, allowing me to relive the moments individually.

Going Abroad

My first trip abroad wasn't until I was a junior at Indiana University. Honestly, I wasn't thrilled about studying in Europe; I had to be convinced. However, spending a semester overseas was part of the college culture. I chose Florence, Italy.

This book is about Paris, so don't worry; I eventually find my way there. I went to Italy without knowing anyone on my trip, and those months abroad were about self-discovery in so many ways. The Browns, a family from St. Louis who often hired me to babysit, sent me on my sojourn with a journal, and my mom bought me my first digital camera to take along. These are two essentials that I still travel with today more than 20 years later.

My study-abroad program required us to spend three weeks in Siena, Italy, for a language-intensive class to learn Italian before going to Florence for the remainder of the trip. In the center of Siena's main square is a large tower. My friends and I climbed to the top with the motivation of gelato waiting for us afterward. At that moment, I looked down at the square and decided I knew what I wanted to do. I loved the idea of travel and seeing the world. I wanted to travel, take pictures, and find a way to make a living doing it—a core memory. In early 2003, e-commerce wasn't a thing, and digital photography still had a way to go. Creating this book was beyond my wildest dreams.

During my time abroad, my grandma was healing from the loss of my grandpa, who had passed away shortly before my first European venture. My grandma and I wrote letters back and forth weekly. I would tell her about my adventures in Italy, giving her details about where I was traveling and the foods I was discovering. I hoped my correspondence gave her something to look forward to. These letters and my storytelling heavily influence my blog to this day. I am still writing to her to share what I have experienced in Paris as if she were still with me.

My First Trip to Paris

I had a terrible case of bronchitis and very little money on my first trip to Paris as a college student, but that didn't stop me from seeing the city. On February 14, 2003, my friends and I took the overnight train from Florence to Paris. We didn't have incredible meals, and our hostel was a bare-bones establishment, but the memories of seeing the city for the first time have stayed with me. I took the double-decker bus tour of Paris and sat on the top, eating a banana and Nutella crêpe and soaking in every detail around me. It was everything Madame Marsh said it would be and more.

On my first excursion, I relied heavily on everything popular travel writer Rick Steves wrote about where to go, eat, and stay. After an afternoon at the Louvre, my friends and I were determined to find the well-known pâtisserie Angelina for hot chocolate. This was before Google Maps, and we spent hours unsuccessfully trying to locate Angelina on Rue de Rivoli. Knowing how close we were but never making it there still makes me laugh.

In one of my many high school French classes, I had an assignment on French Impressionism. I prioritized a visit to the Musée d'Orsay to experience in-person some of the paintings I had studied and to see how many I could identify by each artist. At the top of the Musée d'Orsay was the famous clock, which I didn't know much about or hadn't seen before. I shot the clock with my film camera, not knowing that the image would change my life. That print became an immediate online sales success and spurred the drive in me to continue my travel and photography pursuits.

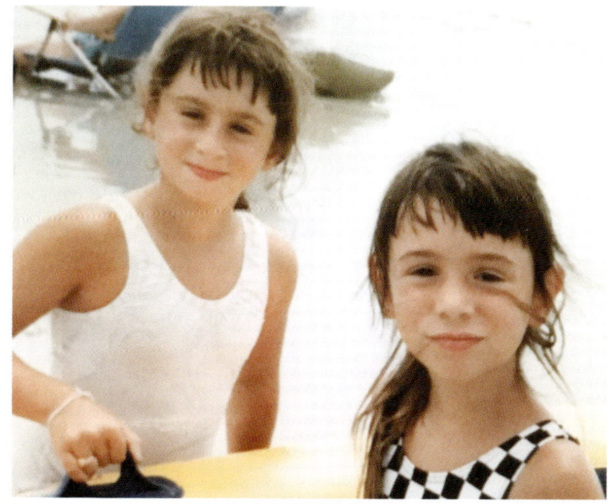

Early Work

My job path after college had little to do with where I am now. I entered a training program to become a buyer/manager at a major department store in Chicago. The numbers side of the job was what I enjoyed the most, and eventually, I became a visual merchandising coordinator, helping with department store displays for a clothing brand. Ambitious and young, my next job was in sales. Unfortunately, that job didn't last long, and I was laid off in the summer of 2008 amid the worldwide financial crisis.

In my early 20s, I had very little savings and did not expect to lose my job. However, my rent still needed to be paid. I struggled to find a position in a tough job market. Babysitting wasn't my first choice to make extra cash, but it was the most stable after a few failed attempts at starting other job paths. I worked as an overnight nanny (10 p.m. to 7 a.m.) for one family two nights a week, just enough to throw off my sleep schedule. Luckily, that family kept me on for an entire year. Baby Jack slept through the night for me very early on, which allowed me to start my online business simultaneously.

In 2008, a friend from my Italy trip told me about Etsy, which changed my life. Before, there was no online marketplace for creatives; Etsy was a new platform. For 20 cents a listing, I could sell my photography online. The price was perfect, and I didn't pay until I sold something.

Babysitting and Etsy

I picked up a few extra babysitting jobs, both days and nights. While the kids napped during the day, I worked on my Etsy shop. It was time chunking at its finest and worked so well for my Attention Deficit Disordered brain. I needed time to focus, and the house required quiet while the kids napped. Afternoons included visiting playgrounds and walking to the post office to drop off my online orders.

Finding my niche and pricing for my photography was not easy. There weren't many artists on Etsy initially. I spent four years in the darkroom learning photography in high school, but digital photography was different. My old digital camera from my study-abroad days still worked, and I practiced my photo skills any chance I got while exploring my city of Chicago. I spent a lot of time creating still lifes of food and flowers at the Green City Market.

As mentioned earlier, numbers are my passion, and I love analyzing statistics. One photograph in my Etsy shop, the black-and-white Musée d'Orsay clock from my first trip to Paris, was getting more clicks than any other piece. What if I went to Paris to photograph the city at length and then listed the images on Etsy to sell?

I told my own family I was going to Paris the following year at the end of 2009 on New Year's Eve. Their first question was, "How will you afford it?" I used airline frequent flyer miles from my previous job, money from my babysitting work, and squeezed every penny to for my first solo trip in 2010.

My First Solo Trip to Paris

My first solo trip was made possible by research and hard work. It was in 2010, before Instagram. I found as many blogs and articles as possible and made lists of what to see and do and about the areas to explore.

I settled in at a tiny hotel on Rue de Bourgogne in the 7th arrondissement. When I checked into the hotel, I asked for a recommendation of where to eat dinner. The staff directed me to the restaurant next door, Le Sac à Dos. I hesitated. Is this a tourist trap, or is it good?

My palate in my 20s was limited, and I rarely broke out of my comfort zone to try new foods. I decided on this trip that I would change this habit. The restaurant served classic French cuisine listed on a chalkboard menu and had tiny tables with red-checkered tablecloths and three people working—the owner, the server, and the cook. The kitchen was super small, and the owner chose the menu daily, depending on what was offered at the market in the morning.

During the day, I would explore as much of Paris as possible on foot, holding a paper map and my camera. In the evening, I would return to Le Sac à Dos for dinner, trying escargot, foie gras, and other standard French dishes on the menu. The owner would sit with me and point out different places on my map to explore the next day. He would also help with my French pronunciation as I ordered and shared details of my day. A few years after my initial visit, the server died of a heart attack, and the restaurant later closed.

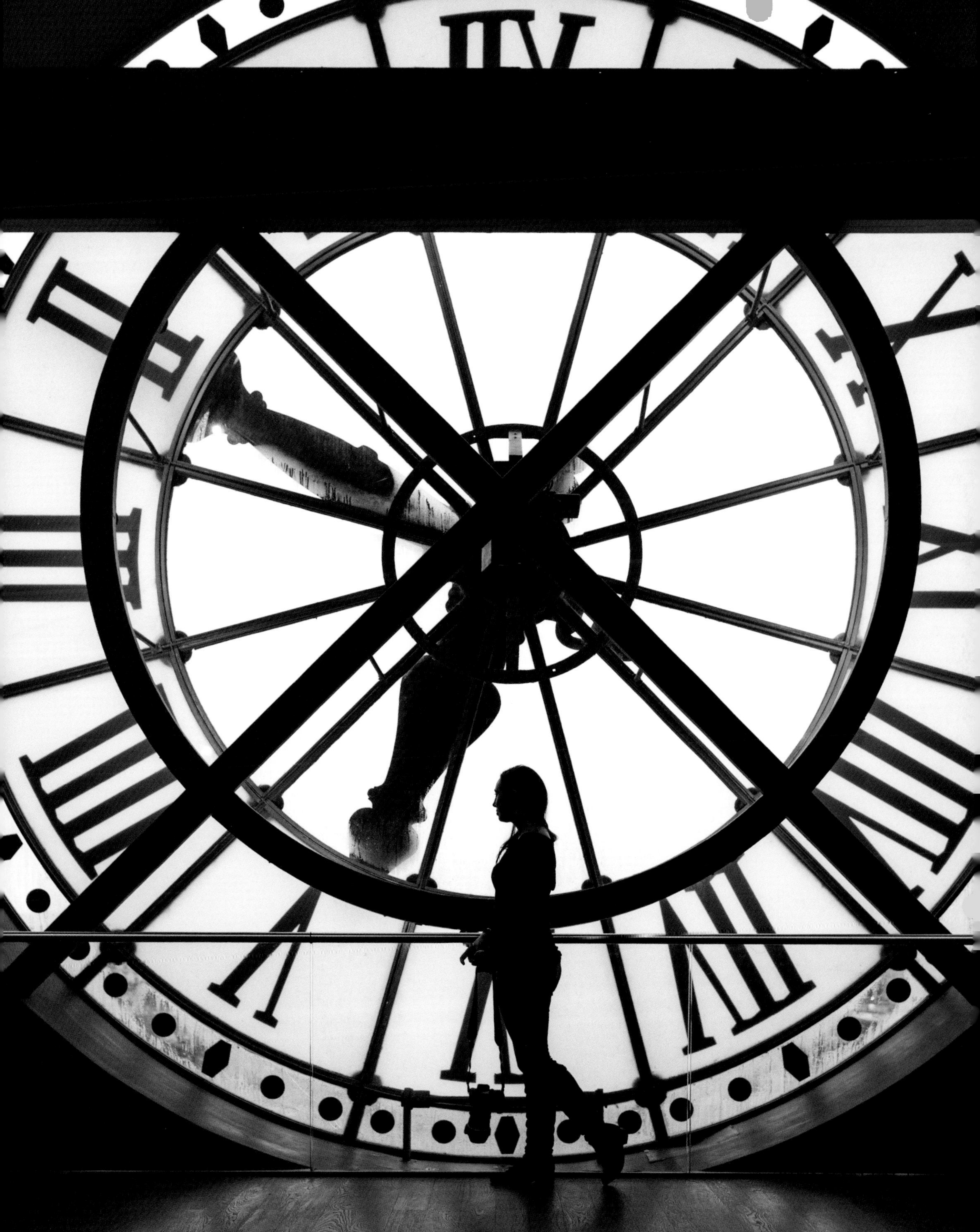

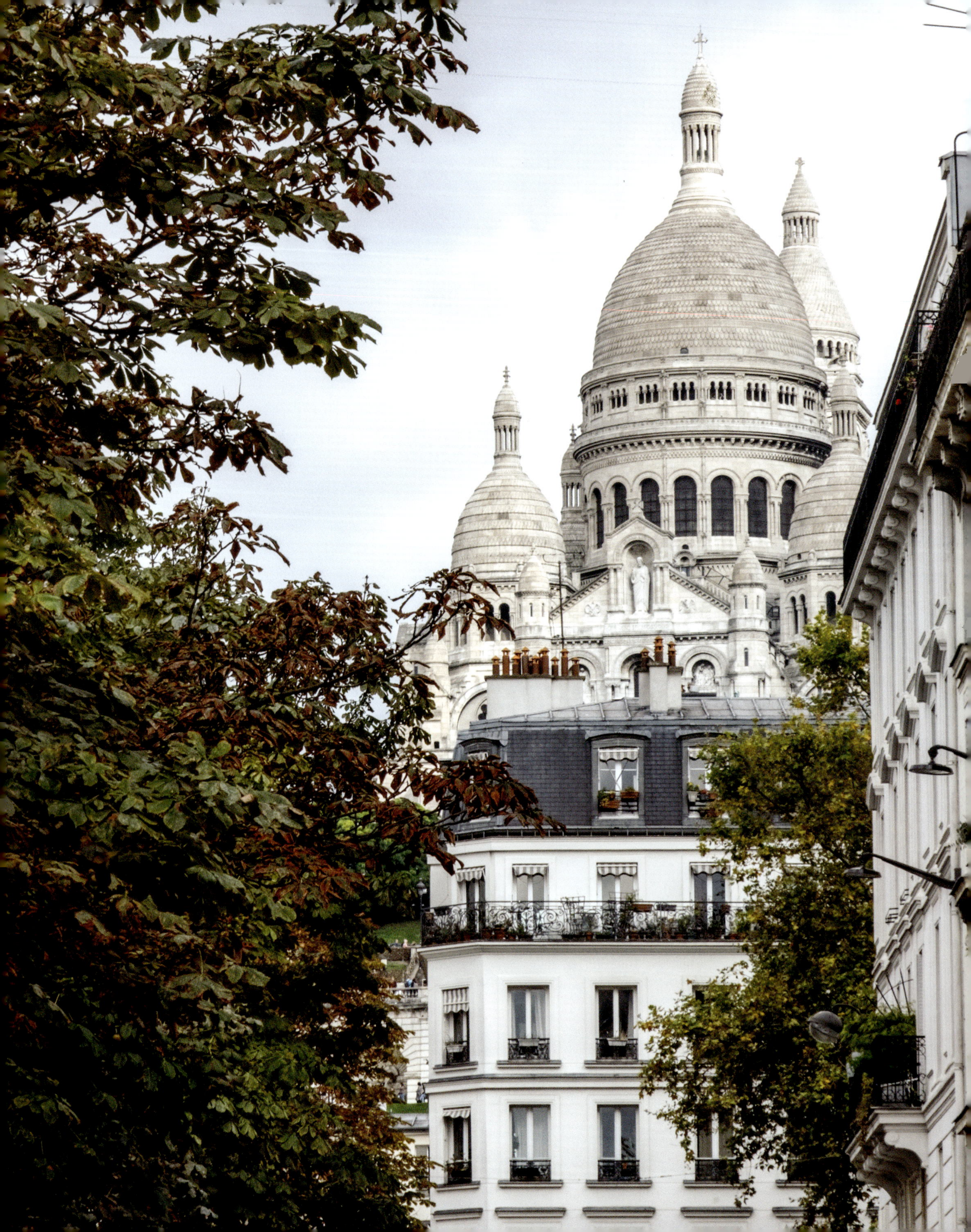

My Early Photos

I had upgraded my first digital camera and bought a new Canon for the trip. Looking back at the images I shot on my first solo trip gives me an idea of how I saw Paris. With a fresh set of eyes, I was seeing the city for the first time. My camera became an extension of me as I learned to frame what I saw through the lens. My photography style is a mixture of macro- and micro-moments. I love patterns, repetition, and color. Since I used a black-and-white film camera in high school, I still gravitate towards black-and-white images, especially on rainy days and for architecture.

Over the years, I have taught myself photography through trial and error. It is an art that I am still learning. I have saved every digital storage card since 2010. When working on this book, I had the gift and challenge of going through every digital card I had saved over the past 15 years. My photography has ranged from blurry and out-of-focus to too dark, too light, and just right.

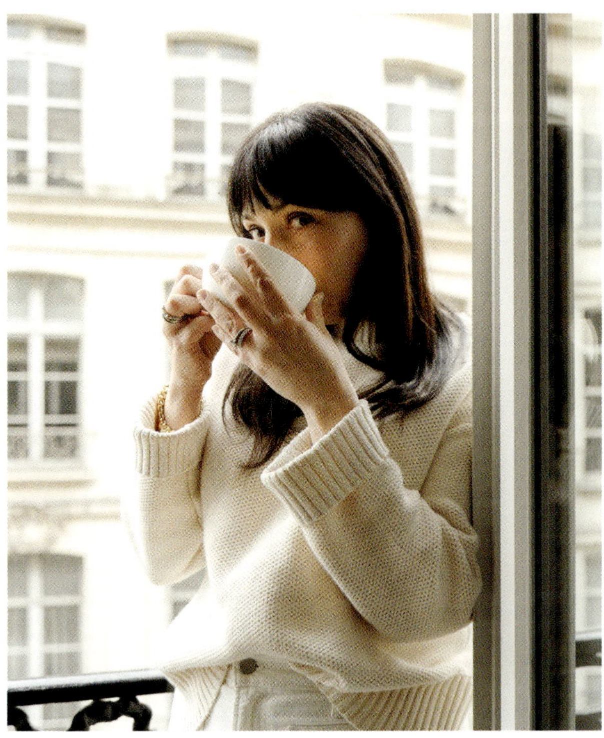

Moving to Paris

When I returned from my first solo trip to Paris in 2010, I was home just in time for my grandma's 90th birthday. Our birthdays are two days apart, and being able to celebrate with her was a priority. I am grateful we had this time together because she passed away the following year. I still think of how she encouraged me in the early days, especially when I was trying to navigate my career.

Etsy was an essential piece of my early success and helped me get to where I am today. Etsy is oversaturated now, but in early 2010, I became a top photographer on the platform. By 2011, I was on my own, supporting myself as a full-time photographer. I developed a formula that worked quite well—travel, shoot, and list prints. I booked a trip to Spain, Portugal, and France for the summer. I took the train from Barcelona to Montpelier, Marseille, and Aix-en-Provence, ending my trip in Paris. During my one-night stay in Montpelier, I saw the Woody Allen movie *Midnight in Paris* before it was released in the US. The film was quirky, but I loved the visuals, especially the opening scene showing Paris, and the movie's style has stuck with me ever since.

On one of the last days of my trip, I sat in the beautifully symmetrical Place des Vosges, surrounded by historical 17th-century buildings, and dreamed about what it would be like to move to Paris. I wanted to live like a local and experience the city now that the highlights had been crossed off my list. I figured out how to run my Etsy shop from Europe, let my lease expire on my Chicago apartment, and put most of my belongings in storage. Letting go of my Chicago apartment was important because I needed to let go if I wanted to grow from this experience. At that point, my full income came from my Etsy shop. Just before arriving in Paris, I signed my first big dream client—Pottery Barn.

Airbnb was just starting in 2013; I settled on a budget-friendly apartment in Montmartre with a balcony overlooking the Basilica of Sacré-Cœur and another overlooking the courtyard.

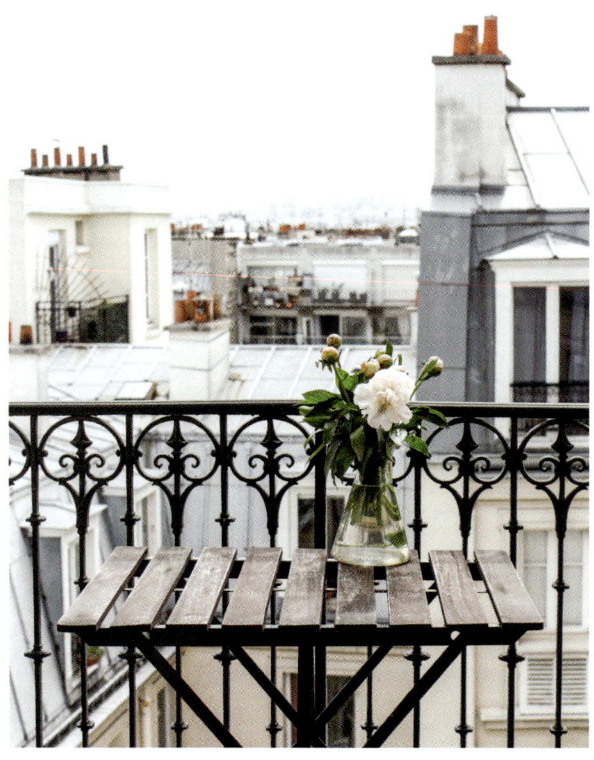

Teach People About Paris

As the move date approached, the idea terrified me. I arrived in Paris without knowing anyone besides one of the families I used to babysit in Chicago. The day I landed in Paris, I saw Nichole Robertson, a fellow Francophile and the author of *Paris in Color*, and asked her to join me for coffee. To my surprise, she agreed. At KB Café near my Montmartre apartment, Nichole and I spoke about Etsy, Pottery Barn (she was also a featured artist), and Paris. She was so kind to give me her time and some great advice. Afterwards, I returned to my apartment and wrote in my journal what she told me: "Teach people about Paris." I am so grateful for that coffee meeting; Nichole's words have stuck with me for all these years, as I write my blog and now as I write this book.

Starting over was a challenge, but no one was watching me fail or succeed. At that time, social media was just beginning to flourish, and I didn't have a blog. In 2013, my first round of living in Paris was for three months, the maximum time I could visit without a visa. Early on, I assumed I would spend most of my time alone, which would be a soul-searching adventure. The family I knew from Chicago quickly became my "Paris family." We saw each other weekly, sharing a common connection to Chicago and both having made the move to Paris.

Although a little lonely at first, I remember I had a turning point on Valentine's Day and decided I needed to stay longer in Paris despite the tug of family back home. While most people spend a short trip in one season, I experienced Paris in snow, the start of spring, in full summer bloom, and through the transition to autumn. I learned how to live out of a suitcase and to resist buying or collecting things that would weigh me down.

Ultimately, my dad put pressure on me to settle down and put roots in one city.

Exploring the City

I arrived in Paris in my early 30s on a tight budget and with no SIM card for my cell phone; I was disconnected from the world when I walked out of the door. In 2013, Google Maps wasn't like it is today, so I spent most of my time getting lost in Paris. The experience was all new and exciting, and there was so much to see. I walked around the city with my camera, capturing everything with my lens. It was very similar to how comfortable we are now with our smartphone cameras as we document our food and tiny moments each day.

Two of the apartments I rented early on were in the hilltop neighborhood of Montmartre, where the Sacré-Cœur Basilica is located, and I learned a lot about the area and the nearby 9th arrondissement. Having an apartment in Paris gave many family members and friends the excuse to visit me, including my aunt and uncle. It was great to have those memories and share "my Paris" with them. My aunt is an incredible cook, so we explored the markets nearby and prepared meals together in my tiny kitchen.

While living in Montmartre, I quickly discovered the Marché Bastille. The market was almost a straight shot from my apartment and always bustling with vendors selling different fruits, vegetables, and cheeses. The atmosphere was so lively, and I enjoyed walking through the market and observing how the Parisians lived—what they bought each week and what stands were most popular and why. I learned how the French eat seasonally.

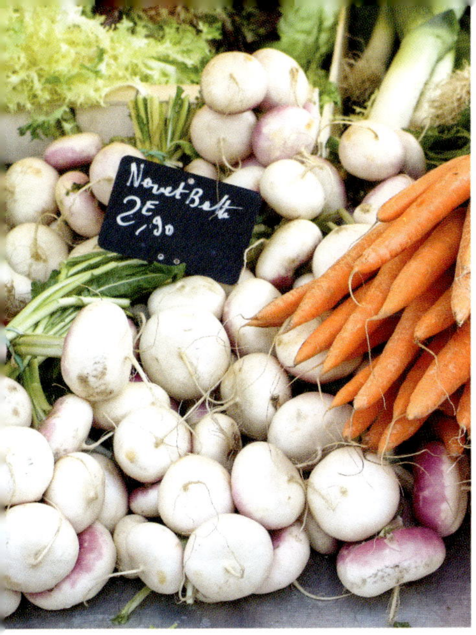
Navet Bolte
2€,90

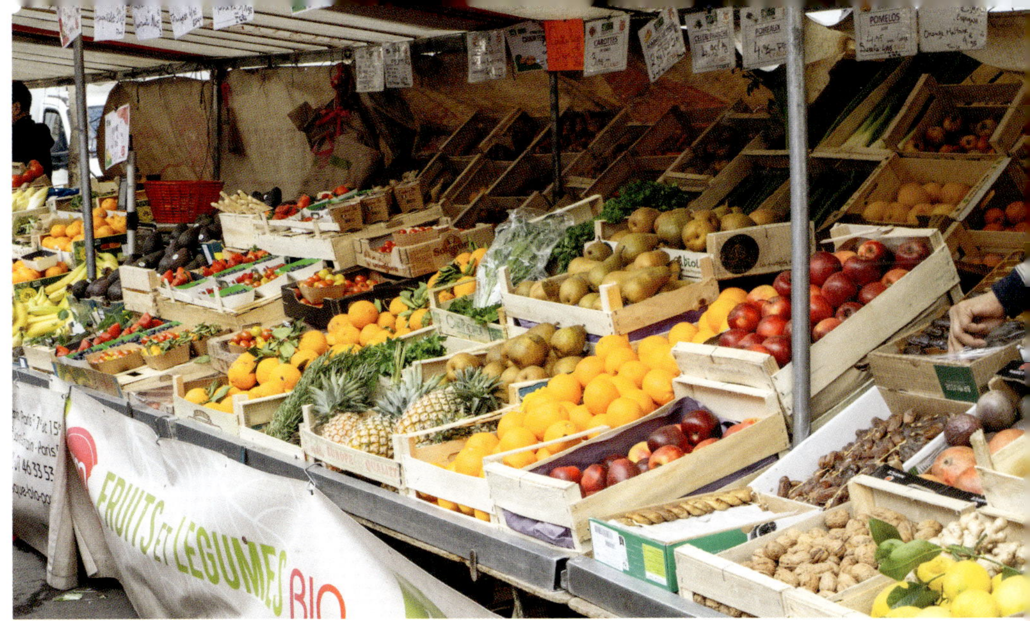
FRUITS ET LEGUMES BIO

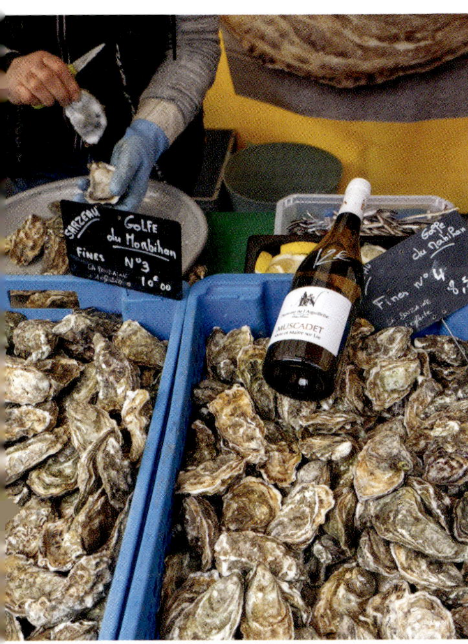
SARZEAU
Golfe du Morbihan
Fines N°3
10€00
Golfe du Morbihan
Fines N°4
MUSCADET

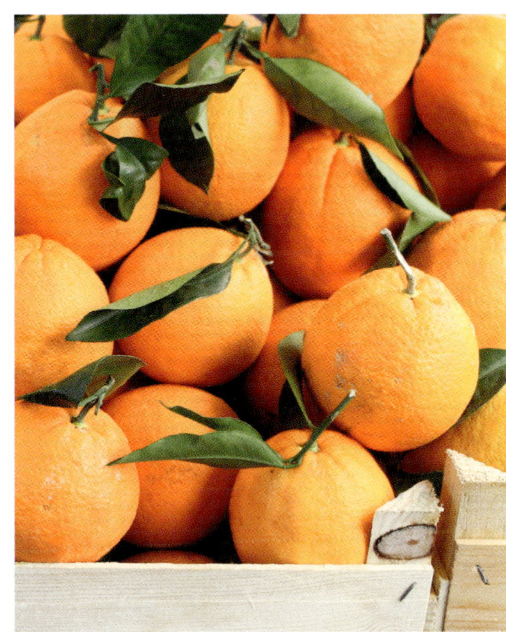

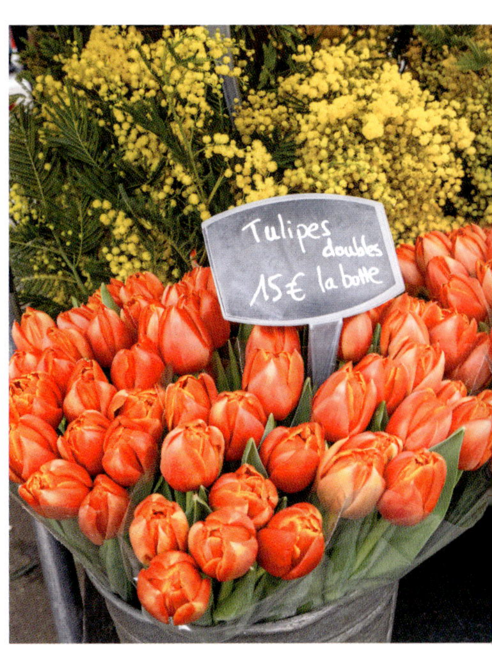
Tulipes doubles
15€ la botte

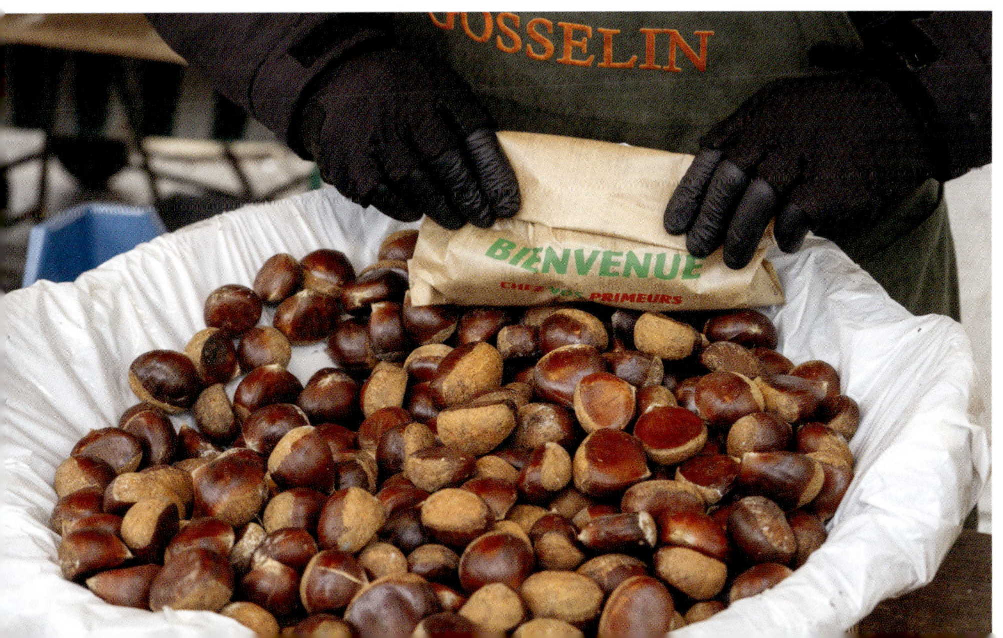
GOSSELIN
BIENVENUE
CHEZ VOS PRIMEURS

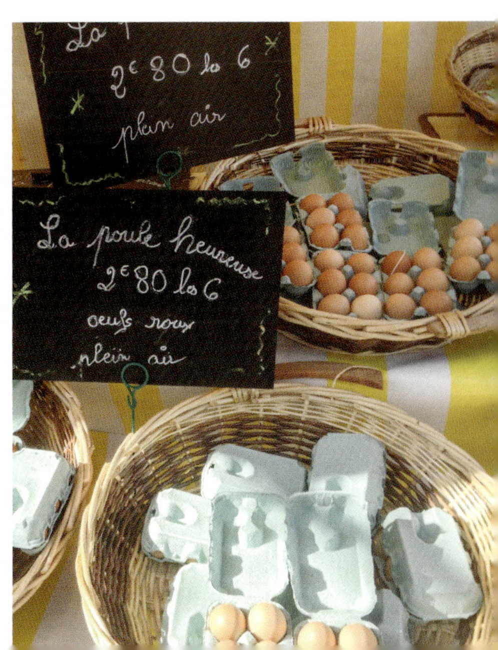
2€80 les 6
plein air
La poule heureuse
2€80 les 6
oeufs roux
plein air

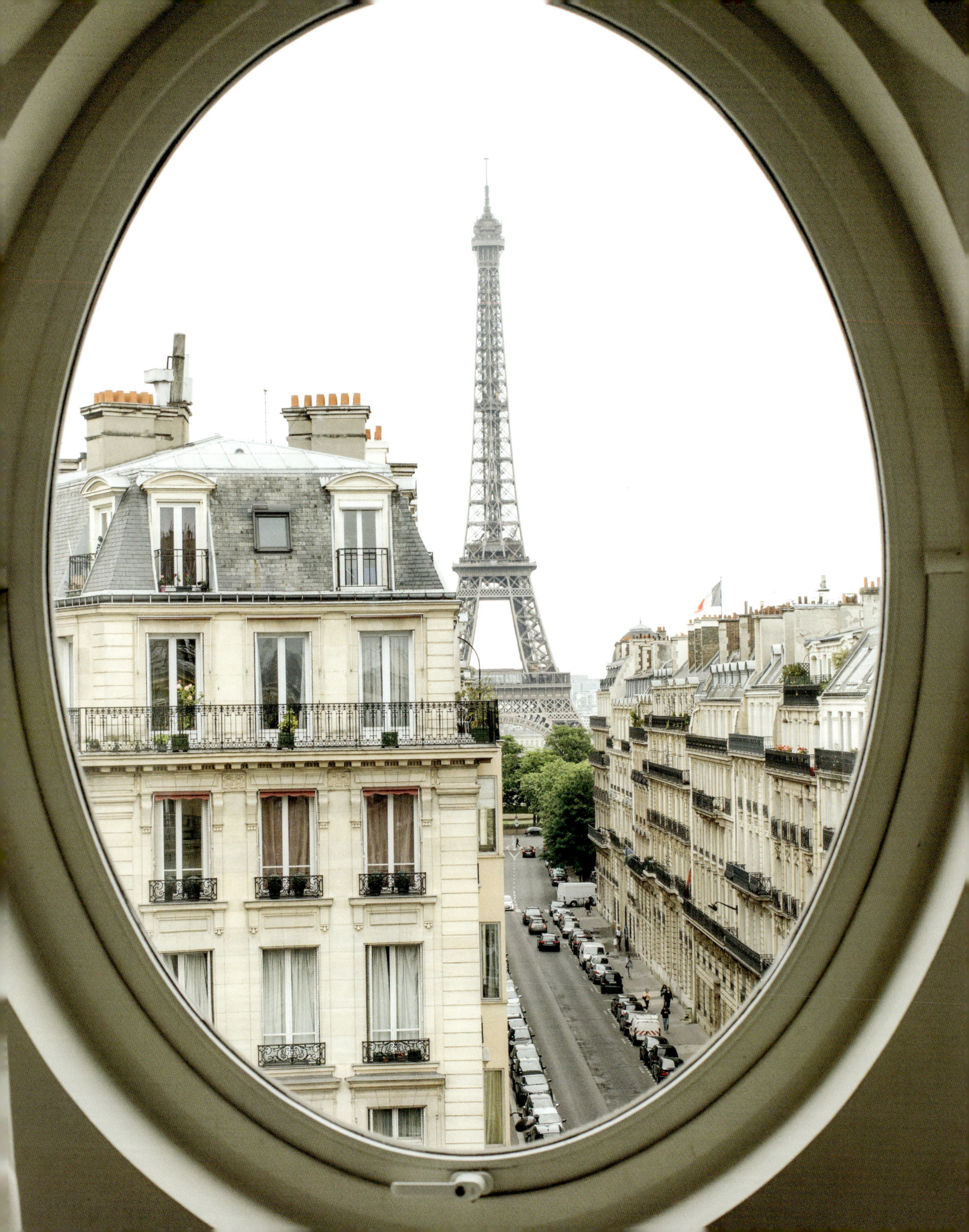

In 2015, my friend Emily and I were walking in the 16th arrondissement when I noticed among the rooftops an oval window at the hotel, Le Metropolitan.

We took a chance, went into the hotel, and asked at the front desk about the oval window. The friendly front desk person offered to let us see a room in the hotel. While riding up in the elevator, I casually asked again about the room with the oval window, and a nod confirmed that we were headed that way. I squeezed Emily's arm as we were led into the empty suite. We had just a few minutes to see the room, and I asked permission to take a photo. The room had a perfect oval-shaped window framing the Eiffel Tower. I snapped this iconic photo, a bestseller in my online store, The Print Shop.

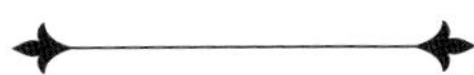

Back Home

In 2015, when I returned from my extended time in Paris, so much of me had changed—my style, mentality, daily habits, including the way I ate and shopped for groceries. There was a little Parisian in me with everything I did. One thing I did not expect after returning was the sense of disconnection from the people around me. My friends and family had continued with their lives while I was in Paris. As I grew with new experiences, so did everyone else.

Now, back in the US, I didn't feel like I fit in.

Finding My Community

Paris had influenced my life, and I was struggling to find a circle of people who were also Francophiles. I considered writing a blog but didn't know much about how it worked. During a restless night, I settled on the name *Everyday Parisian* and pulled myself to my laptop in the dark to type it into the GoDaddy Internet domain registry. Surprisingly, it was available for $12—the perfect price.

I hired one of my expat friends from Paris, Rachelle, who is a graphic designer to set up my blog and website. *Everyday Parisian* launched on July 7, 2016. Finding my voice and the topics readers were most interested in took a while. My only regret is not starting sooner. The blog allowed me to find a community of Francophiles and share our love of Paris and all things French.

Links I Love

At first, I would share articles about Paris on the *Everyday Parisian* Facebook page. As someone who loves stats, I saw these online posts get a crazy number of comments and shares from other Francophiles. Now, each Sunday, I post a roundup of "Links I Love" from the previous week. This special post is a nod to my grandma, who used to clip newspaper articles and mail them to me with sticky notes explaining why I might enjoy the read.

The articles cover fashion trends, beauty finds, travel tips to Europe, new restaurants and hotels in Paris, and more. Reading the list of "Links I Love" while enjoying a cup of coffee and croissant each Sunday has become a reader tradition. My husband, family, and friends participate by sending in articles for consideration. It has been a joy to watch the blog and community grow from my personal feeling of disconnection. I hope to continue to build my community of Francophile friends and family.

Looking for Love

Everyday Parisian and The Print Shop gave me an easy excuse to return to Paris often. When I started the blog, I assumed it would be about living the French lifestyle in the US. It was quickly apparent that blog readers wanted to know everything about Paris. Where to eat, drink, explore, and stay were at the top of their list of questions.

Since I had finally established a career and had two feet on the ground in Chicago, my trips became shorter. The idea of finding love began to occupy my mind. However, dating was always tricky, and I had more bad dates than good ones. On one of my many trips to Paris, I sat at a tiny outside table at one of my favorite spots, Au Petit Fer à Cheval, and made a list of everything I was looking for in a partner. The list idea was something I had shared with friends, but it took forever for me to sit down and do it. I ordered a glass of Sancerre and a bowl of French onion soup and started to write. Finding someone with the same values, goals, religion, and love for family was at the top of my list. Now that I had my list, there was a sense of calm.

Engagement

At the end of 2018, I met my husband at a neighborhood restaurant in Chicago after a nudge by a mutual friend. He covered my short list of what I was looking for and coincidentally shared the same birthday as my grandma. We traveled together to Paris, Amsterdam, and London early in our relationship. Finding someone who loved to travel was significant as it was a part of my life. Our relationship strengthened in 2020 when I moved in with him during the COVID-19 pandemic. We planned and looked forward to international travel when it reopened.

In 2021, I had just finished a girls' trip to Paris, and my husband planned to meet me for the weekend. We settled into the Saint James Paris—a hotel that had been on my bucket list since the pandemic. When my husband didn't put anything in the hotel safe as we checked in, I assumed a proposal wasn't happening.

Our hotel was in the 16th arrondissement, away from the city center. He suggested we take a walk after lunch, and we made our way through the city. It was a beautiful fall day, and the weather couldn't have been more perfect. My husband offered to explore hotel bars, but I refused to go inside on such a nice day. We kept walking, and we found ourselves close to the Louvre. He had found one of my favorite spots in Paris, Palais-Royal, and secretly texted my friend Katie Donnelly, who was waiting to capture a photo of his marriage proposal.

A Special Spot

I had lived in an apartment around the corner from Palais-Royal, and would walk through the gardens daily. It was my dream location for an engagement. As we approached the area, it dawned on me what was about to happen. Tears filled my eyes as we walked through the columns and garden to the fountain. He dropped to one knee and proposed. I looked up, and there was Katie with her camera.

The engagement ring was in his pocket the whole time! He slipped it onto my finger while he kissed me. I did not expect him to have THE ring.

My grandma gave me her engagement ring while she was in hospice care before she passed away. I gave it to my dad and told him to give it to the man who asked for his permission to marry me when the time was right. My dad held onto it for 10 years, and it was unchanged from when my grandma had worn it. While I was in Paris for the girls' trip, my husband met my dad halfway between Chicago and Cincinnati and picked up the ring. I had not expected to wear my grandma's ring in Paris, and it was the best surprise.

We spent the weekend celebrating and soaking up the beautiful fall weather. Now, Palais-Royal is our special place in Paris.

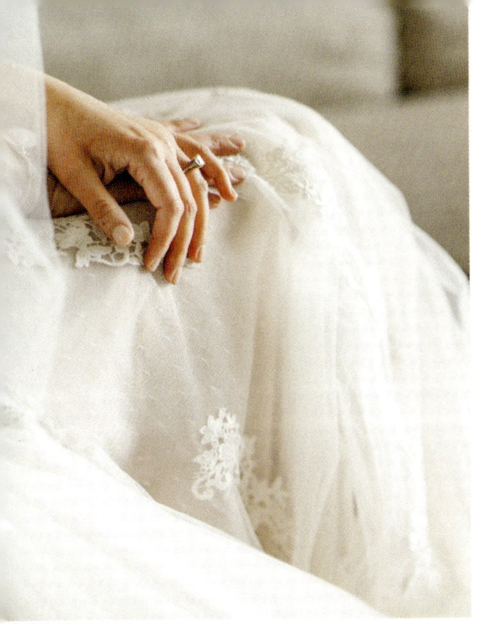

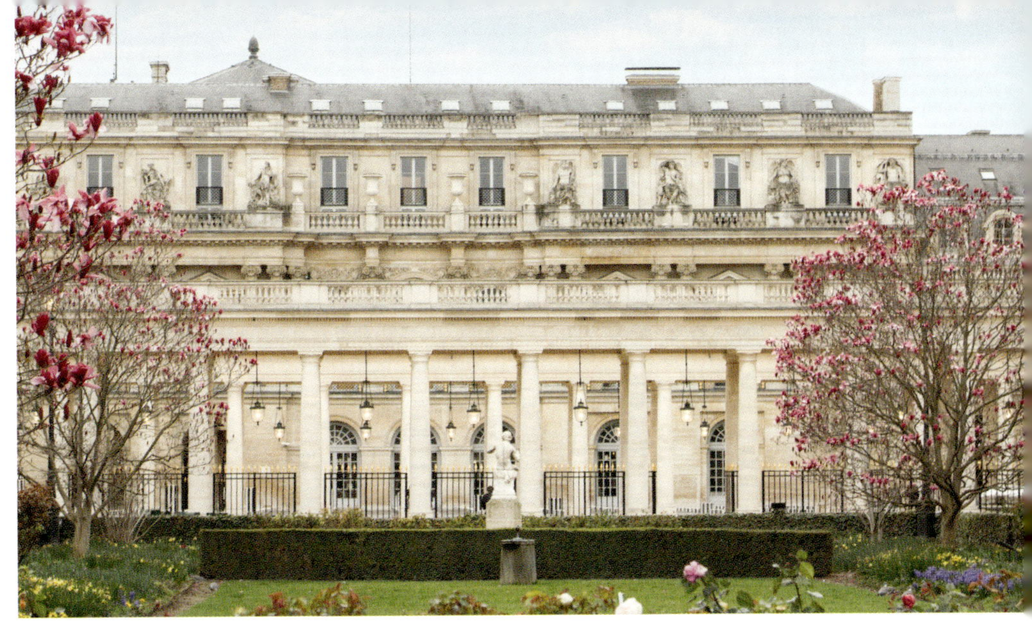

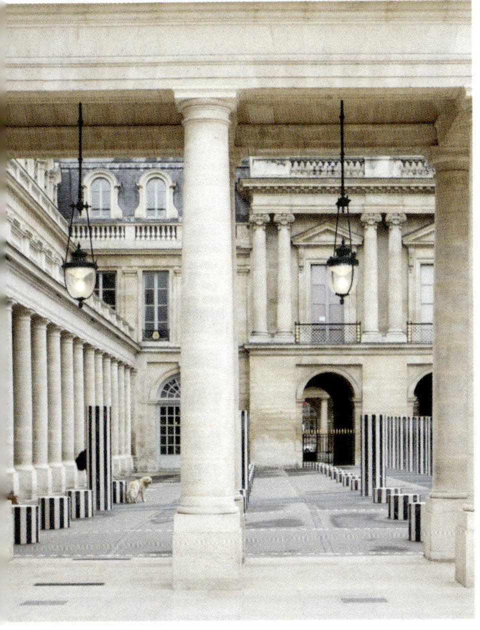

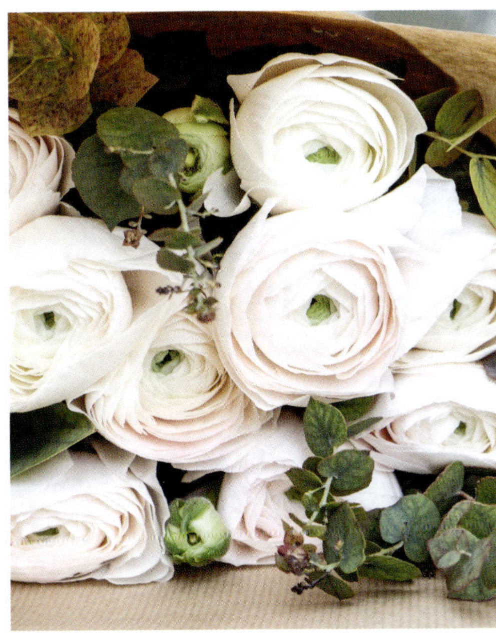

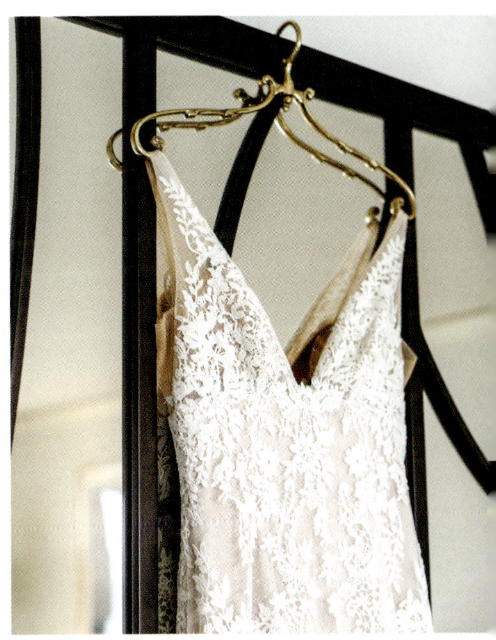

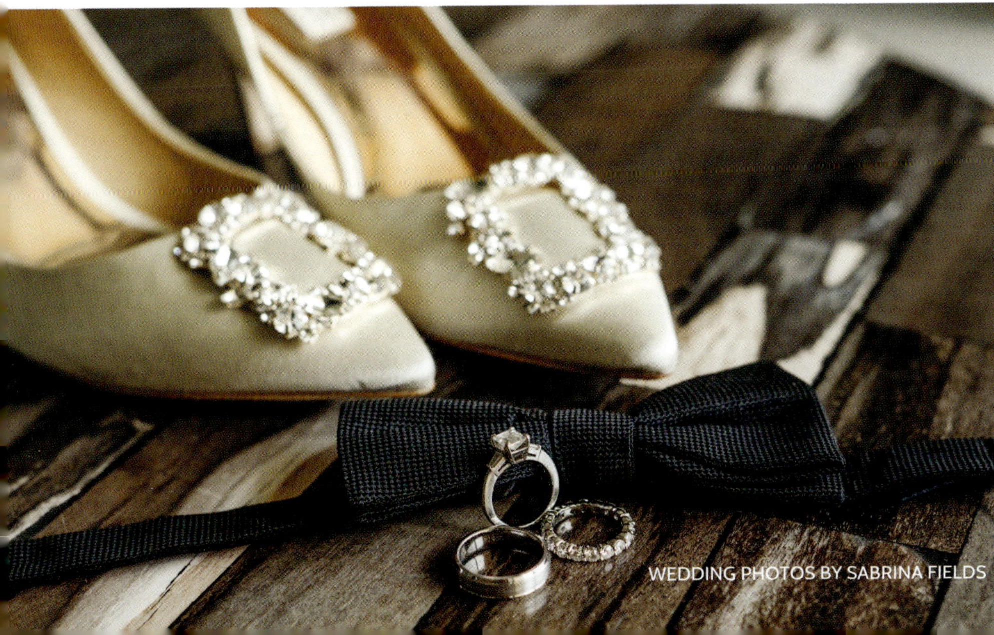

WEDDING PHOTOS BY SABRINA FIELDS

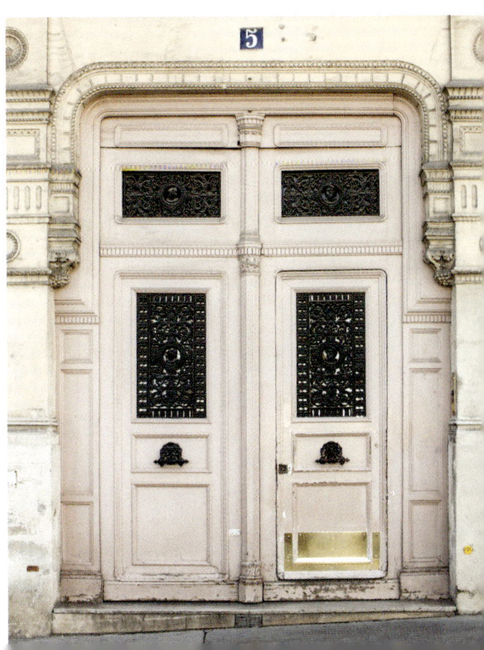

The Light

My photography and style have changed over the years, but my use of light remains the same. I shoot in the early morning when the city wakes up, and the light begins to illuminate the city. I shoot in the evening through sunset and as the city goes to sleep.

"Golden Hour" begins an hour before sunrise and creates that celestial hue in many of my photographs. This can mean very early mornings in the spring and summer. "Blue Hour" is more of a focus for me in the evenings at dusk, when the city transitions into the night. It is a very short window, and I love seeing the lights going on in apartment windows around the city and walking along the Seine River.

I love to wake up early and photograph the empty city streets. When I meet people at art shows, I often receive the question: "Why are there no people in your photos?" It is peaceful and a way for people to envision themselves in the scene.

When I couldn't travel to Paris during the pandemic, I missed the Parisians and their energy the most. I missed the gardens filled with children and friends soaking up the sunshine, the cafés and terraces with tables spilling onto the sidewalks, and the smell of fresh-baked croissants from the boulangerie in the morning.

Now, after years spent in Paris, I welcome Parisians in my photographs and see the city differently.

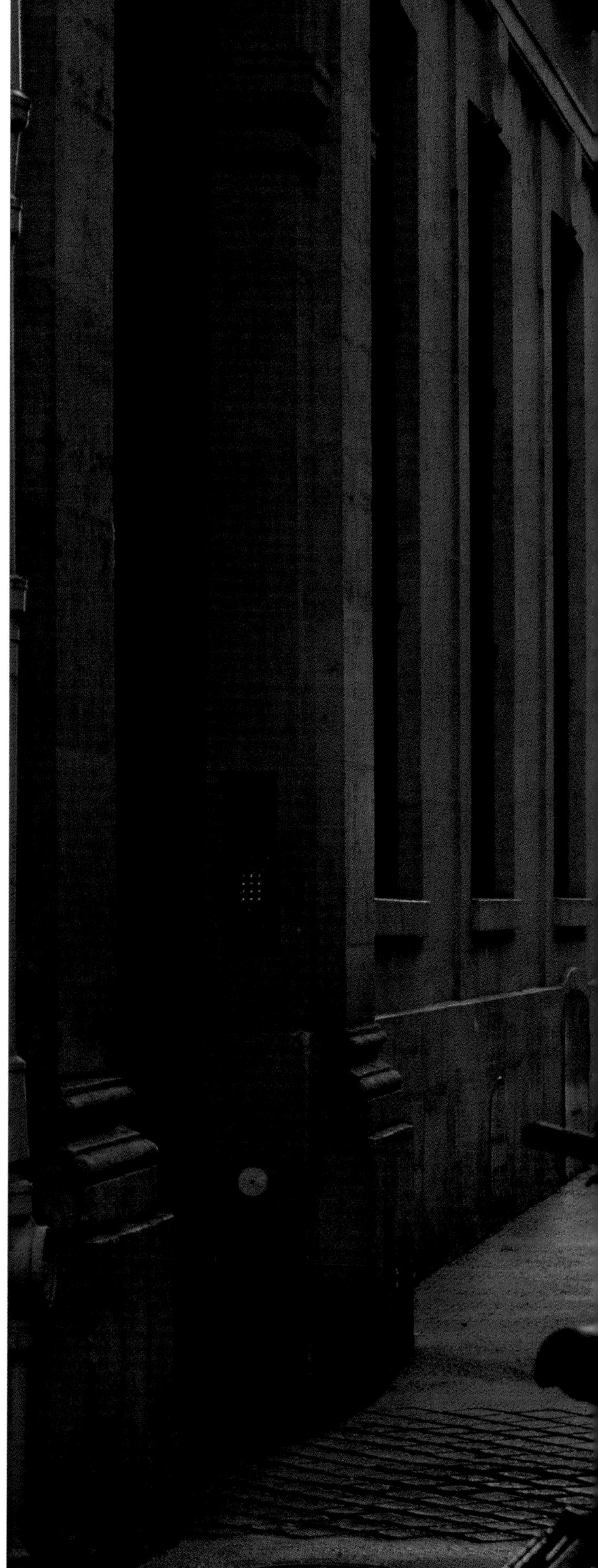

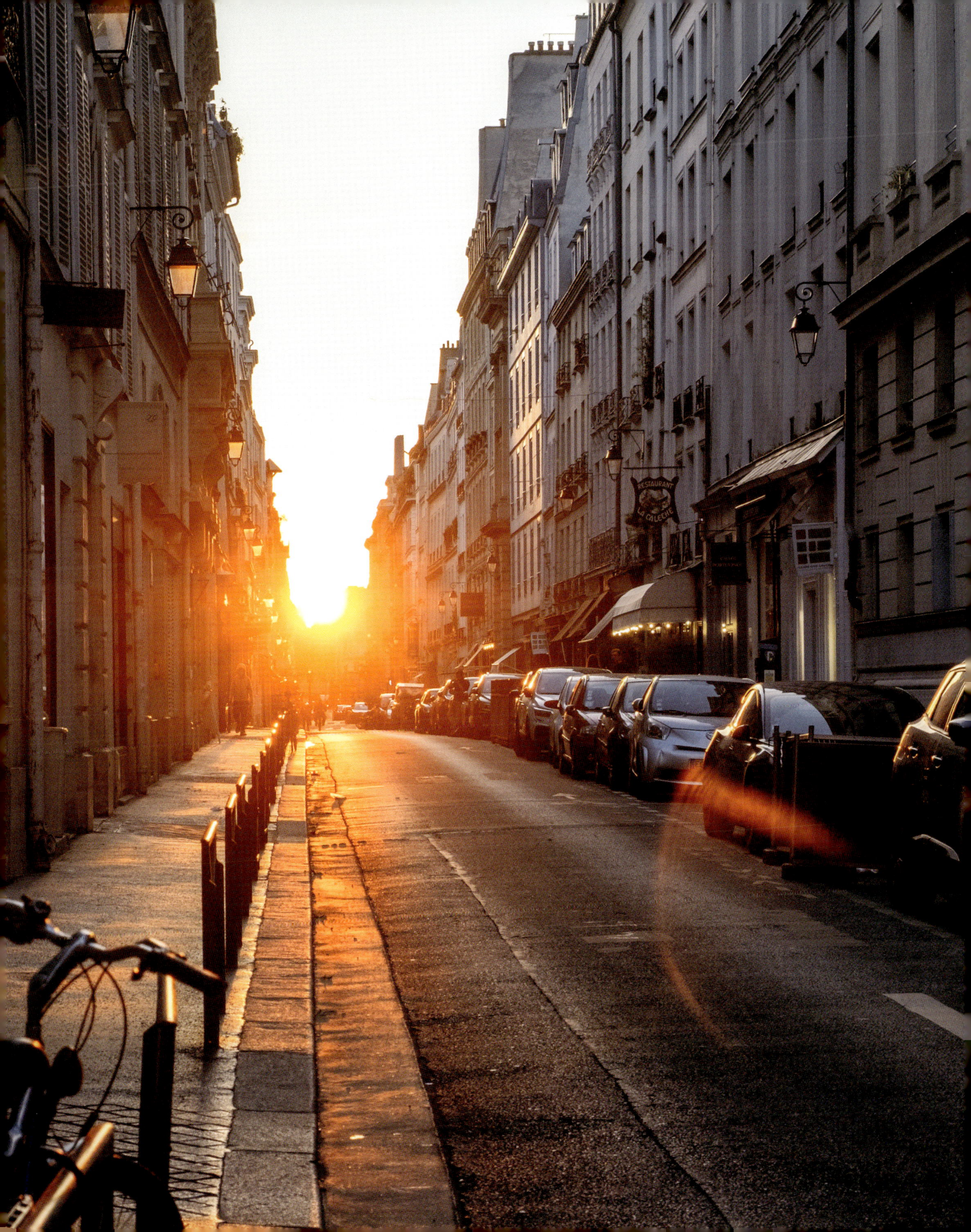
RESTAURANT
LA CALECHE

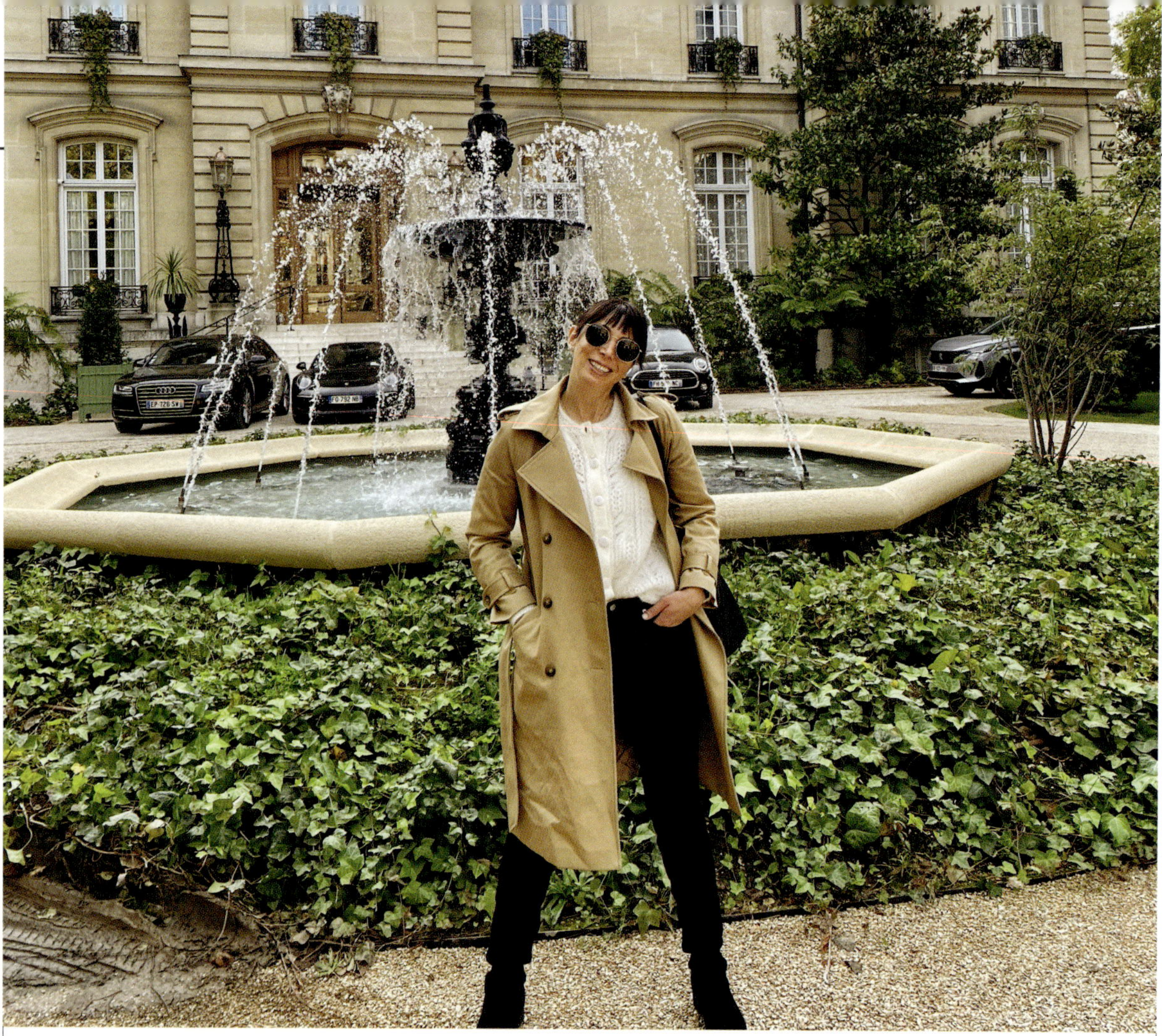

WHERE TO STAY

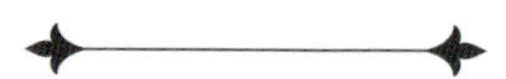

I have stayed at many hotels in Paris over the years, and these are my recommendations:

1st Arrondissement

- **Grand Hôtel du Palais Royal** is in the center of Paris, just behind the Palais-Royal and the Louvre. The rooms have optional balconies and some offer views of the Eiffel Tower. The suites provide a 180-degree view of Paris. It's perfect for solo travelers, couples, or families.

3rd Arrondissement

- **Le Pavillon de la Reine**, in the heart of Place des Vosges, is tucked away for privacy and a retreat from the bustle of the lively Marais. Dine at Anne, the hotel's Michelin-starred restaurant, for lunch or dinner. Boulangeries, bistros, and the Marché Bastille are just steps from the hotel.

4th Arrondissement

- **Le Grand Mazarin Paris** is a colorfully decorated boutique hotel in the Marais. Splurge for a room with a balcony overlooking Paris's rooftops. The hotel has a fitness room, spa, and pool in its basement. Book an evening at Boubalé for a unique dining experience with flavors from the Mediterranean and Middle East. Hôtel de Ville and Le BHV Marais department store are outside the hotel's door.

6th Arrondissement

- **Relais Christine** on the Left Bank, is the sister property of the luxe Saint James hotel. In December, enjoy its courtyard imbued with the smell of pine and decorated with twinkle lights. The hotel is covered with jasmine in the summer and offers an escape from city sightseeing. For the Left Bank lover, you are centrally located to explore the Jardin du Luxembourg and Rue de Buci.

7th Arrondissement

- **Le Pavillon Faubourg Saint-Germain** offers a quiet retreat at the start or end of your day. In the evenings, enjoy cocktails and jazz in the Saint James bar. The lobby is a cozy spot to warm up by the fire on a cold winter day and enjoy the hotel's teatime. Bistros and coffee shops can be found throughout the surrounding neighborhood.

8th Arrondissement

- **Hôtel Balzac Paris** presents a neutral, classic color palette that warms you on the coldest days. For a unique Japanese treatment, visit the pool and Spa Ikoï in the hotel's basement. Some rooms and suites offer rooftop views of Paris and the Eiffel Tower. It's located just steps from the Arc de Triomphe, Champs Élysées, and luxury shopping on Rue Saint-Honoré.

9th Arrondissement

- **Hôtel Adèle & Jules** has been an *Everyday Parisian* community favorite for years. I love the 9th arrondissement for its local vibe and some incredible restaurants. It is a bit off the beaten path for a first-time visit. This hotel is centrally located to visit the Louvre, Montmartre, and Opèra, all within a 15- to 20-minute walk. Upgrade to a club-level room with high ceilings and large windows overlooking the quiet street.

16th Arrondissement

- **Saint James** is a classic Relais and Châteaux property in the upscale 16th arrondissement. This stunning hotel is an escape from the city's center and was on my bucket list of hotels for years. My husband and I stayed here when we became engaged. Don't miss The Library Bar for a cocktail and the garden bar.

Experience Paris on Your Own

My suggestion for your journey through the cobbled streets of the city is to pace yourself. Guidebooks are filled with tips for food, drink, and spots to visit. You will even find some of my favorite restaurants and cafés included in this book. But, I hope this book encourages you to go on your own odyssey. You don't have to cross off every recommendation on the list you made before arriving.

Flâneur

Veer off the typical tourist lists and main streets and experience Paris slowly. *Flâneur* is a French word meaning to stroll the city with no agenda. Stay at a café too long; watch the rain fall or the world pass by. Observe the Parisian way of life from a terrace. Unplug and disconnect; soak in the city. Take out your earbuds. Listen to the city noises. Try a new area you haven't explored. Practice your French by ordering at a boulangerie or café. Quiet your mind and your voice. Parisians speak a bit softer than Americans. I always leave something undone for the next trip. It makes me look forward to planning my next Paris adventure.

Arrondissements

- Paris is divided into 20 arrondissements, spiraling out in a snail shape. Each arrondissement has a unique vibe and its own charm. Parisians are typically loyal to their quartier and will find their favorite boulangerie, café, and bistro not far from where they live.

- Most of the historical monuments are located in the city's center, or, as one friend refers to it, "postcard Paris." The area is easy to navigate on foot, but the metro is also a popular form of transportation.

- The Seine River divides the city into the Left Bank and Right Bank. Explore both sides. The Left Bank is a more quiet and laid-back side with a residential feel. Here you will find: Jardin du Luxembourg, Musée d'Orsay, Musée Rodin, Bon Marché, Latin Quarter, and Eiffel Tower.

- The Right Bank is filled with energy, nightlife, and high fashion. Here you will find: Louvre, Opéra, Champs-Élysées, Arc de Triomphe, Marais, Montmartre, Jardin des Tuileries, and Palais-Royal.

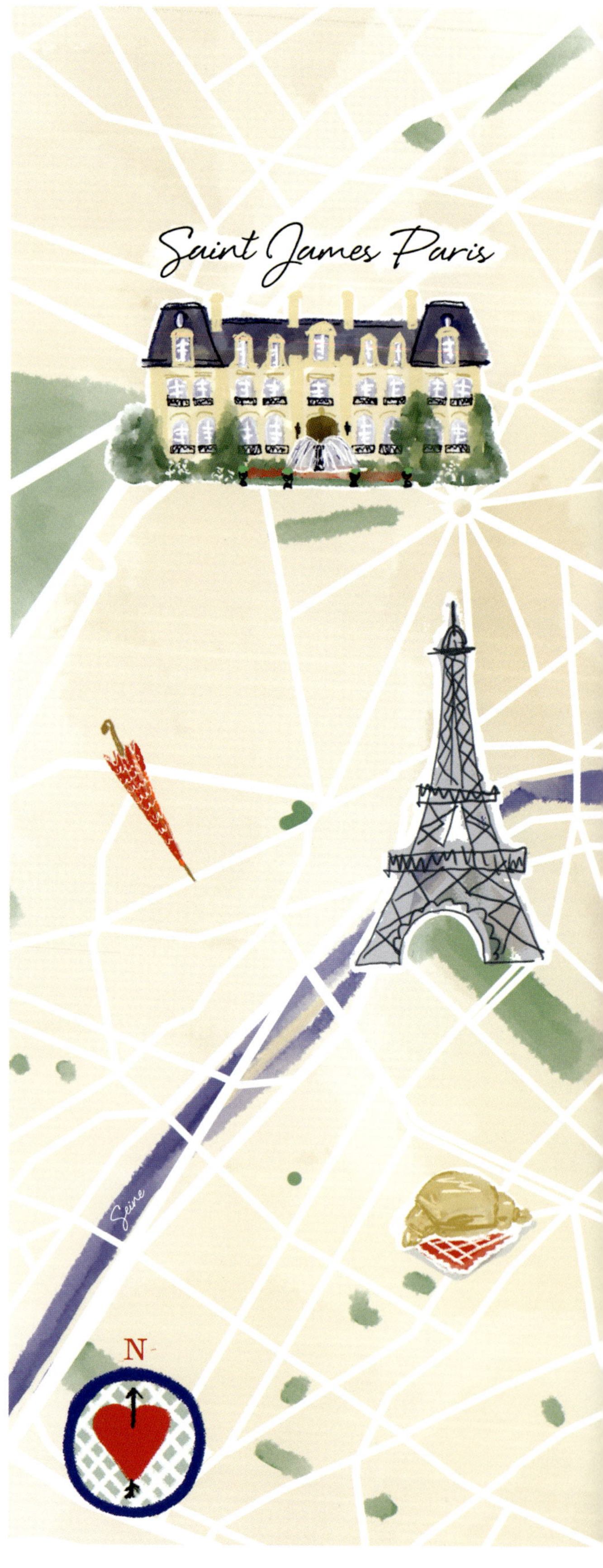

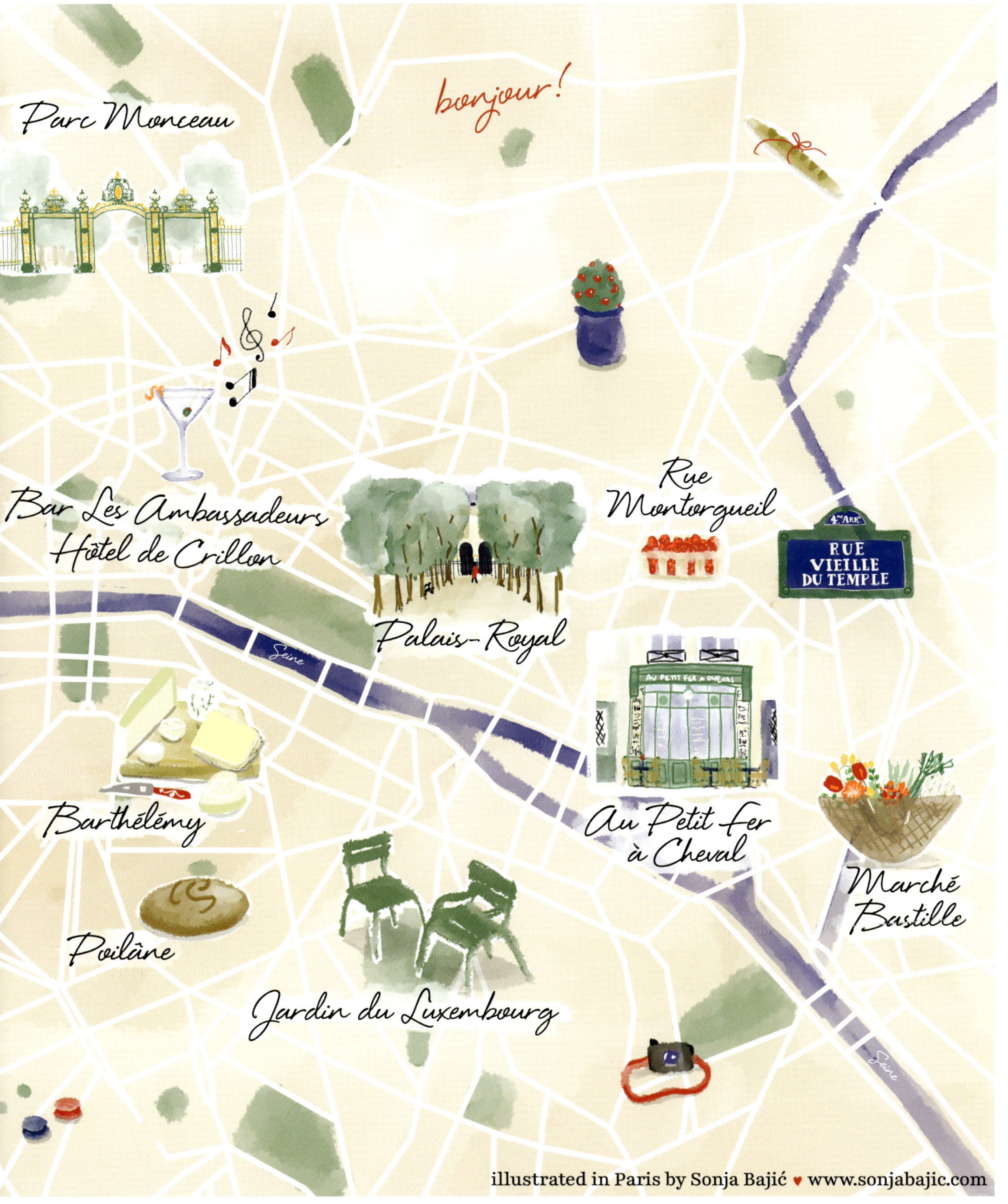
bonjour!
Parc Monceau
Bar Les Ambassadeurs
Hôtel de Crillon
Rue
Montorgueil
4ᵉ ARR
RUE
VIEILLE
DU TEMPLE
Palais-Royal
Seine
AU PETIT FER A CHEVAL
Au Petit Fer
à Cheval
Barthélémy
Marché
Bastille
Poilâne
Jardin du Luxembourg
Seine
illustrated in Paris by Sonja Bajić ♥ www.sonjabajic.com

l'hiver
{WINTER}

The first week of January finds lingering vestiges of the Christmas and New Year's celebrations. Decorations are mostly taken down, but a few reminders of the holidays remain throughout the cold and damp days, like twinkle lights filtering through the empty trees to illuminate the city with a warm glow. Days are shorter, as the sun rises late and sets early.

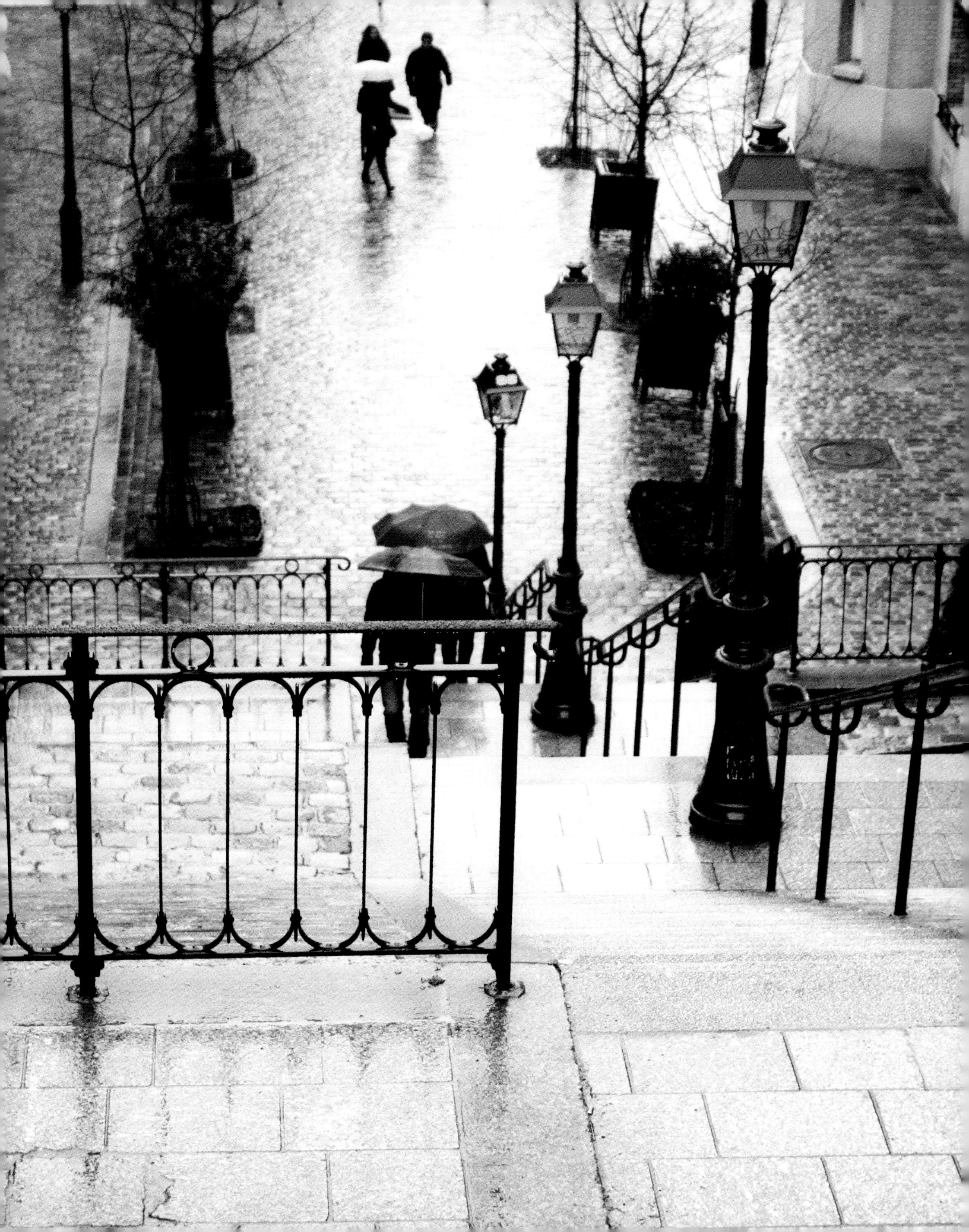

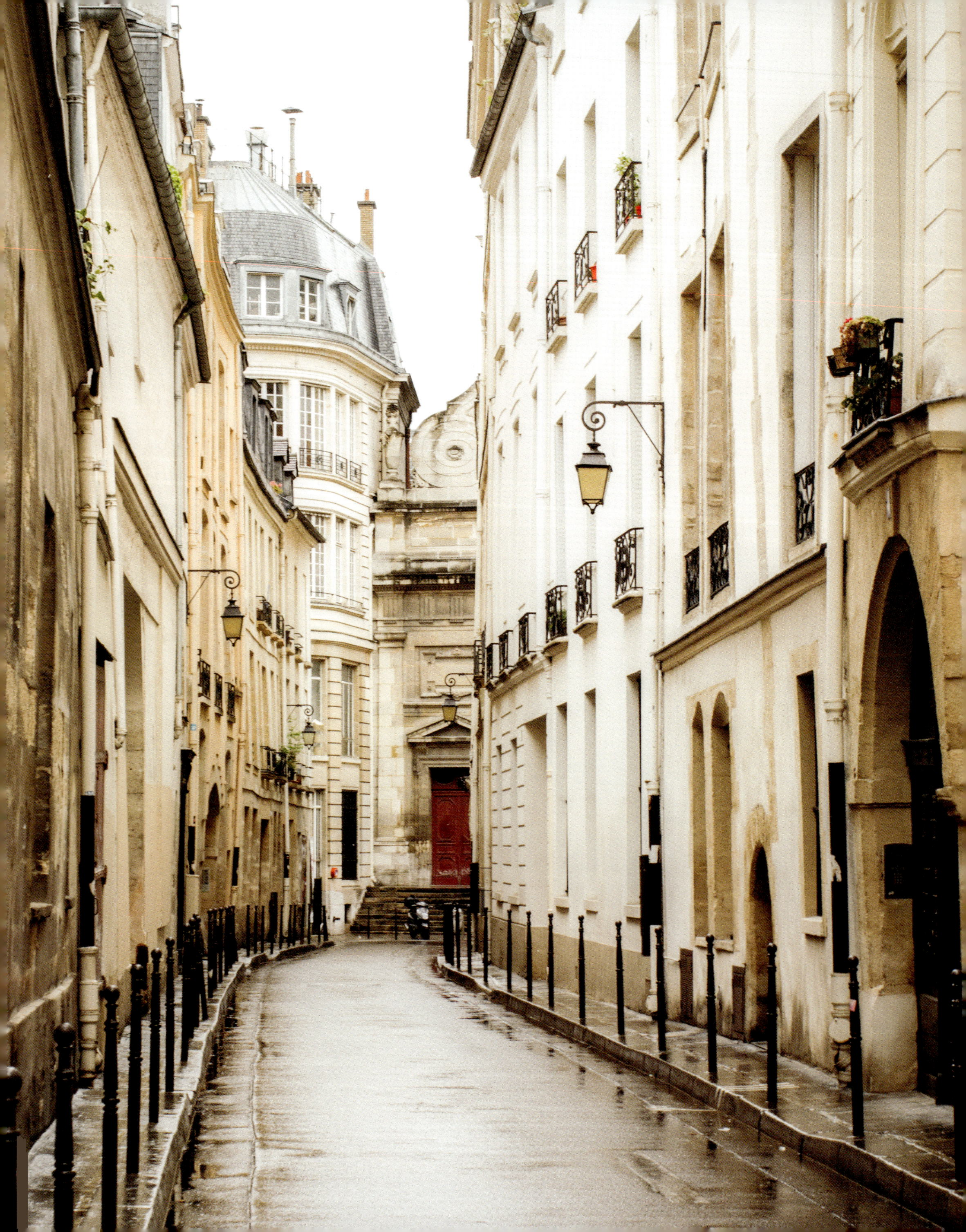

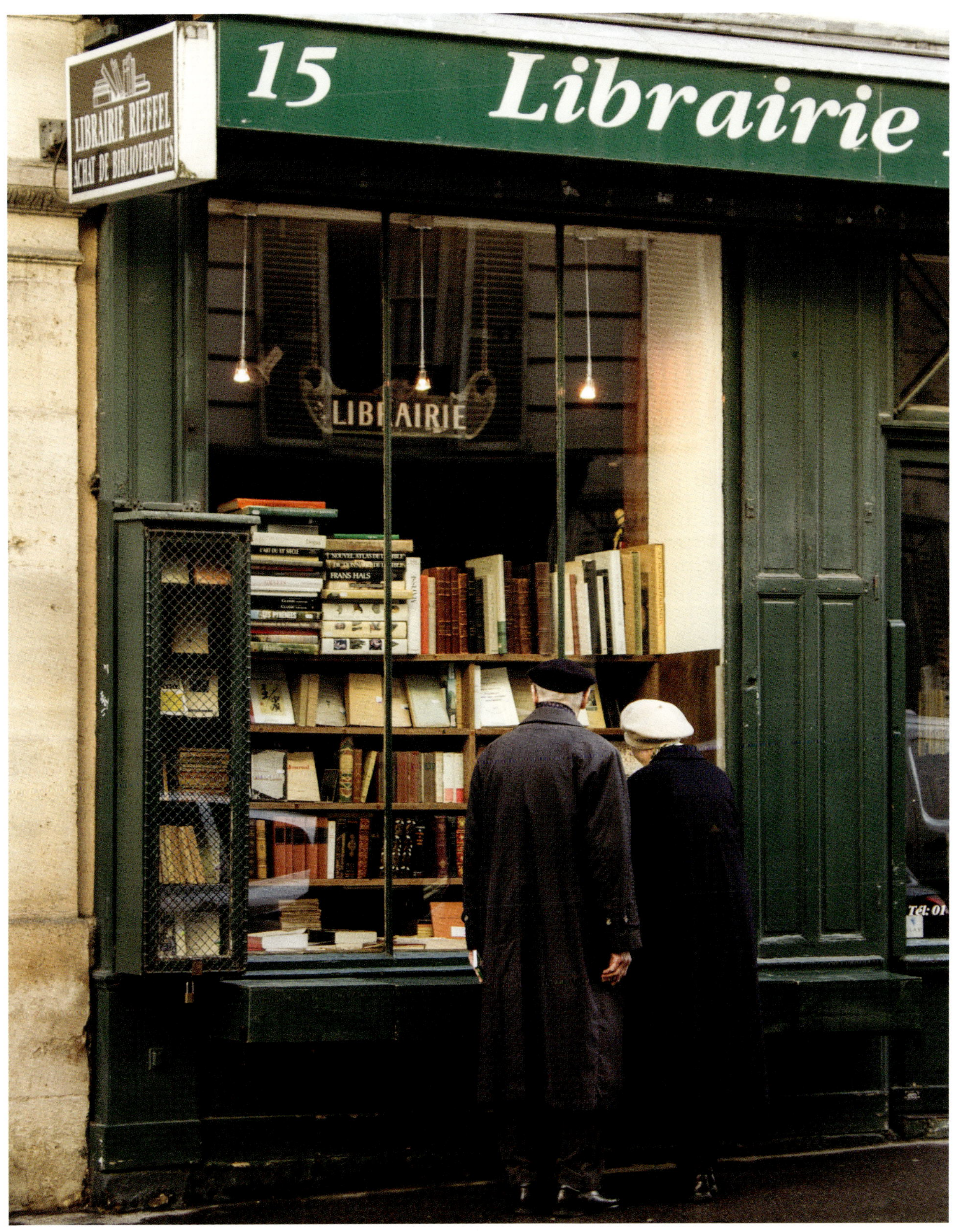
LIBRAIRIE RIEFFEL
ACHAT DE BIBLIOTHEQUES
15
Librairie
LIBRAIRIE
FRANS HALS

A WORLD OF MUSEUMS

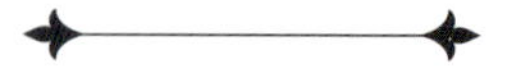

In winter months, get out of the cold and visit museums in the city or join Parisians who enjoy visiting special exhibitions, libraries, and bookshops. Here are few museums to consider:

- **Musée Carnavalet** in the Marais district is free and focuses on the history of the city.
- **Petit Palais** found in the 8th arrondissement houses decorative murals from the early 20th century.
- **Musée des Archives Nationales** displays records of French history. Documents like Marie Antoinette's last letter are rotated every four months to keep them preserved.
- **Musée d'Orsay** will fulfill your desires to see Impressionist works in a space filled with French art.
- **Musée Jacquemart-André** allows you to discover the amazing art collection of a wealthy French couple.

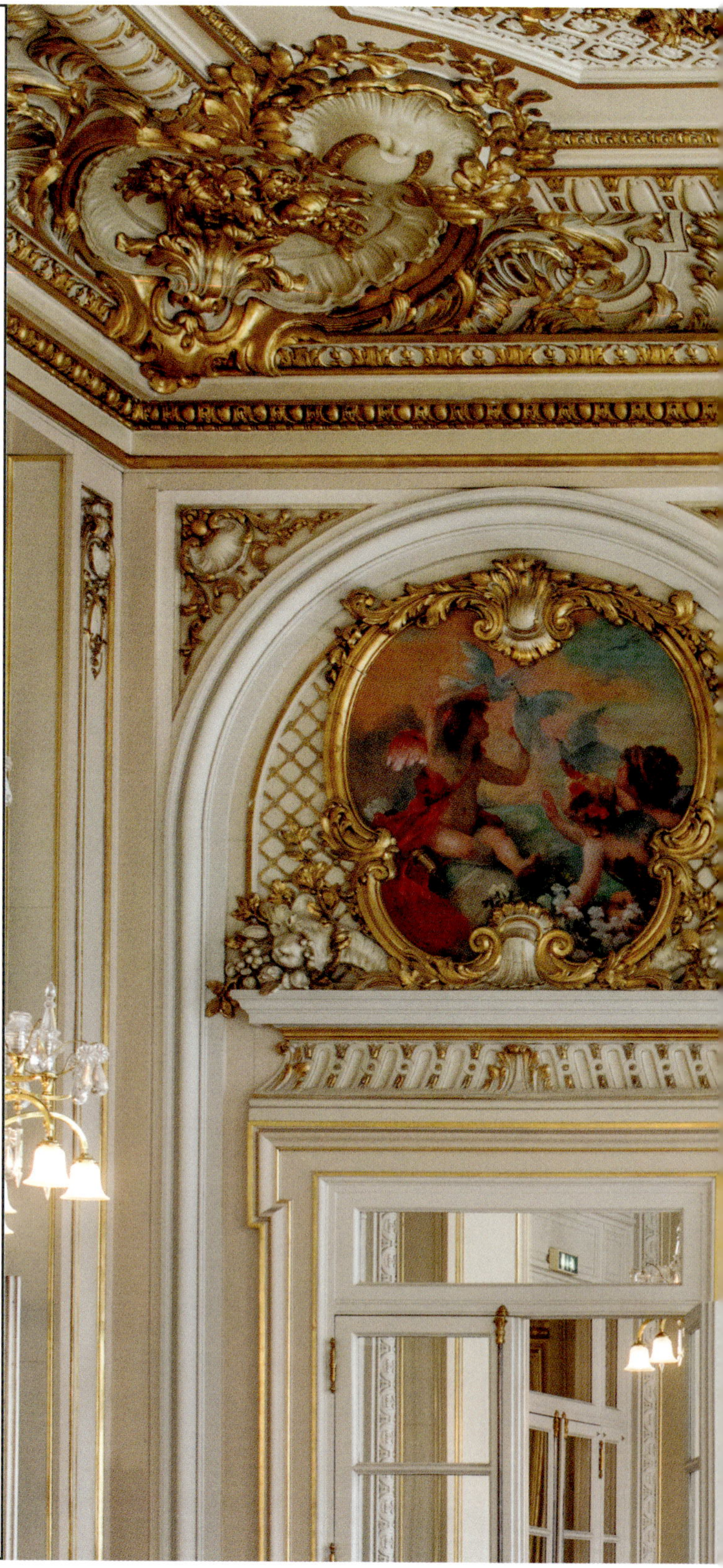

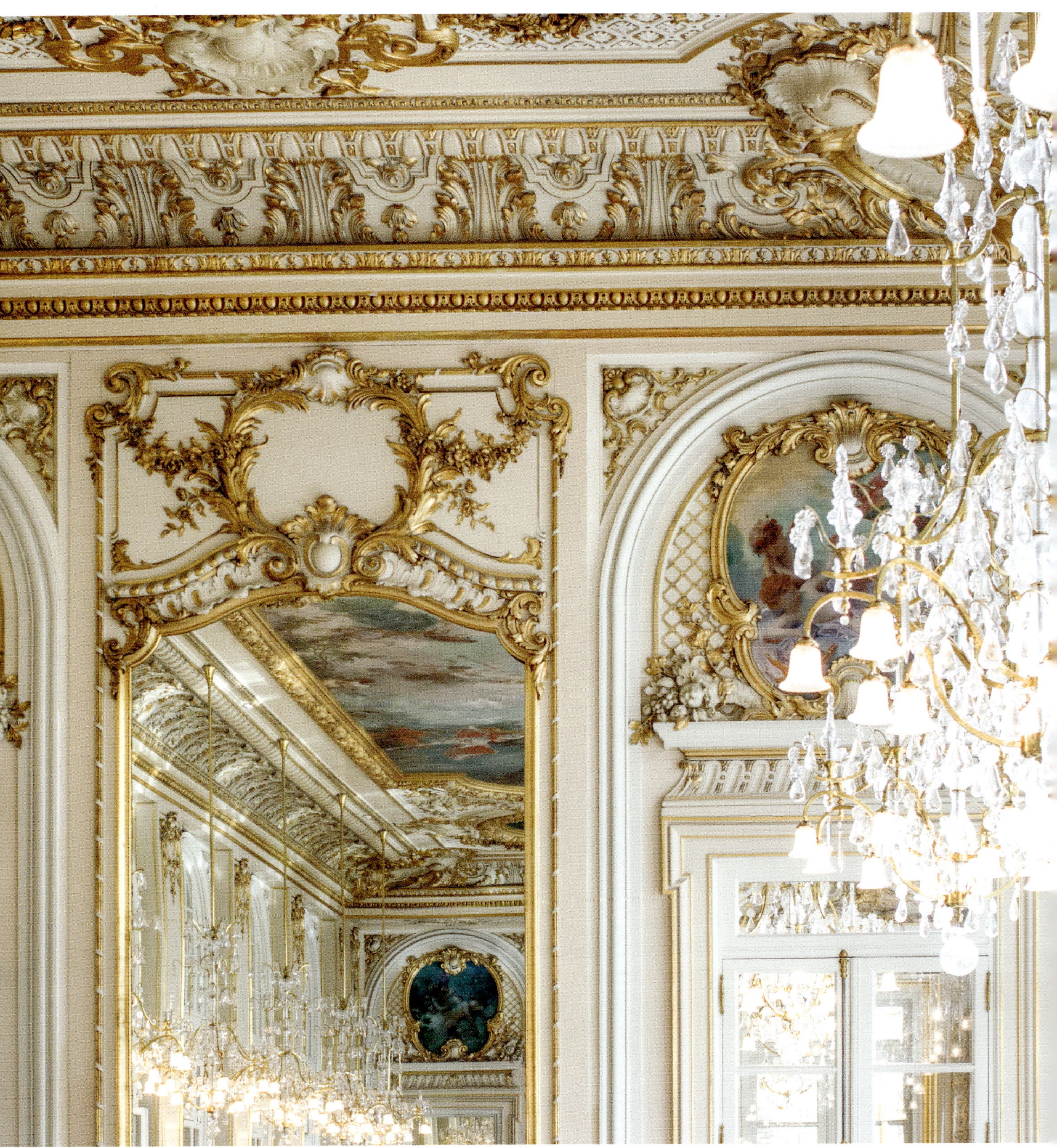

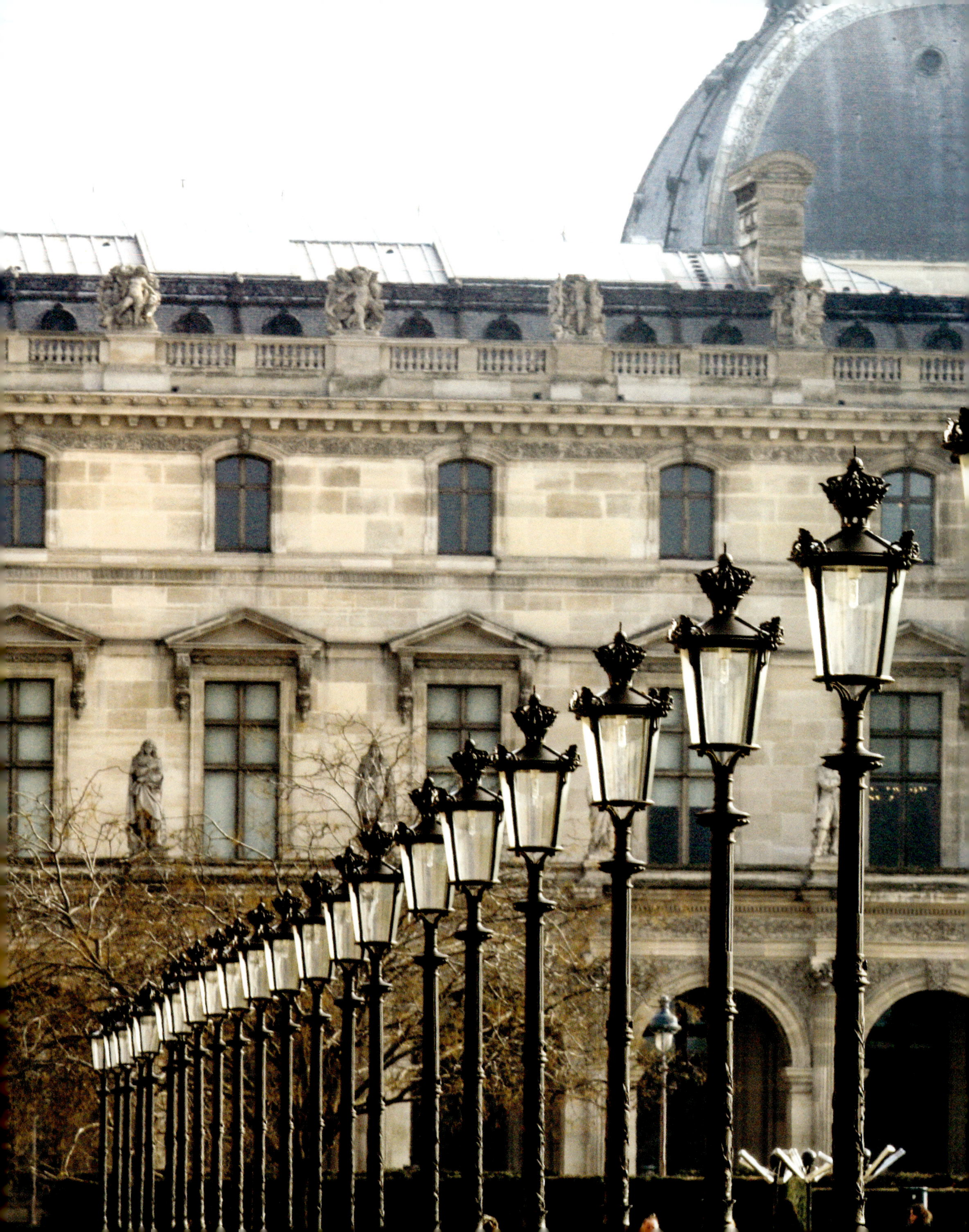

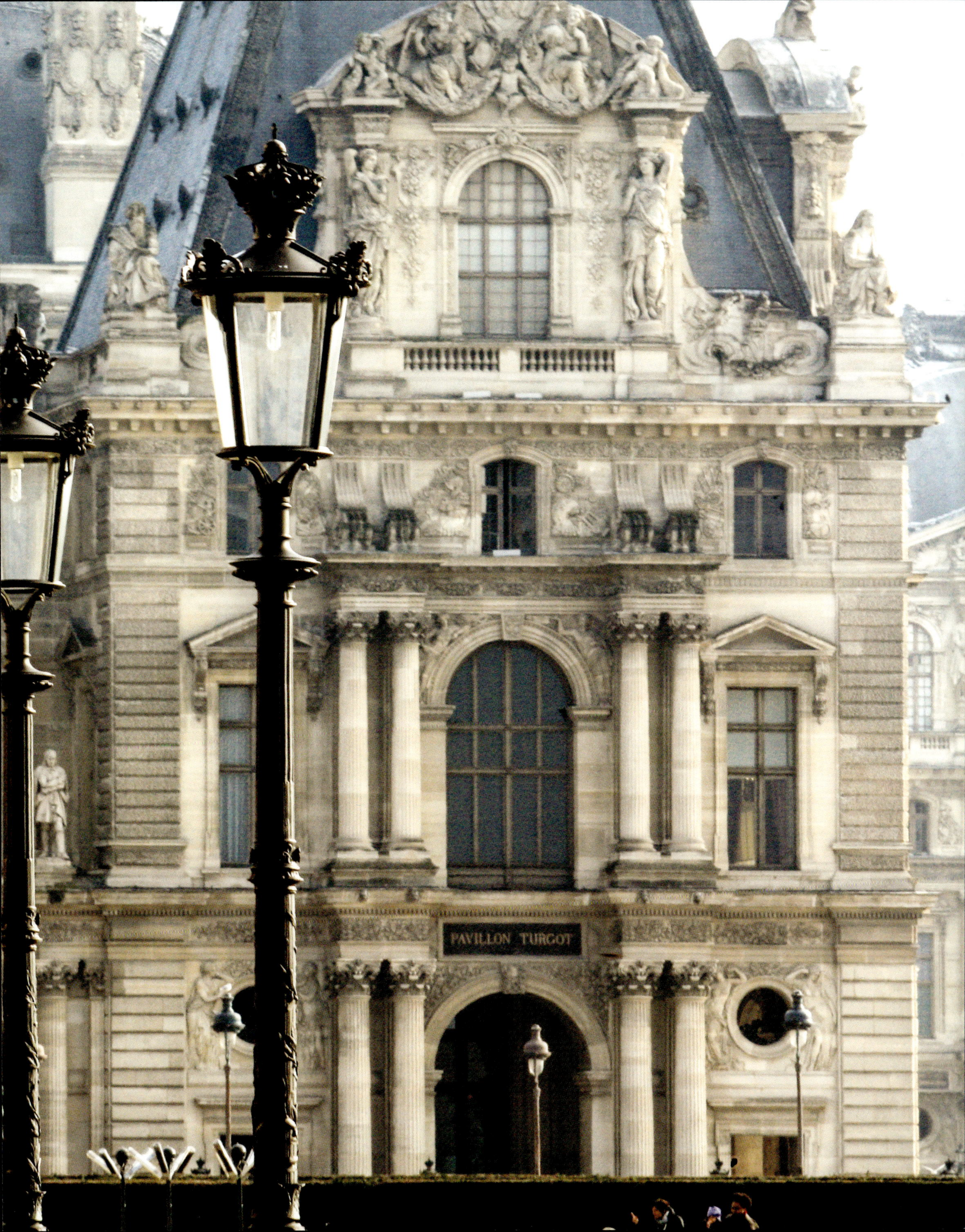
PAVILLON TURGOT

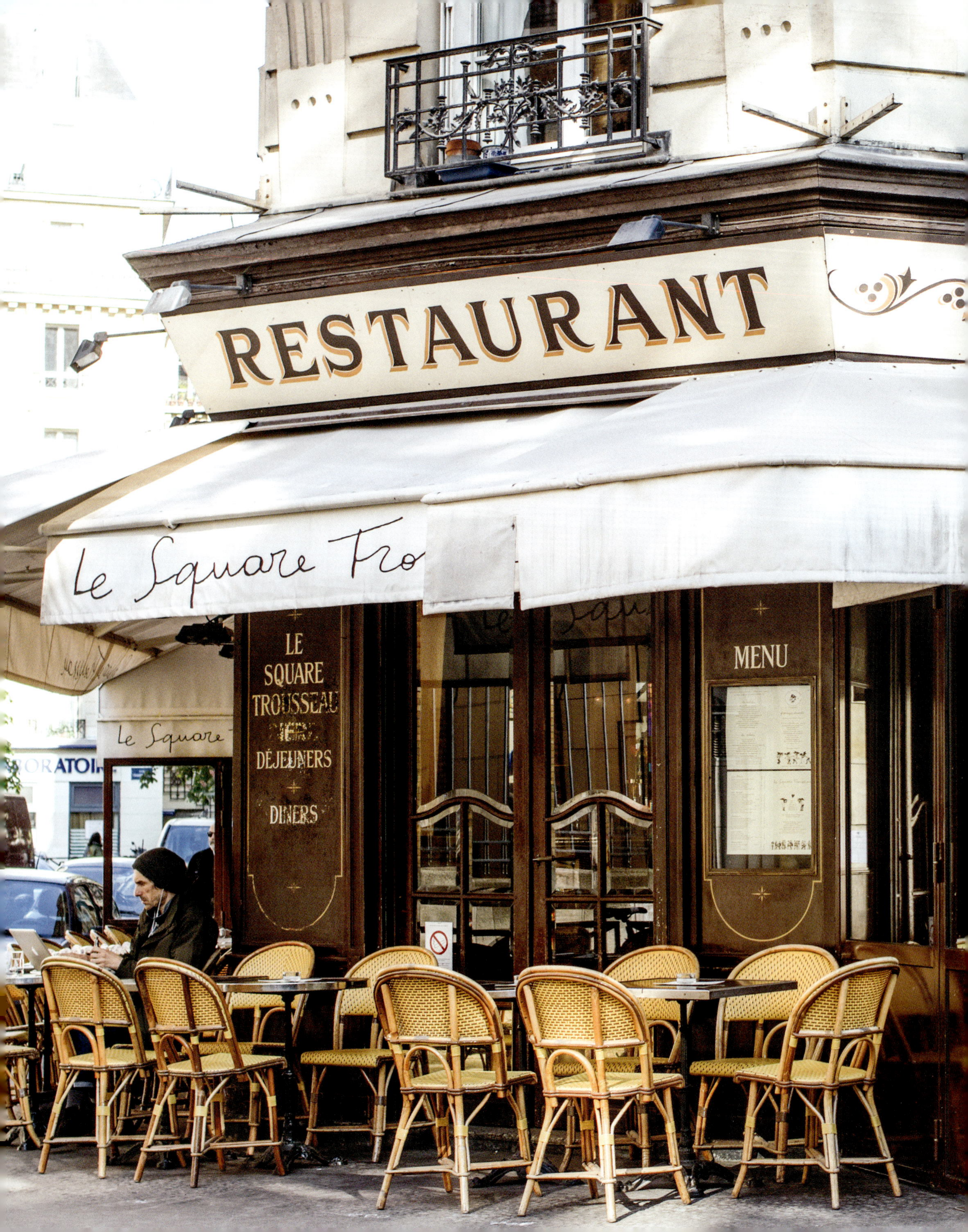

RESTAURANT
Le Square Tro
LE
SQUARE
TROUSSEAU
DÉJEUNERS
DINERS
MENU
Le Square

LES BISTROS

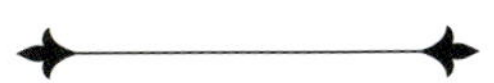

Classic Paris bistros for a comforting winter meal:

- **La Fontaine de Mars** (7th arrondissement): Reservations recommended. You can order various classic French menu items or chalkboard seasonal specials. On warmer days, don't miss the terrace, where some outdoor seats offer a view of the Eiffel Tower.

- **Bistrot des Tournelles** (4th arrondissement): Reservations required. Try the bar for solo dining. The menu stays consistent throughout the year, with a few seasonal offerings.

- **Lorette** (9th arrondissement): Reservations are not required but are recommended. Enjoy a seat on the small terrace or in the cozy interior. Lorette offers a seasonal menu (see the chalkboard) and French bistro items at a reasonable price.

- **Chez Georges** (2nd arrondissement): Reservations are required. Expect typical French menu items in a Parisian dining room with tiny tables and a wood-beam ceiling. It is perfect for a date night, solo dining, or a meal with friends.

- **Le Bistrot Paul Bert** (11th arrondissement): Reservations can be challenging, but walk-ins are possible with the right timing. Enjoy an old-fashioned bistro with a traditional meat and seafood menu.

- A new modern favorite, **Bistro des Lettres** (5th arrondissement): Reservations are recommended, as they have quickly gained a loyal following. The affordable and delicious classic menu items are worth trying, sometimes prepared with a twist. Try their French onion soup. Expect a mix of tourists and locals. During their meal, guests are offered the opportunity to write a letter to themselves, which arrives a year later at their home—a way to preserve a memory and have a time stamp in Paris.

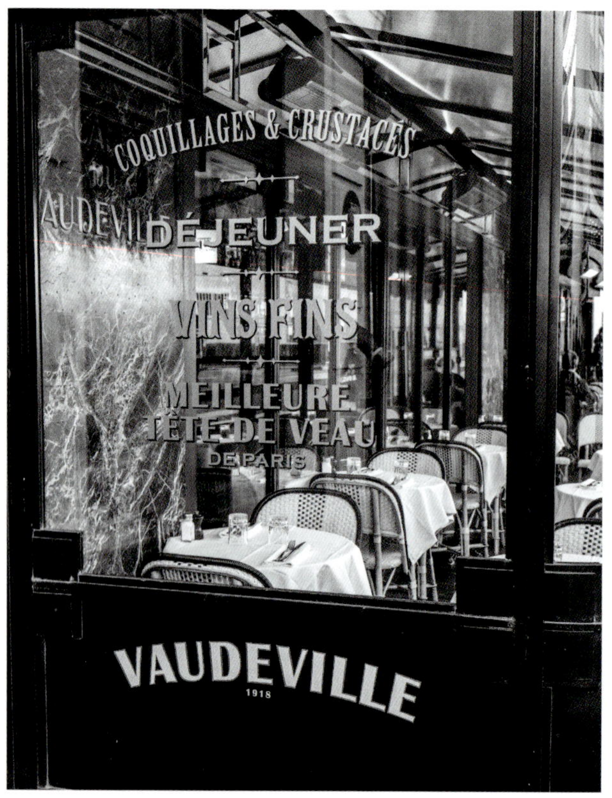

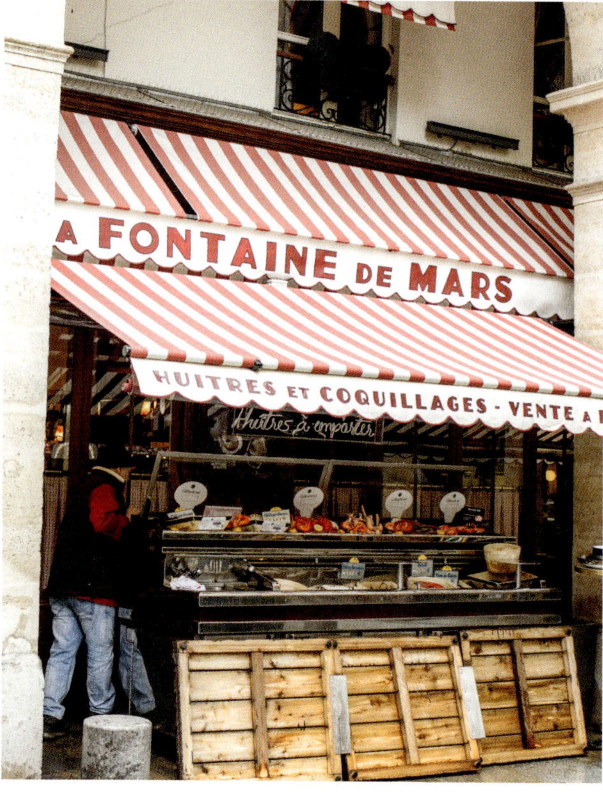

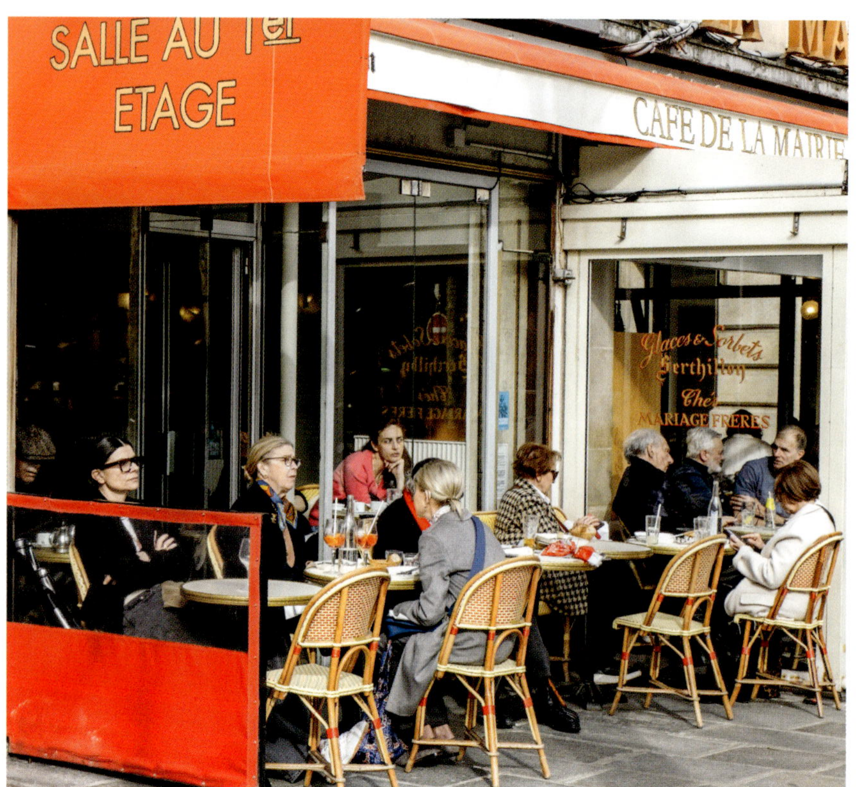

You cannot beat the ambience of a classic neighborhood bistro. Outdoor seating in Paris is enclosed with transparent plastic panels to keep guests warm in the cold months. These terraces used to be heated, but the city recently outlawed the heaters to reduce carbon emissions and save energy. Smokers will typically occupy these outdoor spaces. If you want a non-smoking, warm atmosphere, your best bet is inside a brasserie or café in the winter.

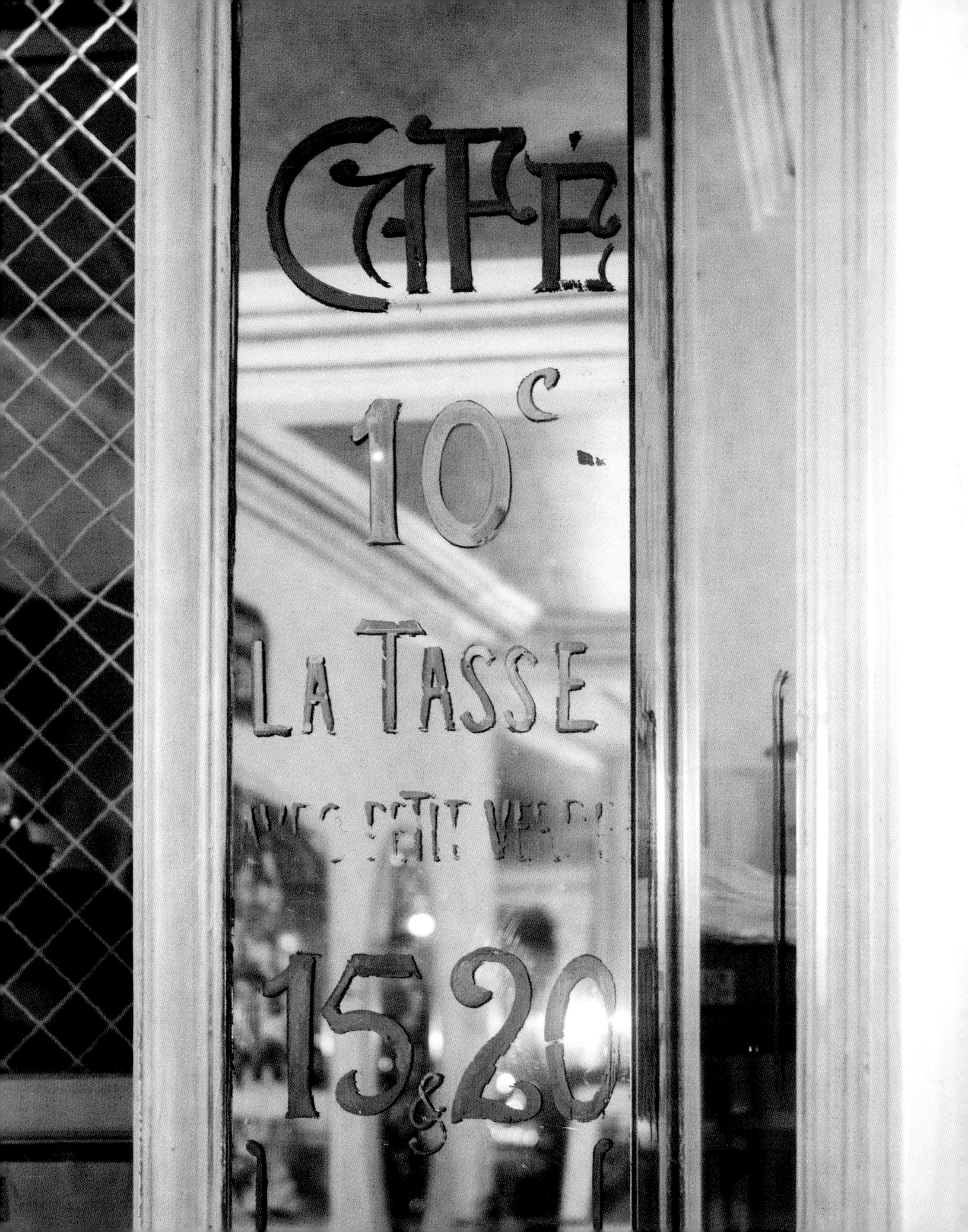

CAFÉ

10c

LA TASSE

15 & 20

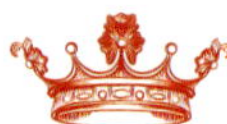

WINTER MENUS

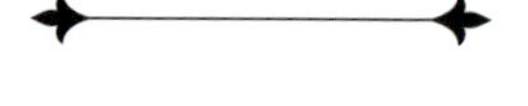

le menu

Soupe à la l'Onion

Velouté de Potimarron
(pumpkin soup)

Cassoulet
(slow-cooked stew with white beans and sausage)

Tarte Tatin
(warm caramelized apple tart)

Aligot
(a heavier potato and cheese dish typically served with meat)

Look for "fait maison" (homemade) on the menu.

- Try some of the stews and braised dishes like boeuf bourguignon, blanquette de veau, and coq au vin.
- Winter-focused cheese dishes include fondue and raclette. Mont d'Or is a cheese baked with garlic and wine and served warm with bread or potatoes.
- Seafood is also popular on menus, including les huitres (oysters) sold at outdoor food markets and brasseries throughout the city.

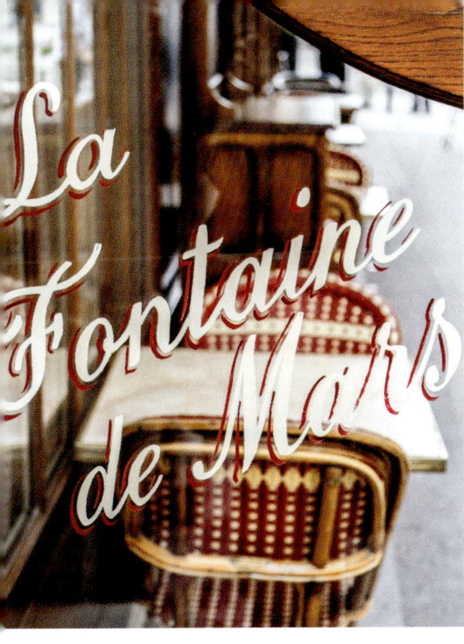
La Fontaine de Mars

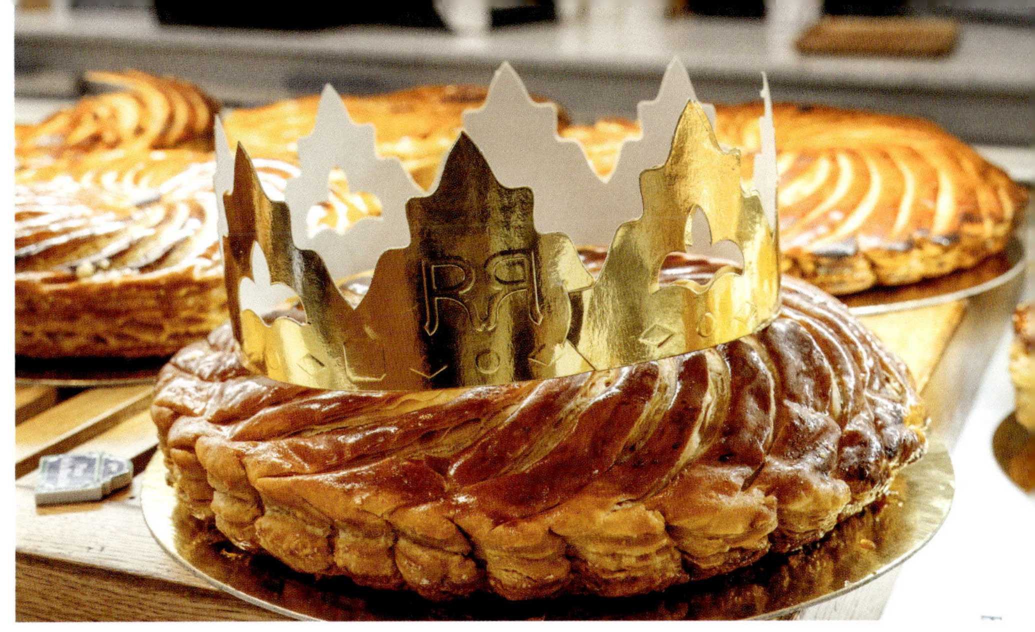

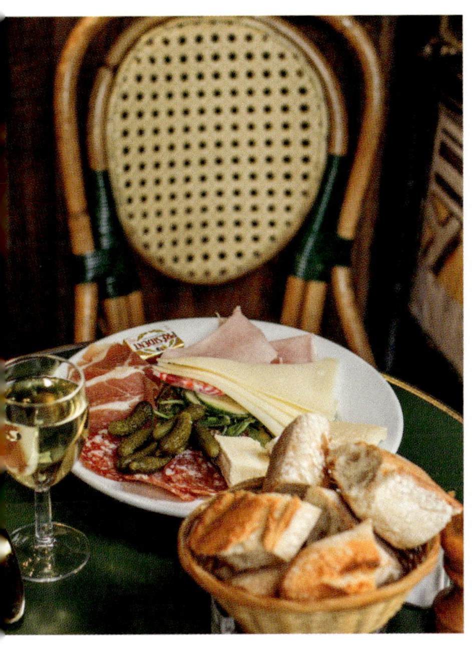

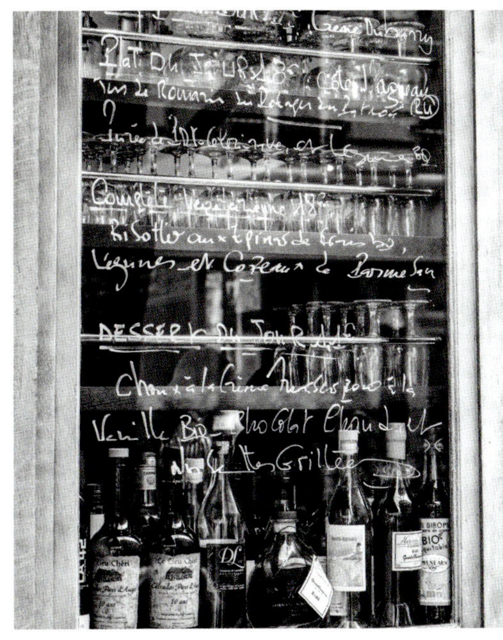

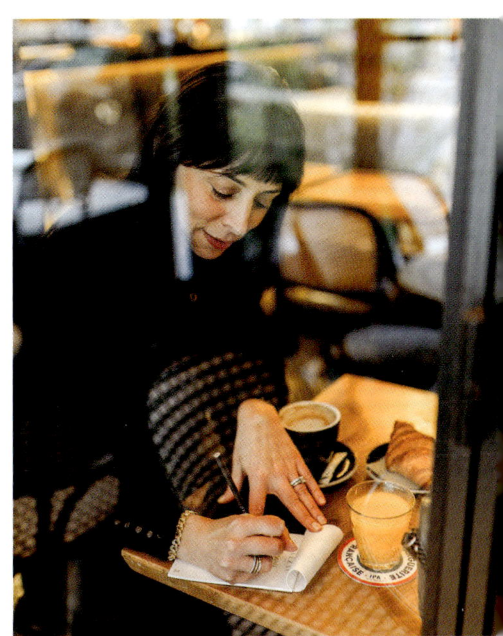

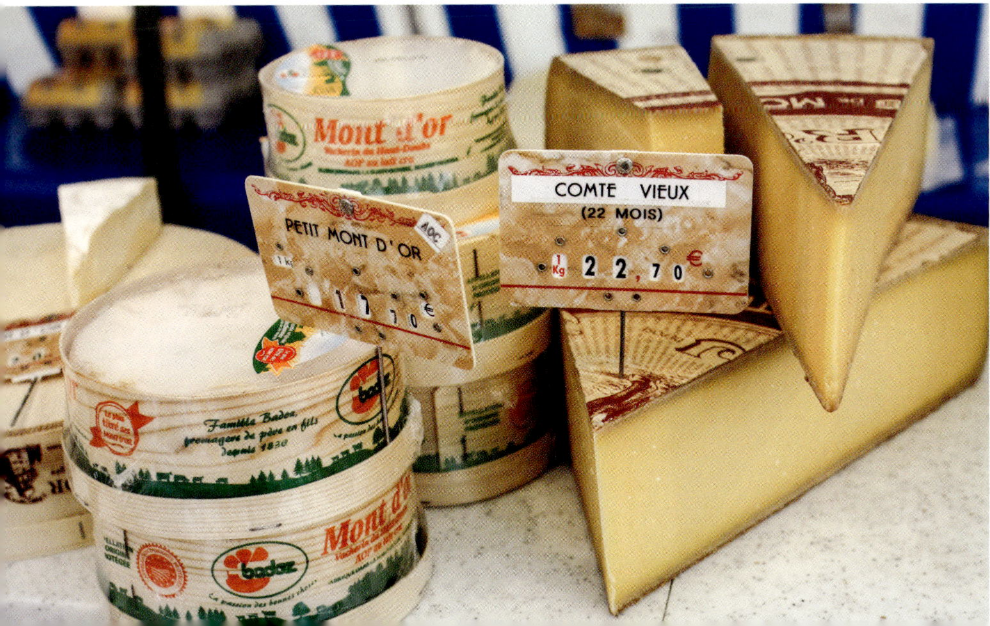
Mont d'or
PETIT MONT D'OR
AOC
COMTE VIEUX
(22 MOIS)
1 Kg 22,70 €
Famille Badoz

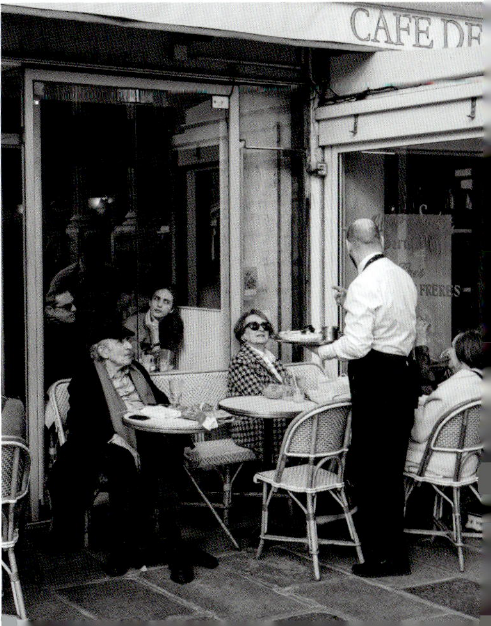
CAFE DE

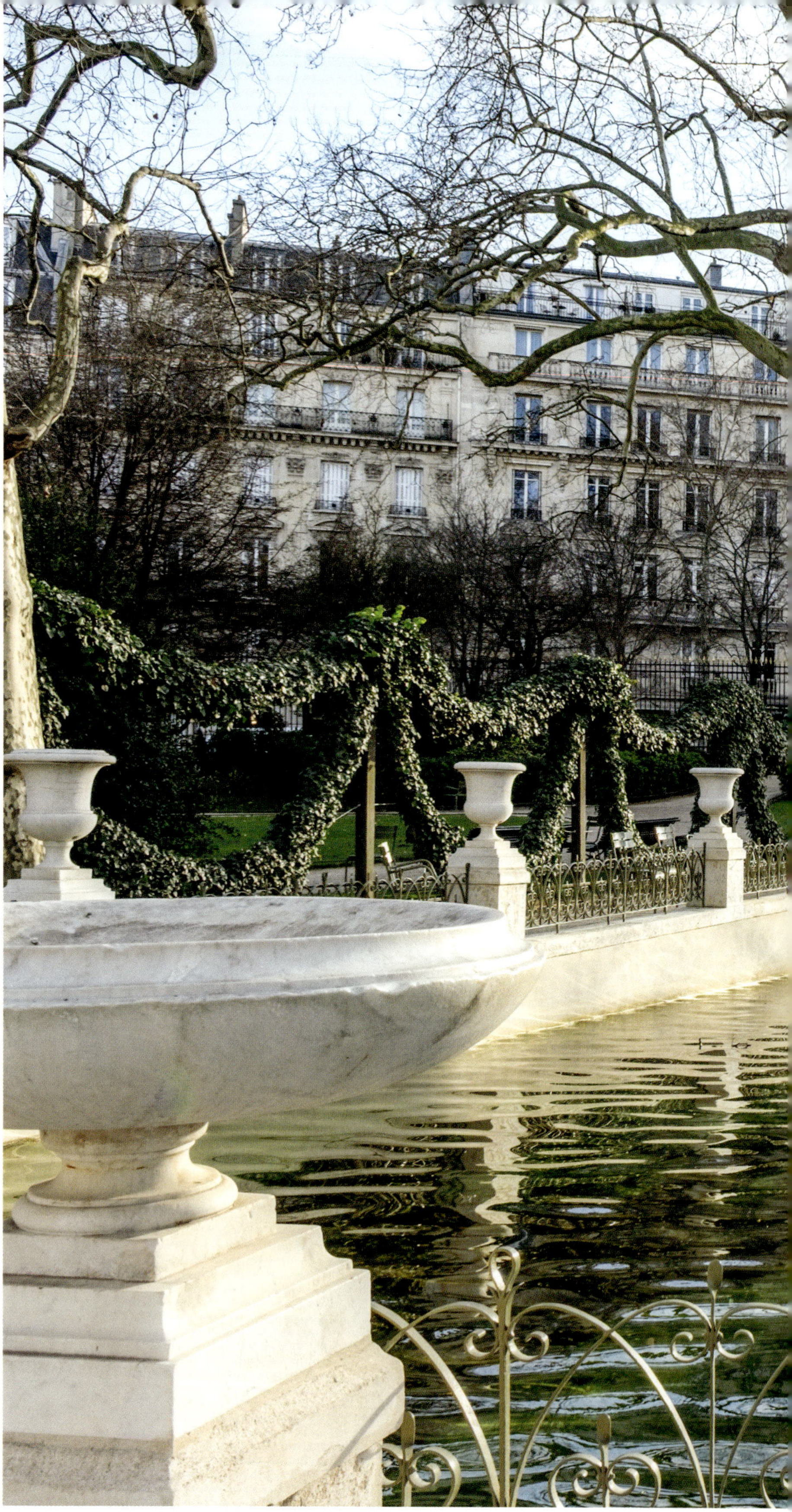

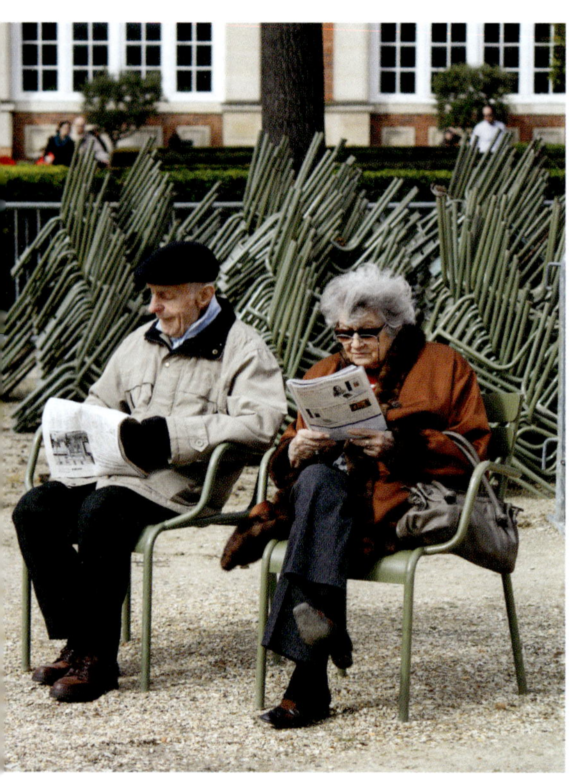

Parks and gardens continue to be enjoyed even in the colder months. Parisians will bundle up and spend the afternoon and early evening here, reading or taking in the fresh air. The Jardin des Tuileries is a great place to enjoy the sunset on a winter evening. The Médicis Fountain in the Jardin du Luxembourg was built in about 1630, and is a favorite spot year-round.

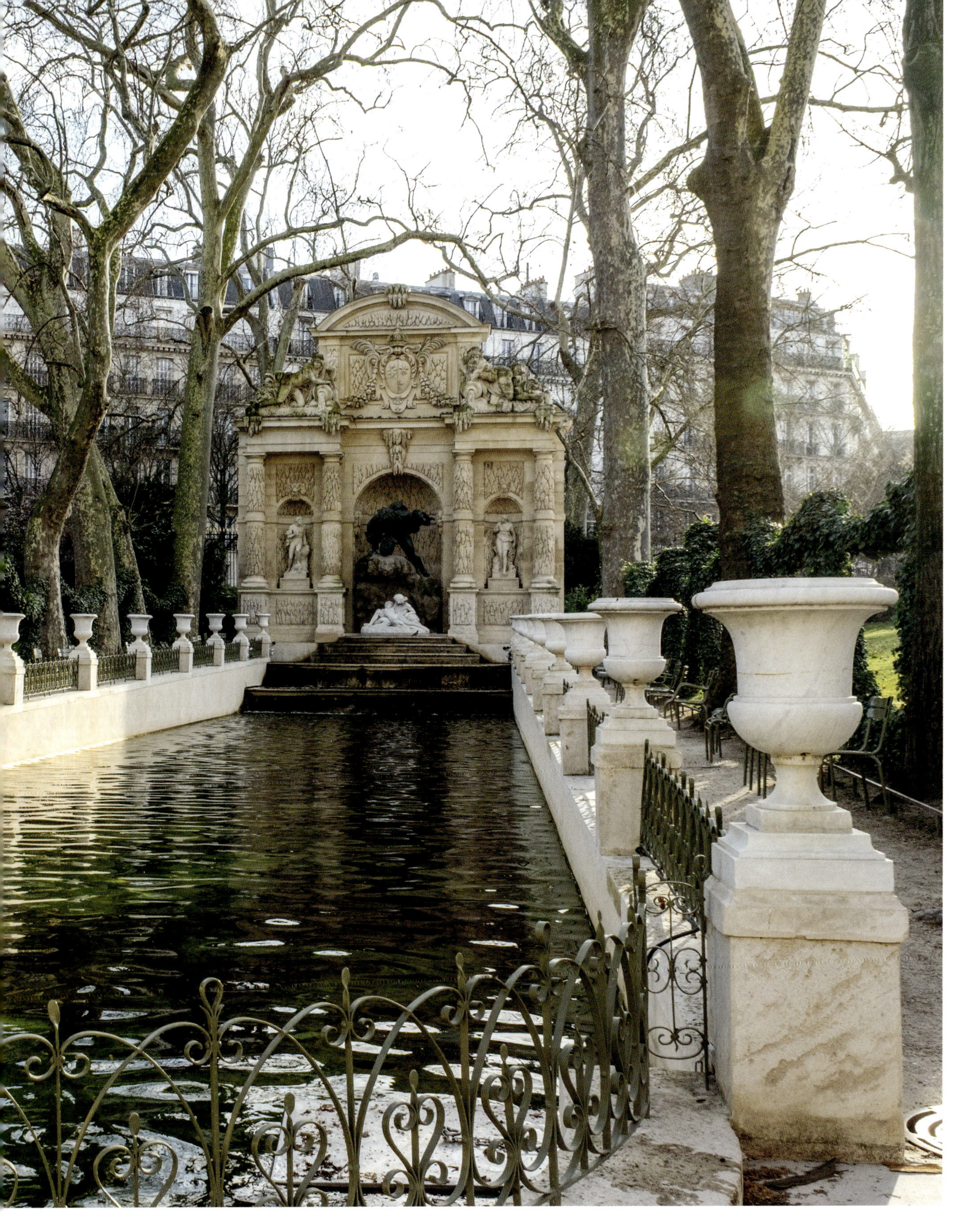

COZY COCKTAIL SPOTS

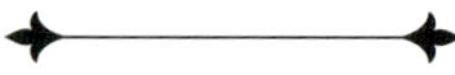

Classic hotels around the city offer comfortable respites with fireplaces, which makes for a perfect space to warm up on a cold winter day. Grab a cocktail, hot coffee, or tea at the following locales:

- **Pavillon de la Rein**—in the heart of the Marais
- **Pavillon Faubourg Saint-Germain**—in Saint-Germain-des-Prés
- **Relais Christine**—in Saint-Germain-des-Prés
- **Hôtel d'Aubusson**—on Rue Dauphine
- **Hôtel Balzac**—close to the Champs-Élysées

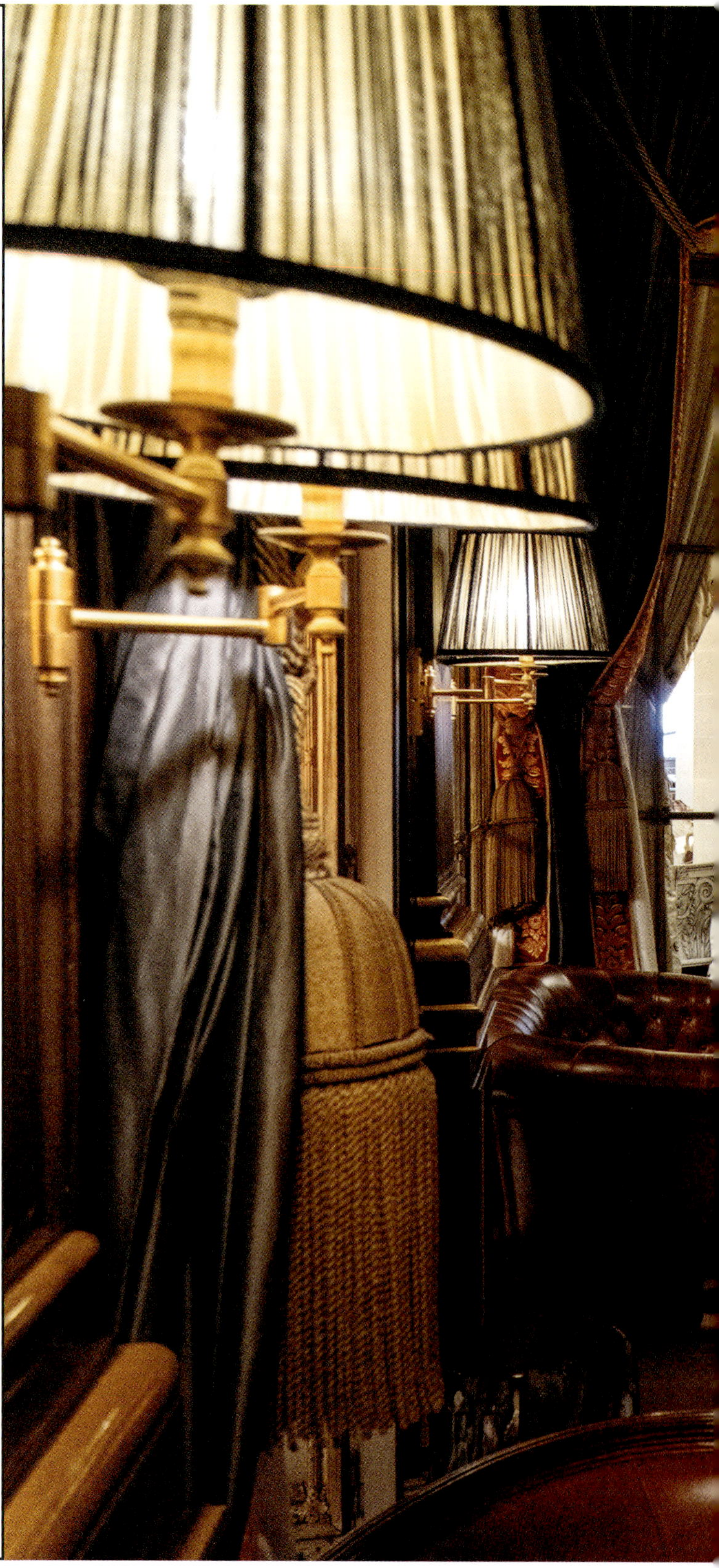

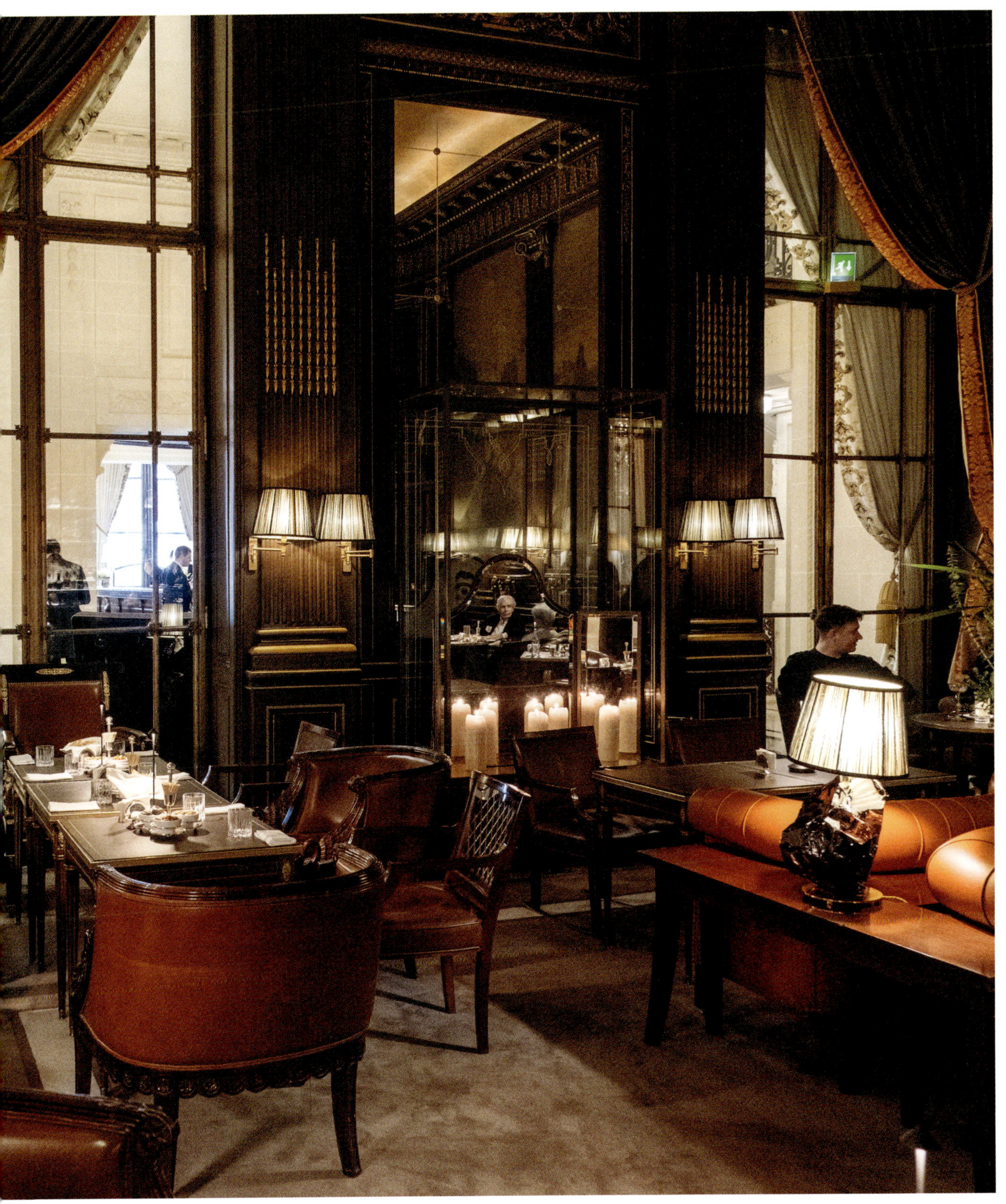

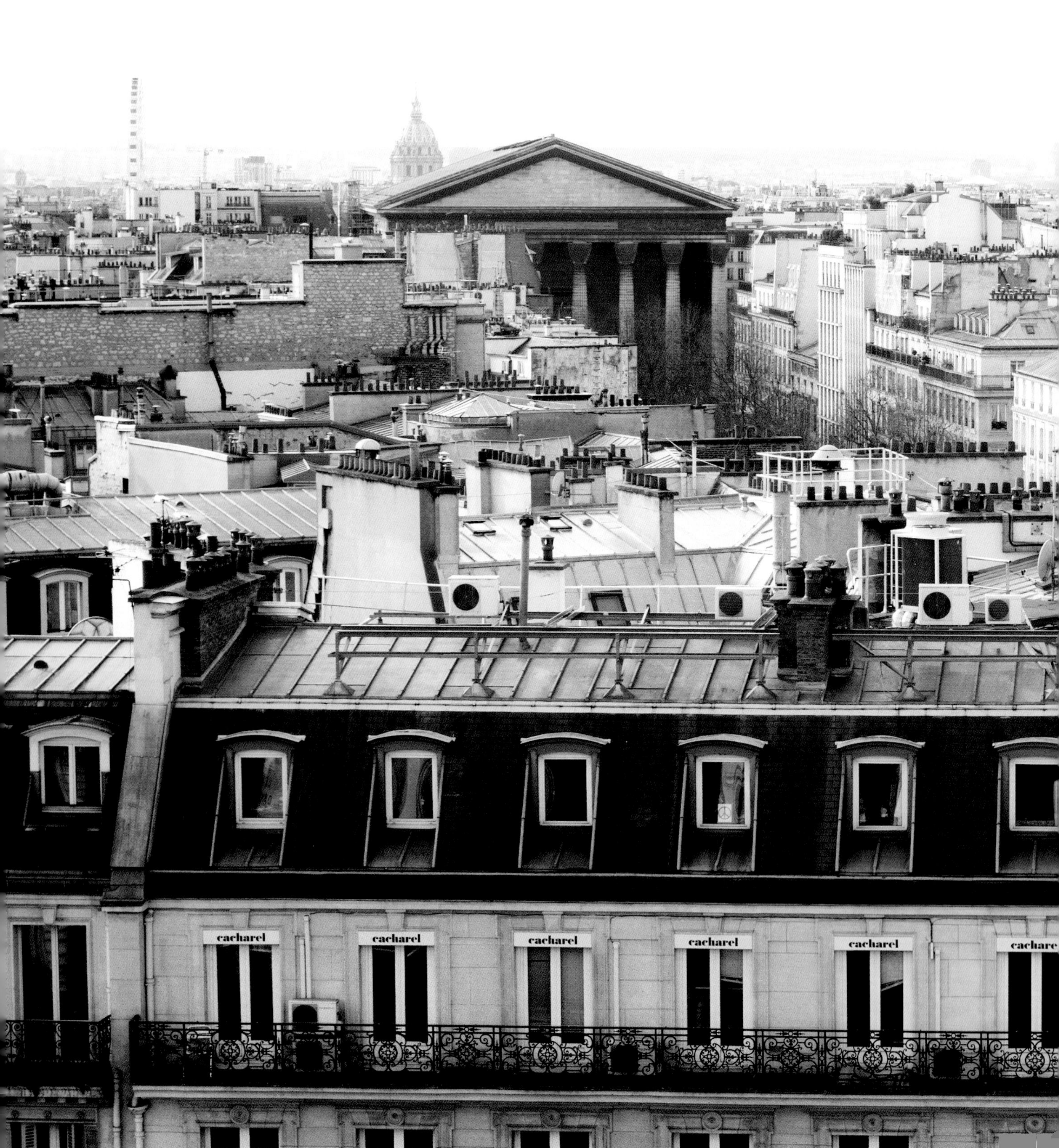
cacharel
cacharel
cacharel
cacharel
cacharel

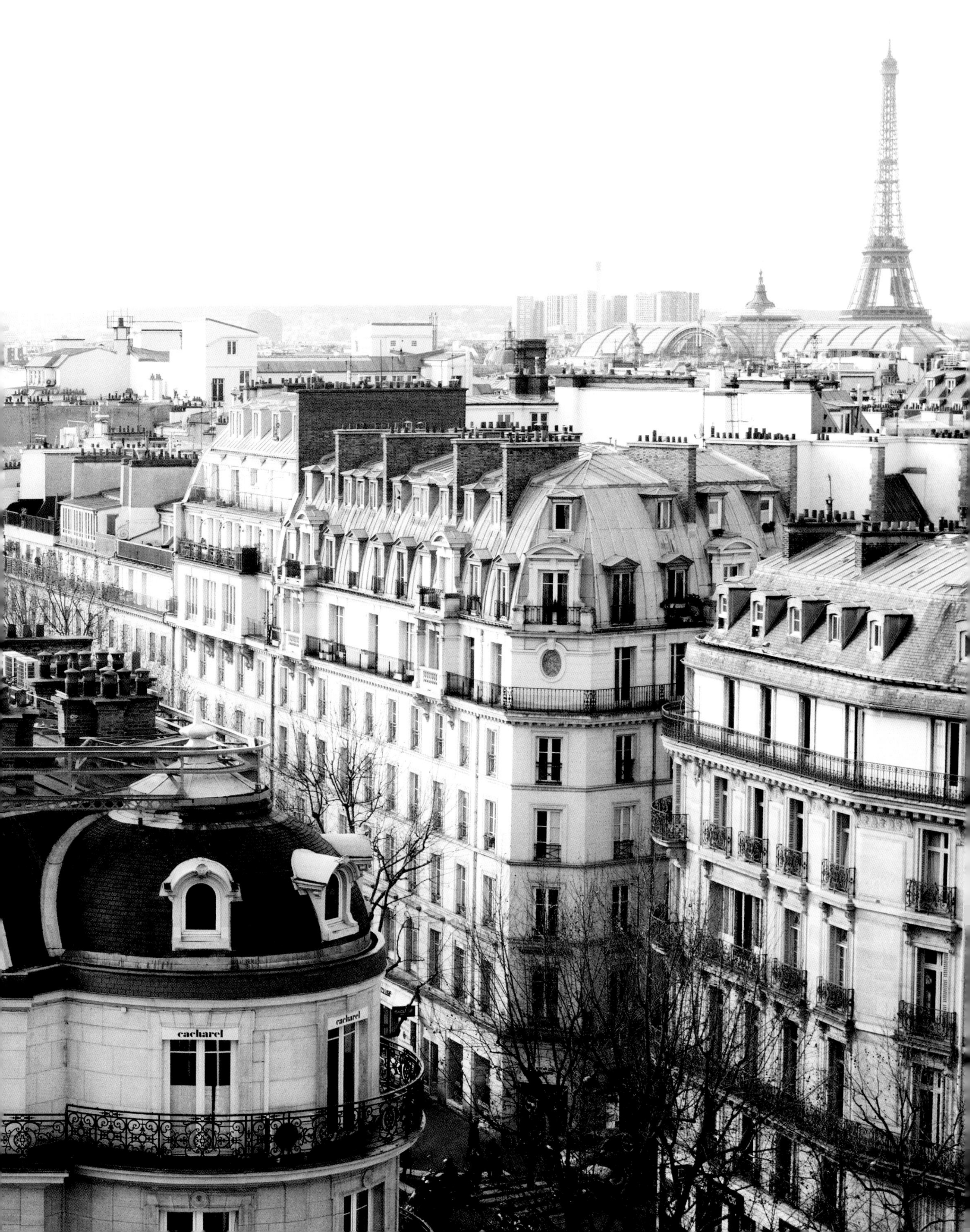
cacharel
cacharel

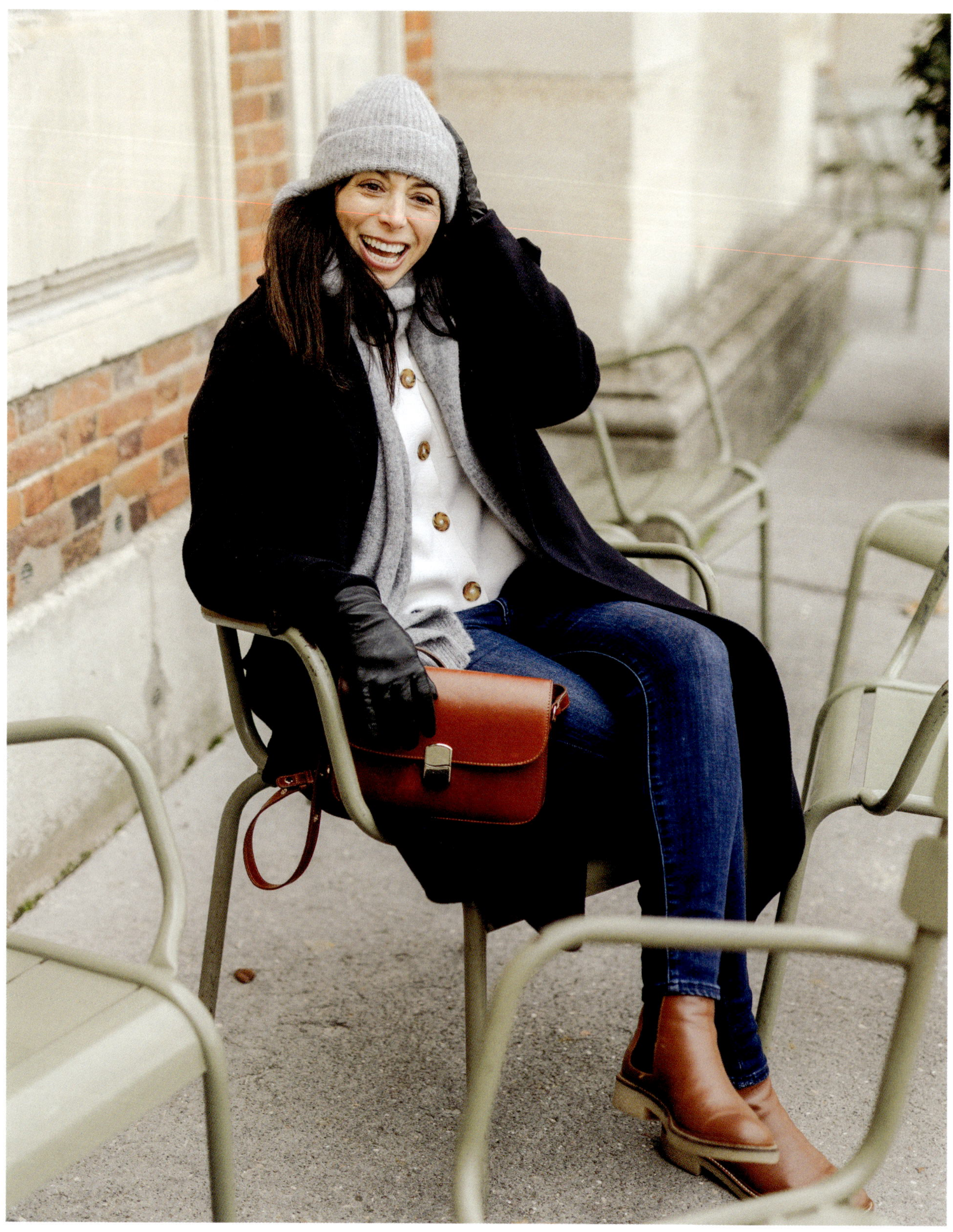

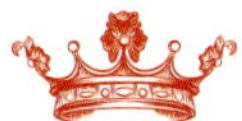

WINTER STYLES

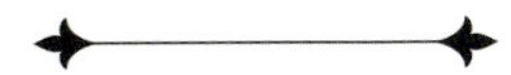

Parisians have a distinct style when it comes to each season. One of my favorite traditions is to sit at a café and spot the trends. In winter, neutral colors such as black, navy, camel, and winter white blend in with the grays and soft blues of the city.

- **Boots:** Chelsea, ankle, and knee-high boots, all primarily black, are part of Parisian winter fashion.

- **Sneakers:** These are becoming more acceptable and common among men and women. Popular brands include Veja and Adidas.

- **Scarves:** The chunkier, the better. Parisians use scarves as a key winter accessory. They typically sit the scarf on top of their coat, instead of tucked in, and tie it in a knot around their neck or drape it over one shoulder.

- **Coats:** The big trend is long wool coats in dark colors, such as black or navy. A wrap coat tied at the waist is also popular.

- **Black Tights:** Wearing them with boots, skirts, and dresses is a trend I have seen year after year in Paris.

- **Sweaters:** They are essential for keeping warm in the winter. Classic camel, black, and navy styles include chunky knits, turtlenecks, and cashmere sweaters.

- **Hats:** Keep warm throughout the winter with a wool or knit beanie. In recent years, baseball hats have become more popular for a relaxed look on the weekends for both men and women.

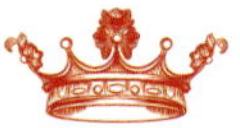

SCARVES

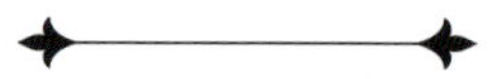

Scarves are an essential part of Parisian fashion. Parisians wear them year-round and change styles according to the weather, layering with a dress, shirt, sweater or coat. The addition of a scarf instantly elevates an outfit. Below are the details by season on scarves and how Parisians wear them.

- **Winter** scarves are made of thick wool or chunky black, charcoal, or navy knits. Parisians wear them draped around the shoulder or tied in a knot under the chin, paired with tailored dark coats and boots.

- **Spring** scarves are are lighter in weight with brighter colors, pastels, and florals. They are often tied around the neck or the handle of a handbag. Vintage designer scarves found at secondhand stores or brocantes (flea markets) are perfect for this.

- **Summer** styles are mostly made of linen or sheer material in light colors. Hair scarves are tied around the head, on ponytails, or wrapped on headbands.

- **Autumn** brings out wool or cashmere scarves to help with the transitional, colder weather. Chunky knits in plaids, navy, camel, and gray are popular.

Where to Shop for Scarves in Paris:

- Brocantes (flea markets) and secondhand shops offer vintage scarves from various designer labels with unique colors and patterns. The shopkeeper should be able to provide some history or time stamp for the scarf.
- Major department stores, such as Galeries Lafayette and Bon Marché.
- Hermès on Rue Saint-Honoré is where you will find the flagship location of the luxury fashion house. Make an experience out of finding the perfect scarf.
- Balibaris has several locations and is one of my husband's favorites.
- Octobre Éditions is also great for men's scarves. It is our tradition to pick up a new scarf for the fall season to remember our trip.

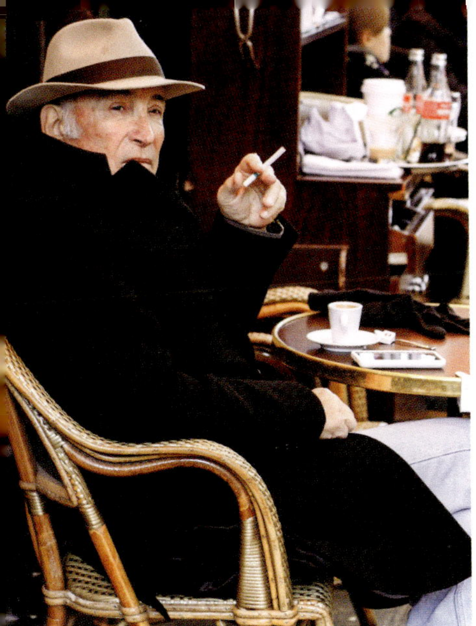

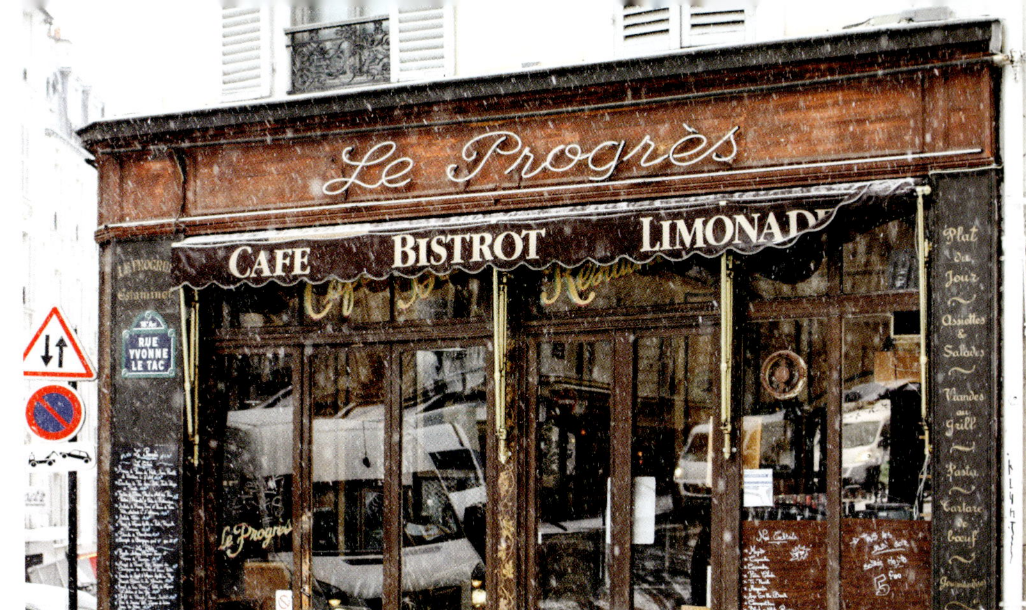

Le Progrès
CAFE
BISTROT
RUE YVONNE LE TAC
Plat du Jour
Assiettes & Salades
Viandes au grill
Pasta
Tartare de boeuf

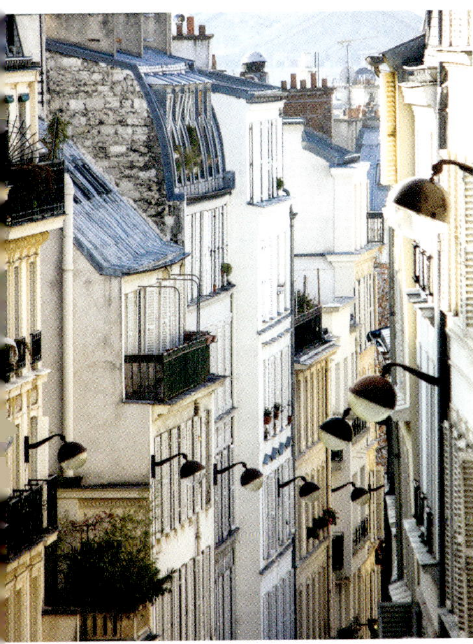

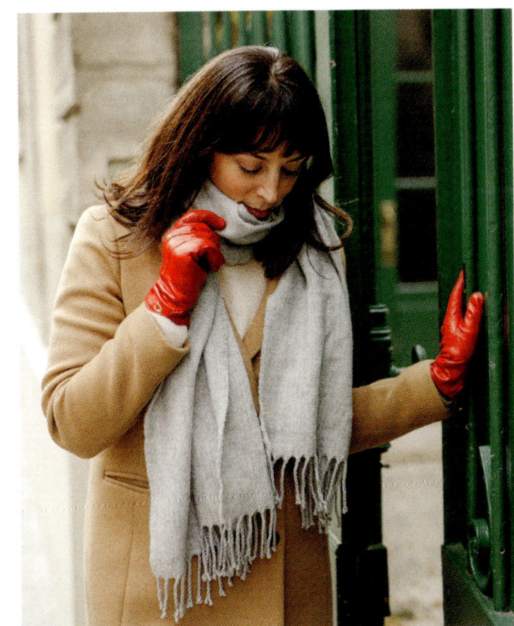

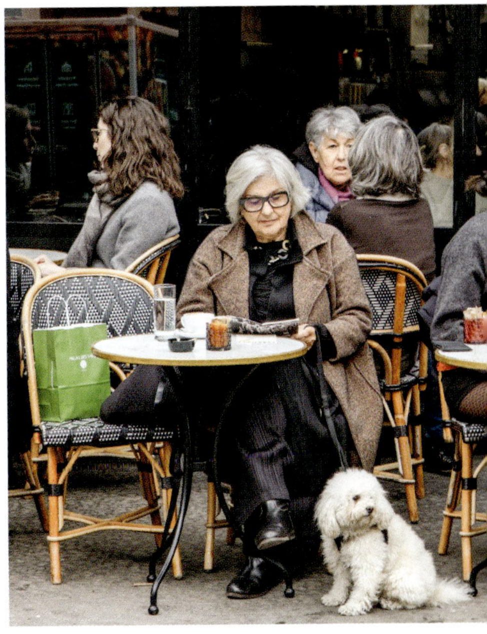

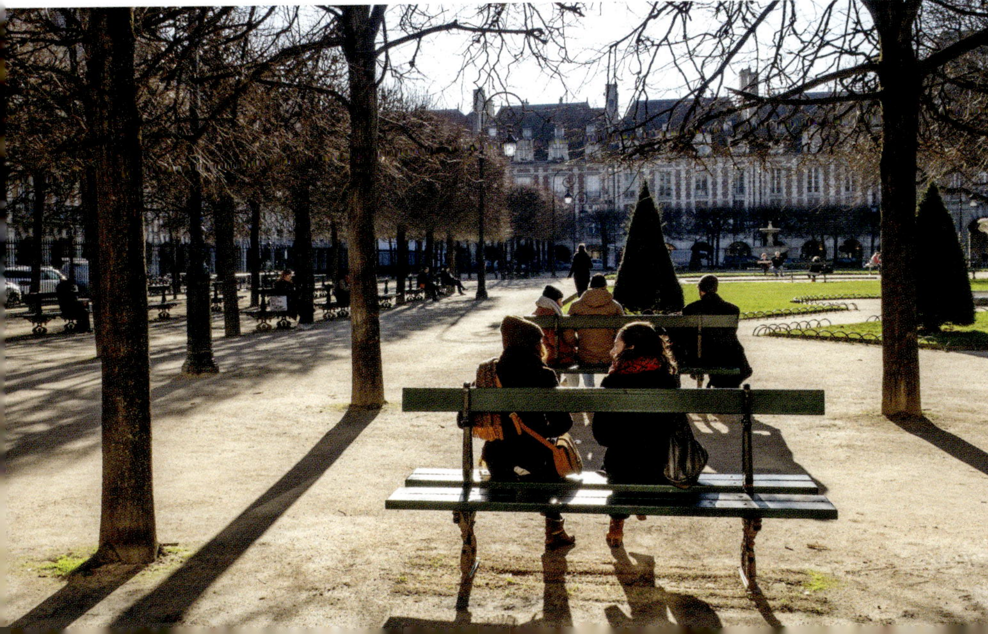

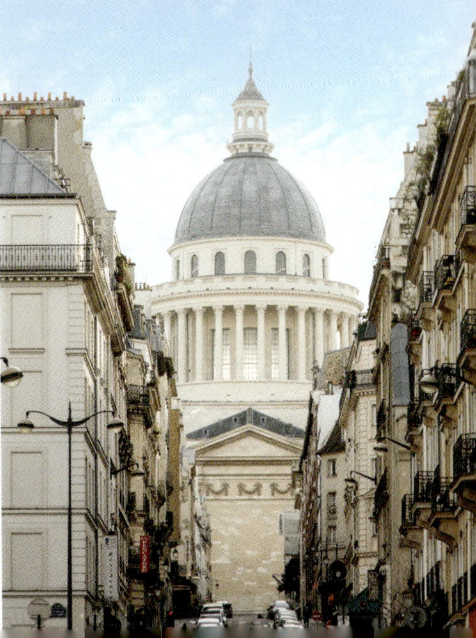

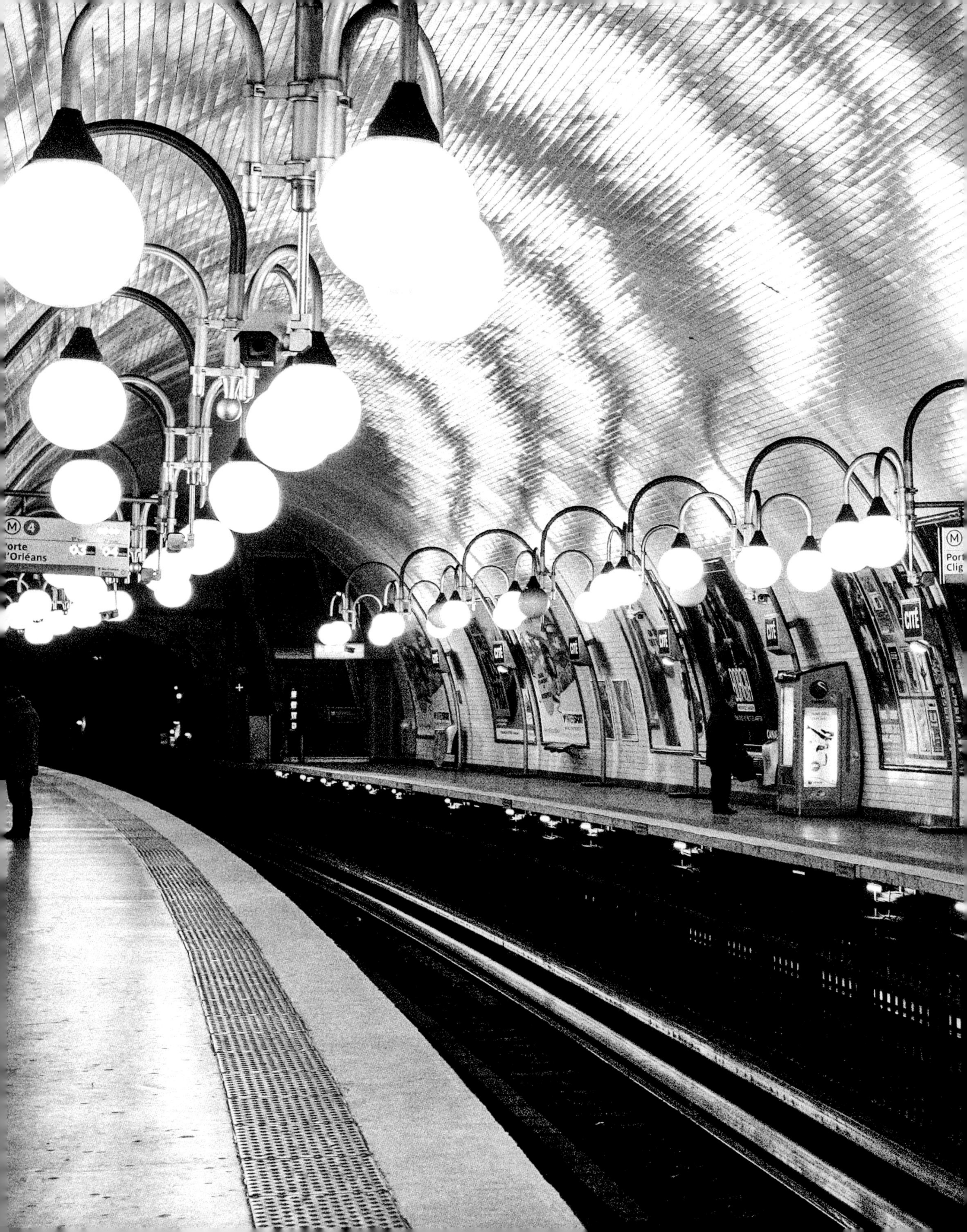
Porte
CITÉ

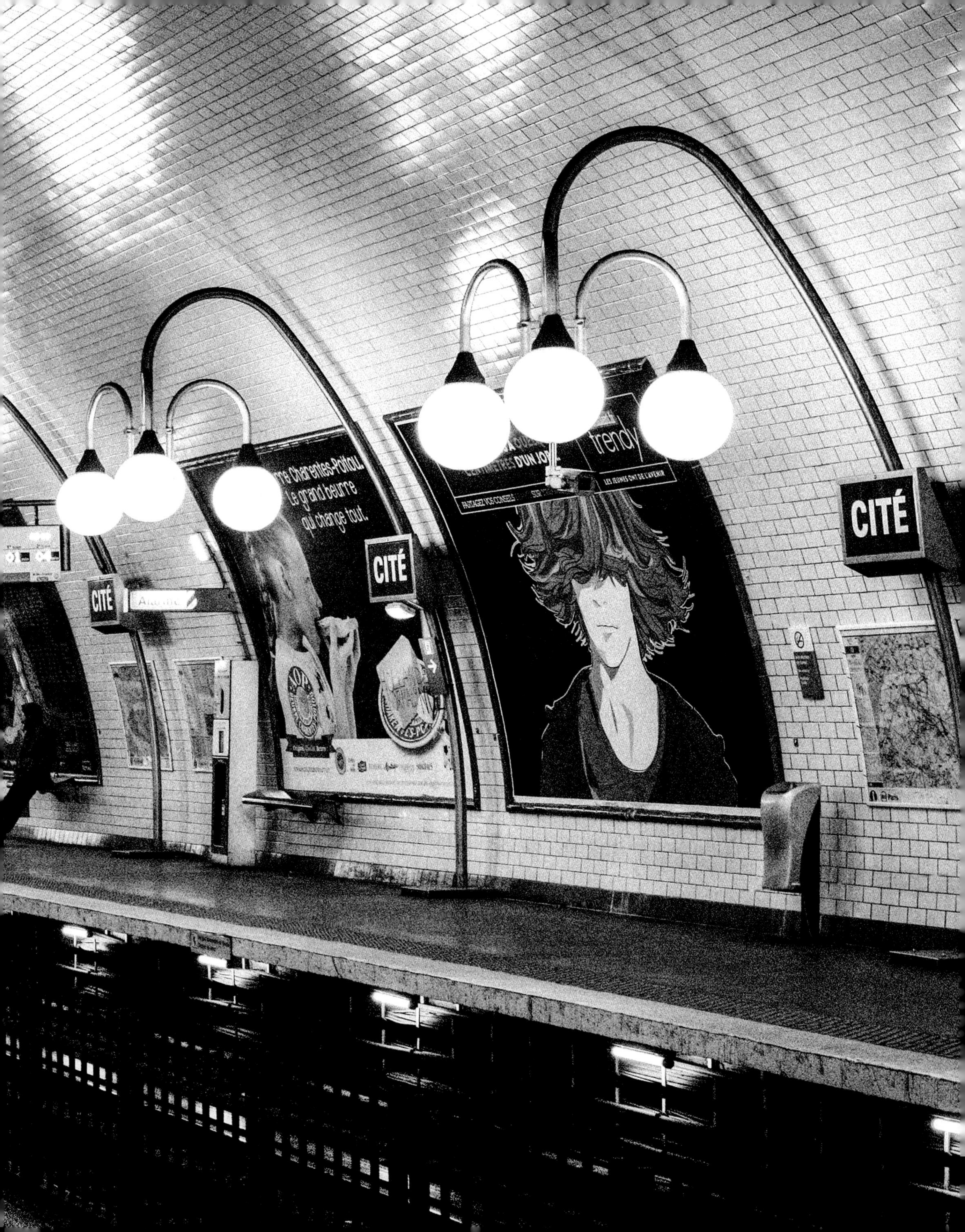
Charentes-Poitou.
Le grand beurre
qui change tout.
trendy
CITÉ
CITÉ
CITÉ

WINTER AT THE MARKET

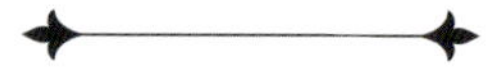

When shopping the markets in winter, look for the signs with the food name and origin. It can help determine flavor and freshness. Eating oysters at the market is a ritual. Flower vendors will have seasonal beauties for your home.

Fruits and Nuts

- Citrus like clementines and oranges
- Apples
- Pears
- Chestnuts

Vegetables

- Cabbage
- Brussels sprouts
- Leeks
- Truffles

Flowers

- Mimosas
- Hyacinths
- Ranunculus
- Chrysanthemums

Seafood

- Oysters
- Fish
- Scallops
- Mussels

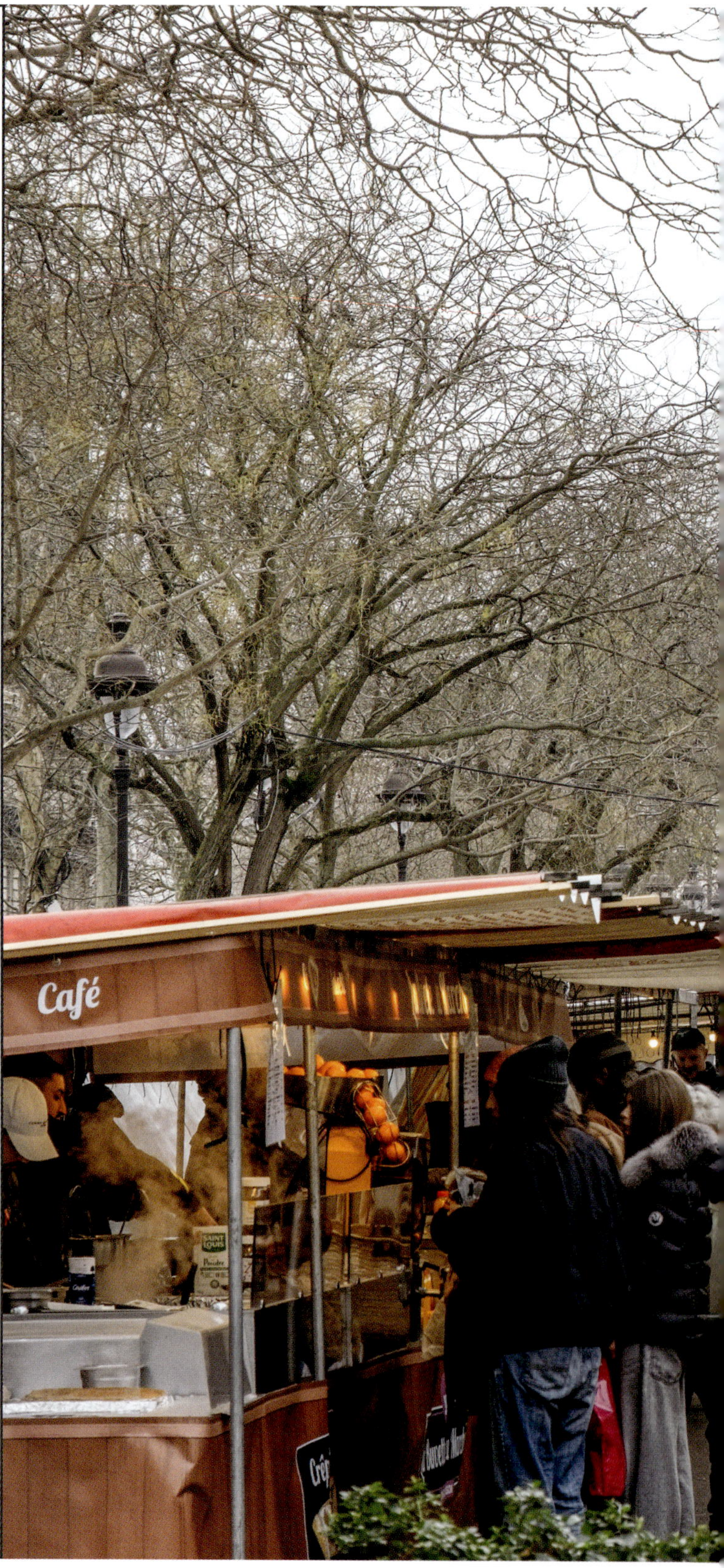

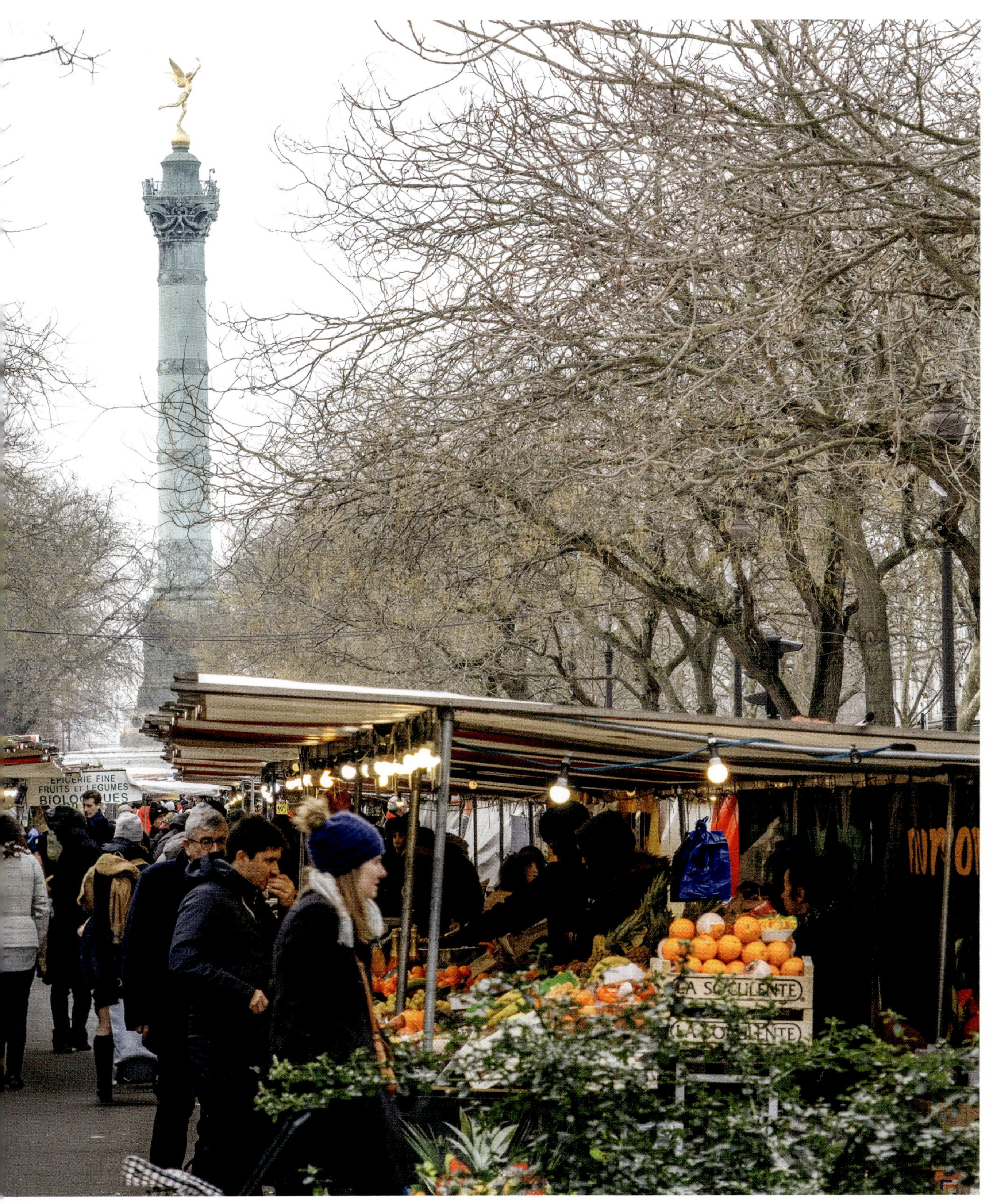
EPICERIE FINE
FRUITS ET LEGUMES

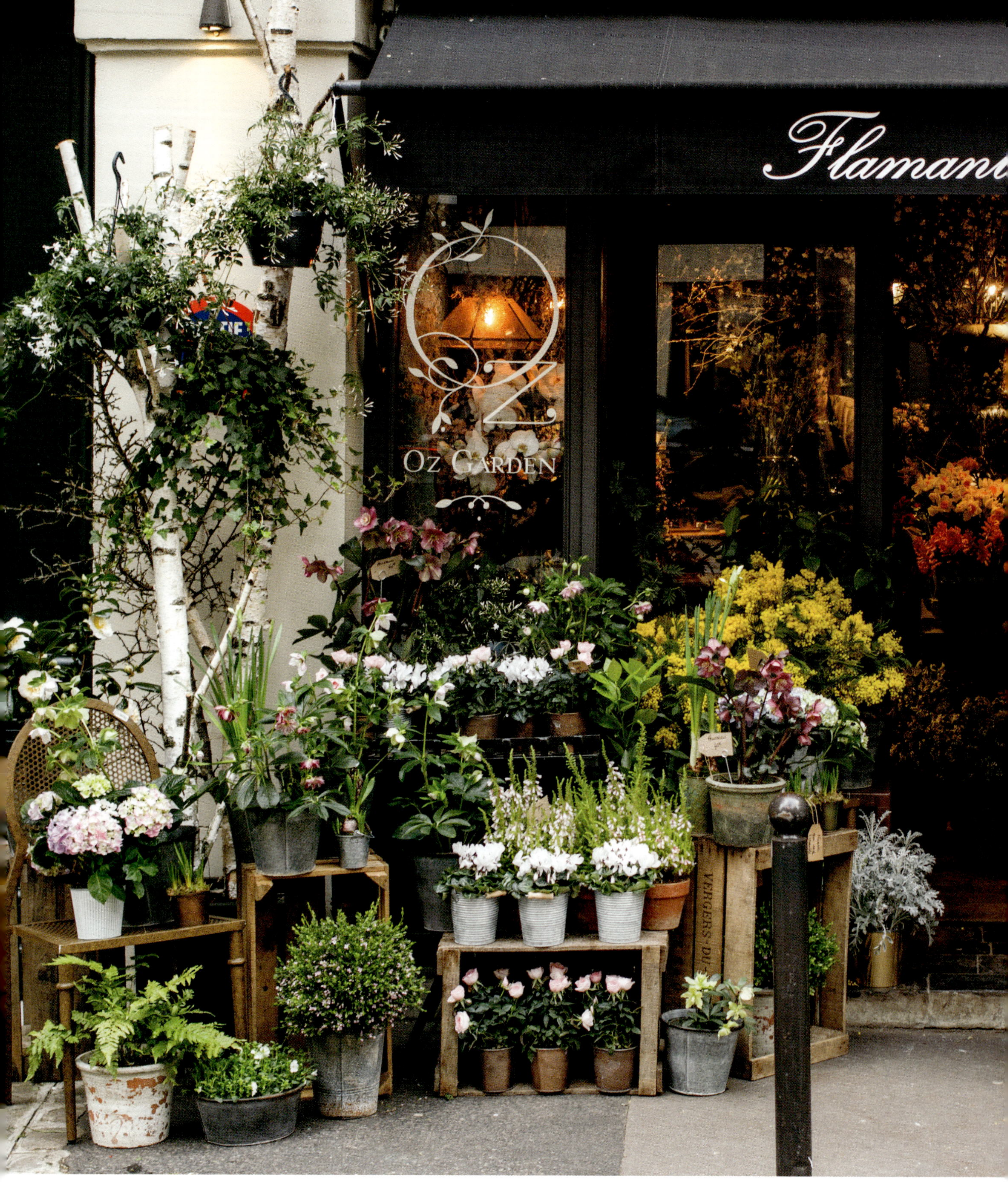
Oz Garden

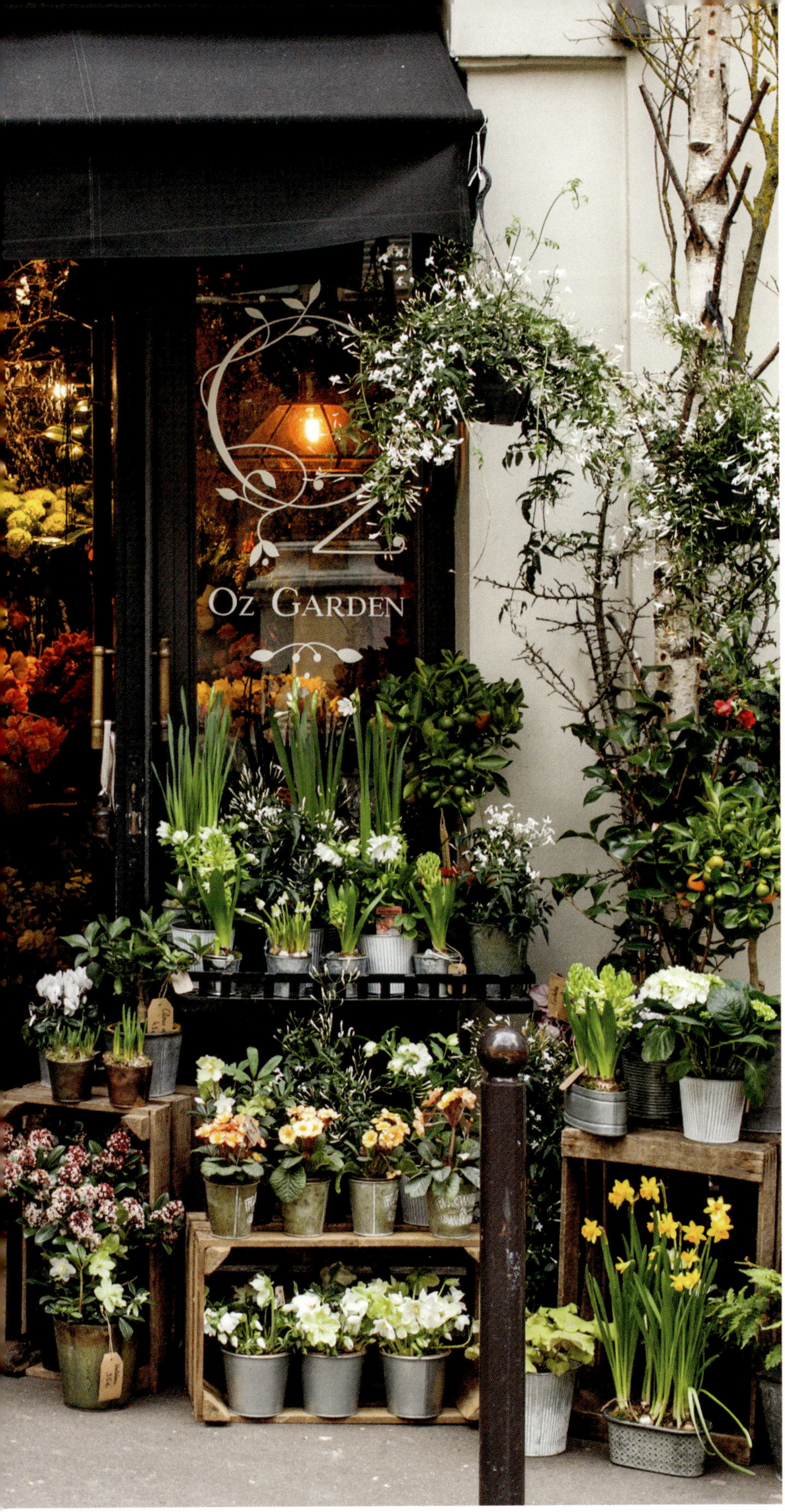

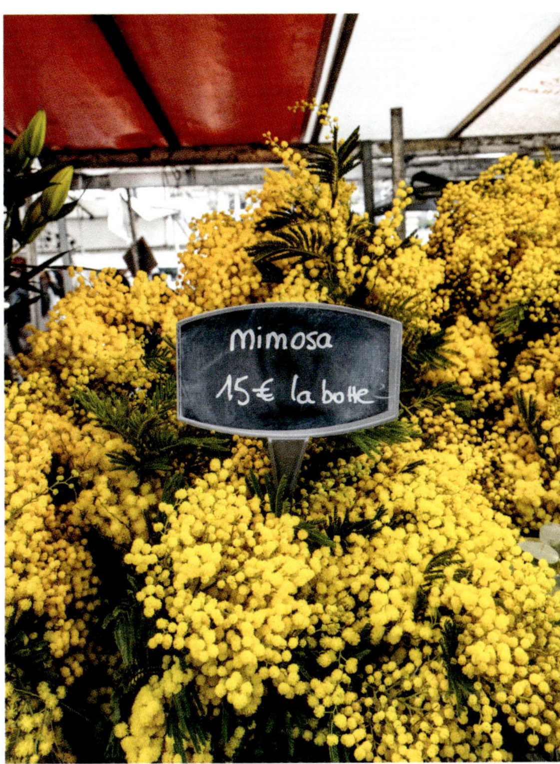

Look out for the bright pop of color from Mimosas, a fragrant winter flower available at corner shops around the city. The smell of its golden blooms is strong and intoxicating, and permeates the air. You'll also find Hyacinths and Ranunculus in season. You will find a flower shop or two in every neighborhood.

Snow in Paris is rare, but it does happen. My wish for it came true twice in early 2013, and I experienced the city covered with snow. This was before Instagram became popular, and the city was pretty quiet during the initial snowfall. I explored my neighborhood of Montmartre with my camera and found my way to Place des Vosges in the Marais.

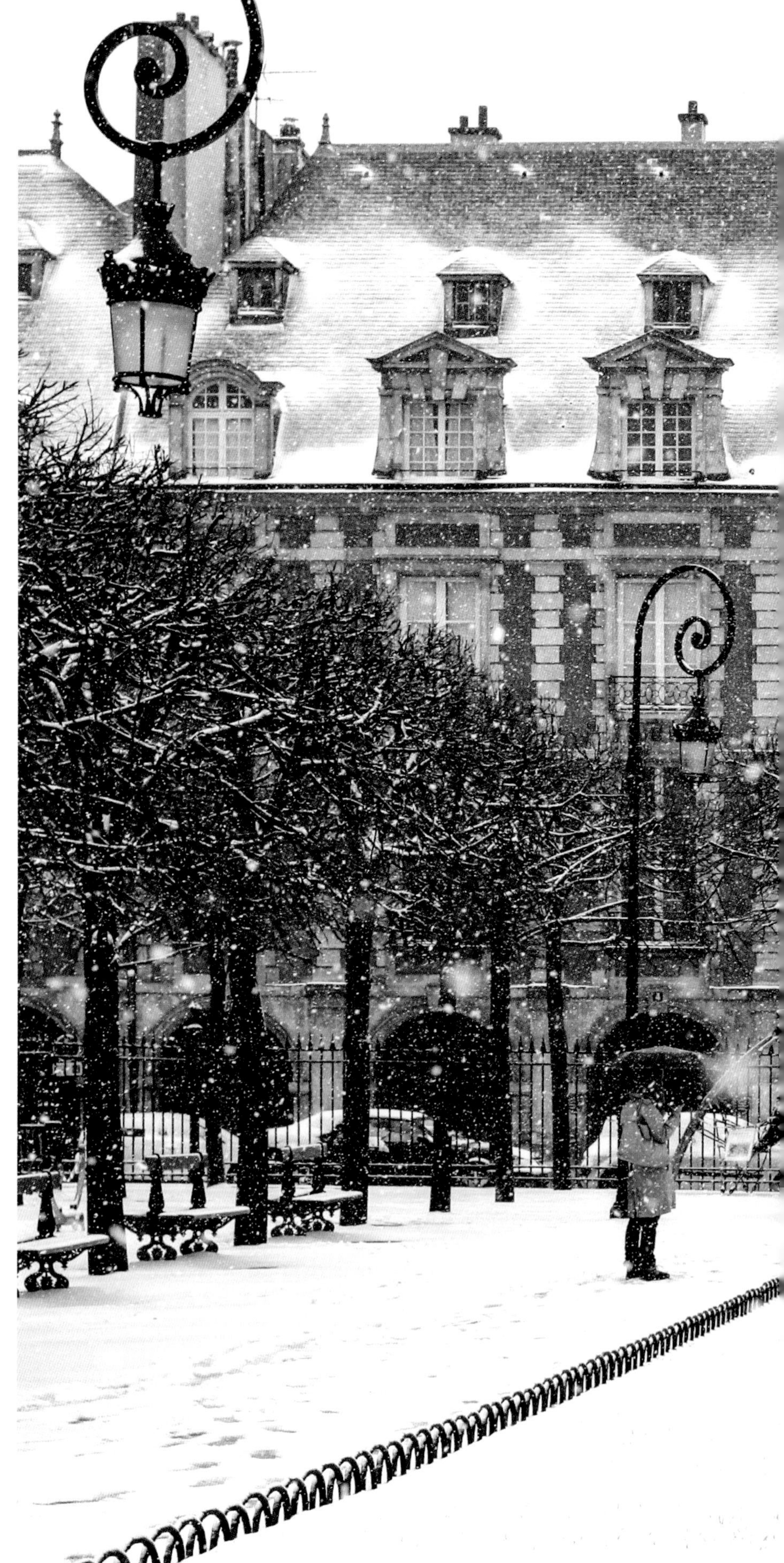

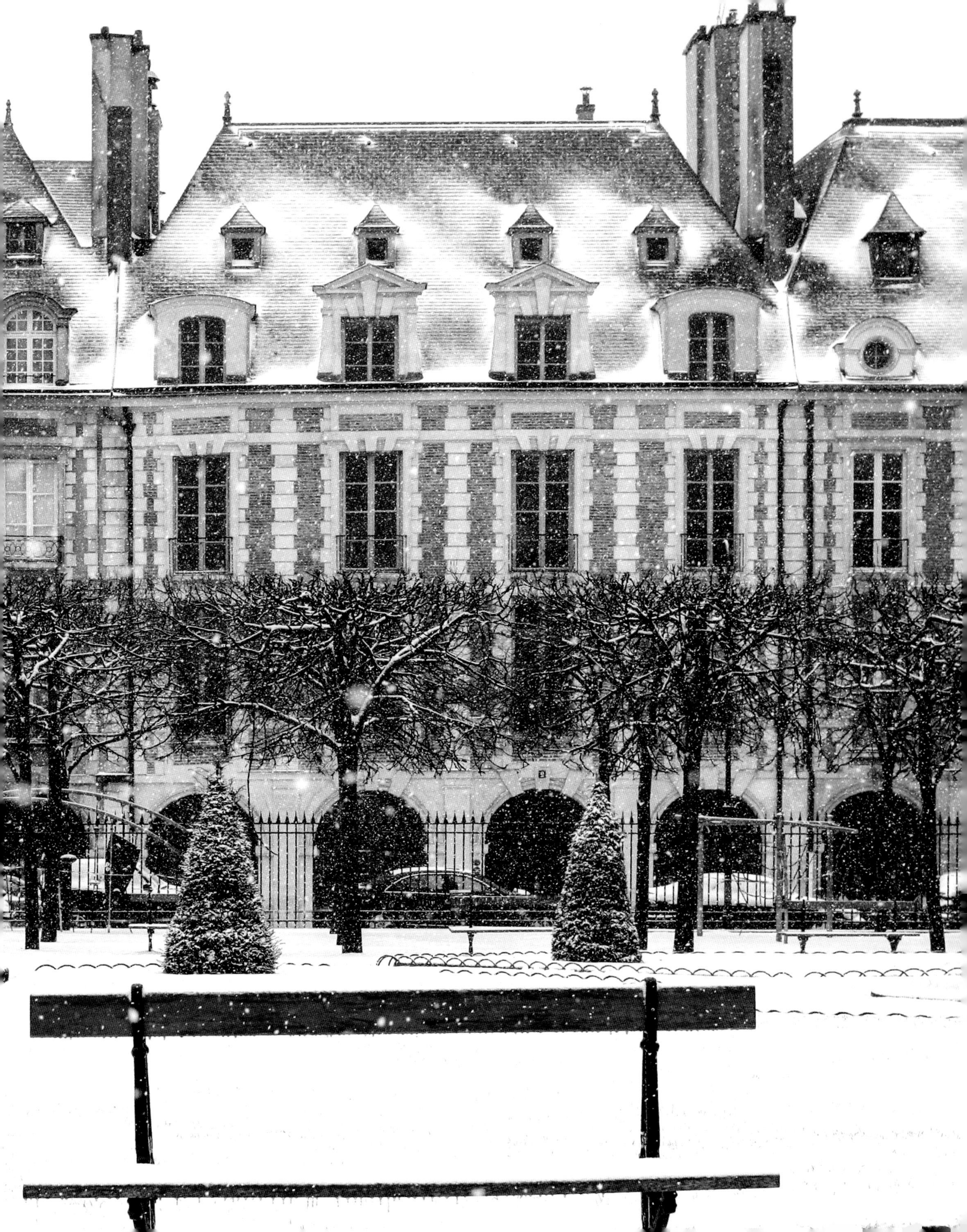

On one January trip, the city had a dusting of snow that coated the roads, cars, and rooftops.

The snow started to fall as I was sitting at dinner at a restaurant in the 9th arrondissement. I looked out the window and could see large flakes falling from the sky at a rapid pace. My solo meal ended without dessert as I was eager to experience the city. Paris was calm and quiet as I walked back to my hotel in the falling snow, soaking in every minute.

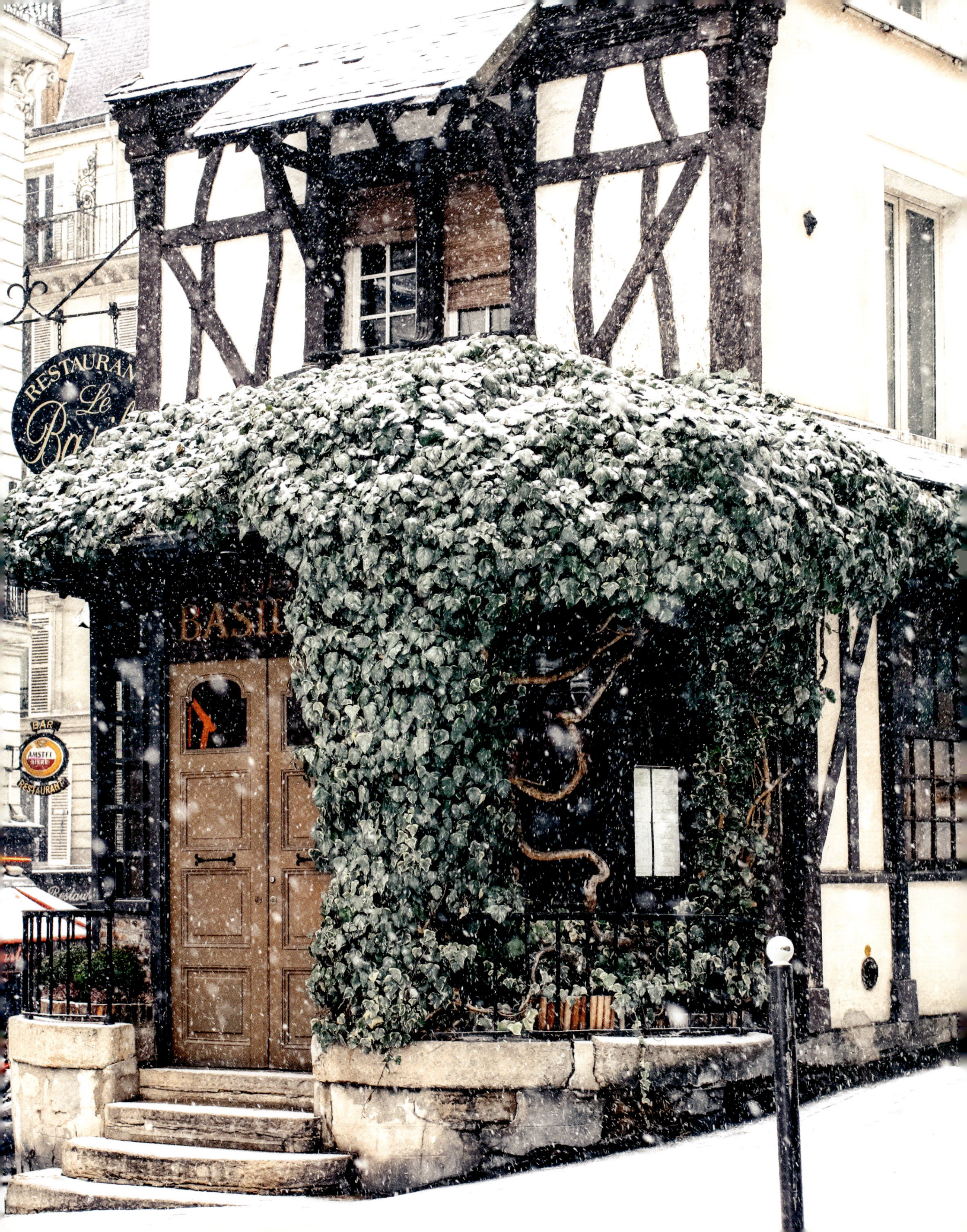
RESTAURAN
Le
BAR

le printemps
{SPRING}

Paris wakes up from a cold winter slumber in March. The city starts to see buds forming on trees, and the bare, brown gardens slowly turn shades of green. Blooms begin to take hold, brightening streets and parks, encouraging all to head outdoors and relish the colorful display.

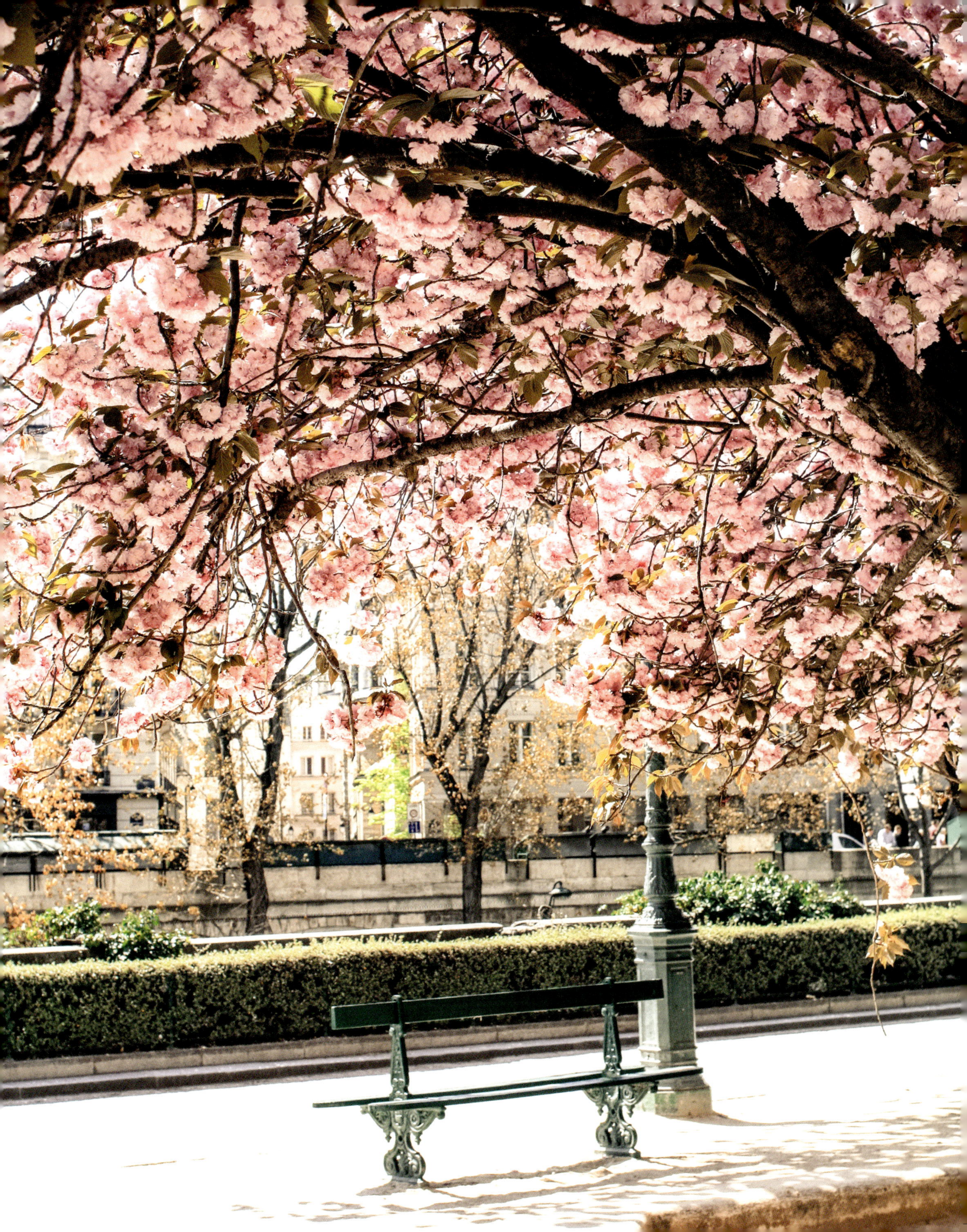

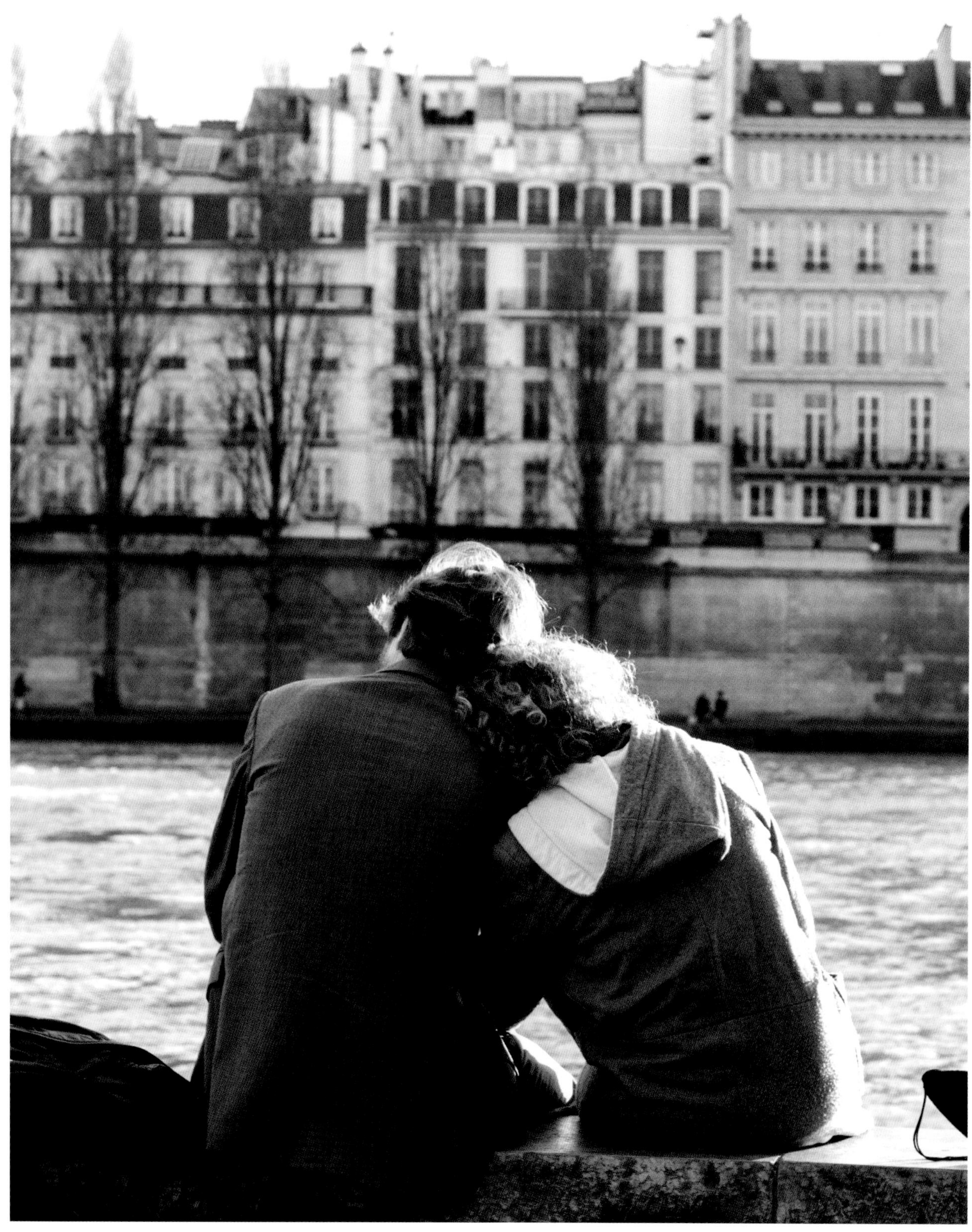

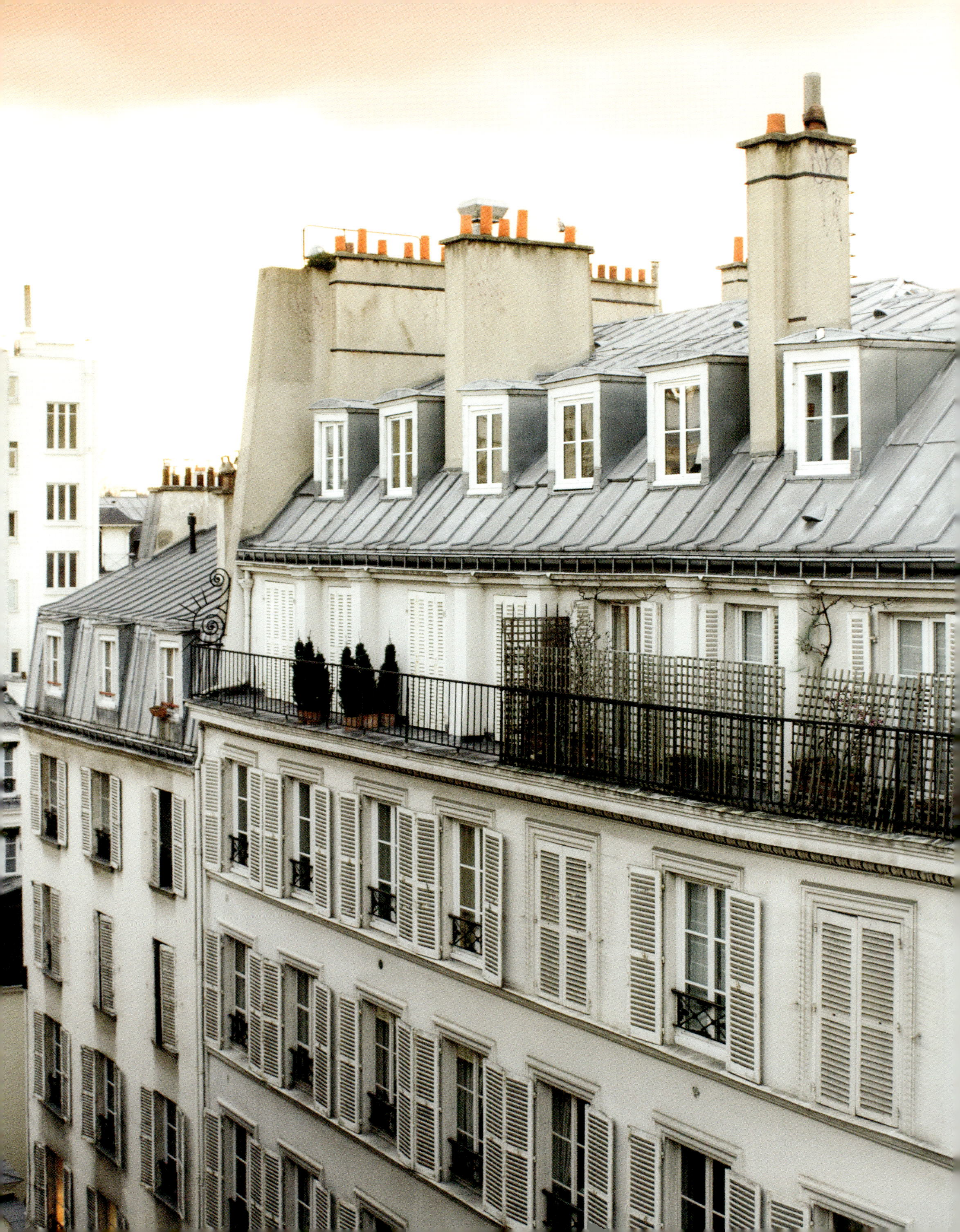

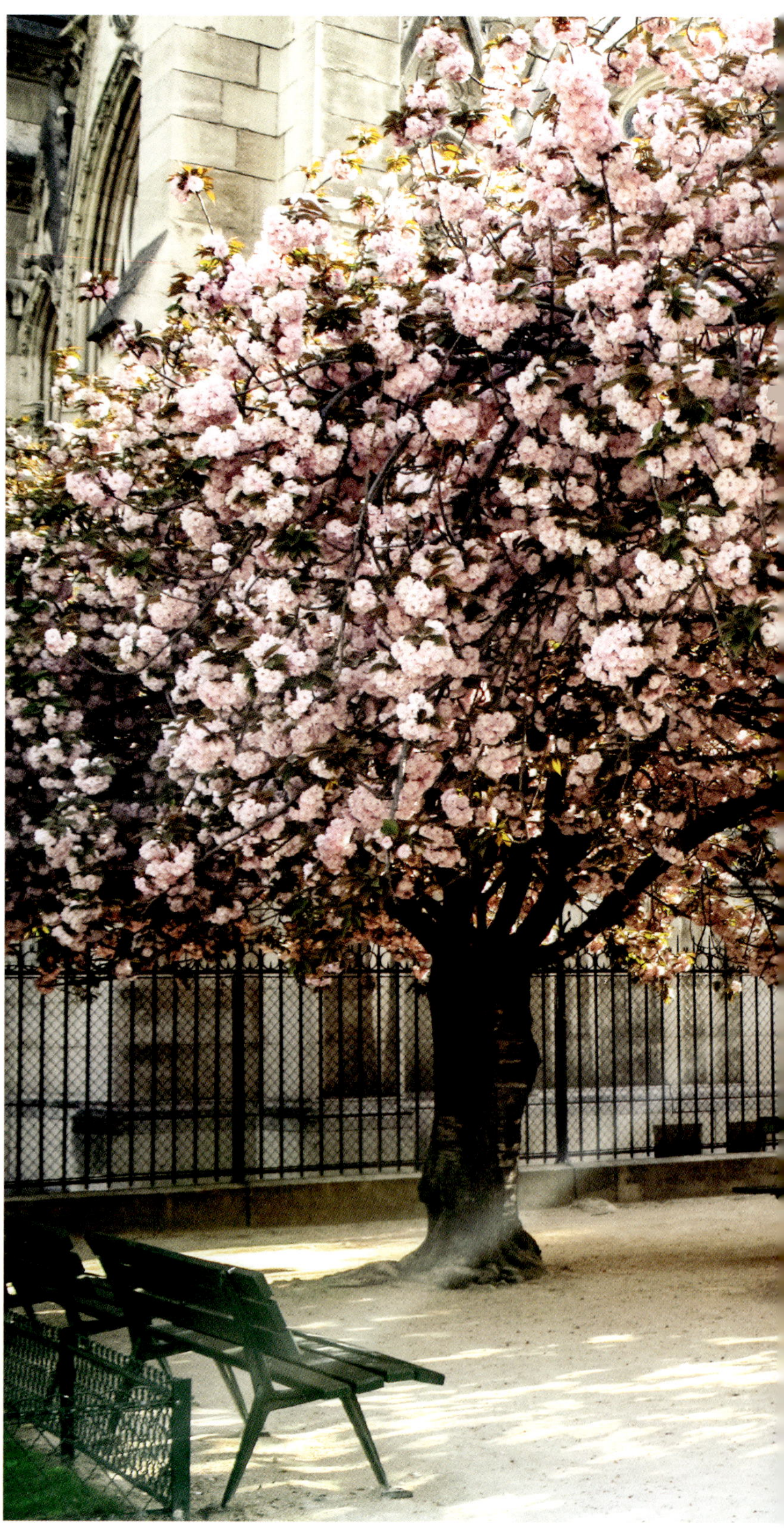

It starts with one bloom, and then the next, in a progression of pink blossoms.

Apple blossoms are tiny pink flowers that come to life in early March and can be found on trees near the Eiffel Tower and throughout the city. Daffodils and tulips add their own bright color to the gray-and-blue palette that fills the city in winter. In recent years, Paris blossom season has begun earlier. While a good portion of the prime offering used to be in April, it now starts in mid-March with the magnolia trees. These aren't all over the city, but you will find them outside the Hôtel de Ville, Eiffel Tower, Champ de Mars, Jardin des Tuileries, and Palais-Royal. These pink blossoms are large and will last for almost two weeks.

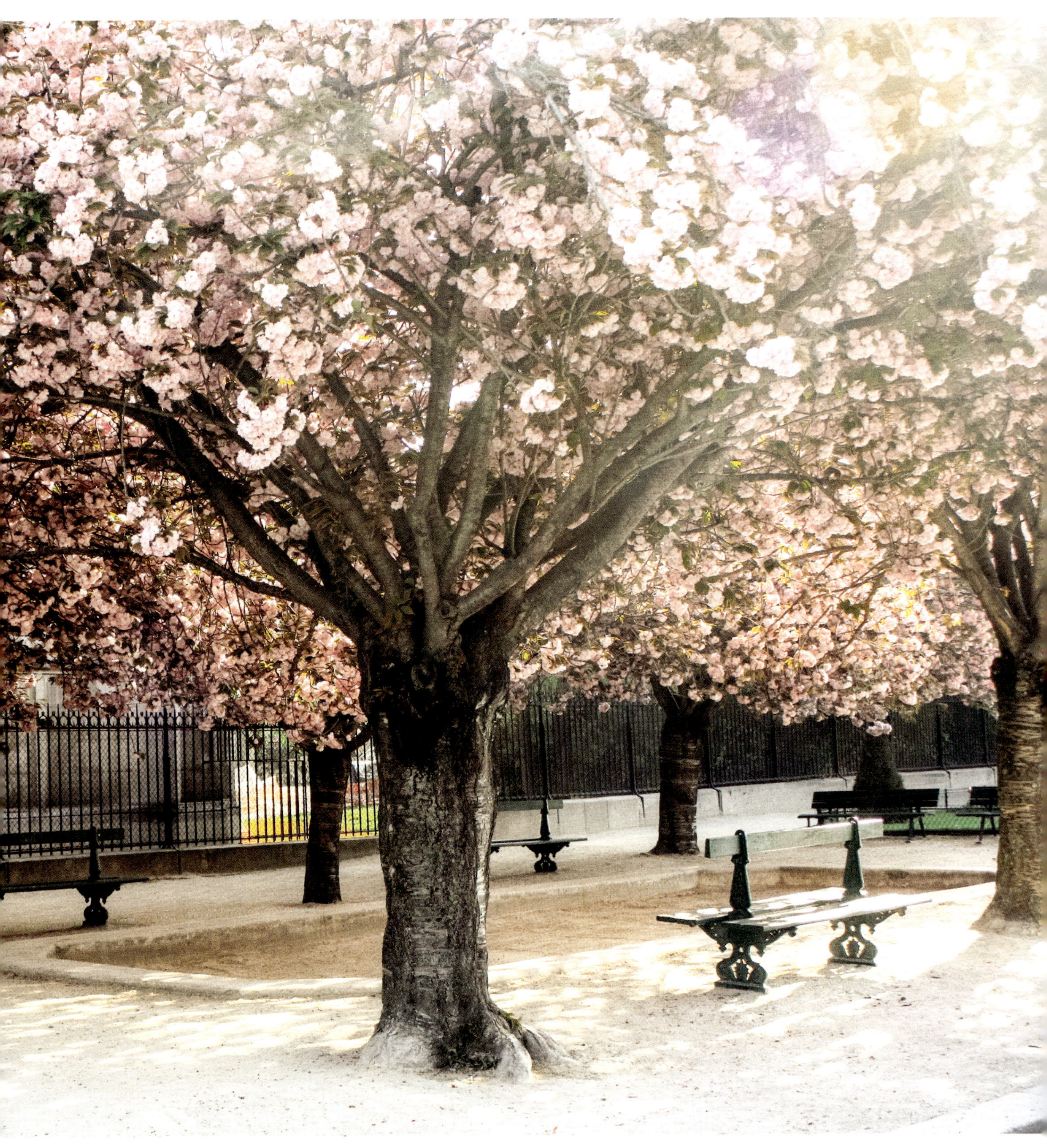

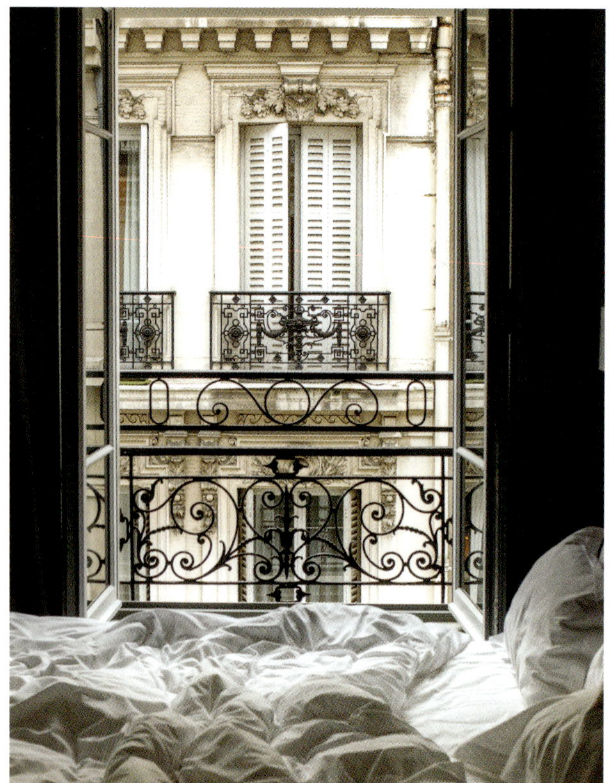

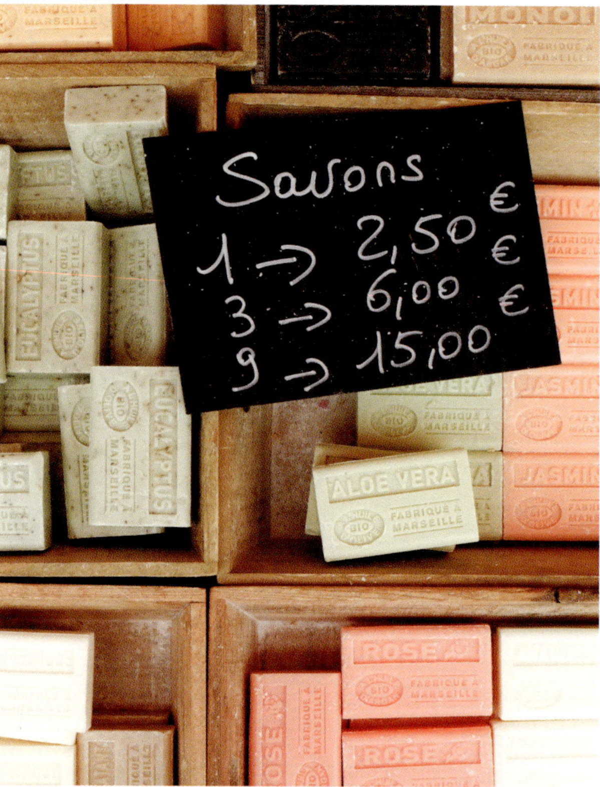

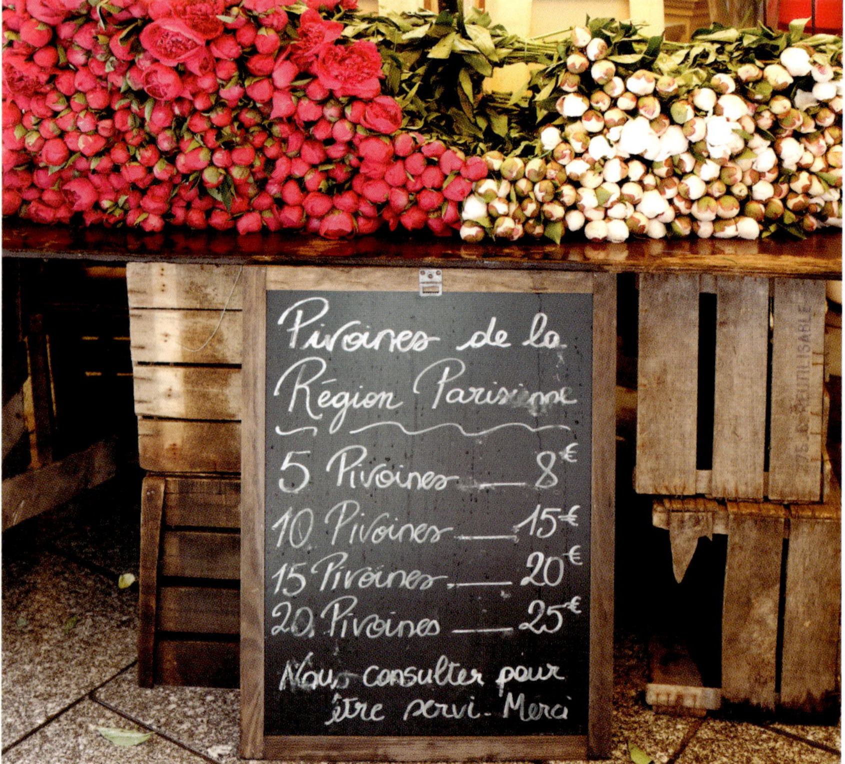

Sundays in Paris are special to me. My first apartment was in Montmartre, and I found the Marché Bastille by walking past it. I loved the energy and the ability to pick up fresh seasonal ingredients each week. The Marché Bastille became part of my Sunday routine, with a trip to the boulangerie for a baguette and a stroll along the Seine.
I found a trip to the market could make a sometimes lonely, solo day feel unique, and it became something I would look forward to each week. A Parisian Sunday isn't about rushing. It is about slowing life down, spending time with friends and family, and preparing for the week ahead.

SUNDAYS IN PARIS

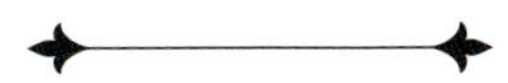

- **Winter**
  The markets are open year-round. On the Left Bank, try Place Monge with its beautiful trees giving shade to stalls where vendors sell meats, cheese, produce, flowers, and other essentials. The Marché Bastille, with more than 100 merchants, is one of the largest markets and has gained popularity over the years on the Right Bank. For a more local experience, explore the Marché d'Aligre in the 12th arrondisement. It's off the beaten path with shops that line the street and a covered market. Roast chicken is a popular Sunday meal. You can pick up a delicious version at the market or at a rotisserie in Paris. La Petit Chaise on Rue de Grenelle is a classic Sunday lunch favorite for Parisians.

- **Spring**
  Paris sheds its winter coat with the start of blossom season. Soak up the sunshine by visiting an outdoor terrace for a coffee and a croissant. Pack a picnic with a baguette, cheese, and rosé and head to Jardin du Luxembourg or Jardin des Tuileries. In the afternoon, explore the lively Marais. Then, cross over to Île Saint-Louis for live music and ice cream at Berthillon. Pop into a bookshop like Shakespeare and Company or browse the bouquinistes selling books and souvenirs lining the Seine.

- **Summer**
  Beat the heat with an early morning market visit. Picnic under a shady spot in Place des Vosges, Champ de Mars, or Parc Monceau. Light salads and a crisp bottle of rosé make the perfect meal for hot summer Sundays. Take in the bowling-like game of pétanque at Place Dauphine.

- **Autumn**
  Visit a brocante (flea market) in a new neighborhood you haven't explored. Take a trip to the city's northern edge and browse the sprawling antiques and secondhand market, Marché aux Puces de Saint-Ouen, and find a souvenir to bring home. Spend an afternoon strolling Saint-Germain-des-Prés and pause for a late lunch on a Parisian terrace with a glass of red wine, a good book, and a bowl of French onion soup.

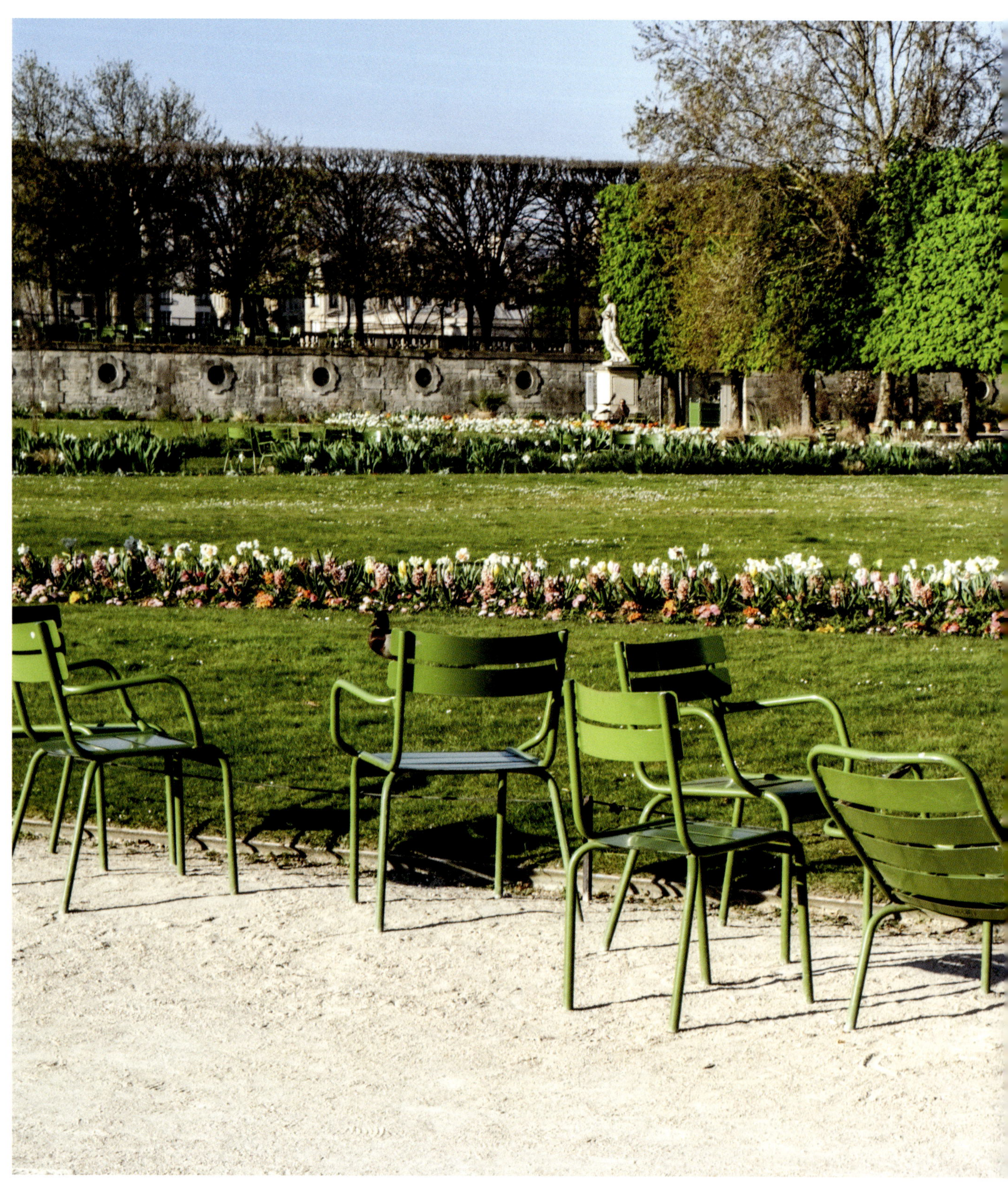

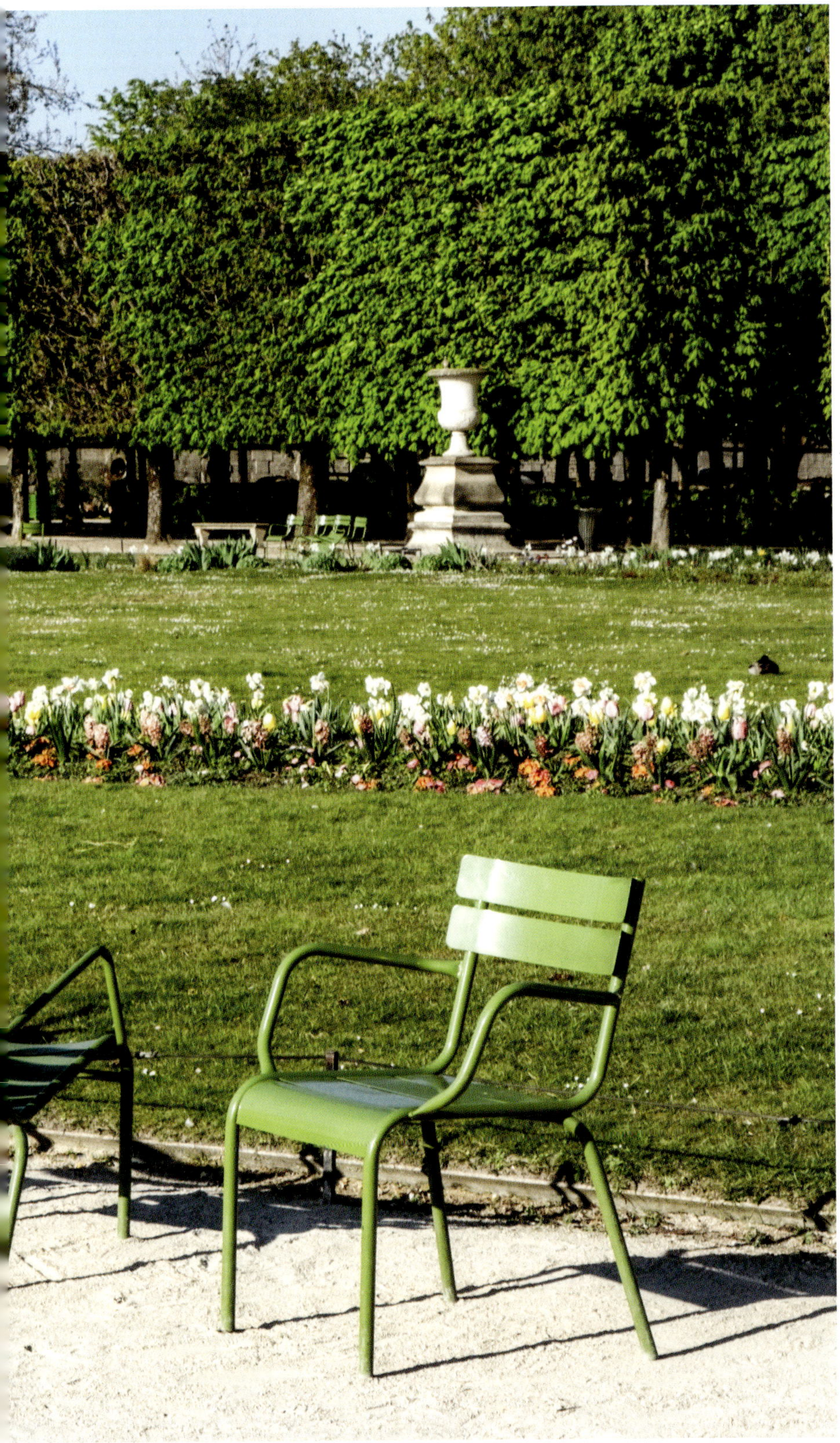

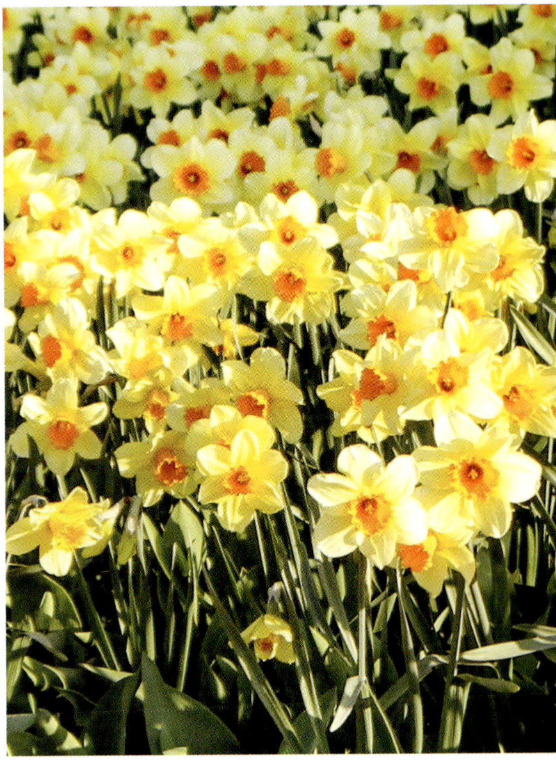

During cherry blossom season at the end of March, the city becomes a sea of pink. What I love most about this short window in spring is that cherry trees all over the town explode with blossoms. It isn't contained in specific areas of the city. You will find them outside grocery stores and on random street corners. By mid-April, daffodils emerge to coat the city with pops of yellow in the many gardens and parks. Parisians will take time to sit on a park bench or chair and enjoy the beauty around them.

SEEKING BLOOMS

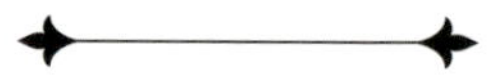

- In front of the Eiffel Tower on the Champ de Mars and surrounding the fountain at Trocadéro, you find a beautiful array of cherry blossom trees.

- Jardin des Plantes has some of the largest cherry blossom trees. You can stand underneath them. The location in the 5th arrondissement is a bit of a destination, but it is worth spending an afternoon or morning here if you have time. One of my many apartments was just around the corner.

- Square Gabriel-Pierné, just off Rue de Seine near the Institut de France, explodes in pink cherry blossoms at the end of March.

- Jardin Anne Frank, a community garden in the Marais, is a bit hidden and worth exploring if you are in the area. It is an excellent spot for kids to play in the morning or afternoon.

- Shakespeare and Company, an English-language bookstore in the heart of the city, has a few large trees in front that bloom in spring.

- One of my top spots to enjoy the cherry blossoms is alongside Notre-Dame. A few trees bloom here yearly, providing shade for a sandbox where kids gather to play.

- Just outside of Paris, the formal gardens of Parc de Sceaux, are a popular picnic destination when cherry blossoms are in bloom. Take the public transit Réseau Express Régional or RER, which translates to "Regional Express Network" in English. Take RER B from the city center, and it is about a 15- to 20-minute walk from the station to the park. Weekends will be busy. I made the solo trip in the pouring rain years ago with no regrets. The town itself on the walk to the Parc is adorable and worth exploring.

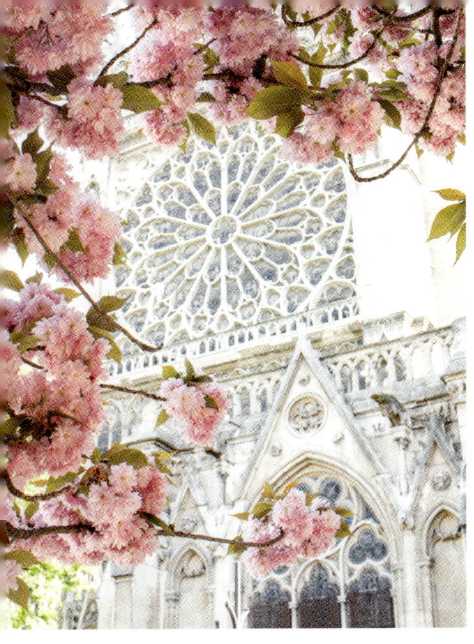
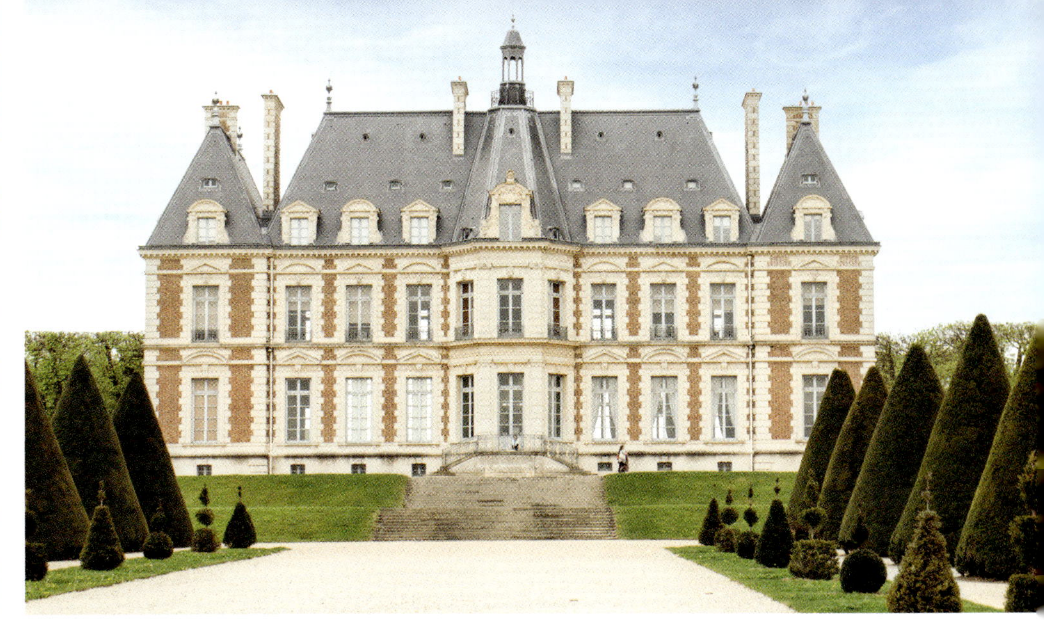
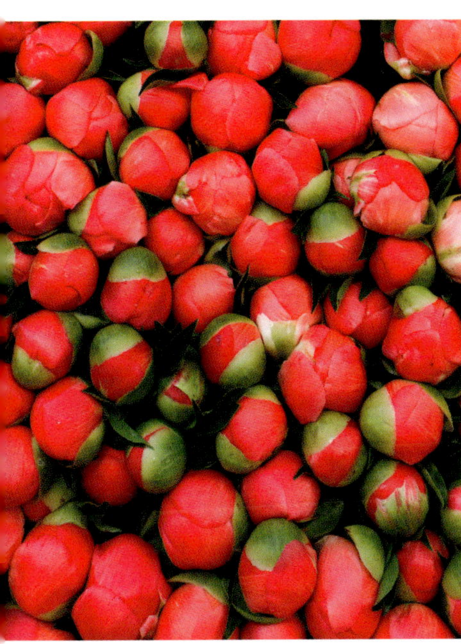
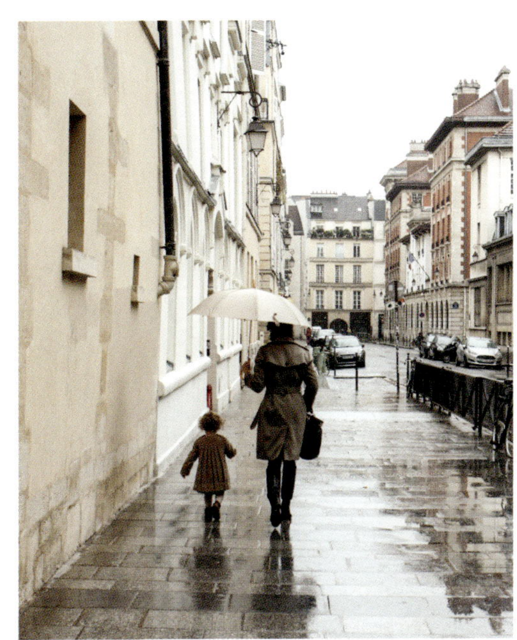
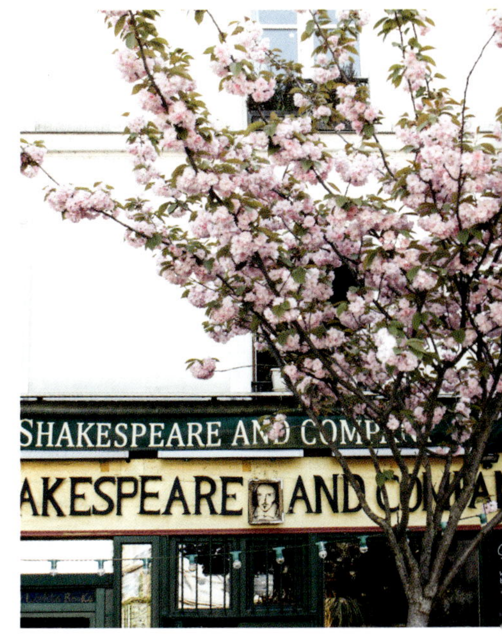
SHAKESPEARE AND COMPA
AKESPEARE AND COMPA
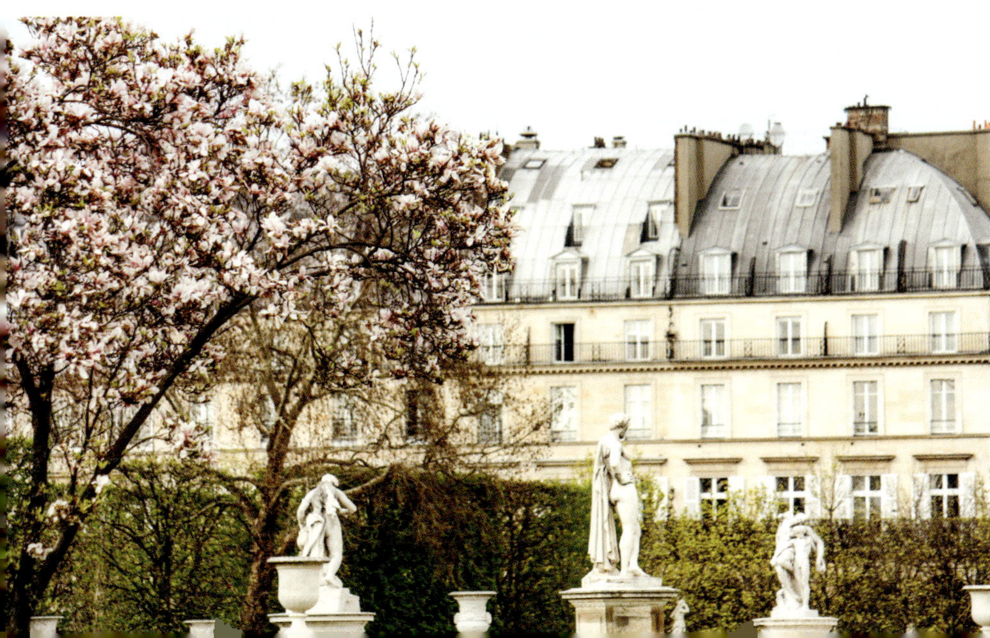
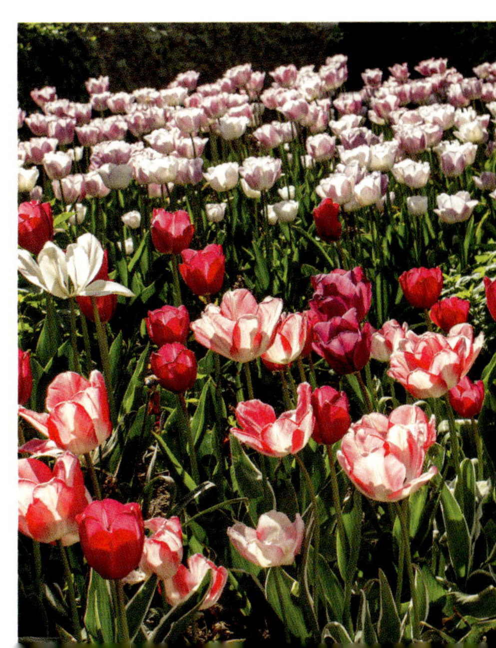

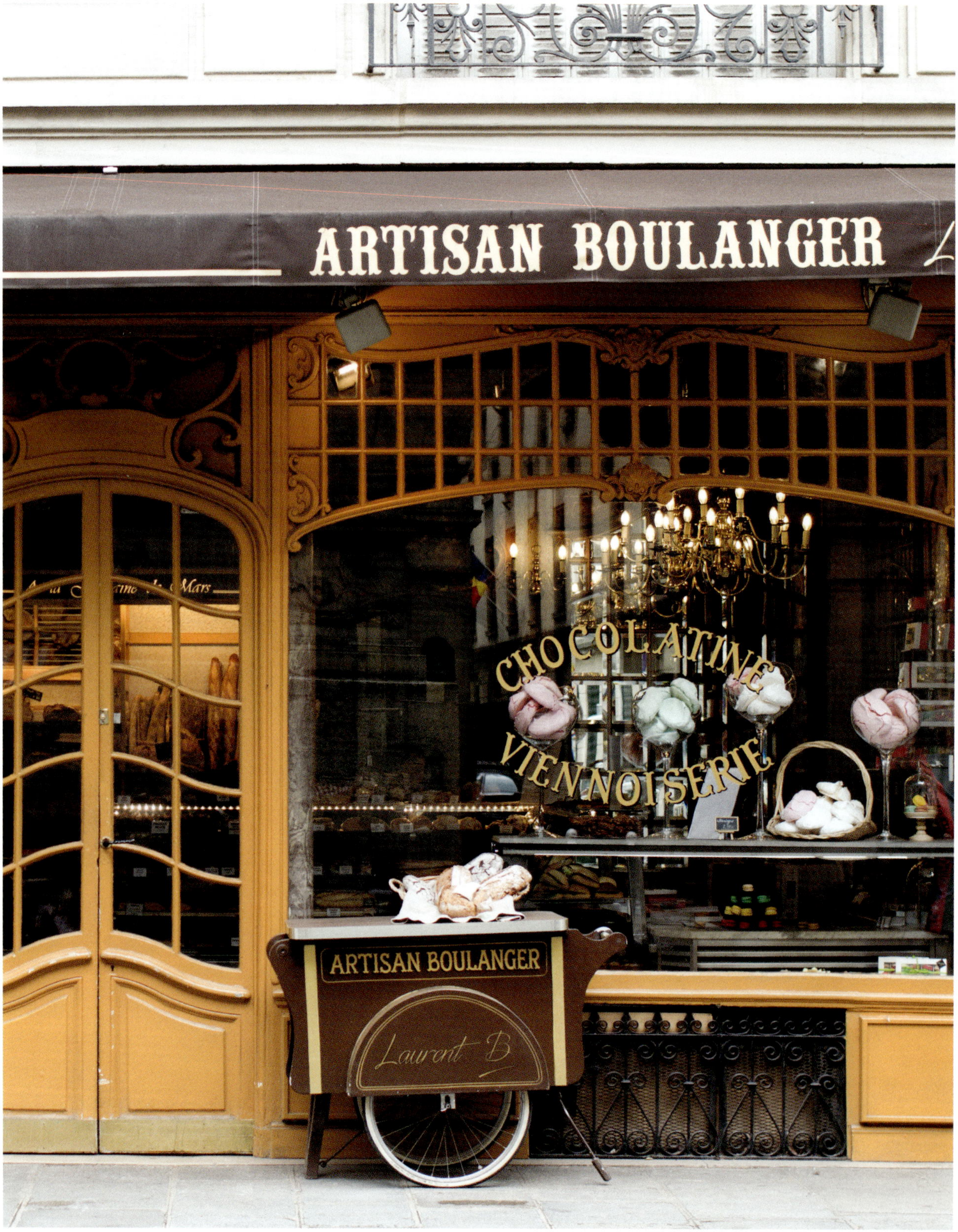

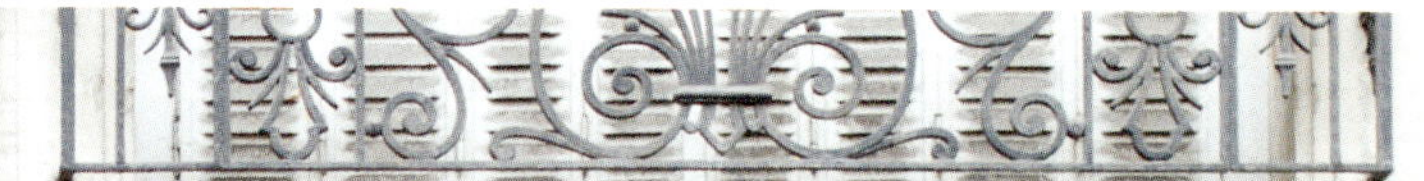
ARTISAN BOULANGER
CHOCOLATINE
VIENNOISERIE
ARTISAN BOULANGER
Laurent B

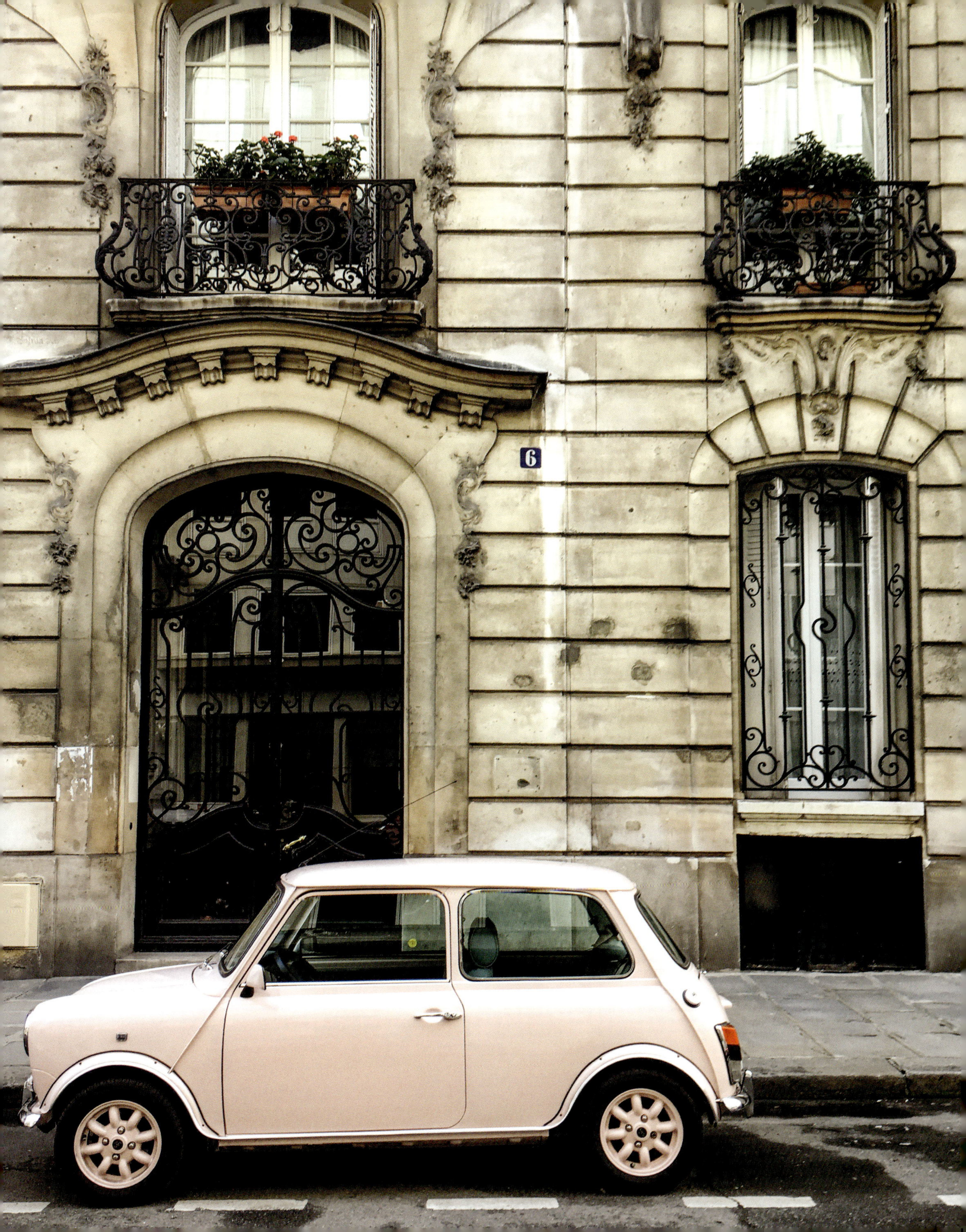
6

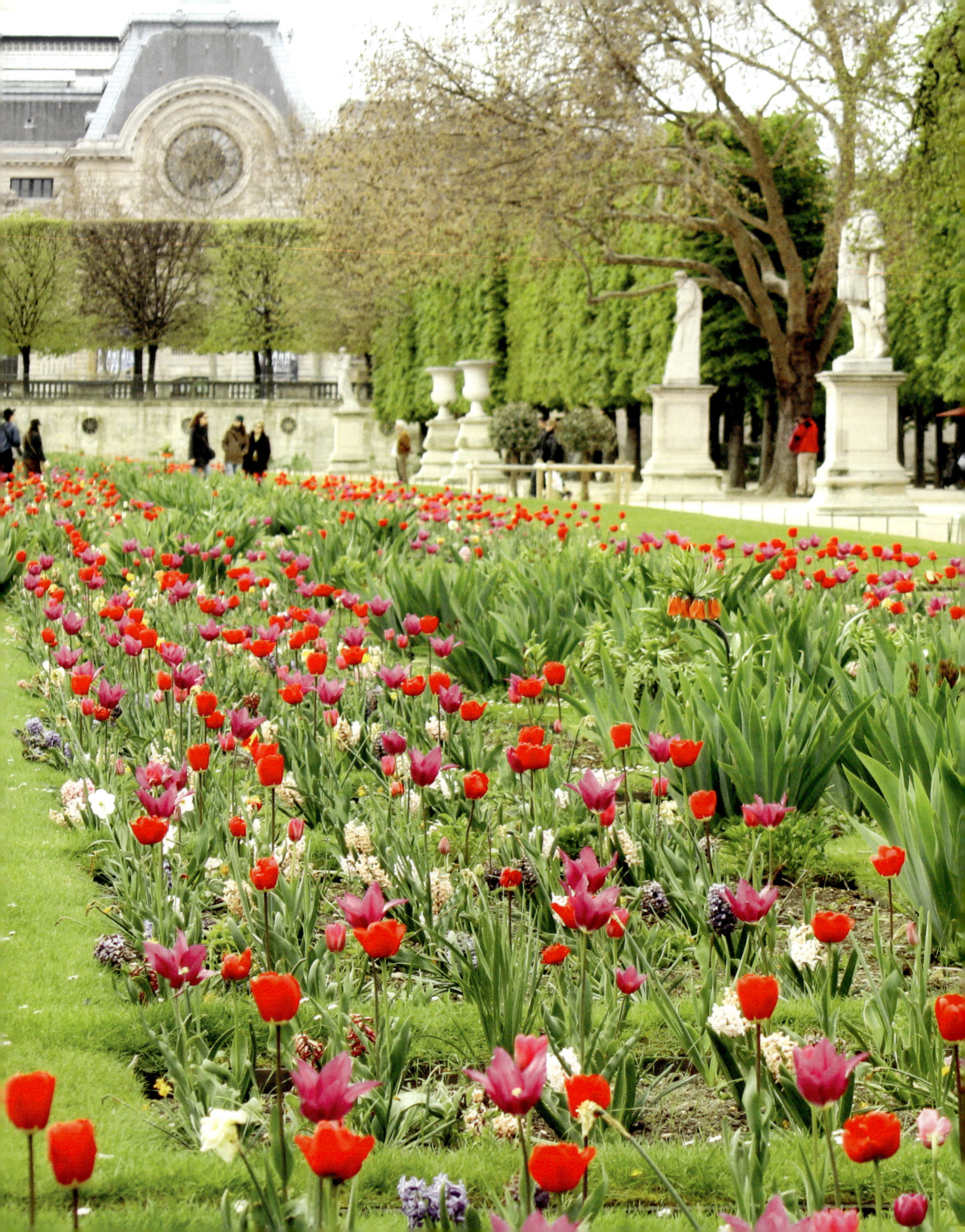

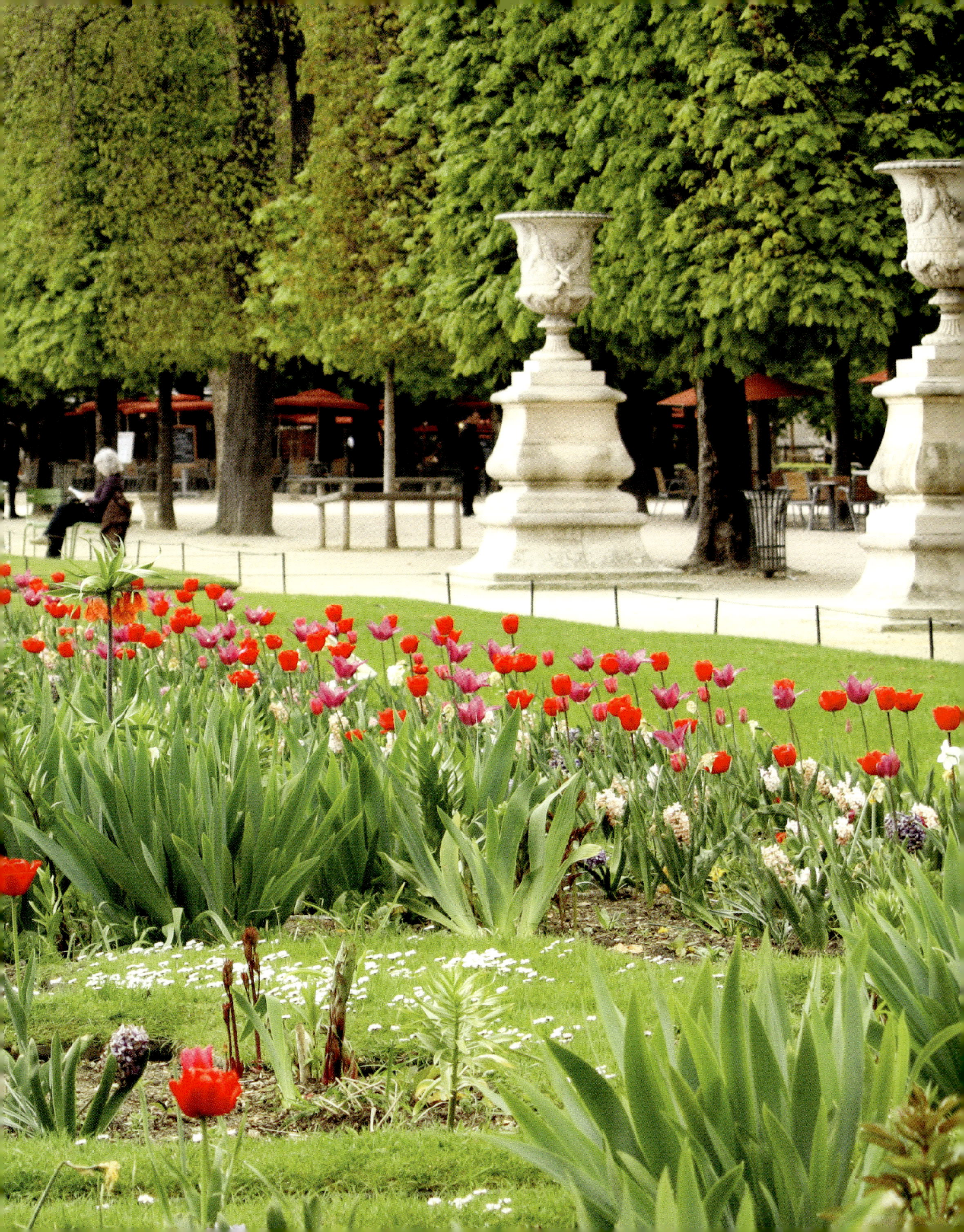

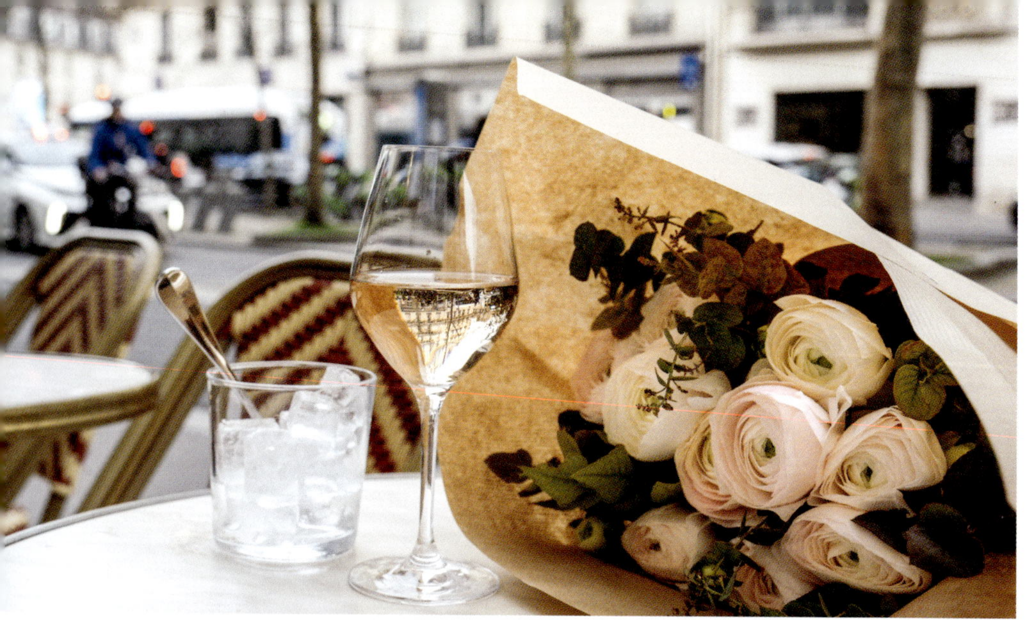

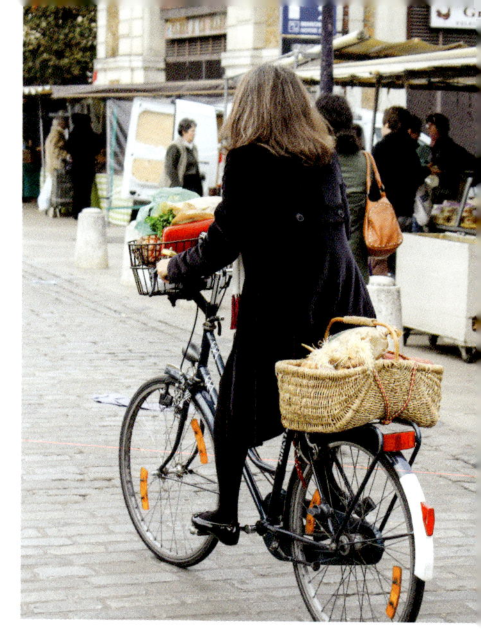

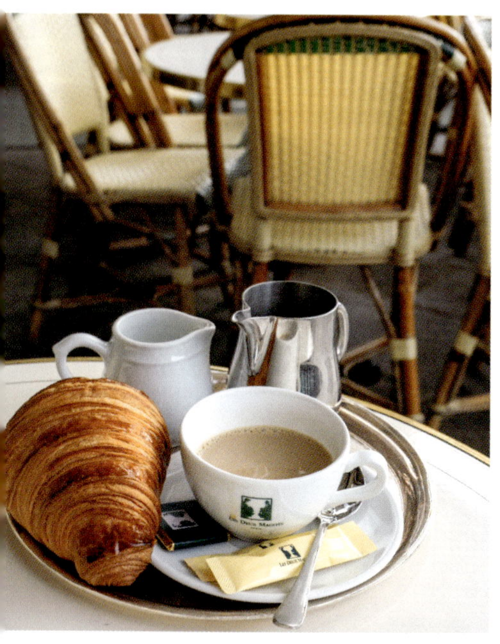

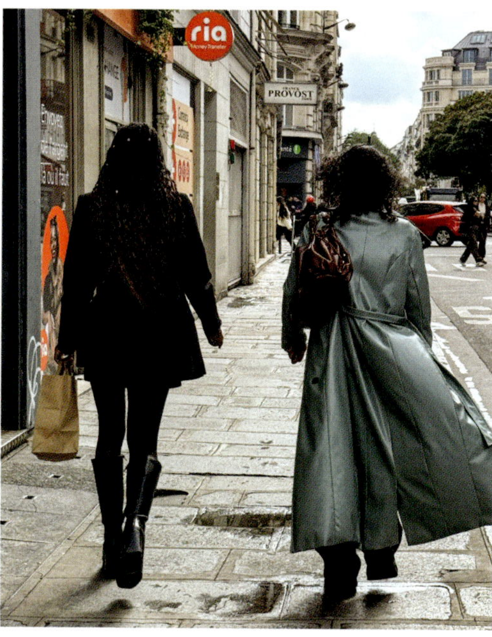
PROVOST

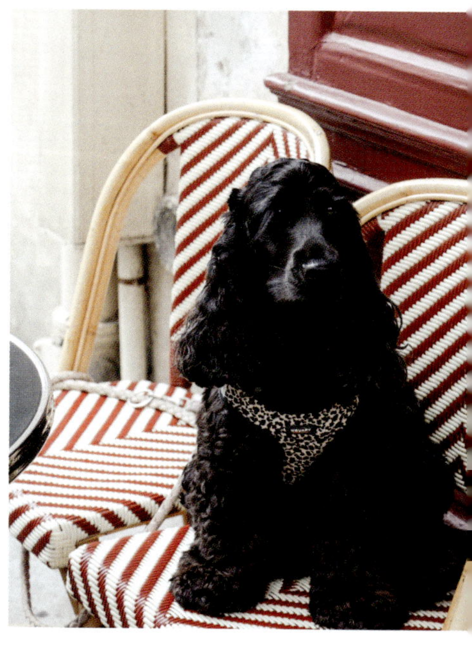

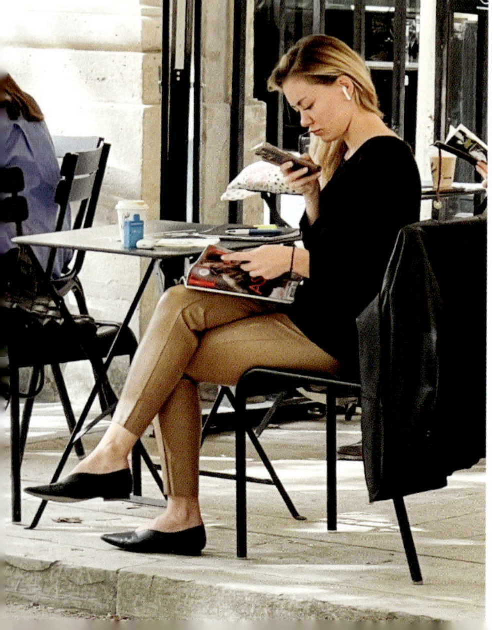

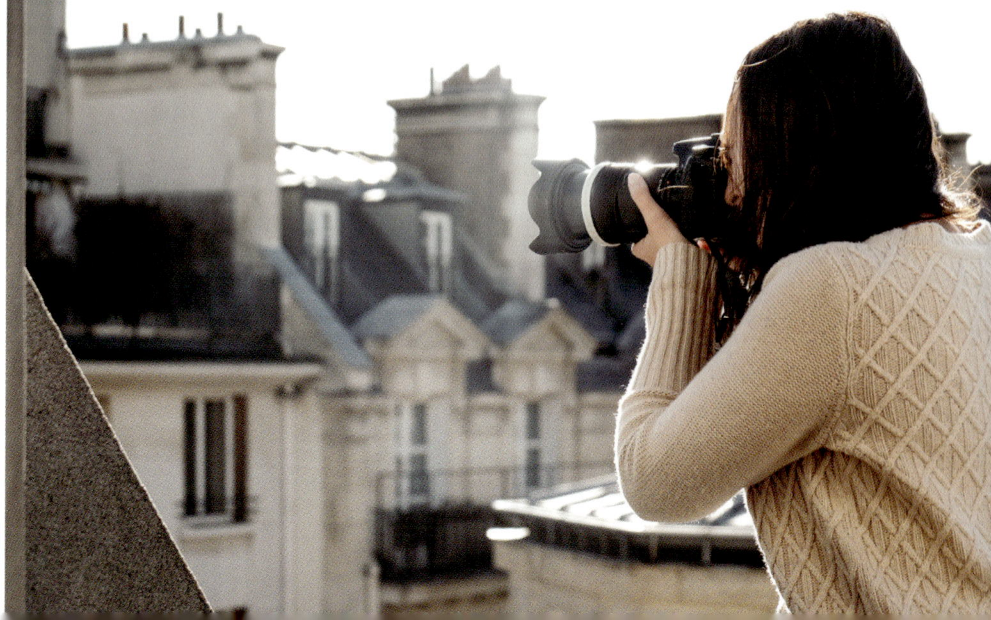

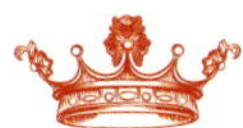

SPRING STYLES

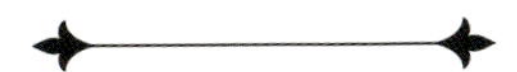

Parisians are thrilled to shed their chunky layers for lighter coats, shoes, and scarves. Here are listed a few key pieces for wardrobe essentials for Paris in the spring.

- **Trench Coat:** It's traditionally in a camel color. Sézane offers two classic styles that are great investment pieces.
- **Light Scarf:** This is for keeping warm on chilly mornings and evenings as the weather transitions.
- **Ballet Flats:** These are always a classic and popular shoe choice in neutral colors or a pop of red.
- **Sneakers:** They are trendy among Parisians and great walking shoes for exploring the city.
- **Crossbody Bag/Canvas Tote:** These are useful for workdays. Parisian women can often be seen carrying both.
- **Blazers:** Choose a relaxed fit and pair it with a button-up blouse or T-shirt.
- **Trousers/Denim:** Wide-legged denim is currently trending.
- **Lightweight Sweaters/Cardigans:** These are a must-have for layering.

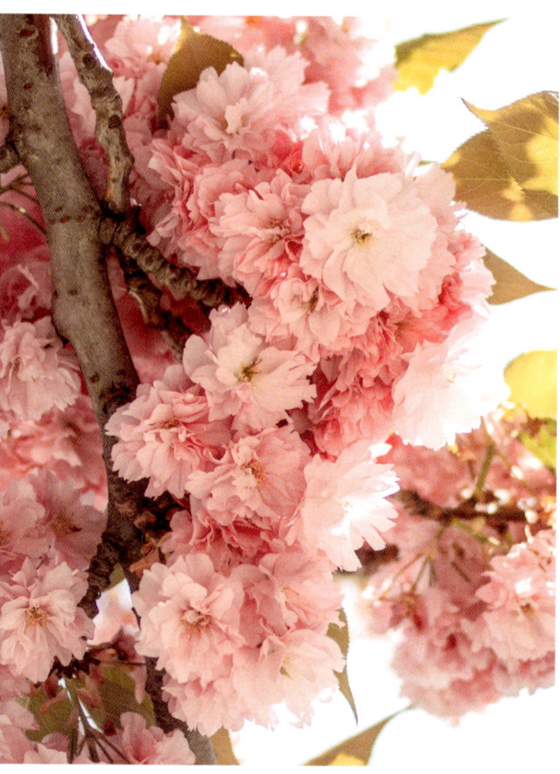

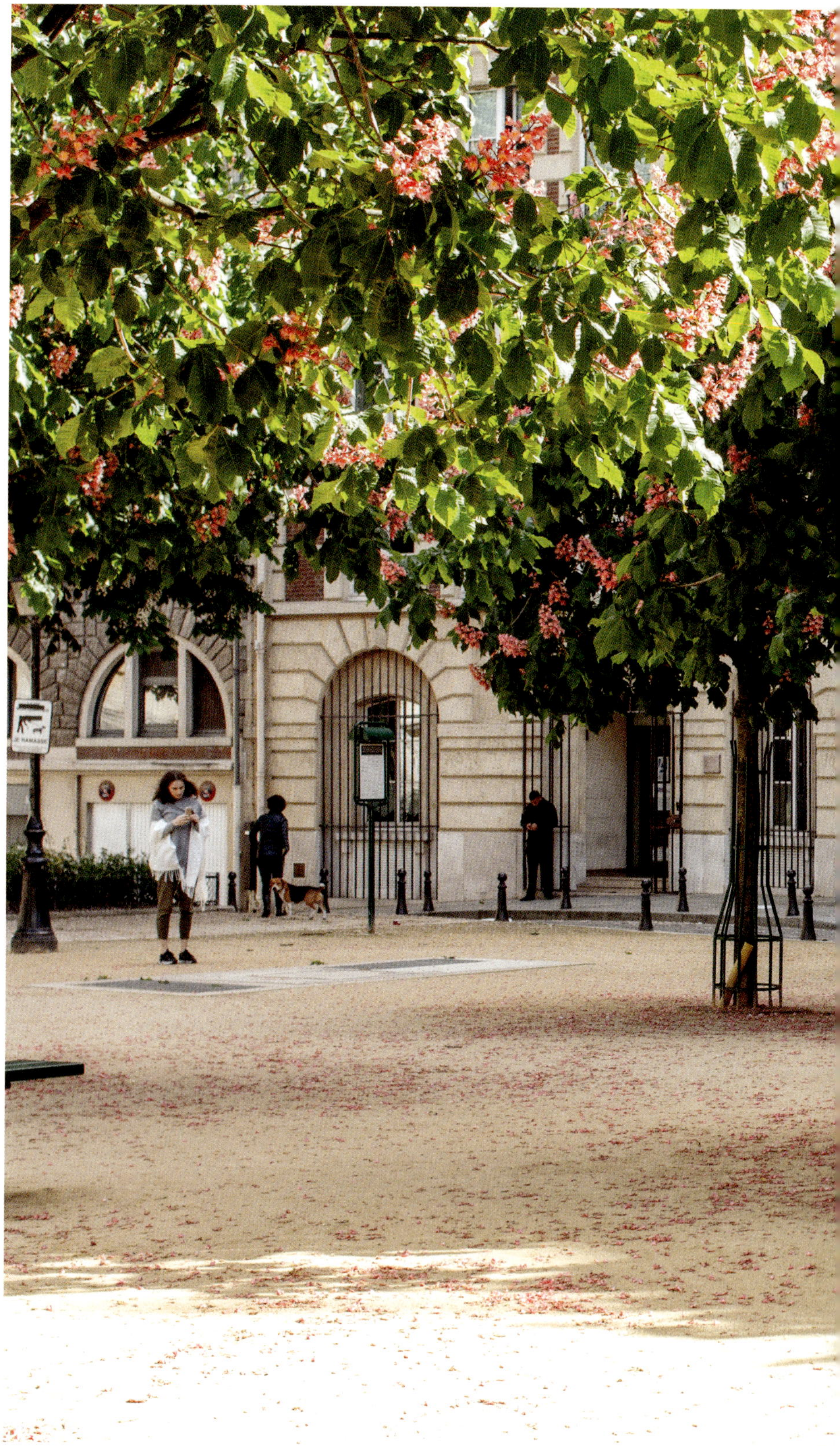

Chestnut blooms may not be as abundant as cherry blossoms in Paris, but they still offer a dab of pink to the atmosphere in spring. Look for these trees in Place Dauphine and the Jardin du Luxembourg in mid-April. Located just off the Pont Neuf, Place Dauphine is a restful spot that is often overlooked. During chestnut blossom season, the area in the center of the public square fills with pink and is worth a visit. Have a seat on one of the green benches to take in the surrounds.

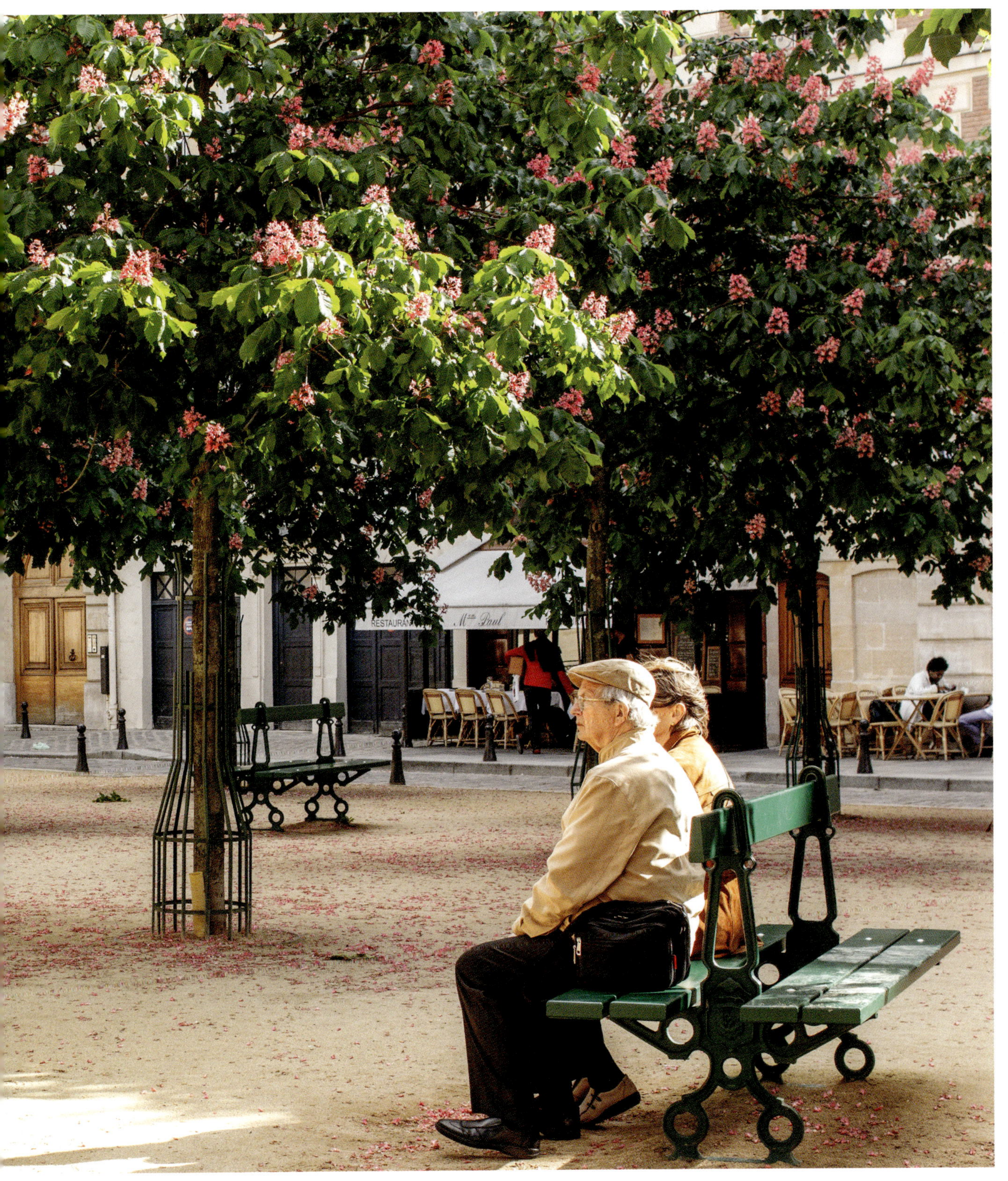

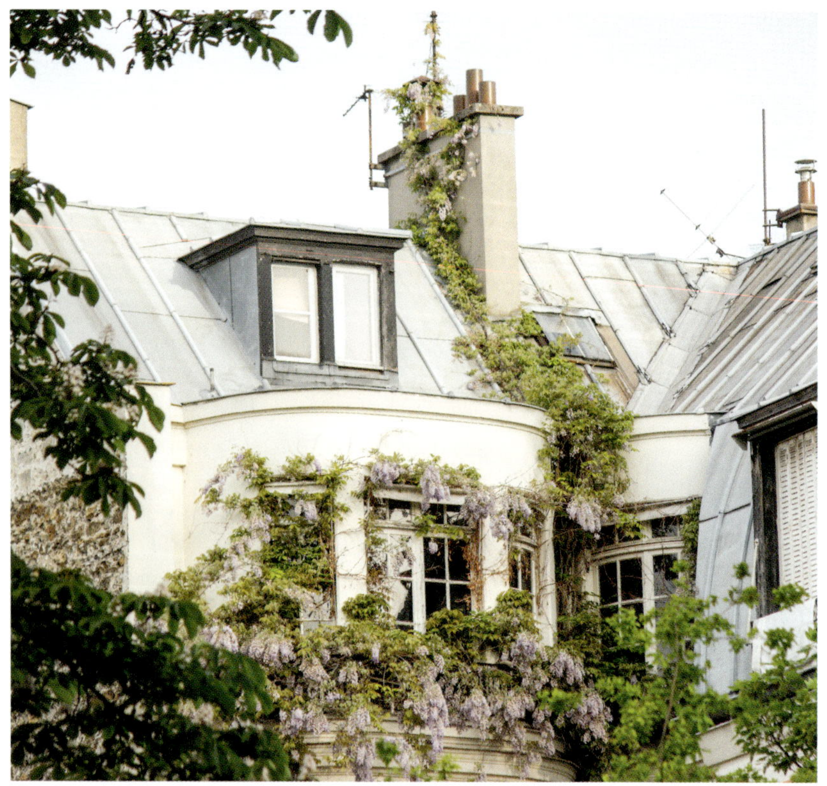

Purple wisteria flowers are the last to show in mid- to late-April. Wisteria blooms have a beautiful, sweet scent that fills the air, especially on warm days. One of the best areas to find wisteria is in Montmartre outside La Maison Rose on Rue de l'Abreuvoir. Outside the restaurant Au Vieux Paris, just on the side of Notre-Dame, wisteria climbs across the exterior, turning the façade a beautiful shade of purple. La Grande Mosquée de Paris, located in the 5th arrondissement, is also covered in wisteria. Enjoy teatime in the outside garden for a real treat.

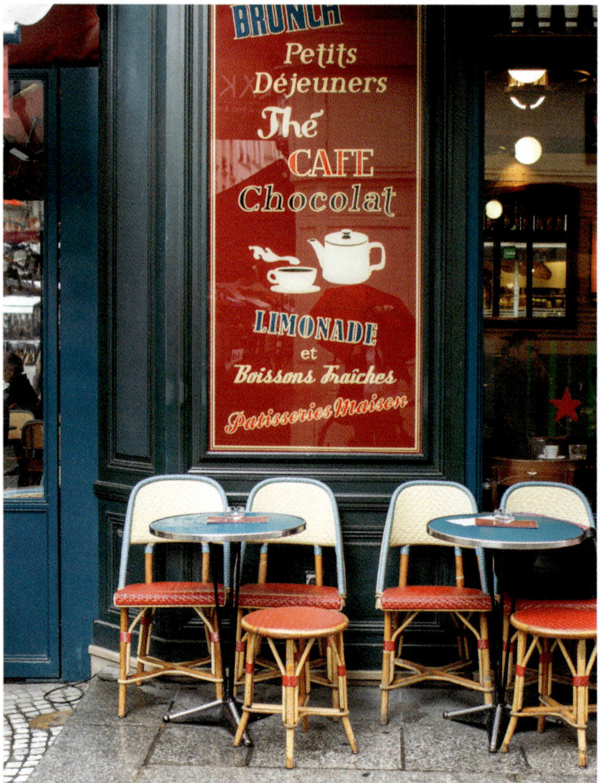

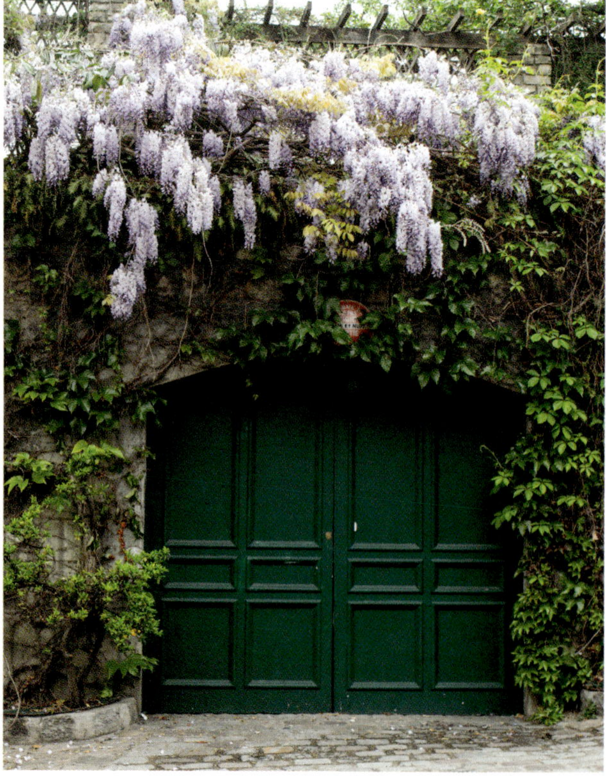

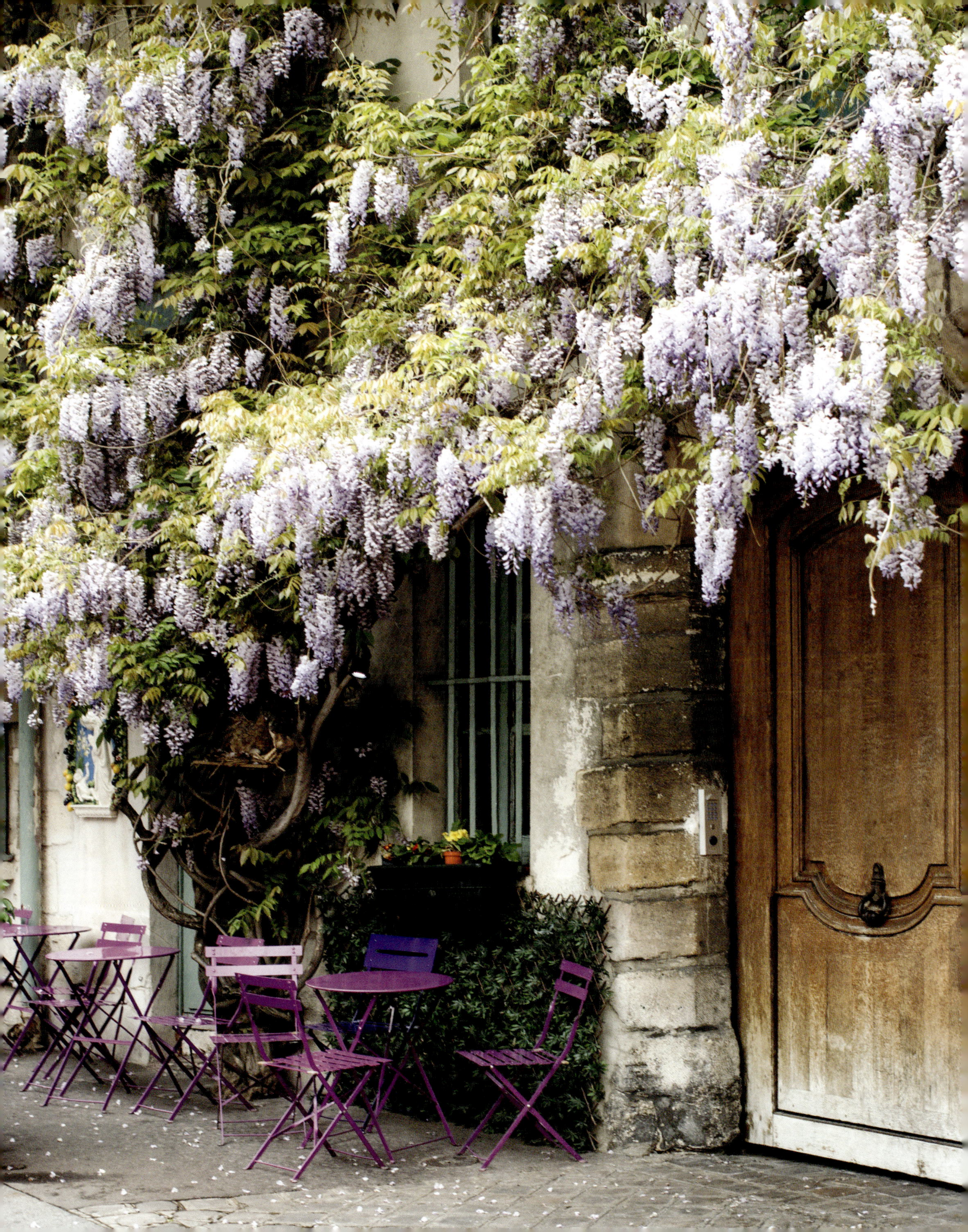

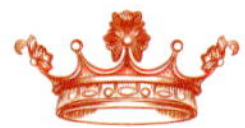

SPRING AT THE MARKET

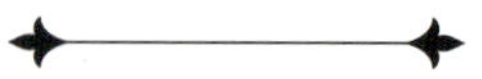

You will find bright, vibrant colors at Parisian markets in spring. Not only are the flowers beautiful but the colorful produce offers fresh spring flavors.

Fruits

- Strawberries (garguette variety in particular)
- Rhubarb
- Cherries

Vegetables

- Asparagus (white and green)
- Radishes
- Peas
- Morel mushrooms

Cheeses

- Chèvres (fresh goat cheese)
- Camembert
- Reblochon

Flowers

- Daffodils
- Tulips
- Peonies (late spring)

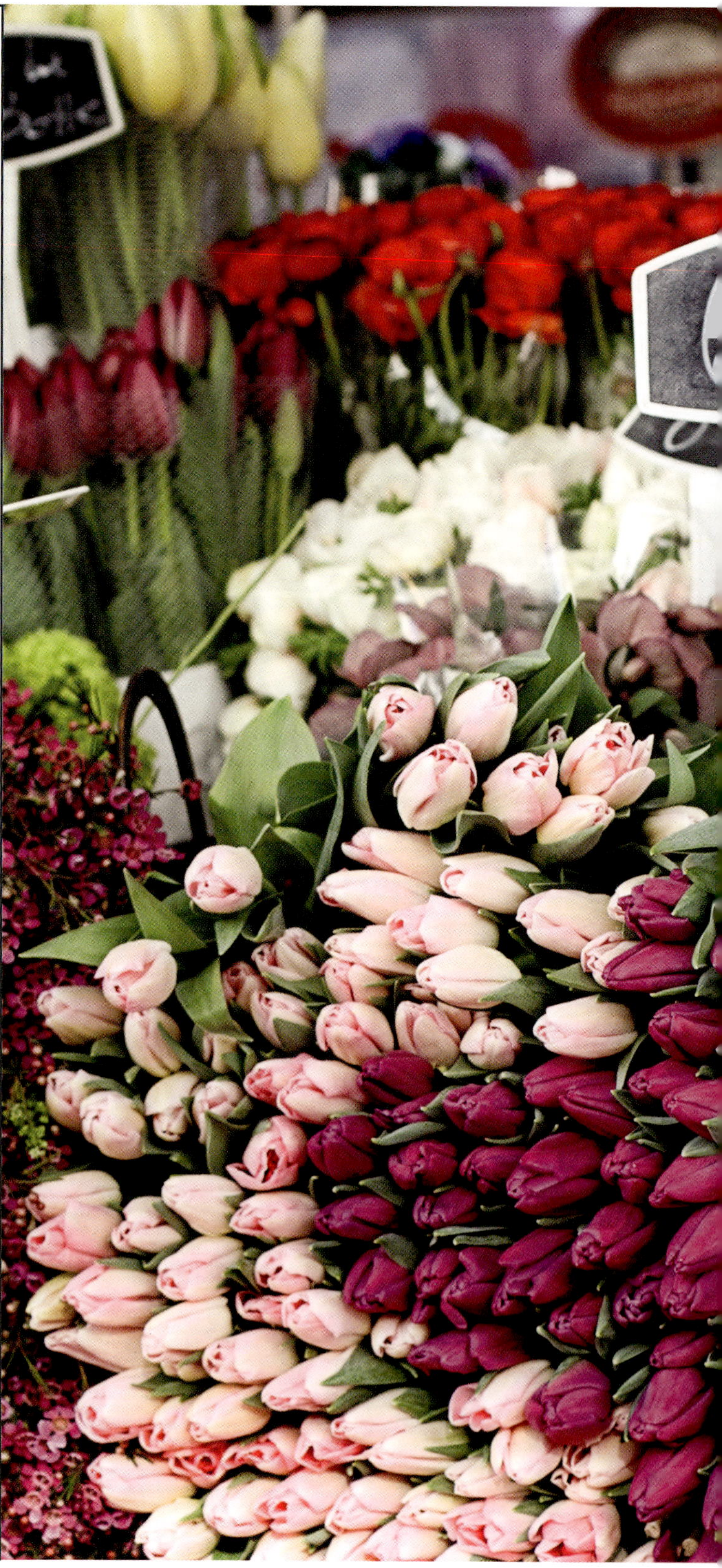

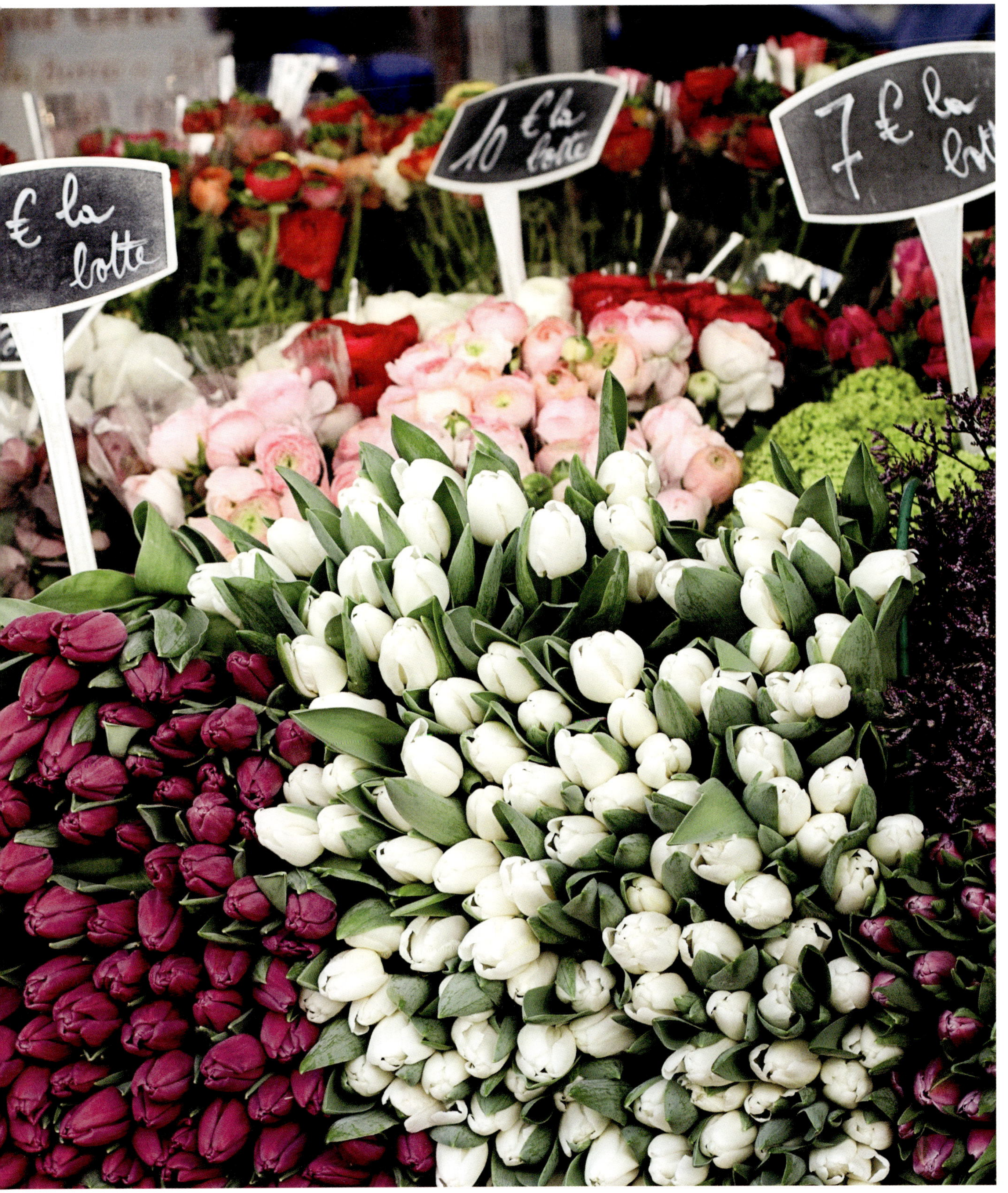
€ la
botte
10 € la
botte
7 € la
botte

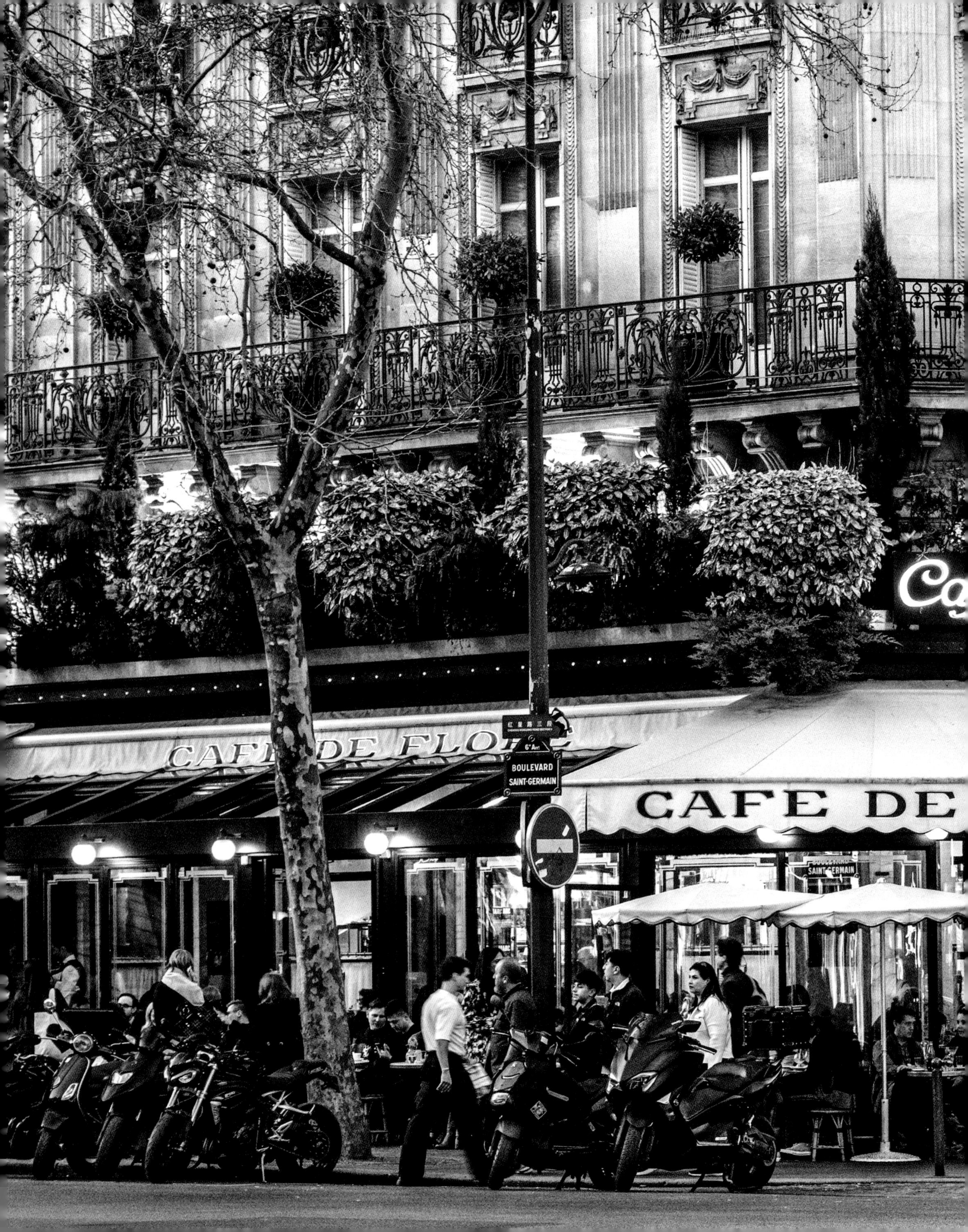
BOULEVARD
SAINT-GERMAIN
CAFE DE

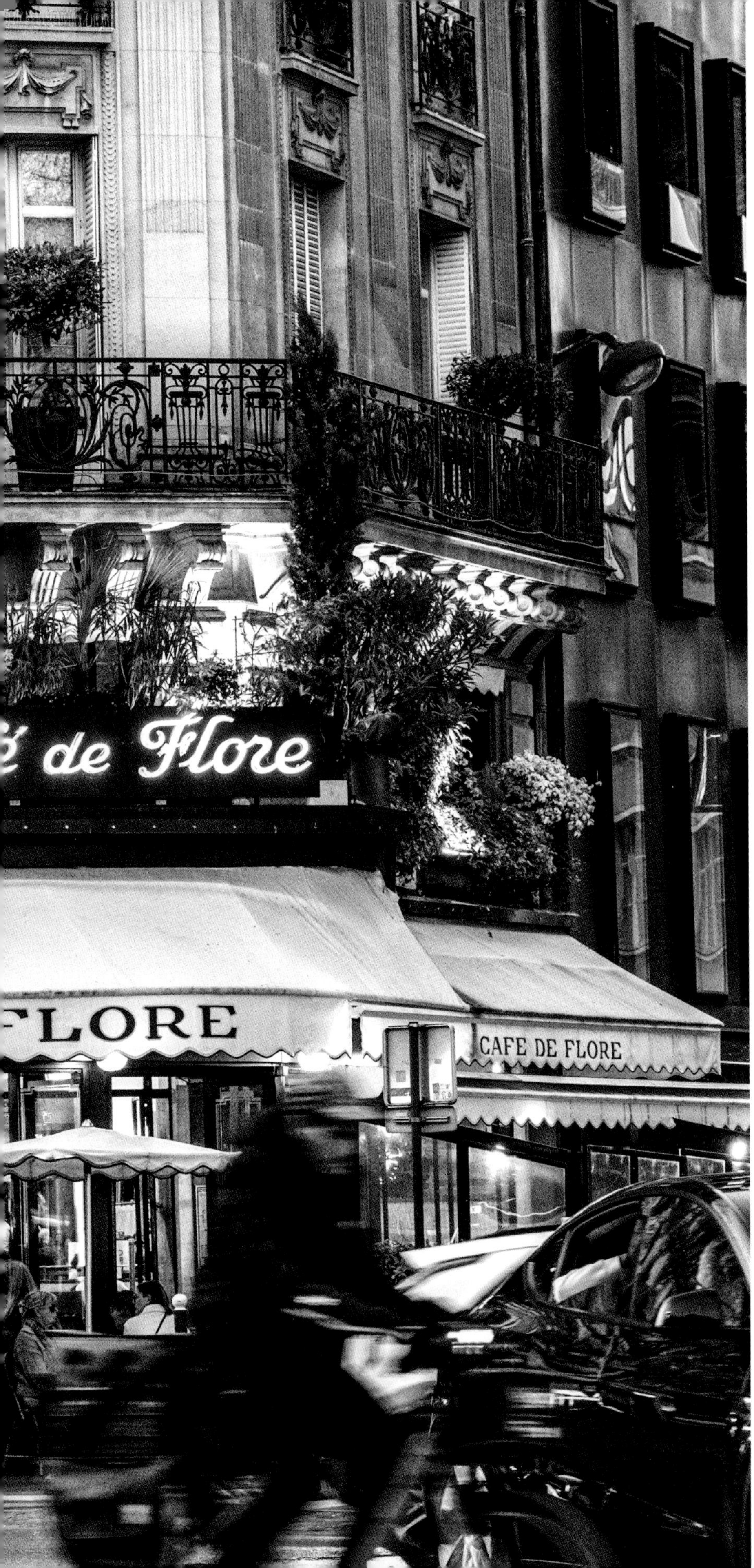

Café culture is very much a part of the Parisian lifestyle. Because apartments are small, meeting friends at a café is more common. Tables can be tight with limited space, and you can often find yourself conversing with a neighbor and meeting someone new.

SPRING MENUS

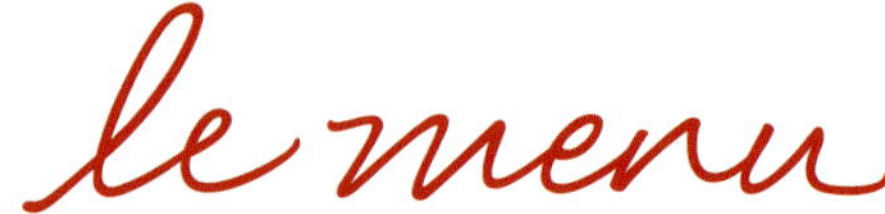

Asperges à la Sauce Hollandaise
(both green and white aspargus varieties)

Salade de Chèvre Chaud
(warm goat cheese atop a bed of greens)

Quiche aux Légumes du Printemps
(quiche with spring vegetables)

Tarte à la Rhubarbe
(rhubarb tart)

- Restaurant menus will be filled with fresh spring produce. Aspargus, particularly the plump white variety, signal the coming of spring.
- Try some of the chèvres, or goat cheeses, that are released in spring.
- While Quiche Lorraine is one of the most popular menu items, enjoy a version featuring fresh vegetables like peas and mushrooms.
- Strawberry desserts are popular at this time of year.

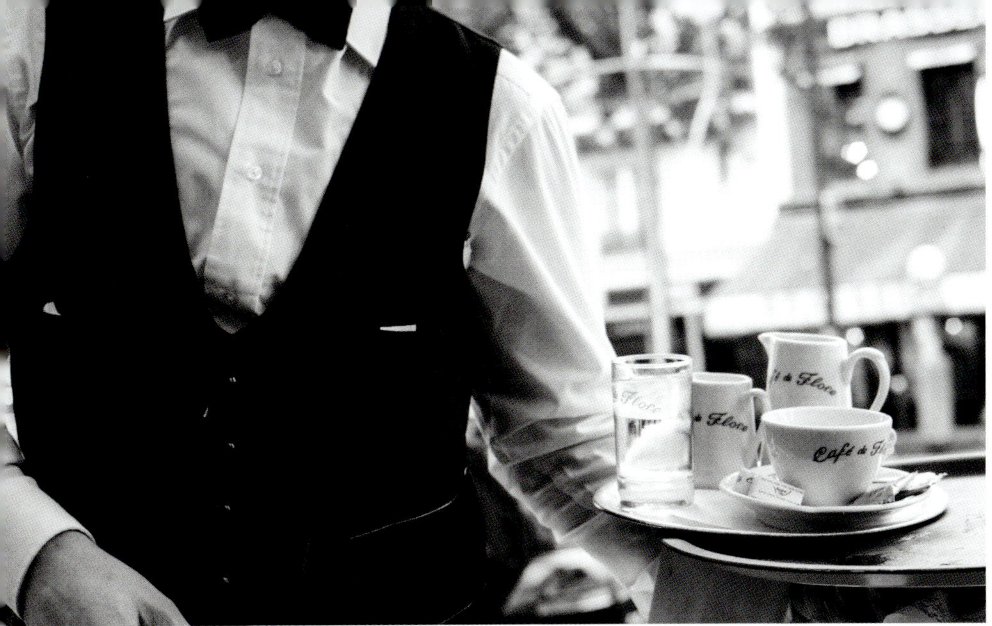
Flore

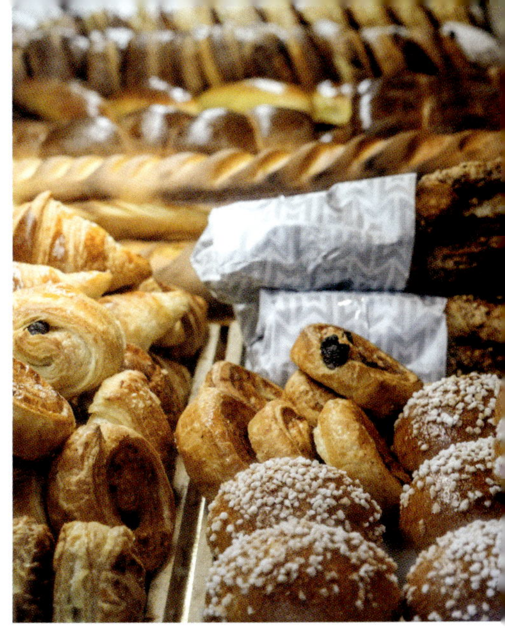

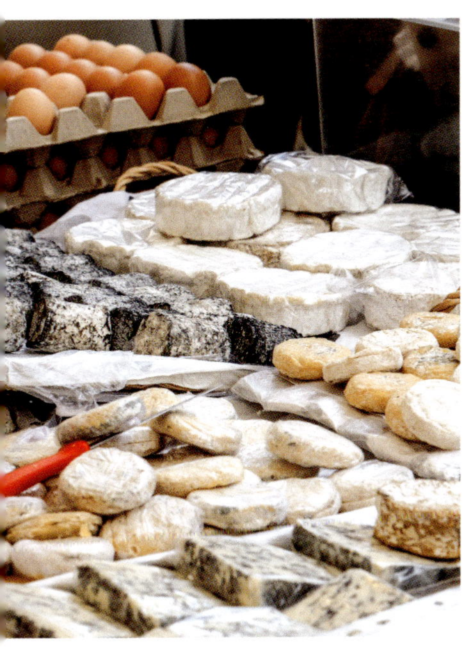

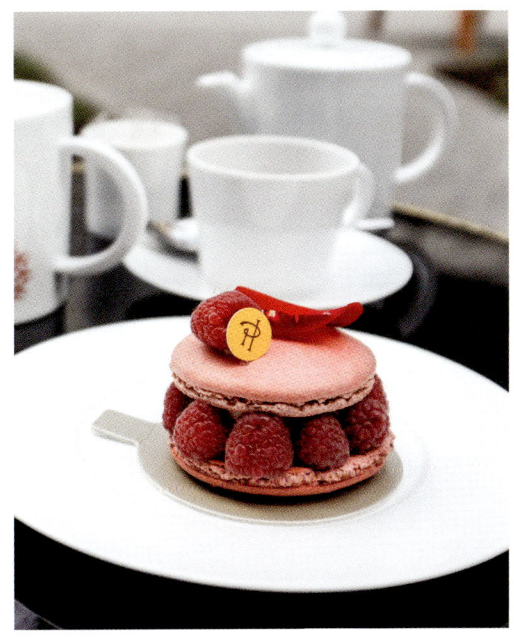

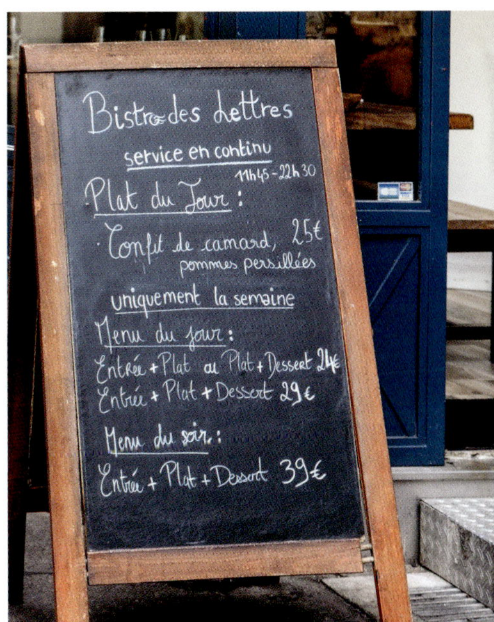
Bistro des Lettres
service en continu
11h45 - 22h30
Plat du Jour :
· Confit de canard, 25€
pommes persillées
uniquement la semaine
Menu du jour :
Entrée + Plat ou Plat + Dessert 24€
Entrée + Plat + Dessert 29€
Menu du soir :
Entrée + Plat + Dessert 39€

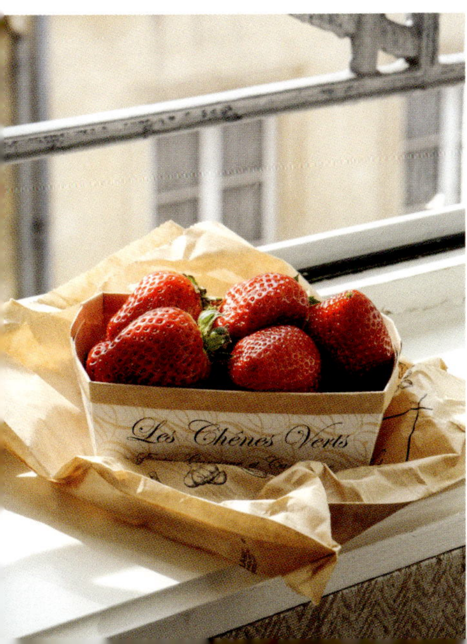
Les Chênes Verts

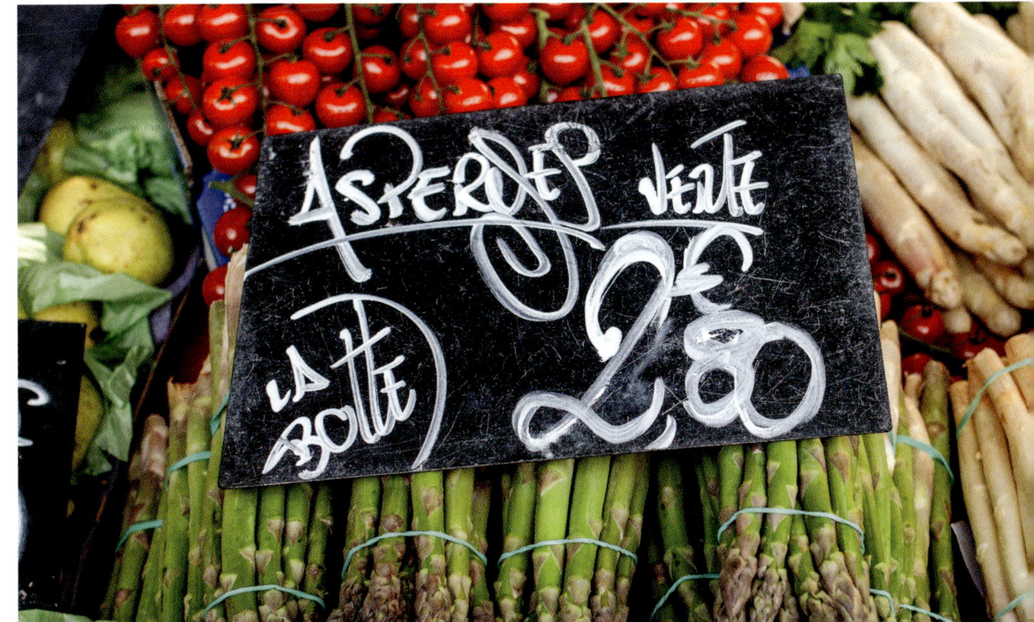
ASPERGES VERTE
LA BOTTE
2€80

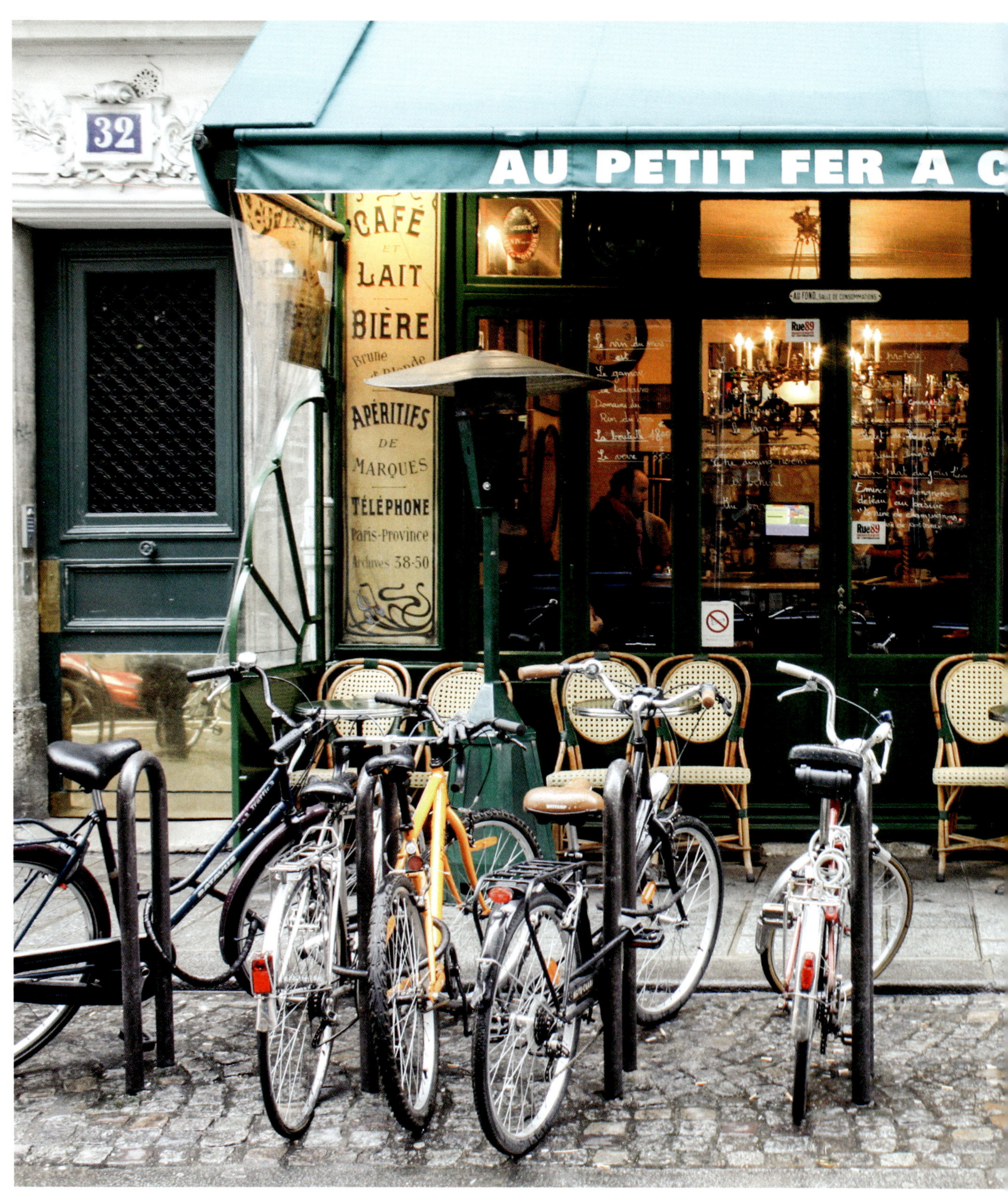
32
AU PETIT FER A C
CAFÉ
ET
LAIT
BIÈRE
Brune
APÉRITIFS
DE
MARQUES
TÉLÉPHONE
Paris-Province
Archives 38-50
AU FOND, SALLE DE CONSOMMATIONS
Rue89

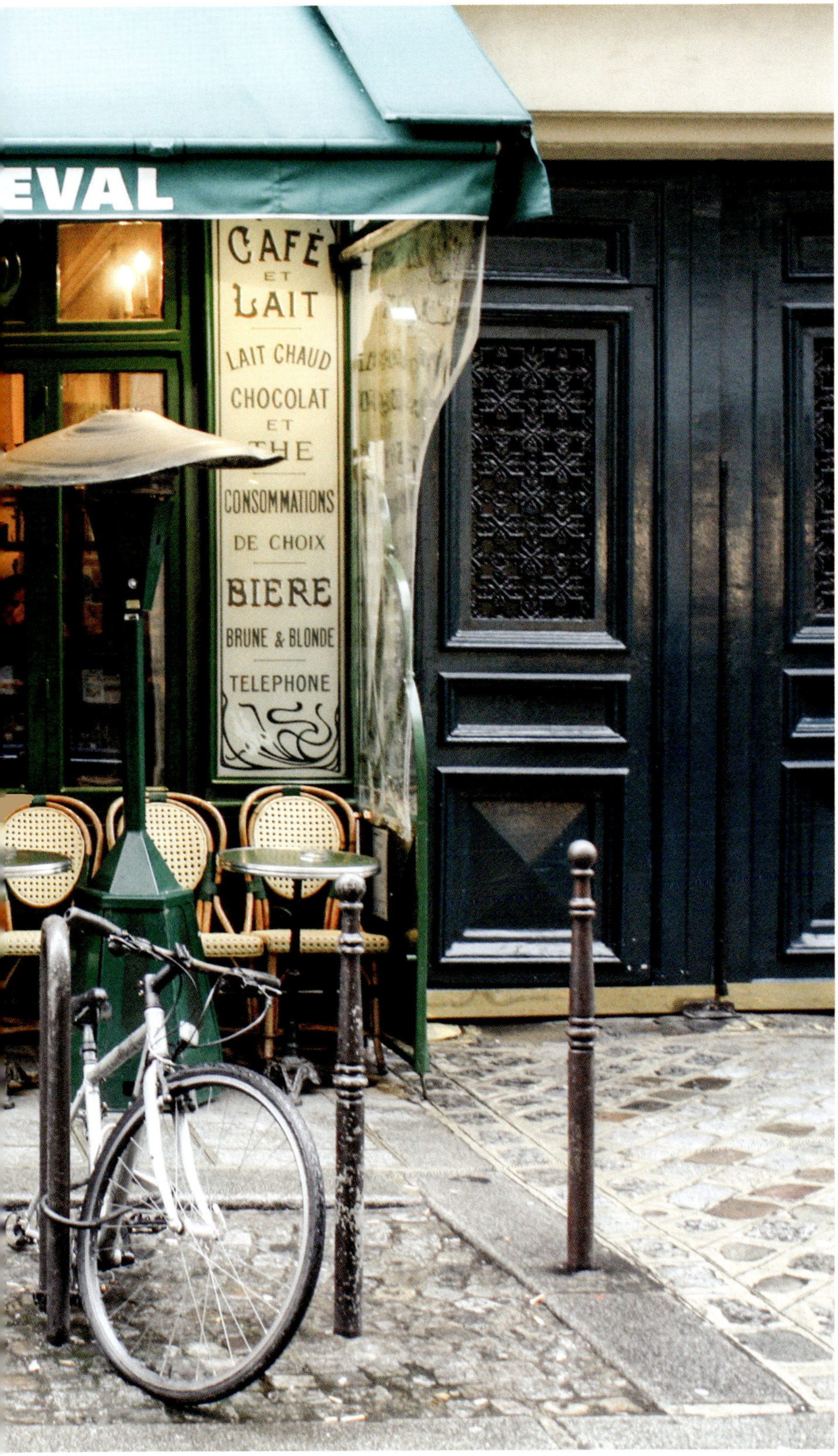

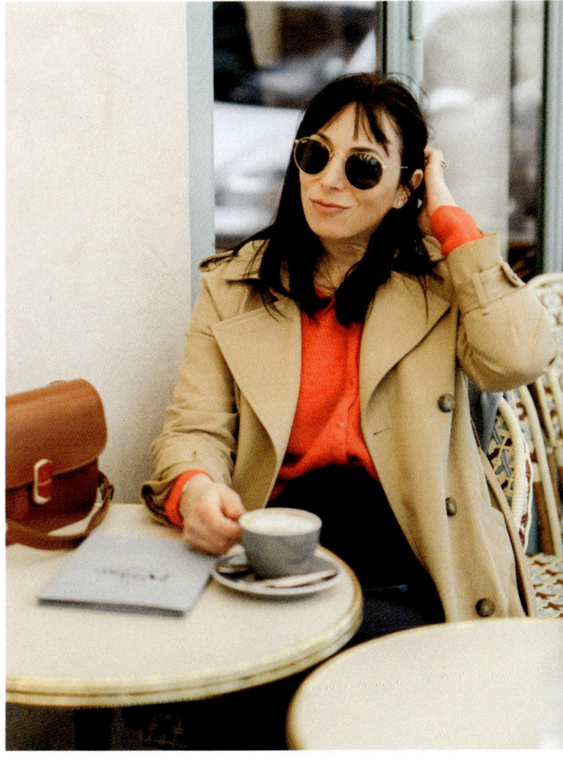

One of the most delightful spots from my many years in Paris is Au Petit Fer à Cheval. I initially took this photo of the shop's exterior in the winter of 2012, but during my stay in 2013, I decided to go inside for a coffee. My apartment was in Montmartre, but I quickly became a regular here. Per Parisian culture, ordering coffee at the bar is cheaper than sitting outside. I would soak in Paris by watching people come in and out of the shop and anyone who walked by my stool.

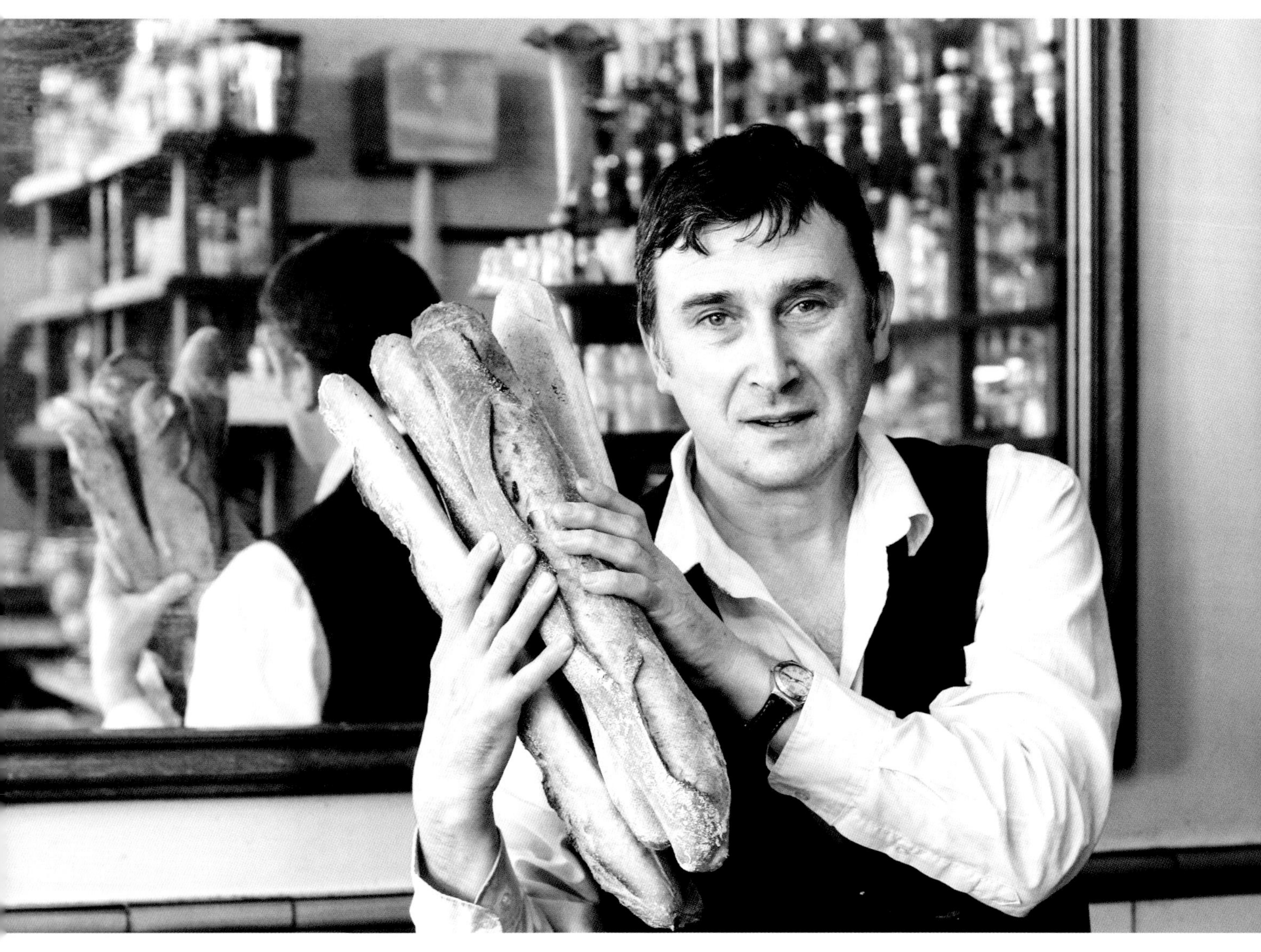

Didier was one of the waiters who helped run the place until a fire closed the kitchen and he retired in 2020.

He is part of my own personal story of the city, "My Paris," and I love that he has an image in the book. Didier often let me practice speaking French with him as he made coffee and poured wine for patrons during my visit. An extra square of chocolate for me slid onto the zinc bar when "the big boss" wasn't looking. I often sent friends and family to visit him on their Paris trips, and he warmly welcomed them.

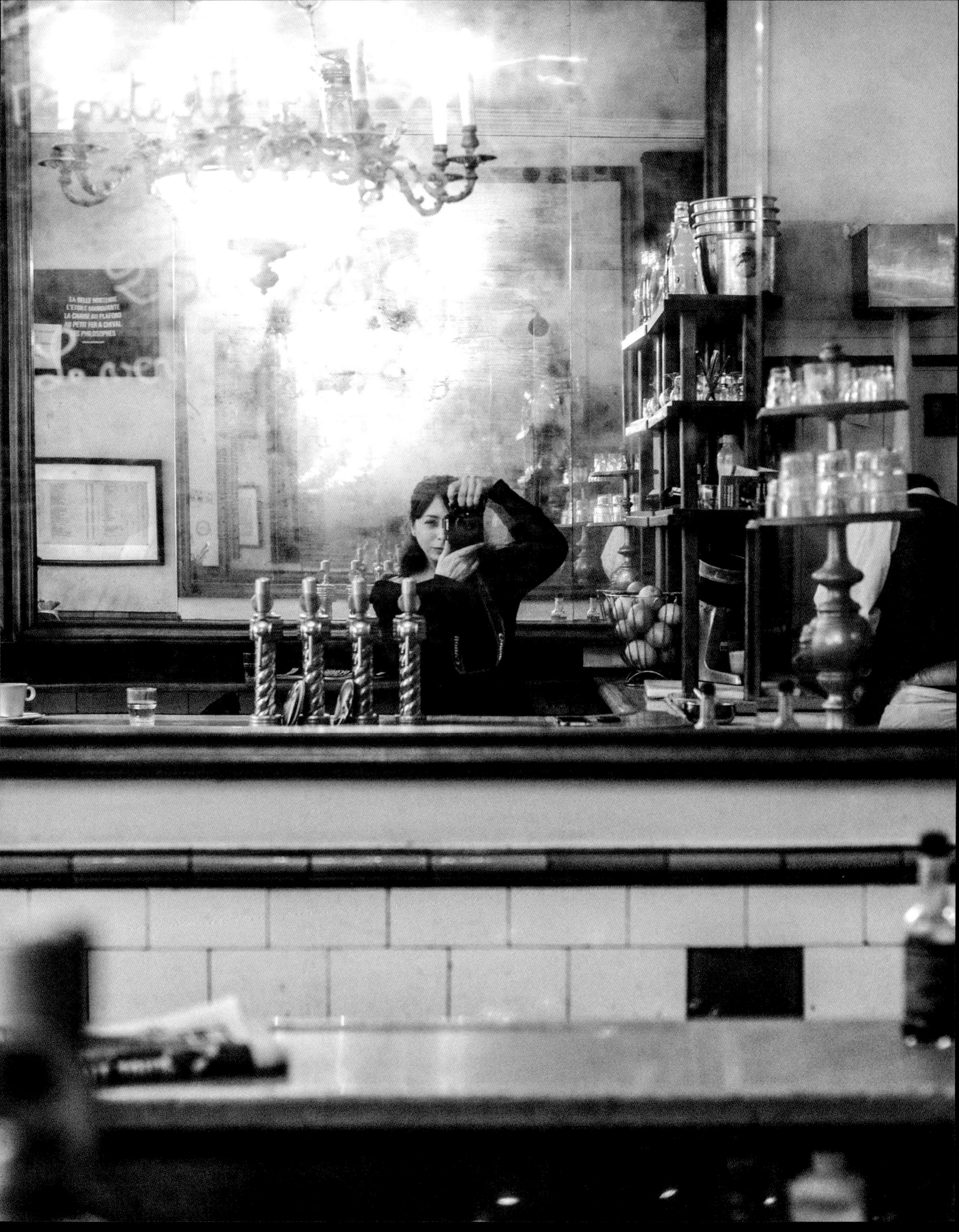

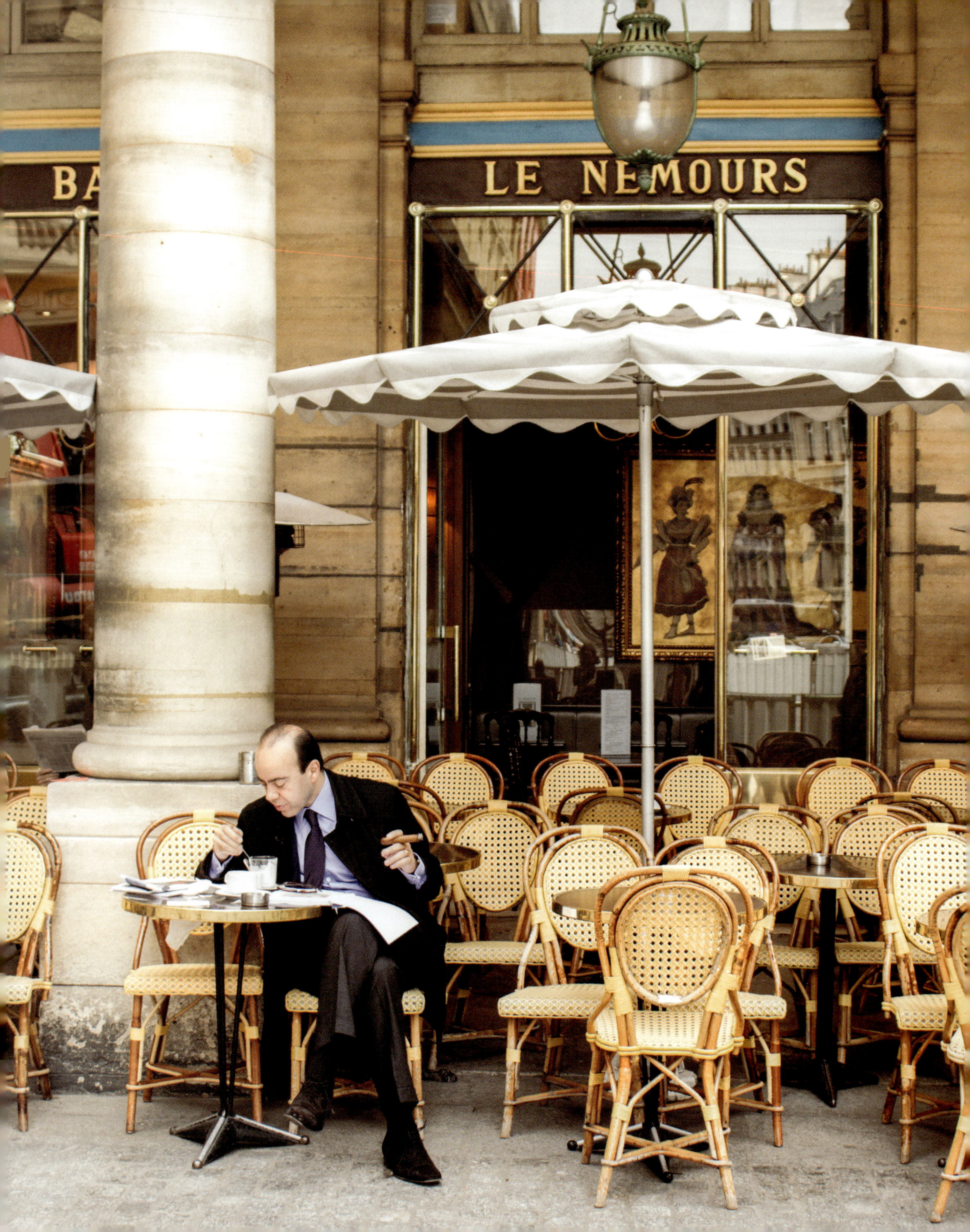
LE NEMOURS

PEOPLE-WATCHING

Recommended cafés in Paris for watching people go by:

- **Le Nemours** can be found just behind the Louvre, close to the Palais-Royal. Rest your feet at this café in between sightseeing.

- **La Palette** is a classic Left Bank café on Rue de Seine in the 6th arrondissement. In the warmer months, the terrace spills down the street.

- **Les Philosophes on Rue Vieille-du-Temple** has the same owners as Au Petit Fer à Cheval. With a more extensive outdoor terrace, the corner location is high traffic for tourists and locals walking the Marais.

- **Café Saint-Régis**, located on Île Saint-Louis, is perfect for coffee and croissants in the morning or wine as you watch the sunset behind Notre-Dame.

- **Le Bonaparte**, tucked right behind Les Deux Magots, offers a classic French vibe, an excellent terrace for the warmer months, and a glass of rosé.

- **Café de Flore and Les Deux Magots** are both located on Boulevard Saint-Germain. Each has a unique vibe that attracts visitors worldwide as well as local Parisians. I prefer Café de Flore.

- **Bar du Marché** can be found on the corner of Rue de Seine and Rue de Buci. It's a small but lively café for an afternoon drink or weekend stop. The terrace gets quite busy during peak times.

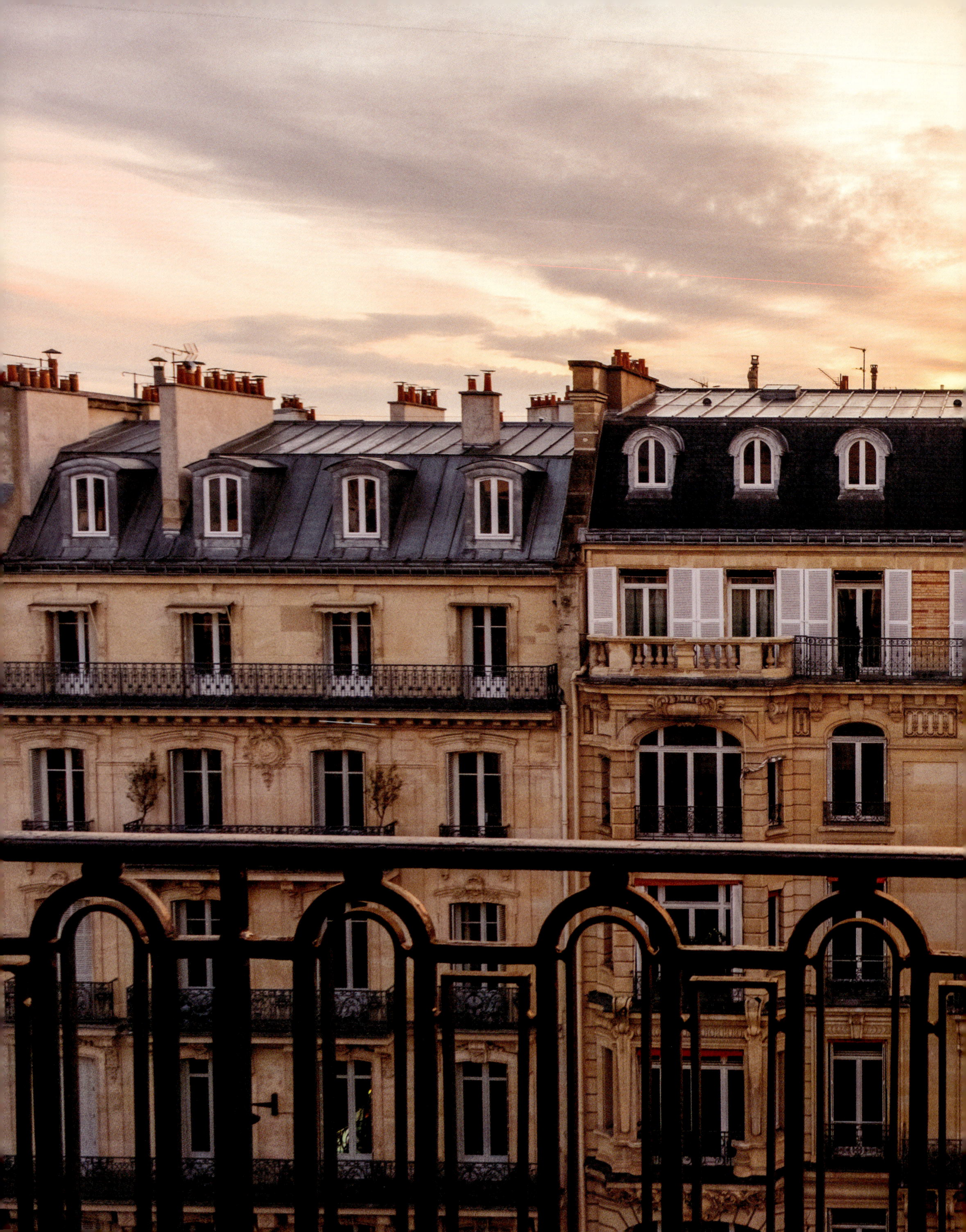

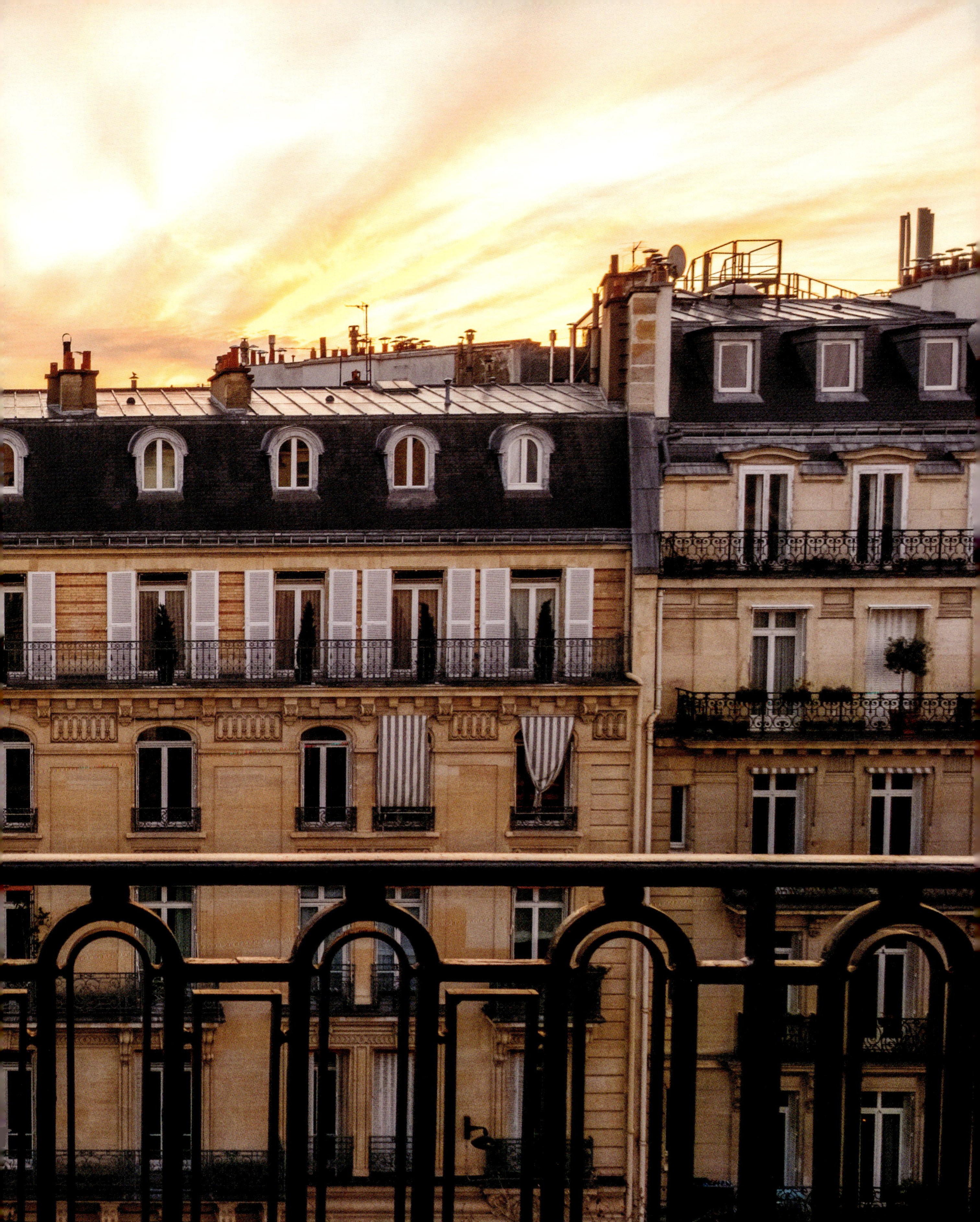

The first warm day of spring in Paris is filled with energy and possibility.

Sunlight warms my face as I step outside and breathe in the sweet scent of the city. Café terraces overflow with Parisians and travelers, faces tilted toward the sun, soaking in the long-awaited light of a new season. There's a shift in the air.

During my weekend visits to the Marché Bastille, I look forward to the first strawberries of the season. Bright red, sweet, and bursting with flavor. I wait for their arrival all year. On my walk, I pick up a warm baguette from Maison Landemaine, paired perfectly with salted butter.

My Sunday routine in spring brings me to one of my favorite parks in the Marais, Place des Vosges, to mark the beginning of picnic season in mid-April. The sounds of the fountains splashing with water, accompanied by kids playing in the background, make for the perfect weekend morning soundtrack.

The first tastes and smells of the spring season remind me to slow down and savor the season.

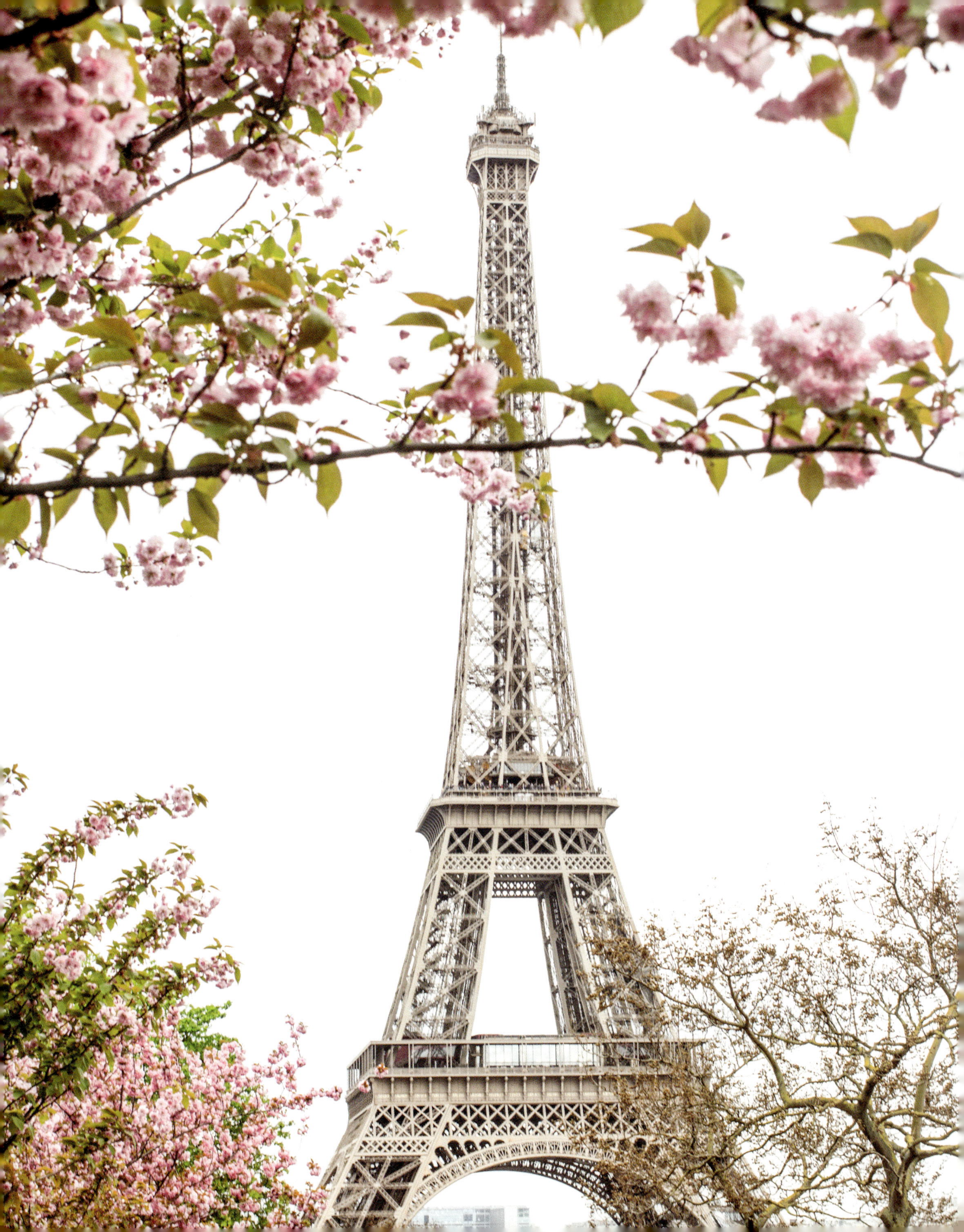

l'été

{SUMMER}

Summer in Paris begins with the noises and laughter of children celebrating the end of the school year in late June and early July. It's the time of year when Parisians pack up and head south for a vacation *à la plage*—at the beach.

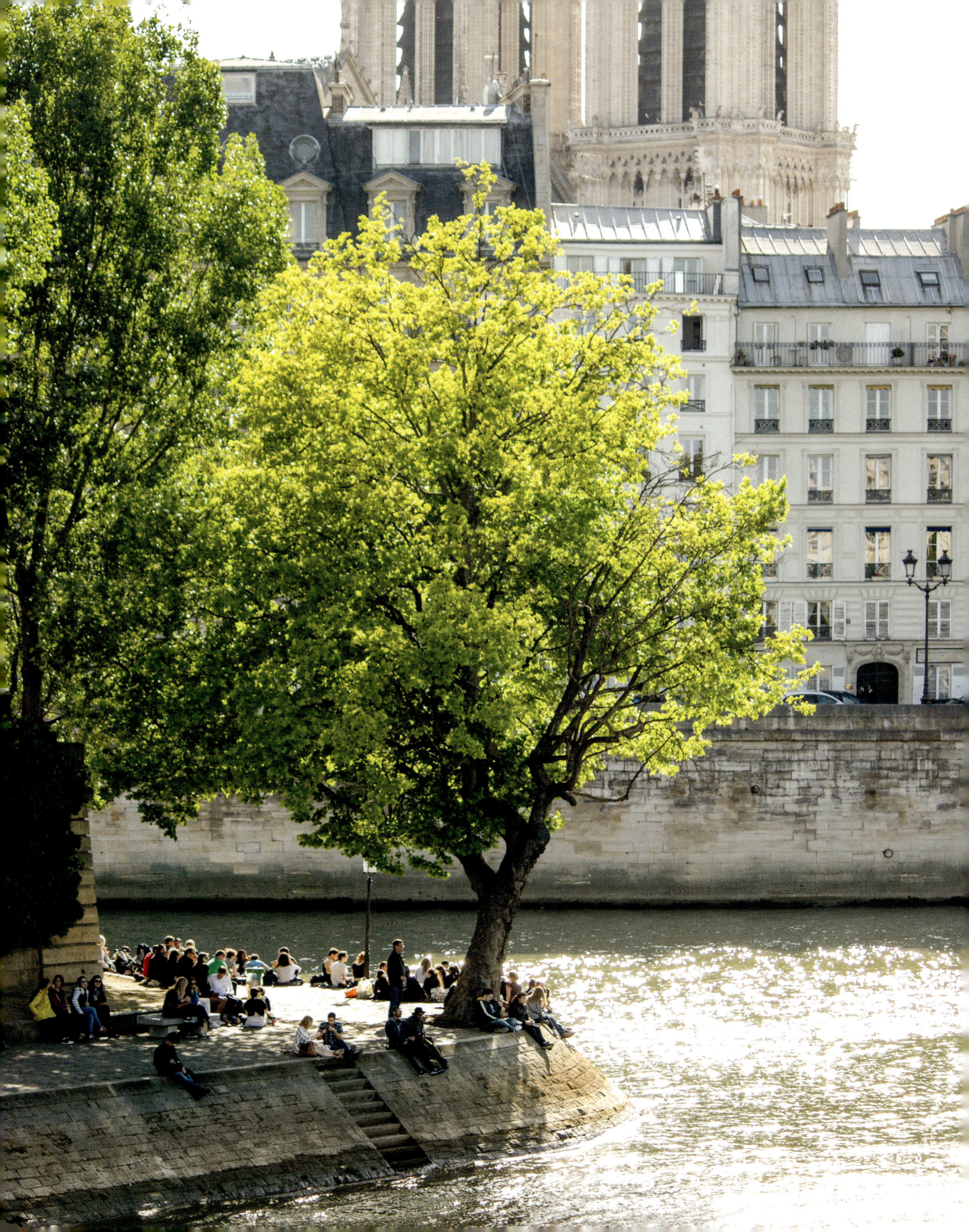

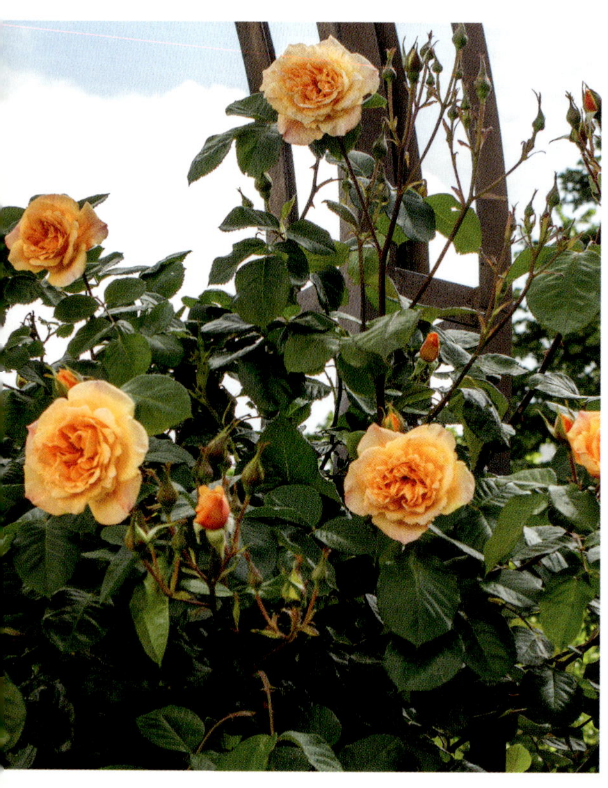

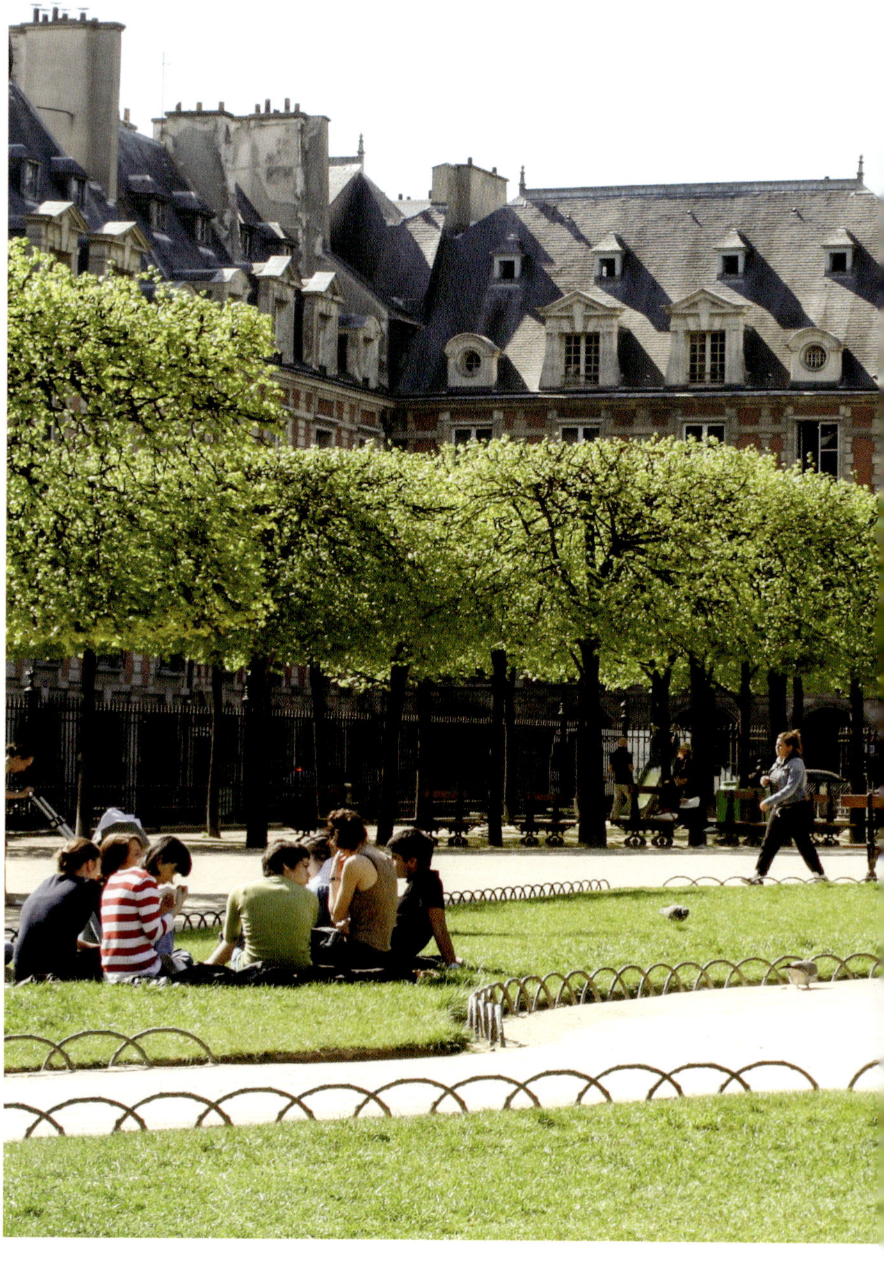

The days are long, and daylight spills into the evening.

At the height of summer, sunset is around 10 p.m. or even later. Everything comes alive at night when the temperatures drop. During the day, the natural light in the city is brightest in the summer months. The city's parks are filled with energy, endless greenery, and roses.

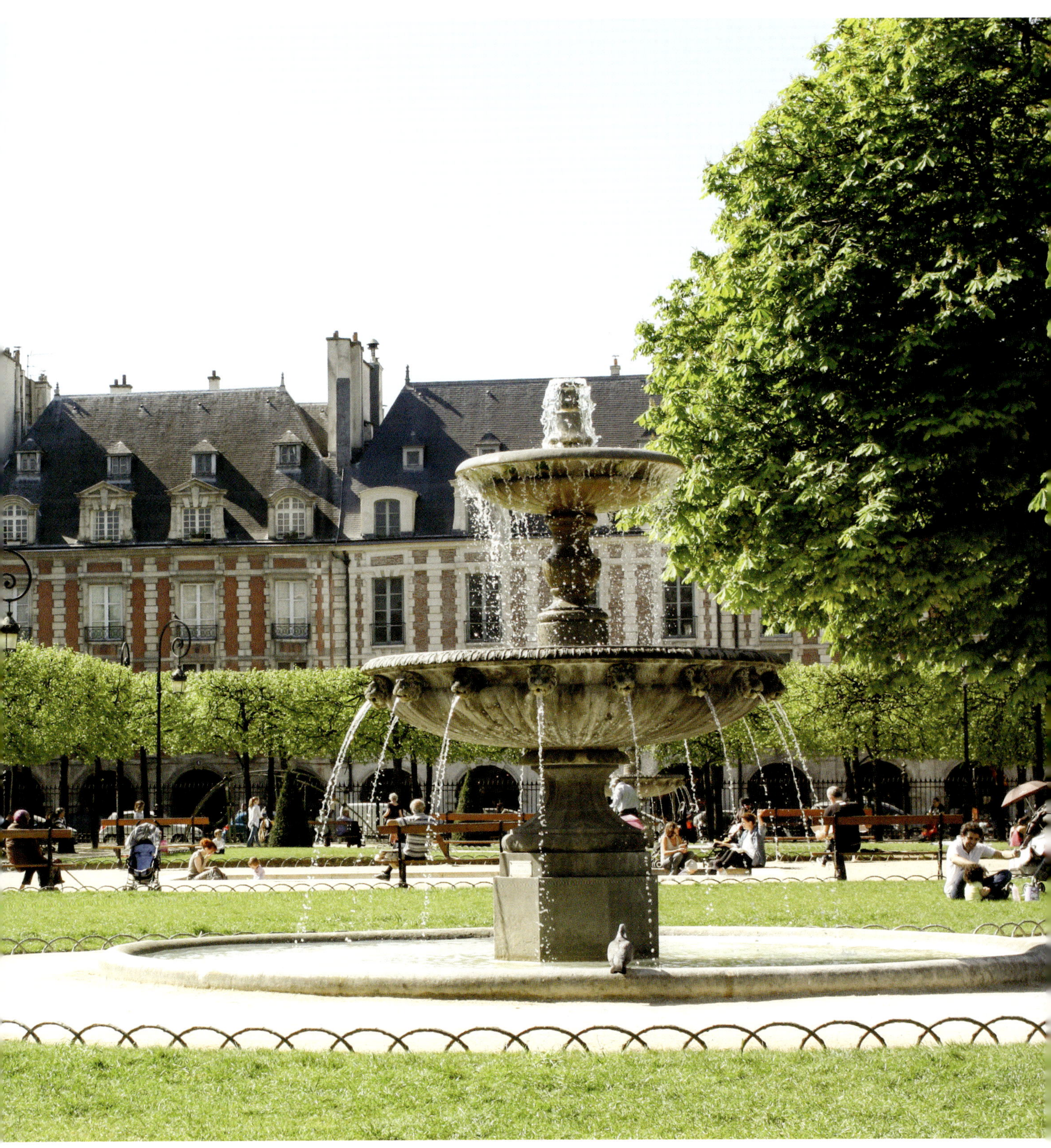

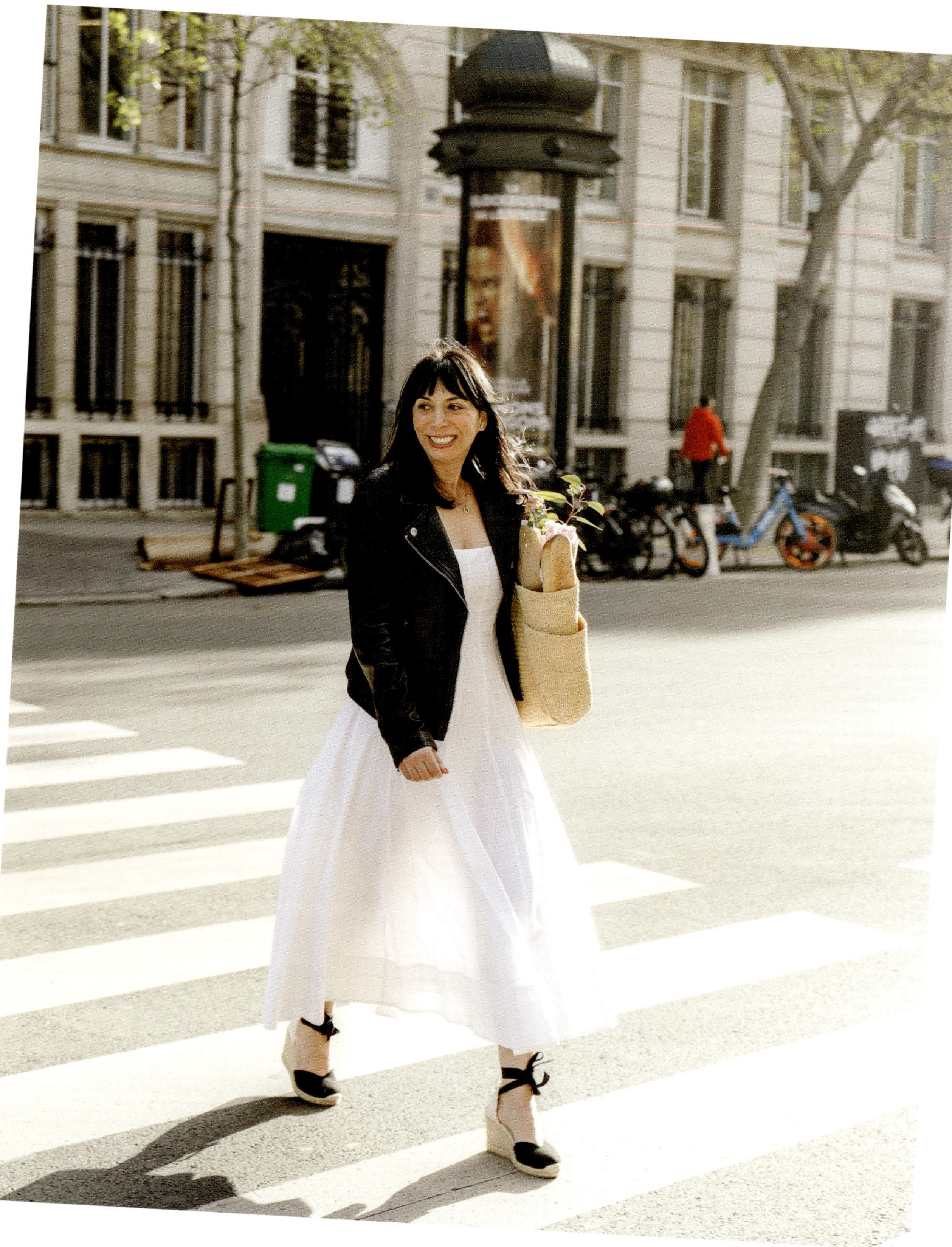

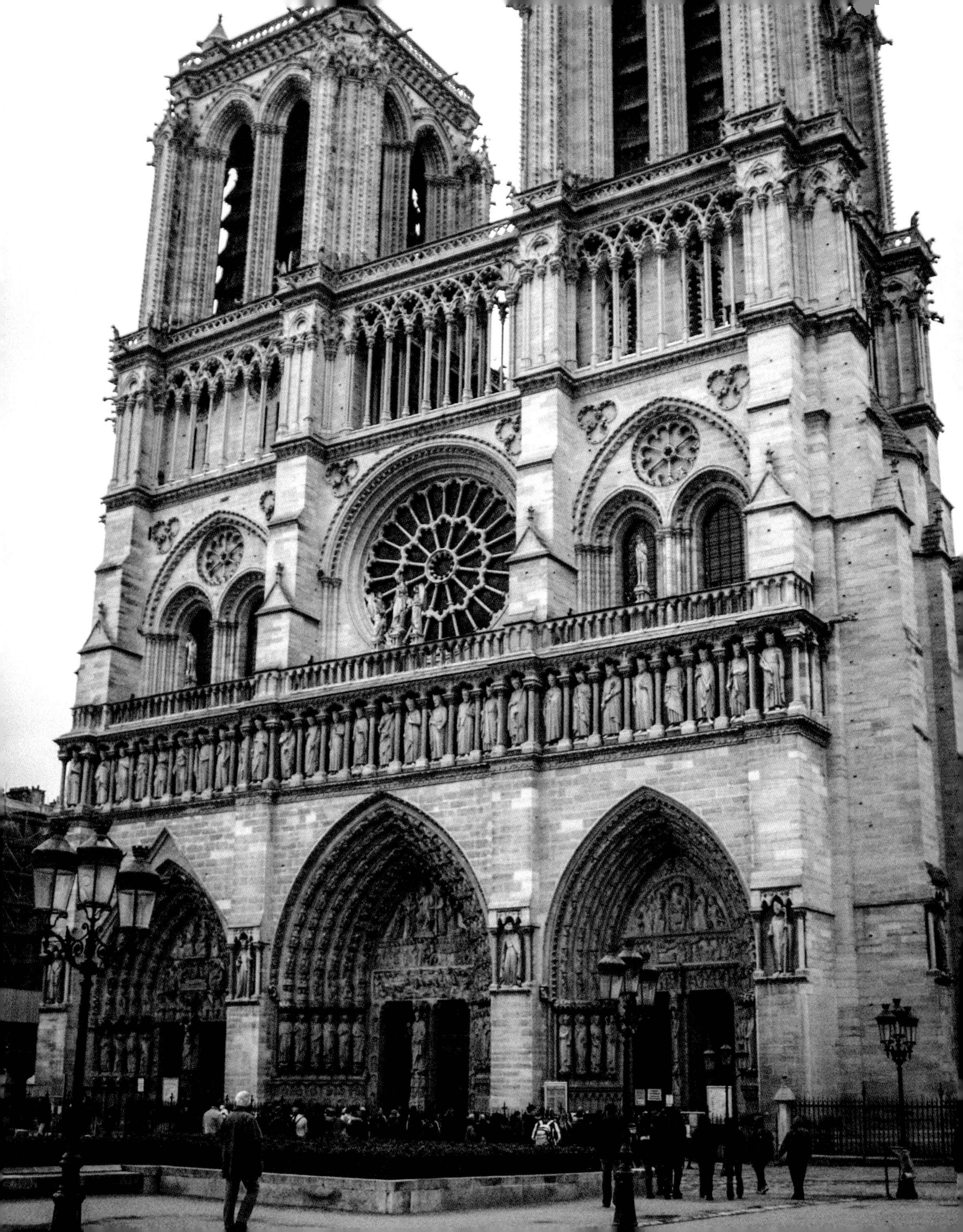

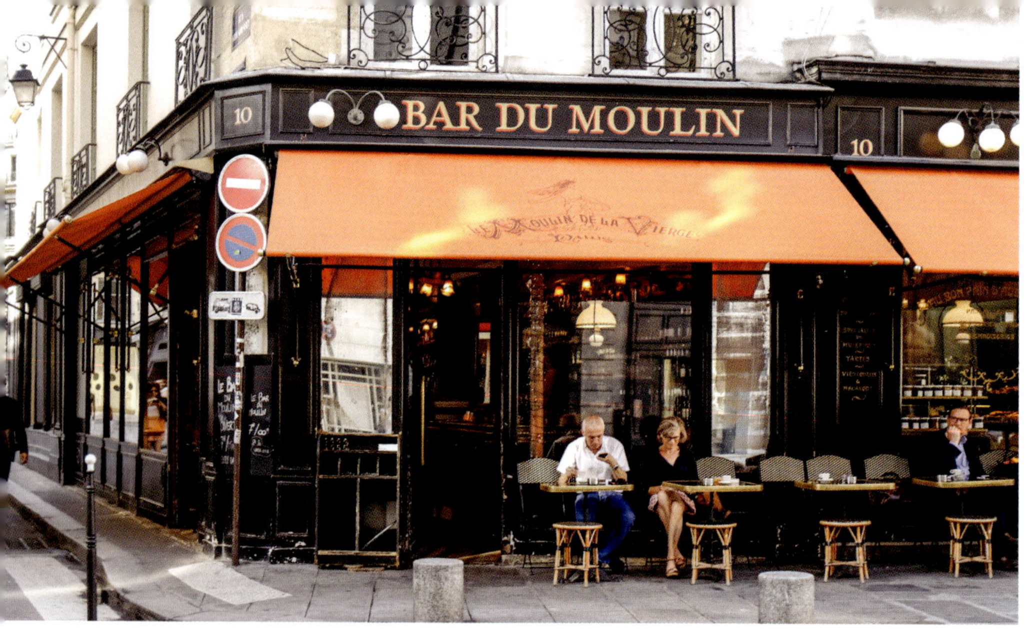
BAR DU MOULIN
10
10
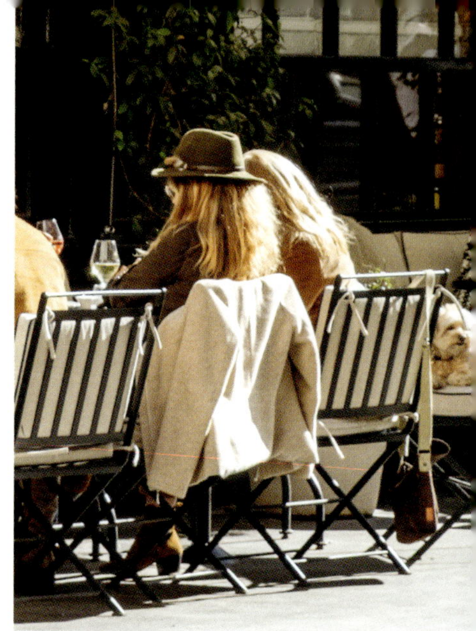
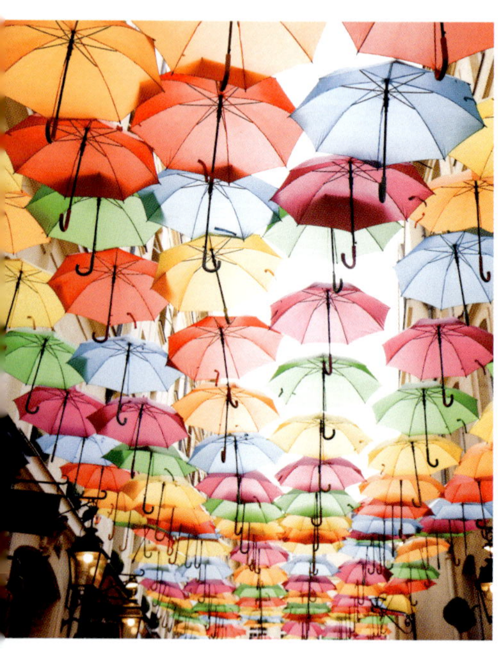
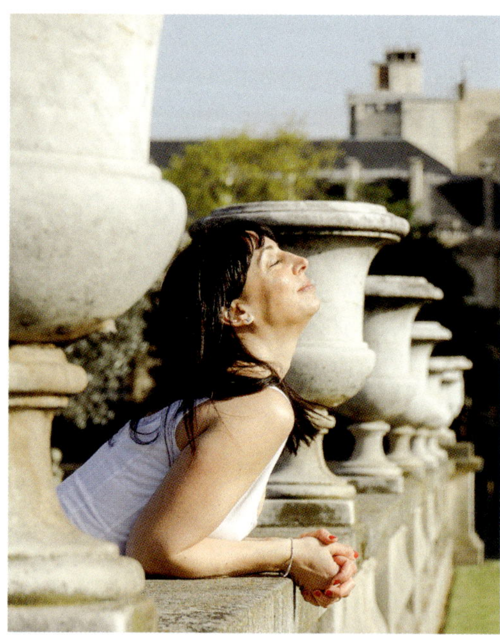
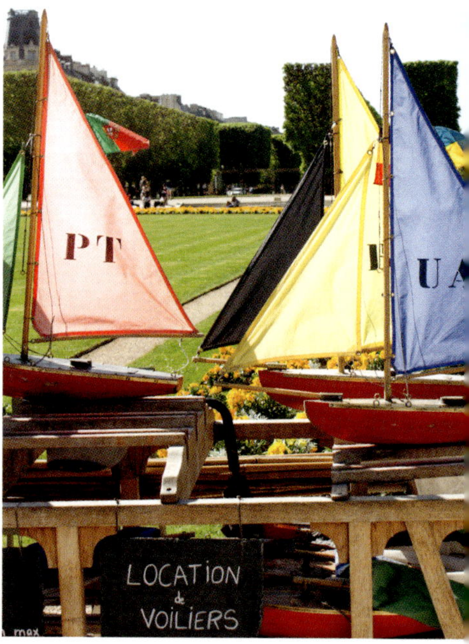
PT
UA
LOCATION
de
VOILIERS
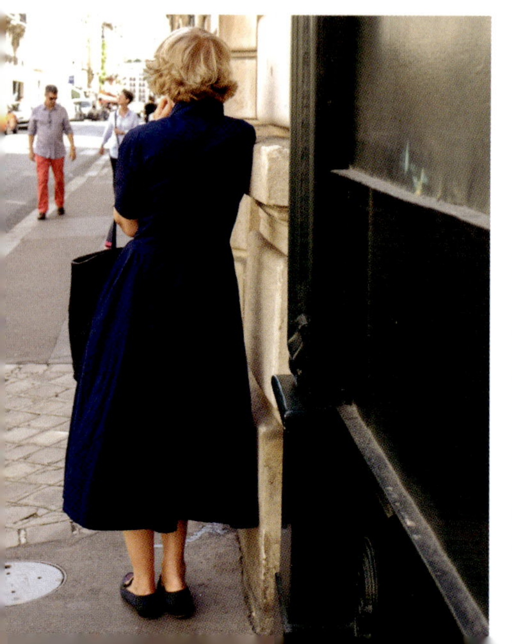
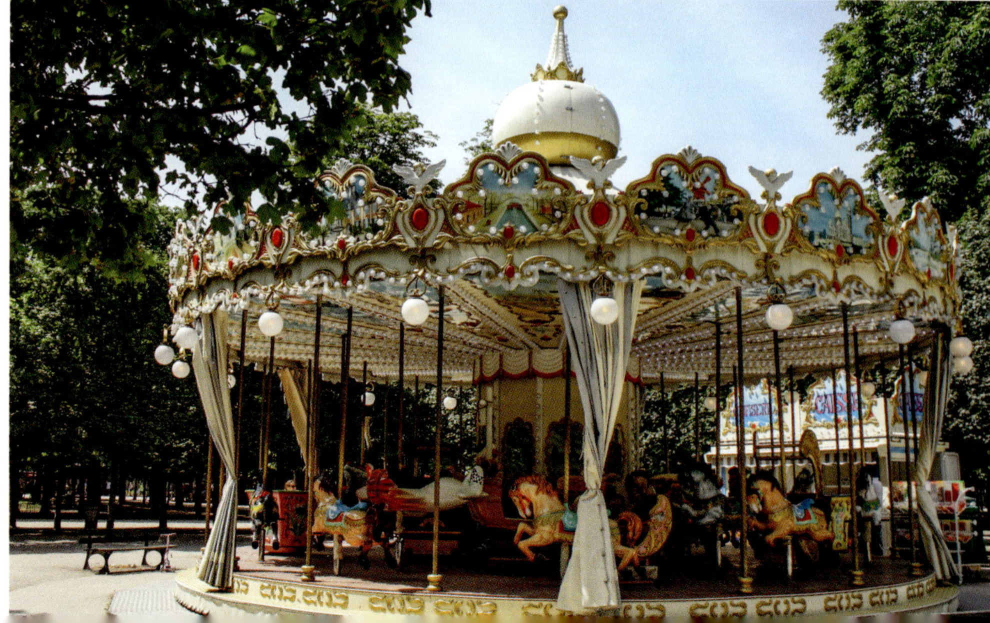

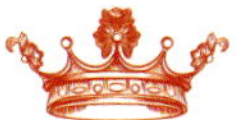

SUMMER STYLES

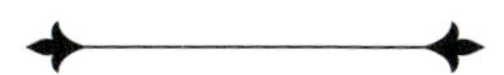

Neutral colors and light fabrics are key in the warm months of summer. Here are a few wardrobe essentials for Paris in the summer.

- **Dresses:** Light and flowy midi and maxi lengths are popular. Slip dresses and cool linen fabrics are perfect for warm days.

- **Tops:** Cotton or linen blouses and button-down tops pair perfectly with skirts made of flowy fabric.

- **Bottoms:** Pant styles include high-waisted trousers or shorts in linen or light fabric.

- **Shoes:** Espadrilles, white sneakers, flats, or leather sandals are great for strolling streets under lush green trees.

- **Accessories:** Makeup is always minimal with sunscreen, sunglasses, and a hat. Hats can range from straw hats to baseball caps. Woven bags are essential pieces in summer for packing picnics, shopping markets, and running errands.

- **Scarves:** A silk scarf tied to a bag or in the hair helps complete any outfit.

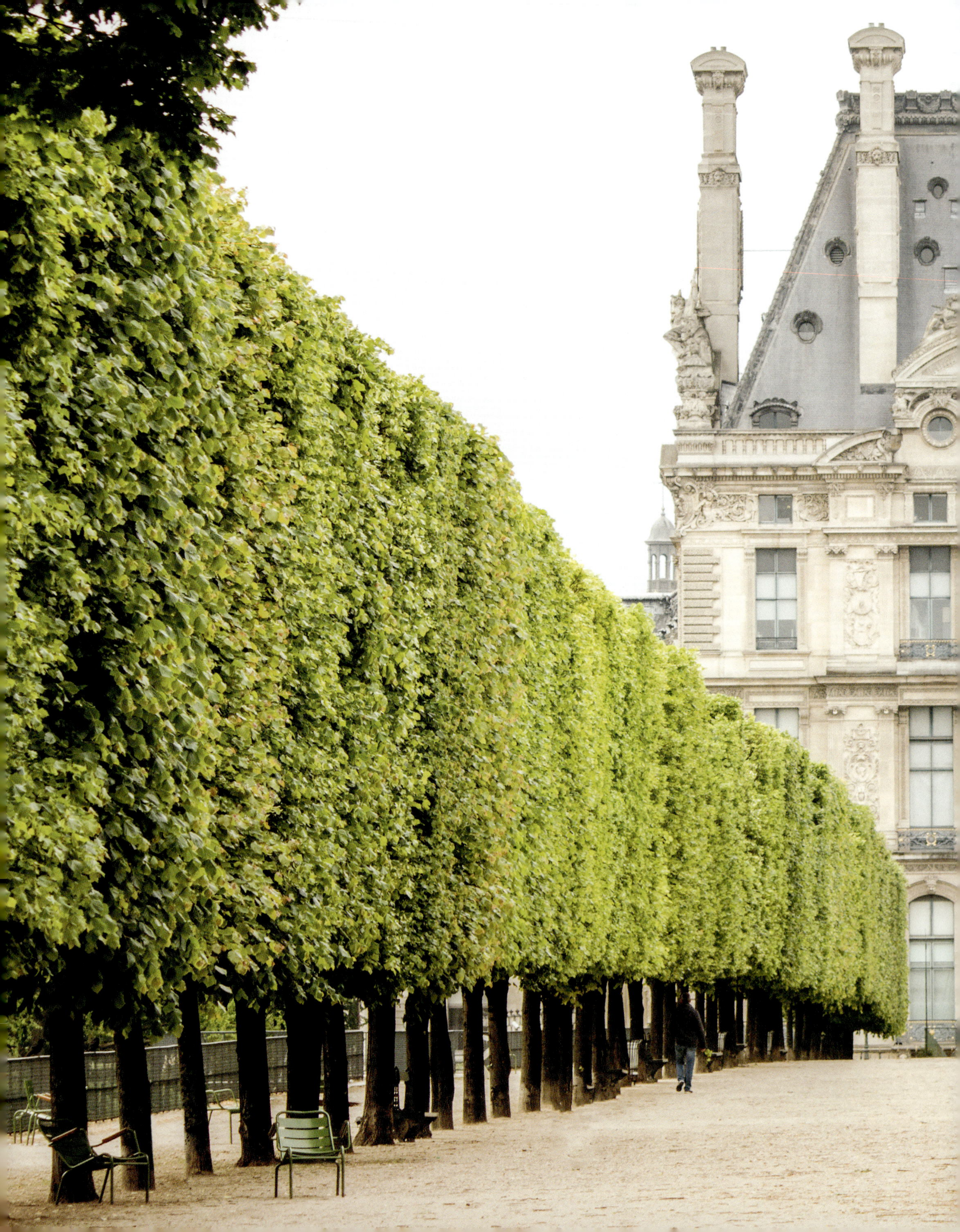

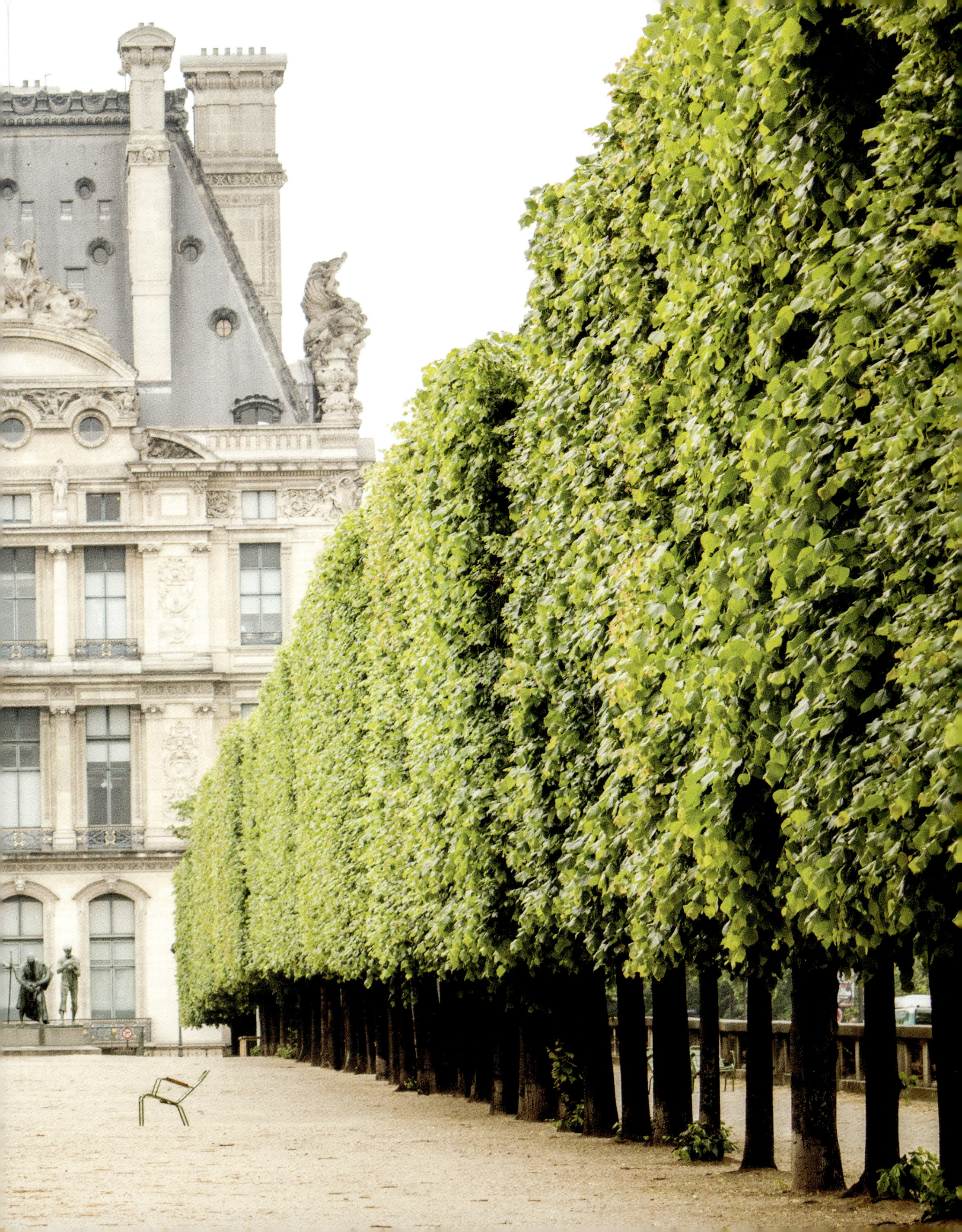

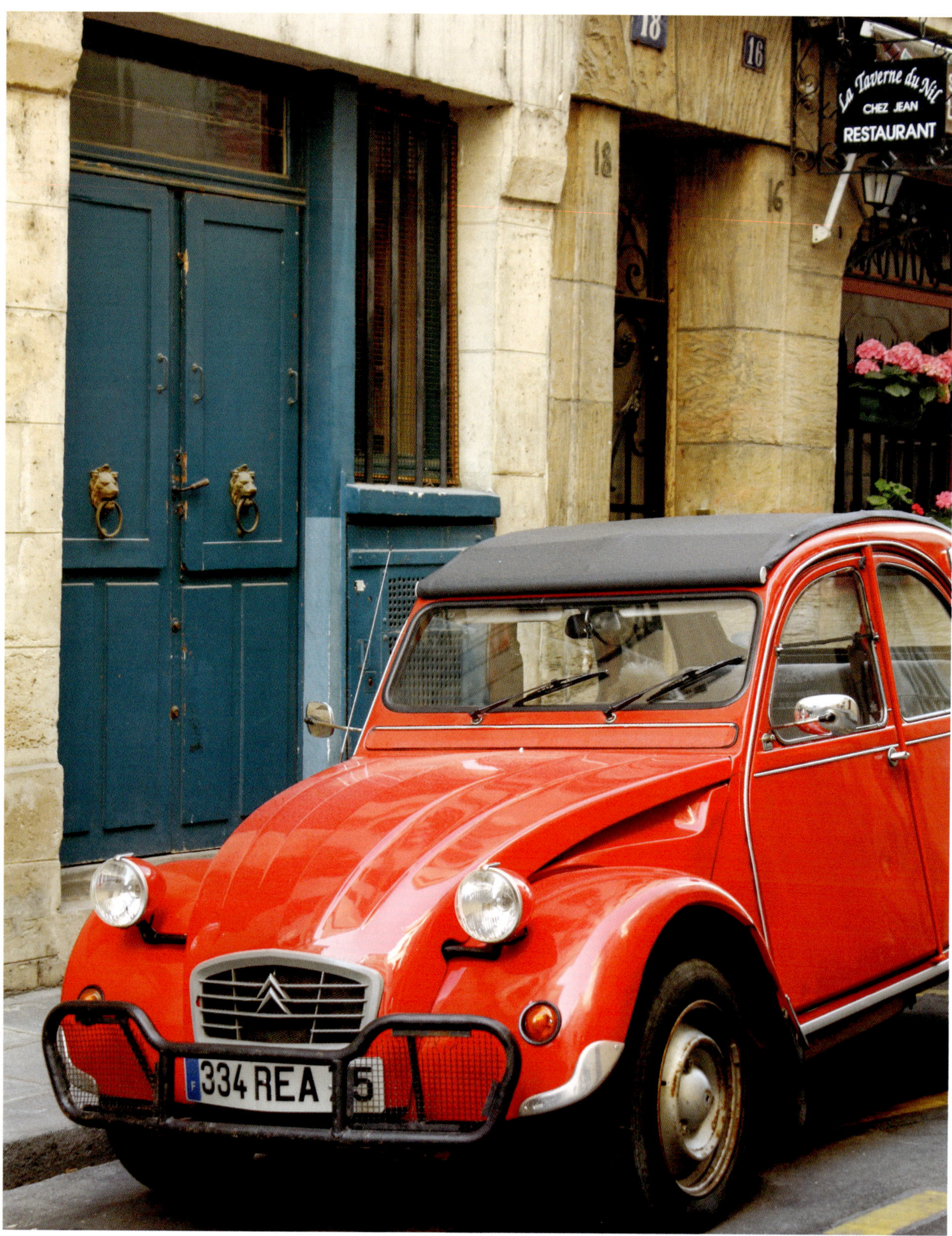
18
16
La Taverne du Nil
CHEZ JEAN
RESTAURANT
18
16
334 REA

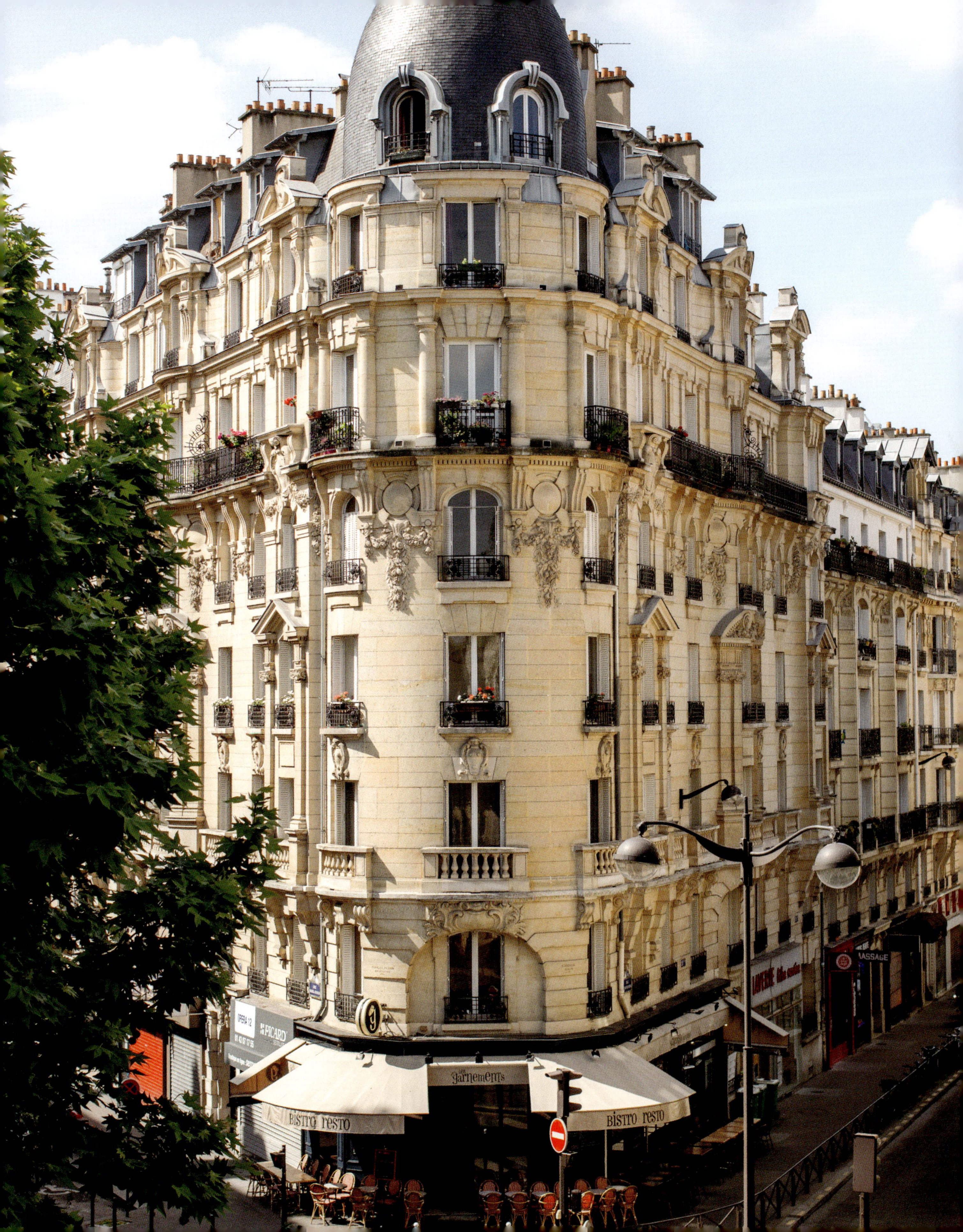
OPERA 12
PICARD
01 42 97 17 55
Les Garnements
BISTRO resto
BISTRO resto
MASSAGE

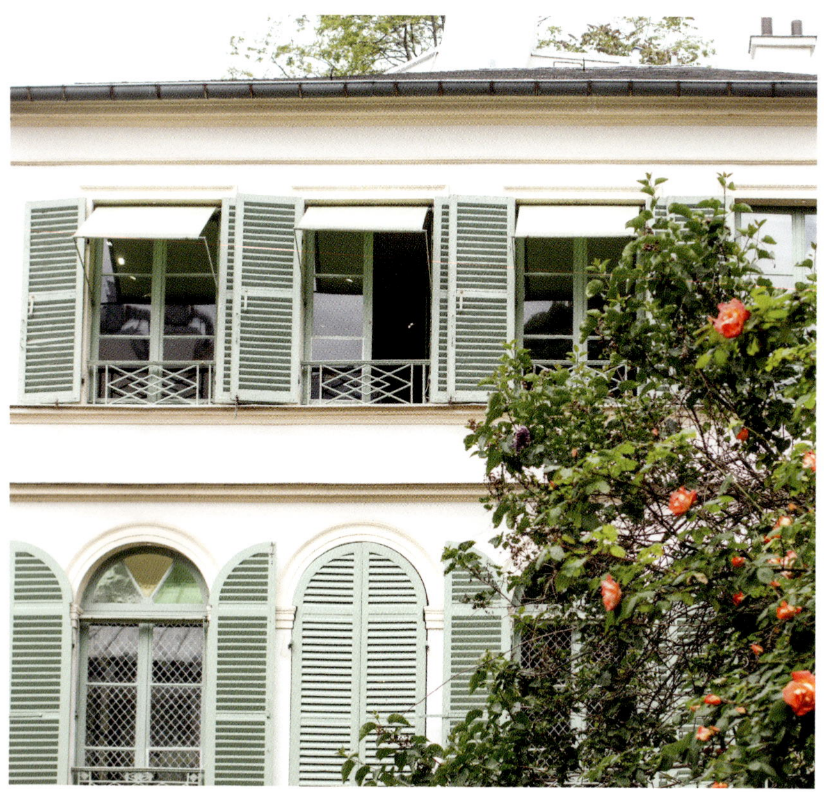

Air-conditioning is a luxury in Paris. Not all hotels or apartment rentals will have it, and the Parisians will keep their windows open for fresh air and to keep cool. A *canicule*, or "heat wave" in English, is not out of the question during summer in Paris. I experienced this weather during a summer visit, and late evening was the only break from the heat. Parisian parks were filled until after dark.

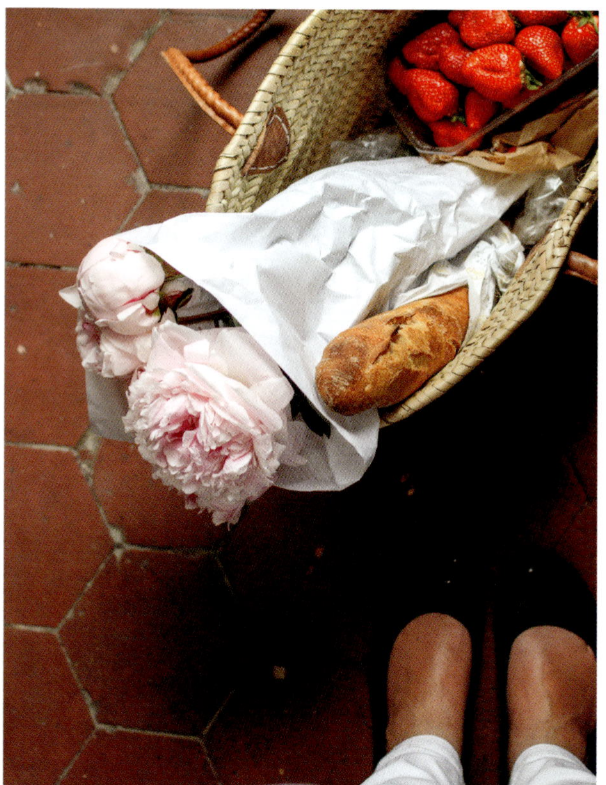

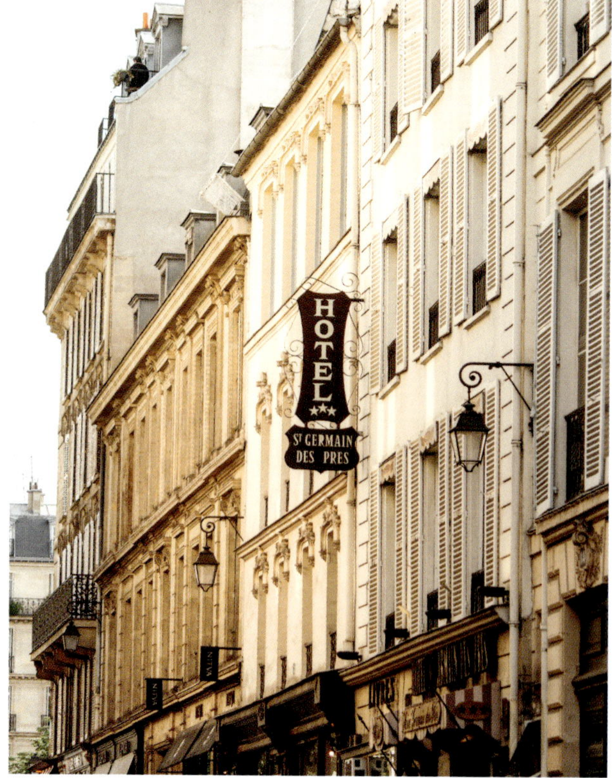

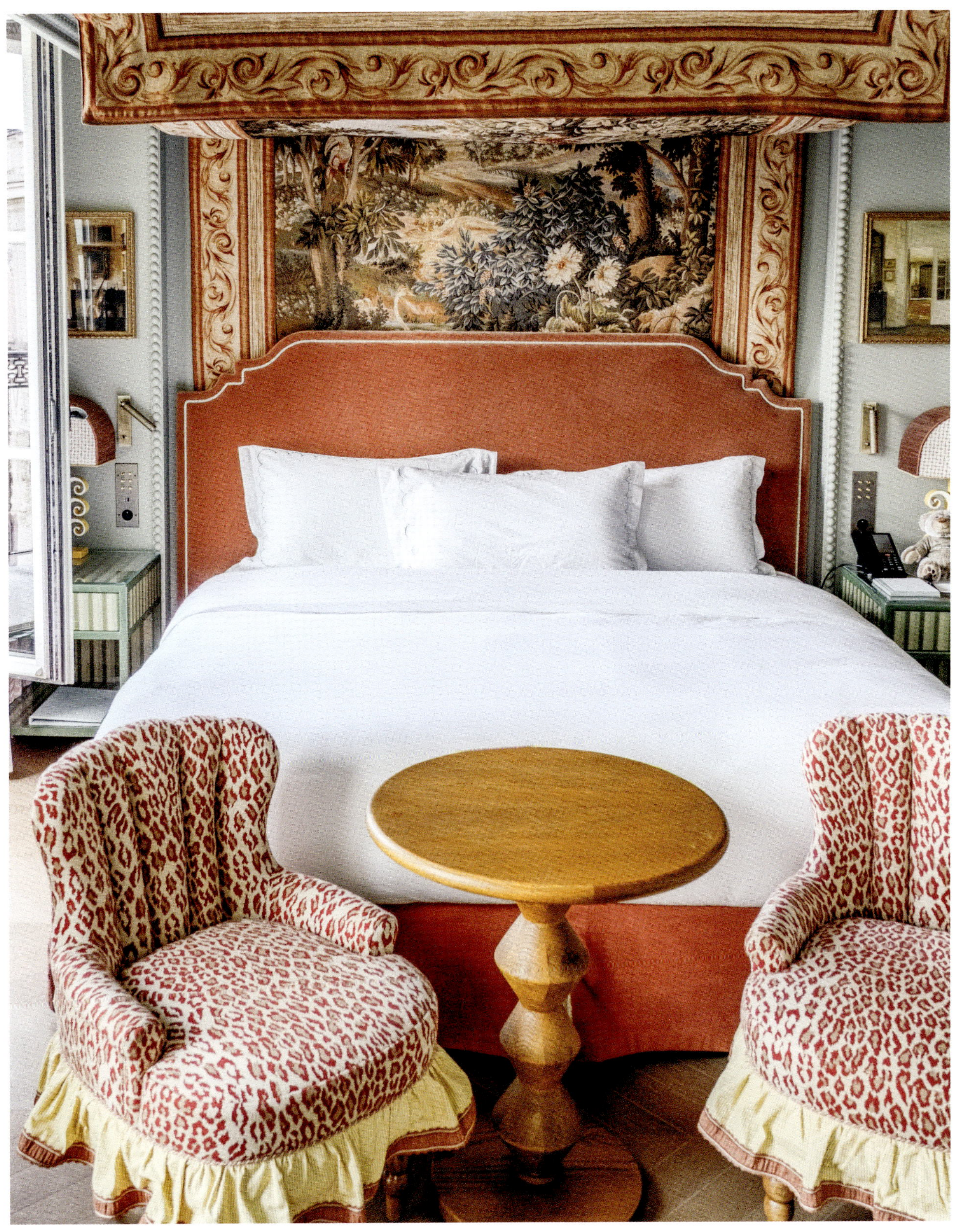

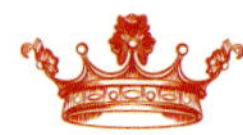

TRY TO SPEAK FRENCH

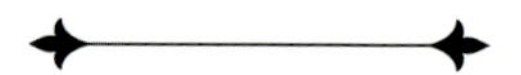

Trying to use a little French goes a long way in the city. "Bonjour" and "merci"—hello and thank you—will help to engage a Parisian when you are looking for public bathrooms or need directions. Using French words opens the doors to a warmer interaction. English is more commonly spoken now, especially with the younger generation. Don't be surprised if they notice your accent and slip into English. If you want to practice your French, just say so. Simple daily interactions, such as ordering at a boulangerie or chatting with a waiter at a restaurant, are great places to try out your French. I have found one of the best times to practice conversational French is with my rideshare driver during transportation to and from the airport.

French Phrases for Paris:

- **Bonjour**—Hello
- **Bonsoir**—Good evening
- **S'il vous plaît**—Please
- **Merci**—Thank you
- **Non merci**—No, thank you
- **Bonne journée.**—Have a good day.
- **Où sont les toilettes?**—Where are the restrooms?
- **Je voudrais un café, s'il vous plaît.**—I would like a coffee, please.
- **Une carafe d'eau**—A pitcher of water
  *The drinking water in Paris is safe, and it will save you money to order tap water instead of ordering a bottled water.
- **Une table pour deux, s'il vous plaît.**—A table for two, please.
- **Excusez-moi, combien ça coûte?**—Excuse me, how much is this?

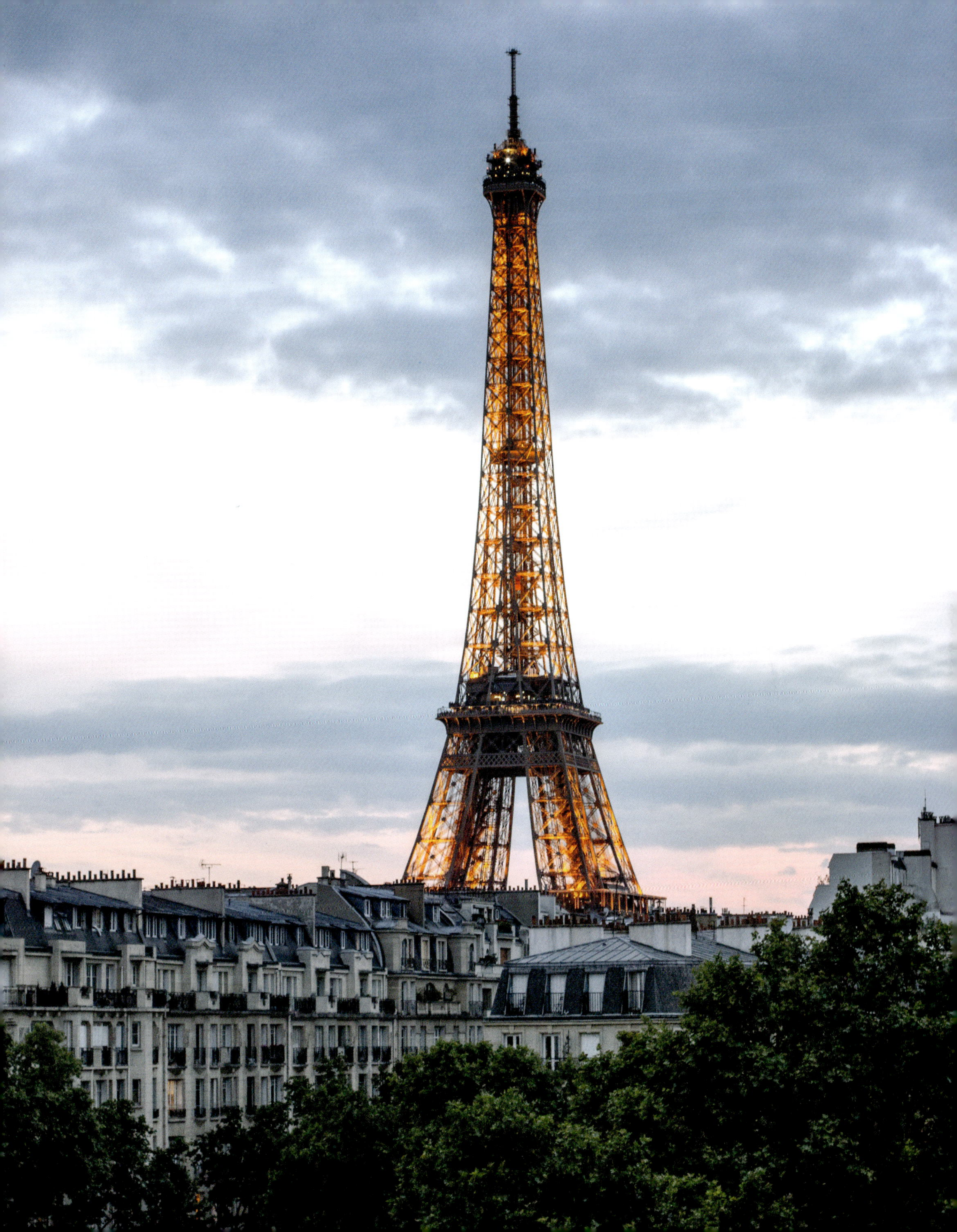

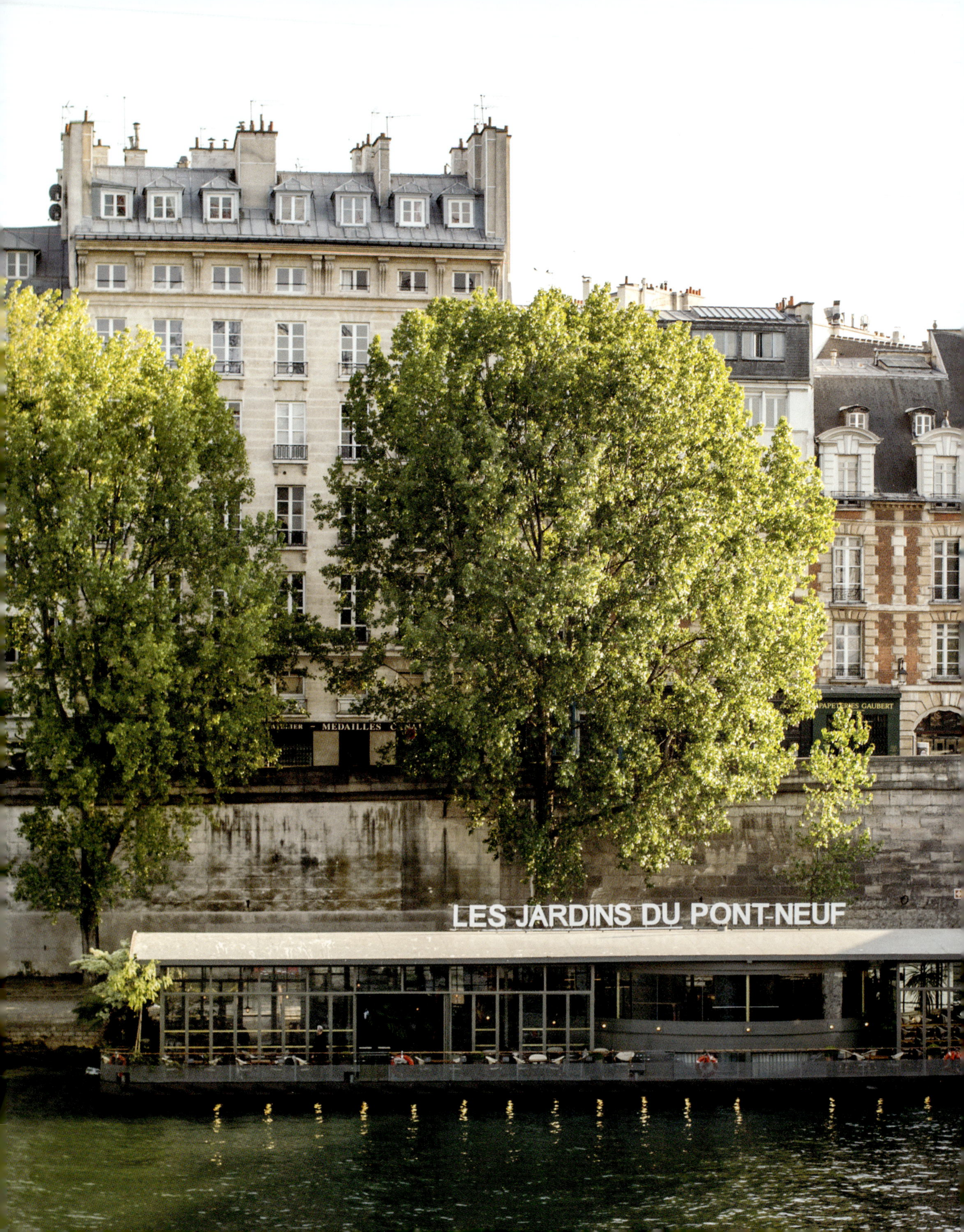
MEDAILLES
PAPETERIES GAUBERT
LES JARDINS DU PONT-NEUF

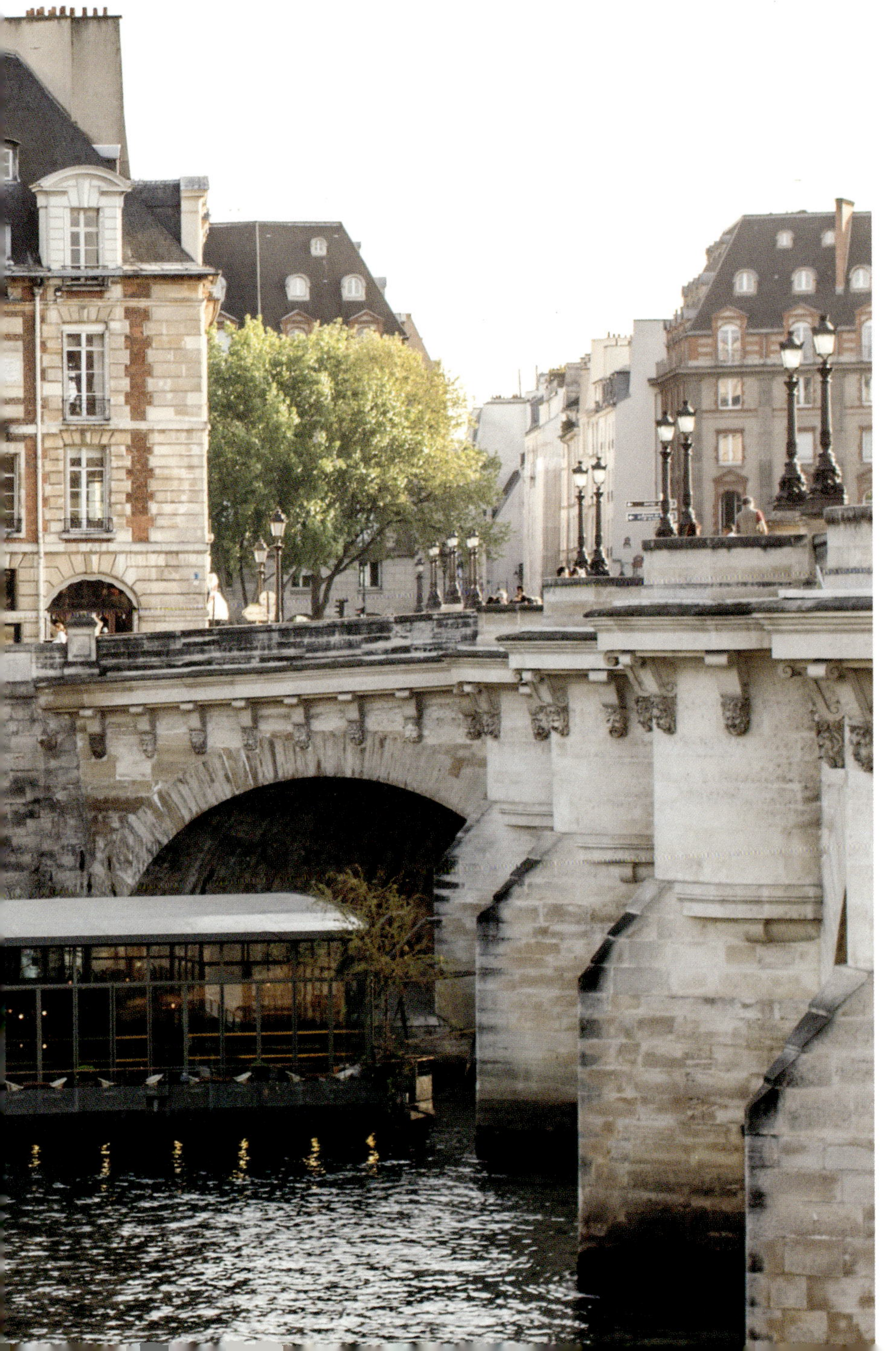

August typically is quiet in the city as many shops and restaurants close for vacation. The closures may last as long as a month as Parisians enjoy their holiday. Some hotels and restaurants that serve tourists stay open, but it's always a good idea to check before heading to your favorite establishment in late summer.

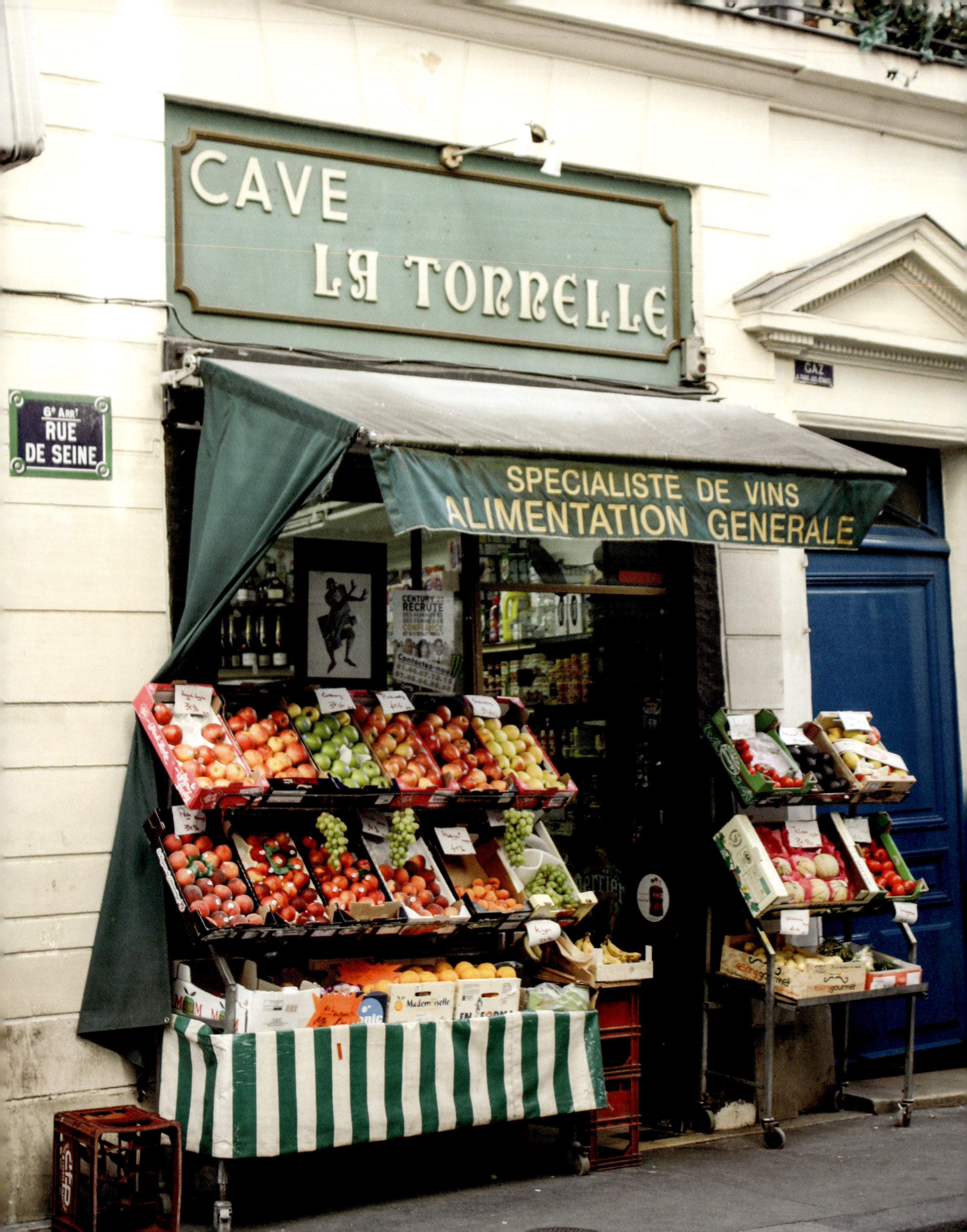
CAVE
LA TONNELLE
6e ARRt
RUE
DE SEINE
SPECIALISTE DE VINS
ALIMENTATION GENERALE
GAZ

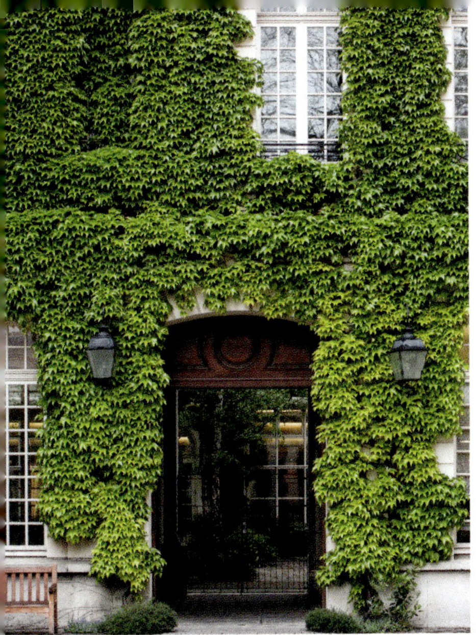

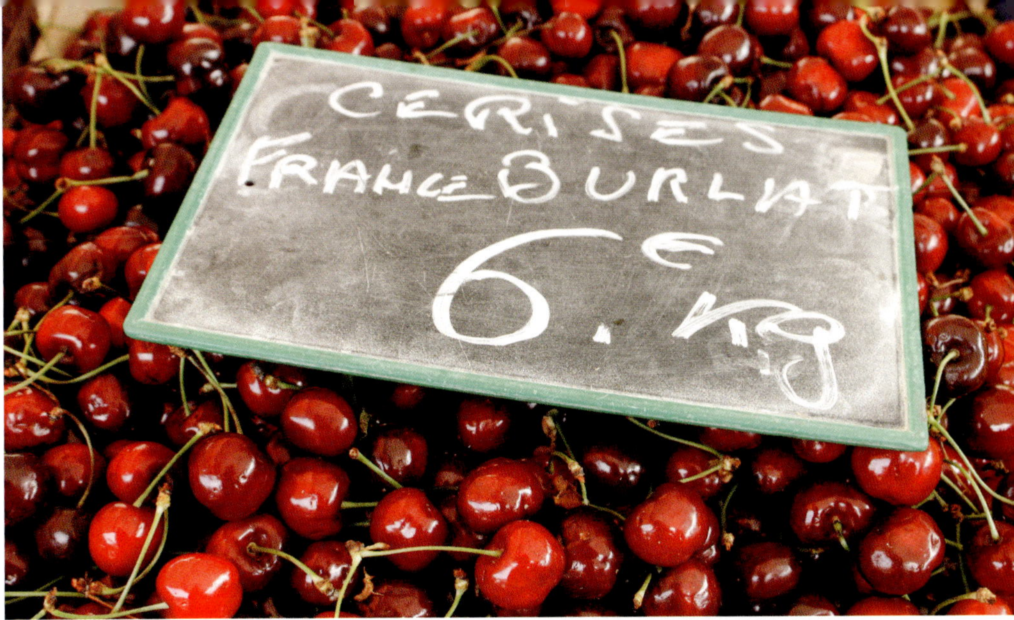

Summer is a time of year when markets are filled with fresh berries, stone fruit, and colorful flowers. Parisians keep cool by spending time on covered terraces, seeking shade under trees in the parks around the city, or enjoying the “Paris Plages” along the Seine, while sipping crisp rosé and eating ice cream. Paris radiates joie de vivre in the summer.

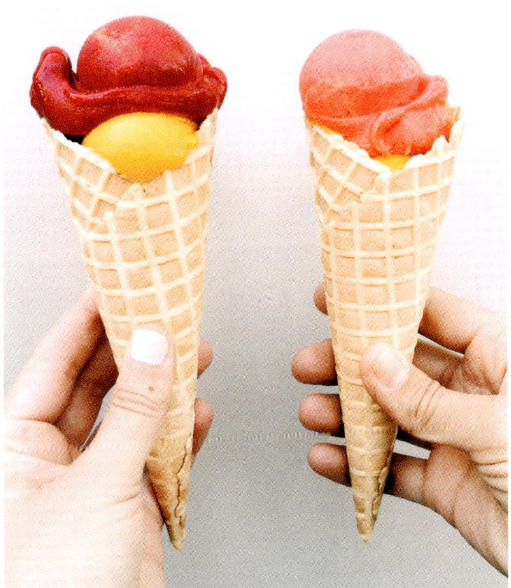

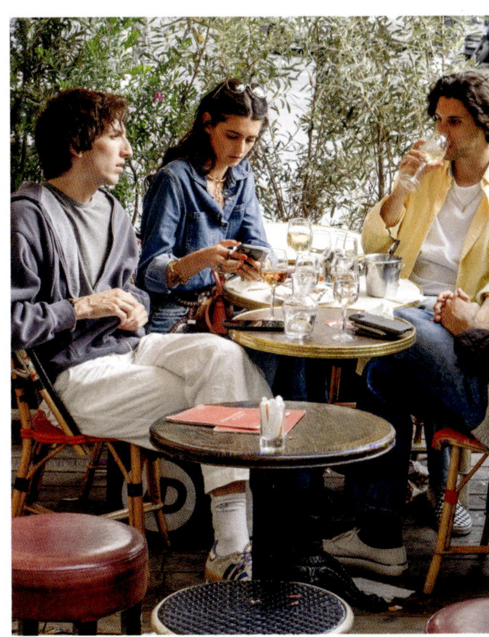

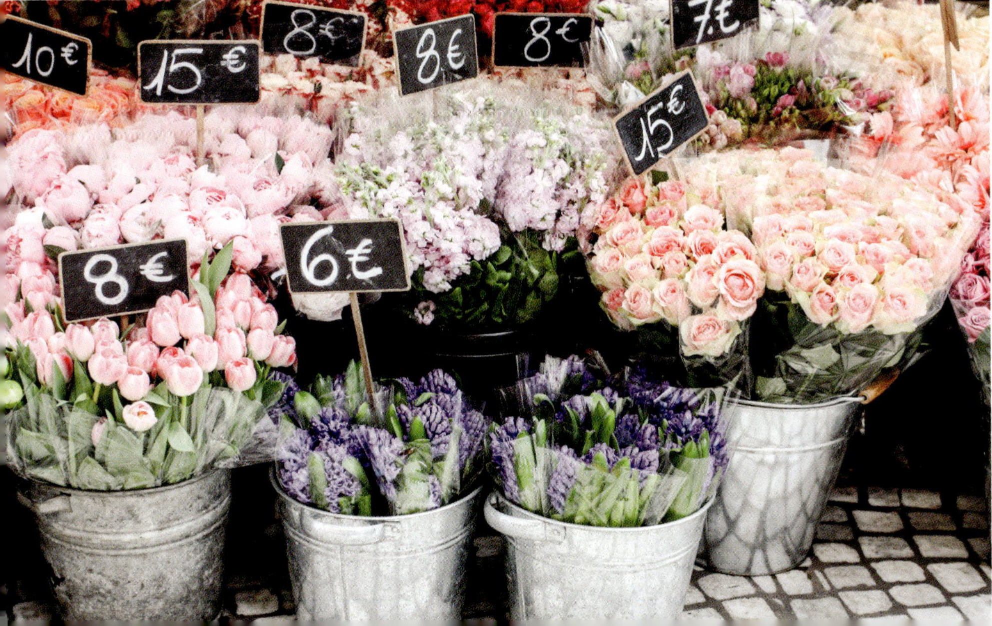

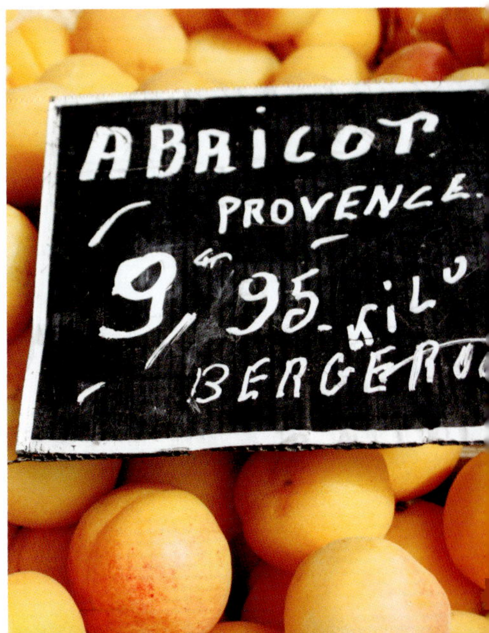

SUMMER MENUS

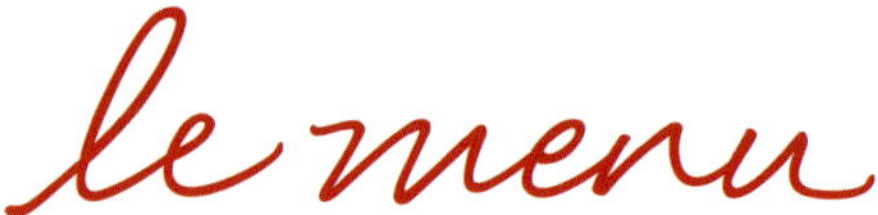

Dorade Grillé
(grilled sea bream)

La Tarte Provençale aux Courgettes
(savory zucchini tart)

Artichauts Vinaigrette or Salade Niçoise
(artichokes with vinaigrette or Niçoise Salad)

Clafoutis
(a baked custard dessert often served with cherries)

- Grilled seafood tops Parisian menus with fish and scallops as leading choices. Ceviche is also a popular choice along with cold soups.
- Fresh market produce like tomatoes or eggplant are blended with goat cheese and herbs in savory tarts. A Provençal dish of stewed vegetables, ratatouille is a summer staple.
- Beverages range from rosé wine with a small glass of ice to keep it cool (which some think is more of a South of France drink than Parisian) or my favorite, Citron Pressé, fresh lemon juice served with water and sugar to mix yourself. Try mixing it with Badoit sparkling water for a bubbly, nonalcoholic drink. Café Glacé, an iced coffee, can now be found on many café menus.

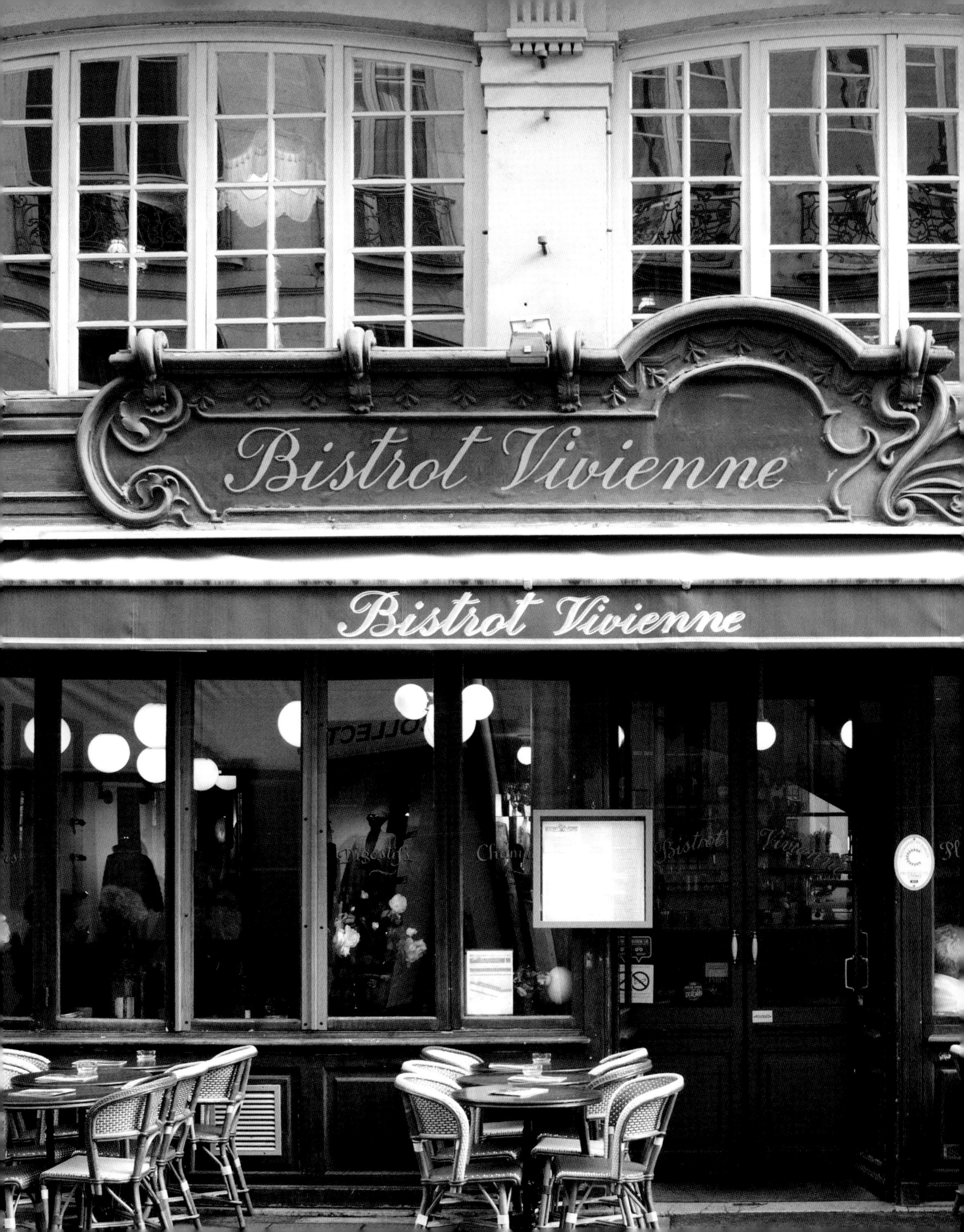

Bistrot Vivienne
Bistrot Vivienne

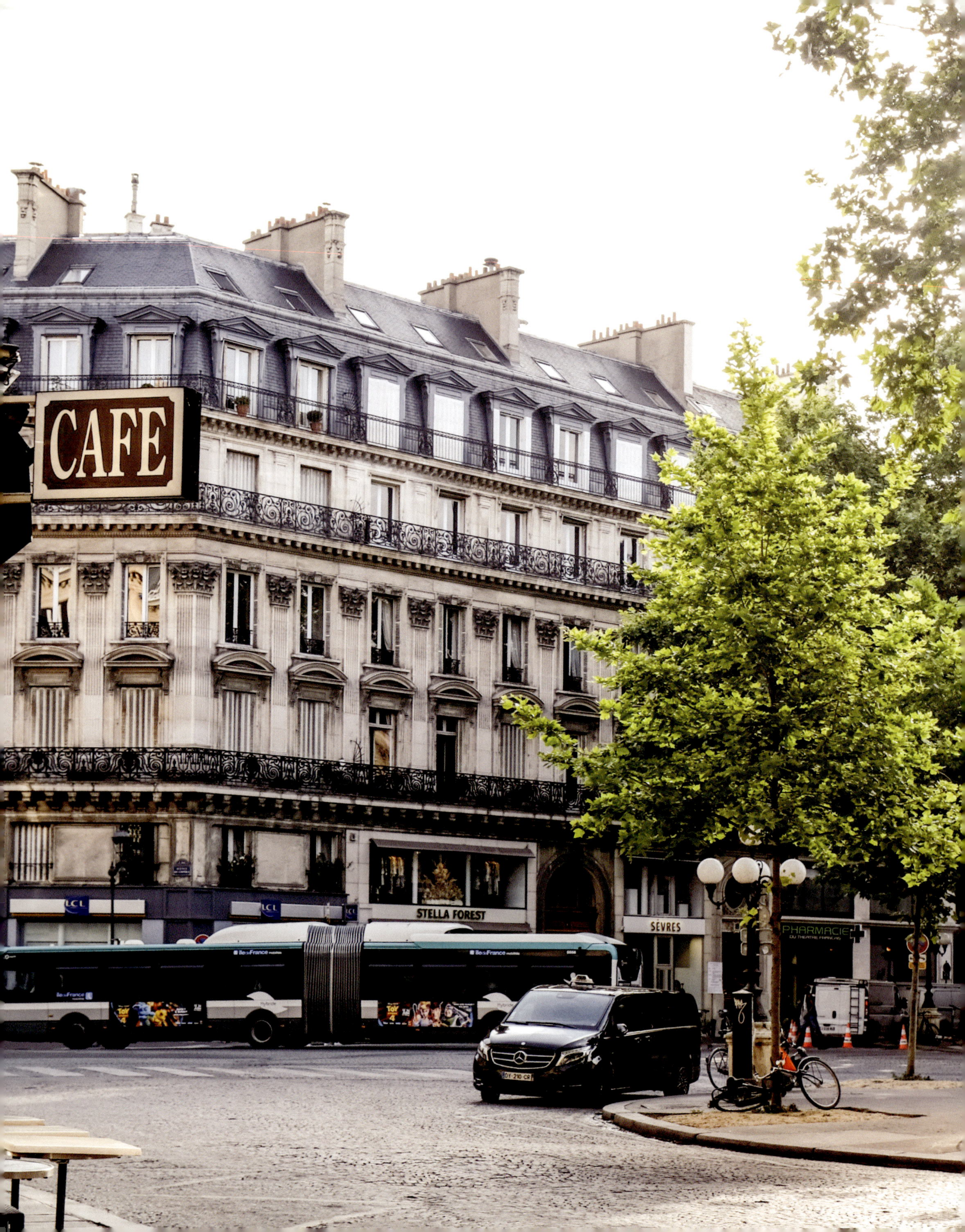
CAFE
LCL
LCL
STELLA FOREST
SÈVRES
PHARMACIE

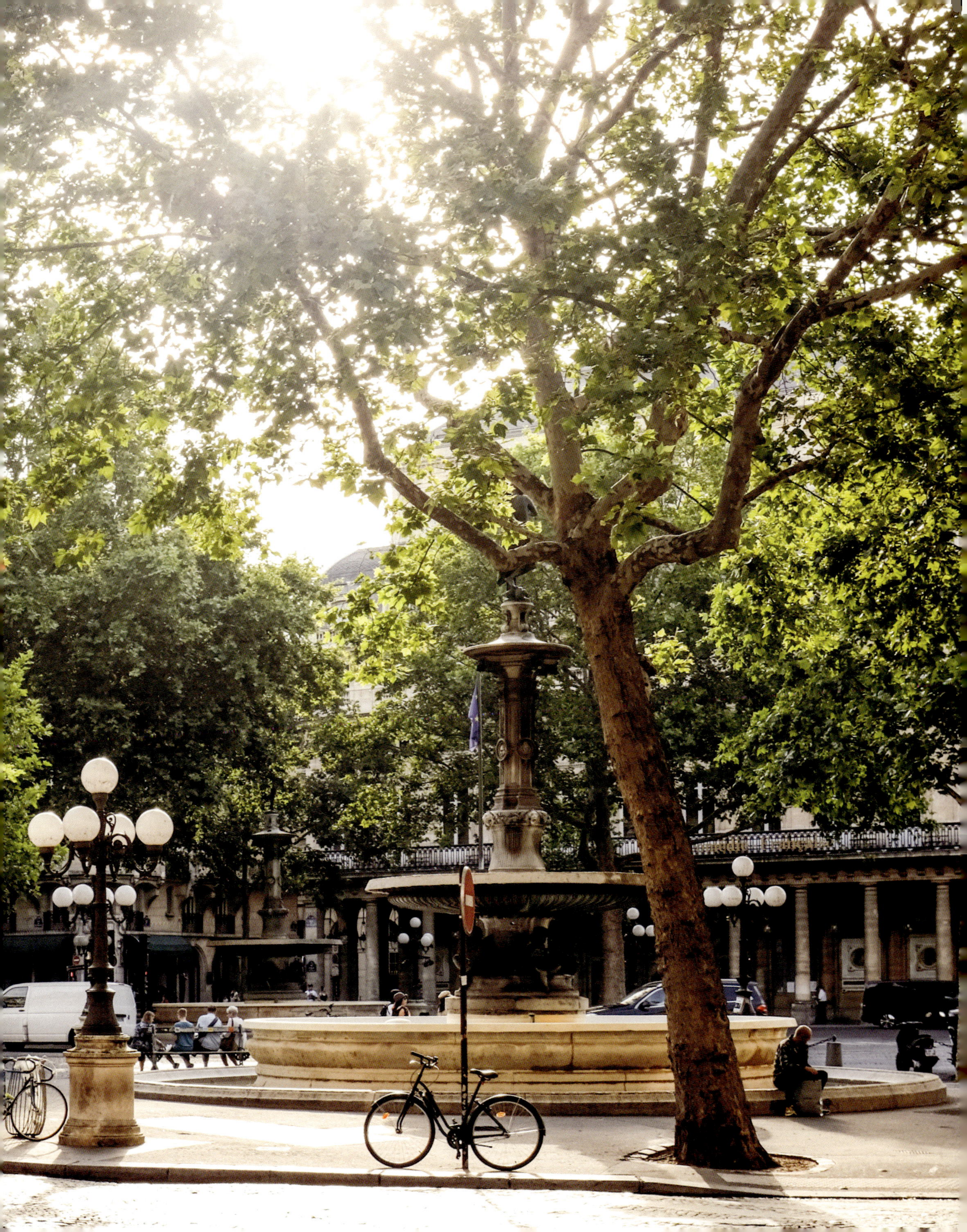

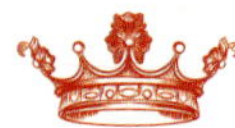

ICE CREAM ADVENTURES

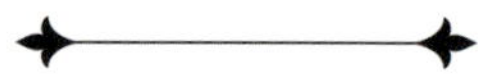

The ice cream scene is always expanding, and I am here to help you find the best! For a classic Parisian ice cream shop, visit Berthillon on Île Saint-Louis, but it is worth exploring and tasting other shops throughout Paris. If you spend time in the city during the warmer months, go for an ice cream crawl and choose your favorite. Here, you'll find some of my recommendations:

- **Une Glace à Paris** is located in the Marais. The shop creates their ice cream on-site using the freshest ingredients. Try their sorbet and ice cream flavors year-round.

- **La Glacerie Paris** offers simple and quality ingredients to make their ice cream stand out. Located just behind Hôtel de Ville, this is one venue you'll want to add to your Marais itinerary.

- **La Glace Alain Ducasse** can be found close to the Marché Bastille on Rue de la Roquette in the 11th arrondissement. I first discovered La Glace Alain Ducasse at an ice cream cart in the Palais-Royal area. The lemon sorbet is still a flavor I can't stop dreaming about once summer hits. Try the Alain Ducasse chocolate store on Rue des Petits-Champs in the 1st arrondissement for ice cream and sorbet as well.

- **Glace Bachir** is a Lebanese-style ice cream eatery in Paris that has gained quite a following for their crushed pistachio topping. I tried their sorbet recently without nuts, and it was delicious.

- **Méert** has ice cream carts in the city during warmer months. I have seen ice cream and sorbet offered at outside locations through September at Méert, a sweet shop known for their waffles, and at the oldest pastry shop in Paris, **Pâtisserie Stohrer** on Rue Montorgueil.

- **Folderol** is technically a wine bar that also offers homemade ice cream. The flavors rotate daily and range from traditional to creative. I love the Olive Oil ice cream paired with a fruit sorbet. My husband recently got the Carrot Cake ice cream, which was incredible. Discover their website for various flavors, past and present, or visit and prepare to be surprised. I highly recommend getting two flavors.

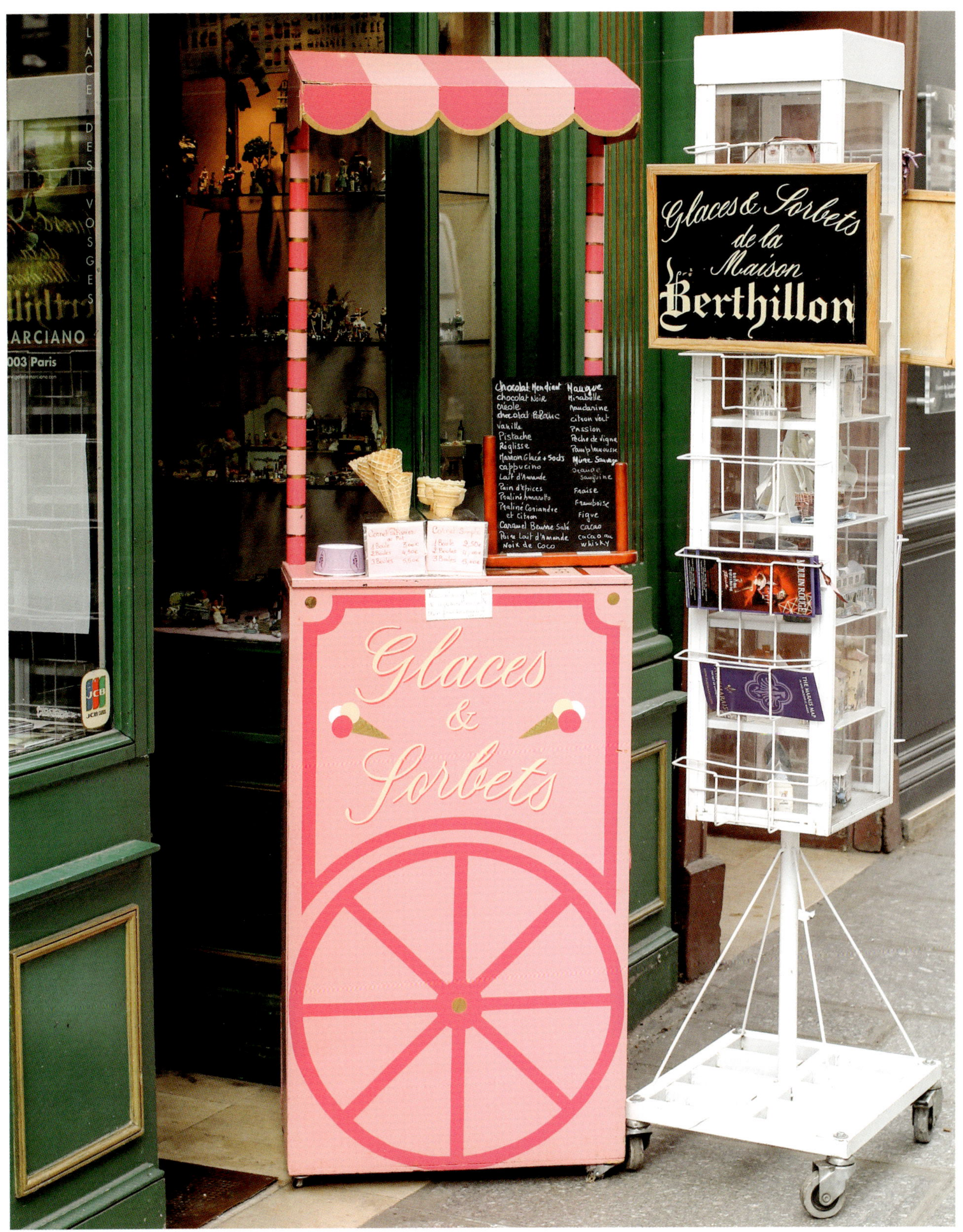
PLACE DES VOSGES
Glaces & Sorbets
de la
Maison
Berthillon
Glaces
&
Sorbets

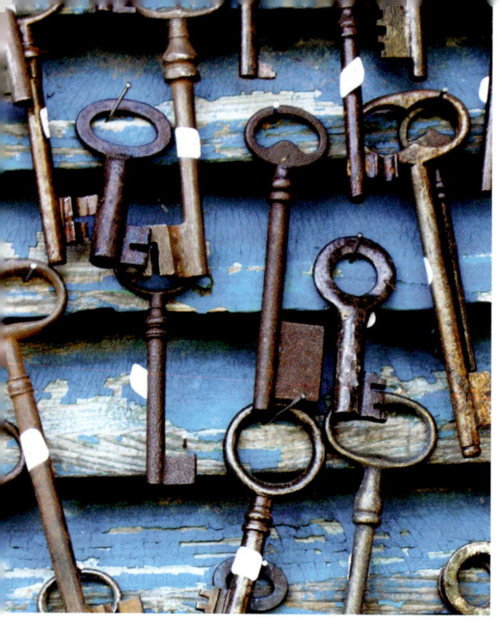

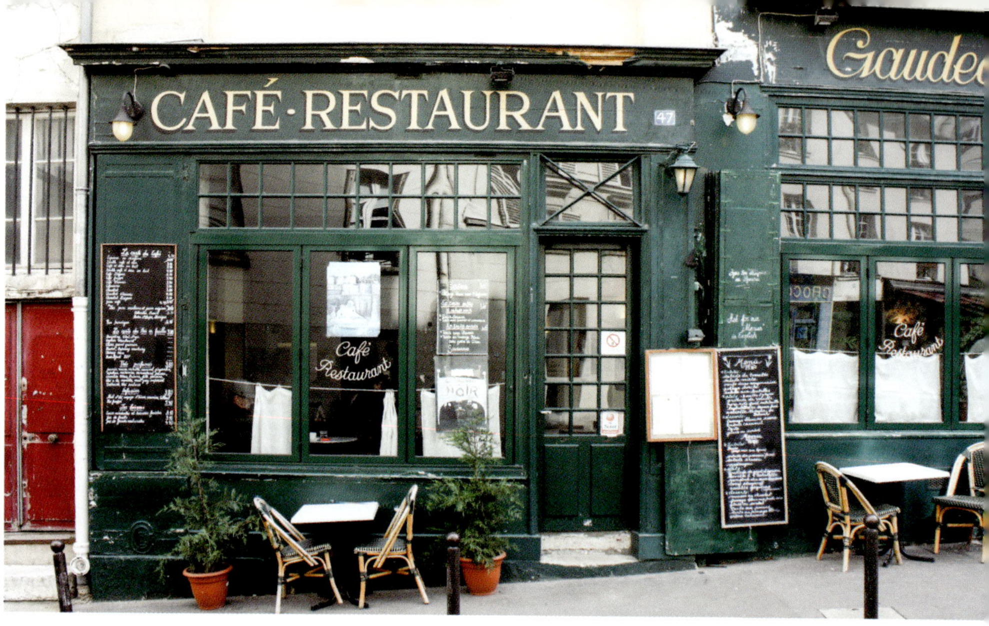
CAFÉ·RESTAURANT
Café Restaurant

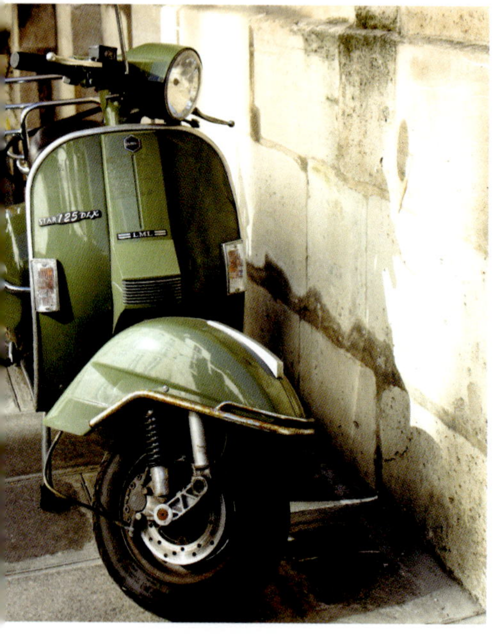

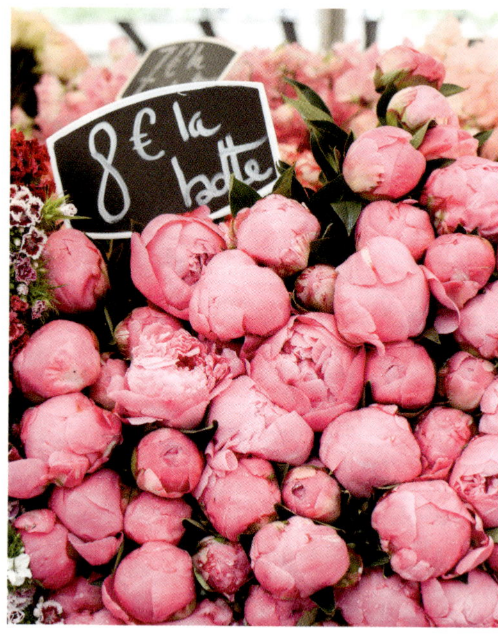
8€ la botte

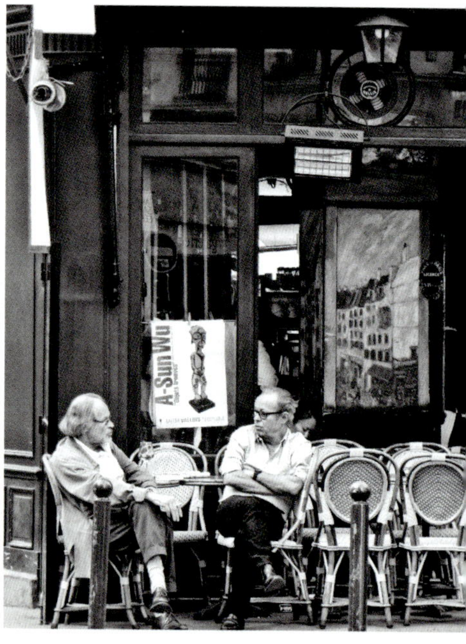

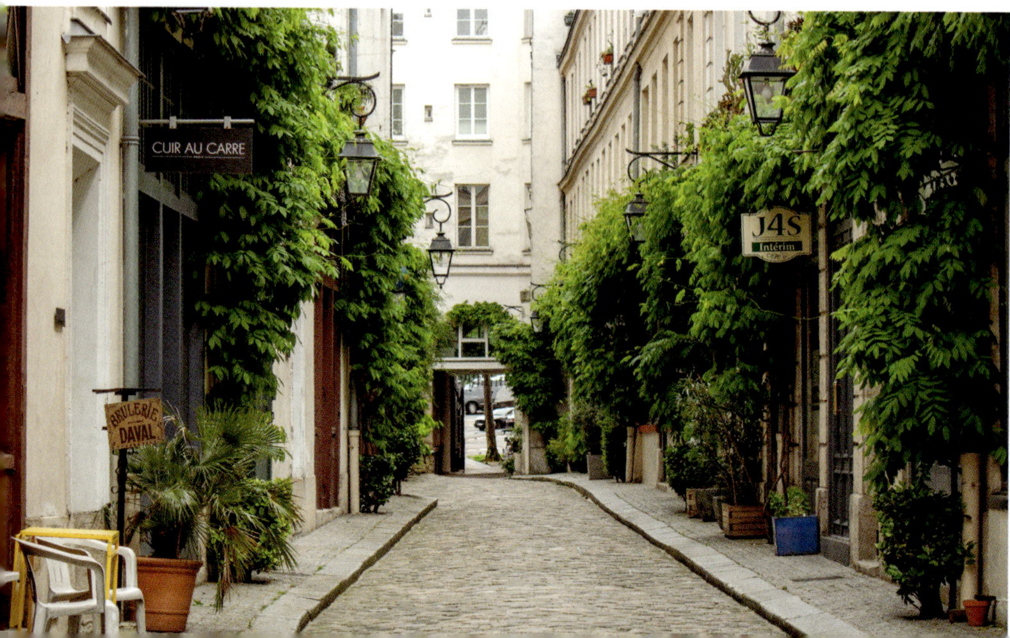
CUIR AU CARRE
J4S
Intérim

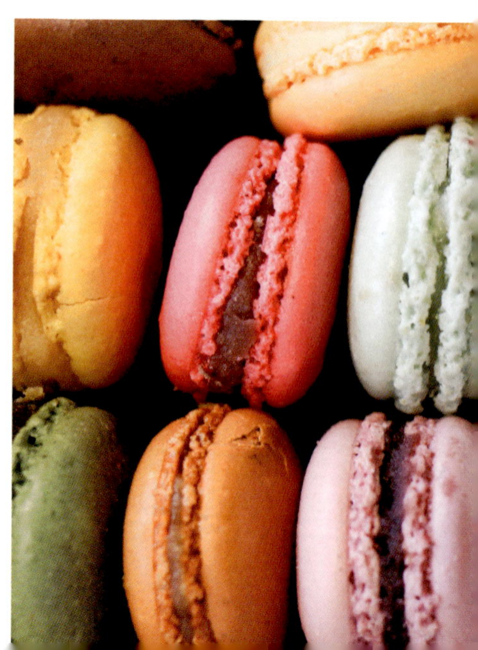

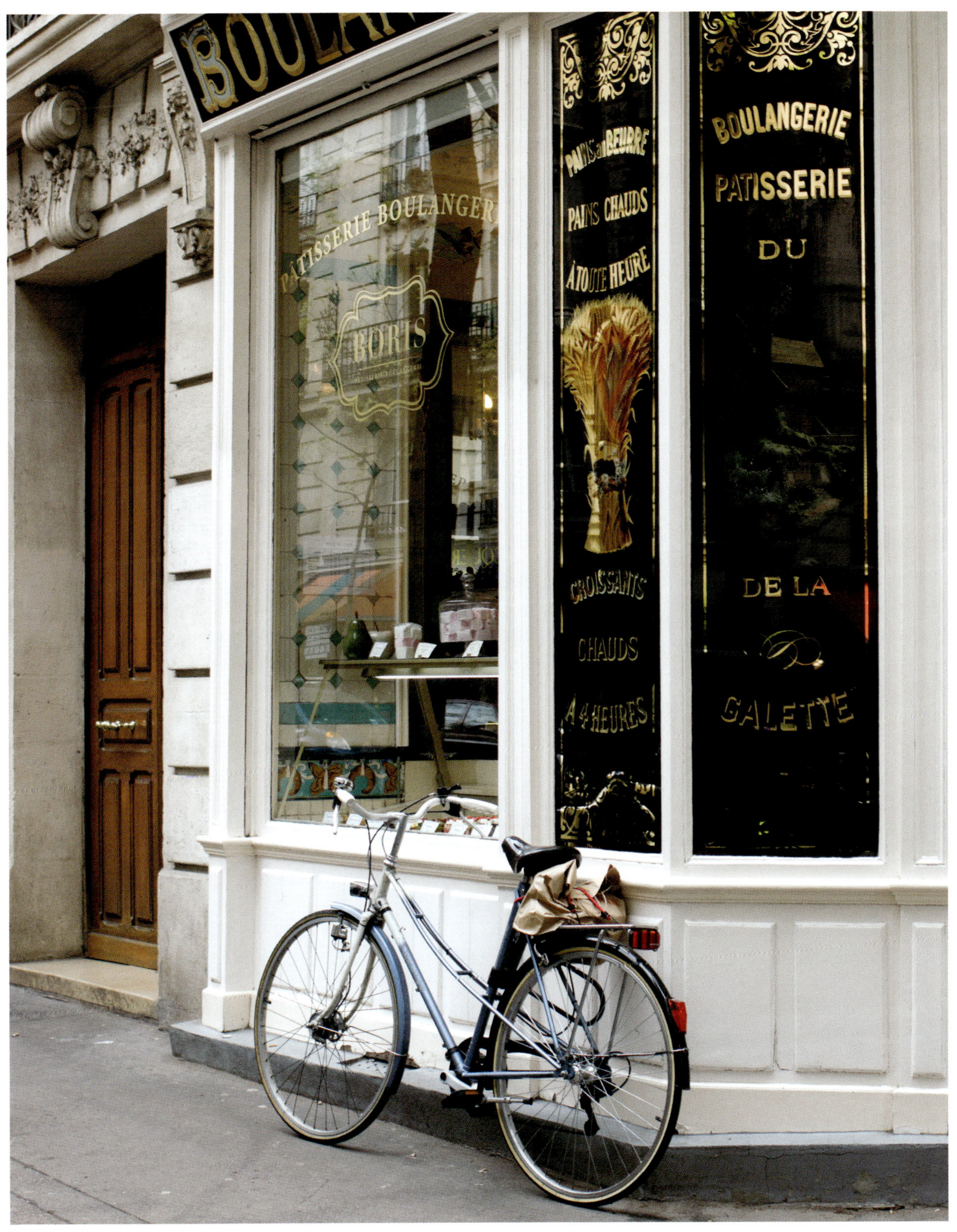
PÂTISSERIE
BORIS
PAINS au BEURRE
PAINS CHAUDS
À TOUTE HEURE
CROISSANTS
CHAUDS
A 4 HEURES
BOULANGERIE
PATISSERIE
DU
DE LA
GALETTE

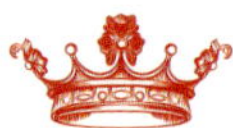

PICNIC SPOTS

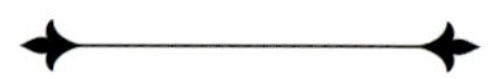

- **Jardin des Tuileries** is just in front of the Louvre, close to the Seine. It is perfect for solo travelers, couples, and families. Grab a bench or collect a few empty green chairs for an impromptu picnic. The grass area between the Louvre and the Tuileries offers an excellent option for larger groups. Also, bring a picnic blanket. In the warmer months, you can set yourself up for a view of the sunset over the Seine and Eiffel Tower.

- **Champ de Mars** near the Eiffel Tower is a classic picnic spot in Paris, especially as spring turns to summer when the evenings are long and warm. It is also a prime venue for Bastille Day fireworks and festivities.

- **Place des Vosges** in the heart of the Marais is a preferred picnic locale for many. Grab picnic essentials at the Marché Bastille, one of the biggest food markets, open on Sundays and Thursdays. Boulangeries close by offer great takeaway options to enjoy in the park. Expect the crowd to be a mixture of Parisians and visitors of all ages. It is an excellent area for young kids to burn some energy.

- **Palais-Royal** is a quieter option to the more extensive Tuileries garden nearby. The trees offer shade in the warmer months, making it a great place for a picnic lunch on a park bench or green chair surrounding the fountain. Palais-Royal is a dog-friendly area, so expect a few adorable pups to crash your picnic. Inside the center of Palais-Royal is a garden with ever-changing blooms: magnolia trees in early spring, roses in the summer, and dahlias in the early fall.

- **Jardin du Luxembourg** is an iconic picnic site on the Left Bank. On weekends, it is bustling with Parisians and visitors. The gardens and the fountains are kid-friendly spots, as ponds dotted with wooden toy sailboats offer a fun activity for an hour.

- **The Seine River** is an easy destination on the Left or Right Bank. Parisians are out on its banks on warm days, no matter the season. Stake out a place for the afternoon or evening. Mind your belongings, as it is easy for something to go missing. The Seine's banks are great for solo travelers open to meeting locals and visitors. Share a bottle of wine and make friends with your picnic neighbors.

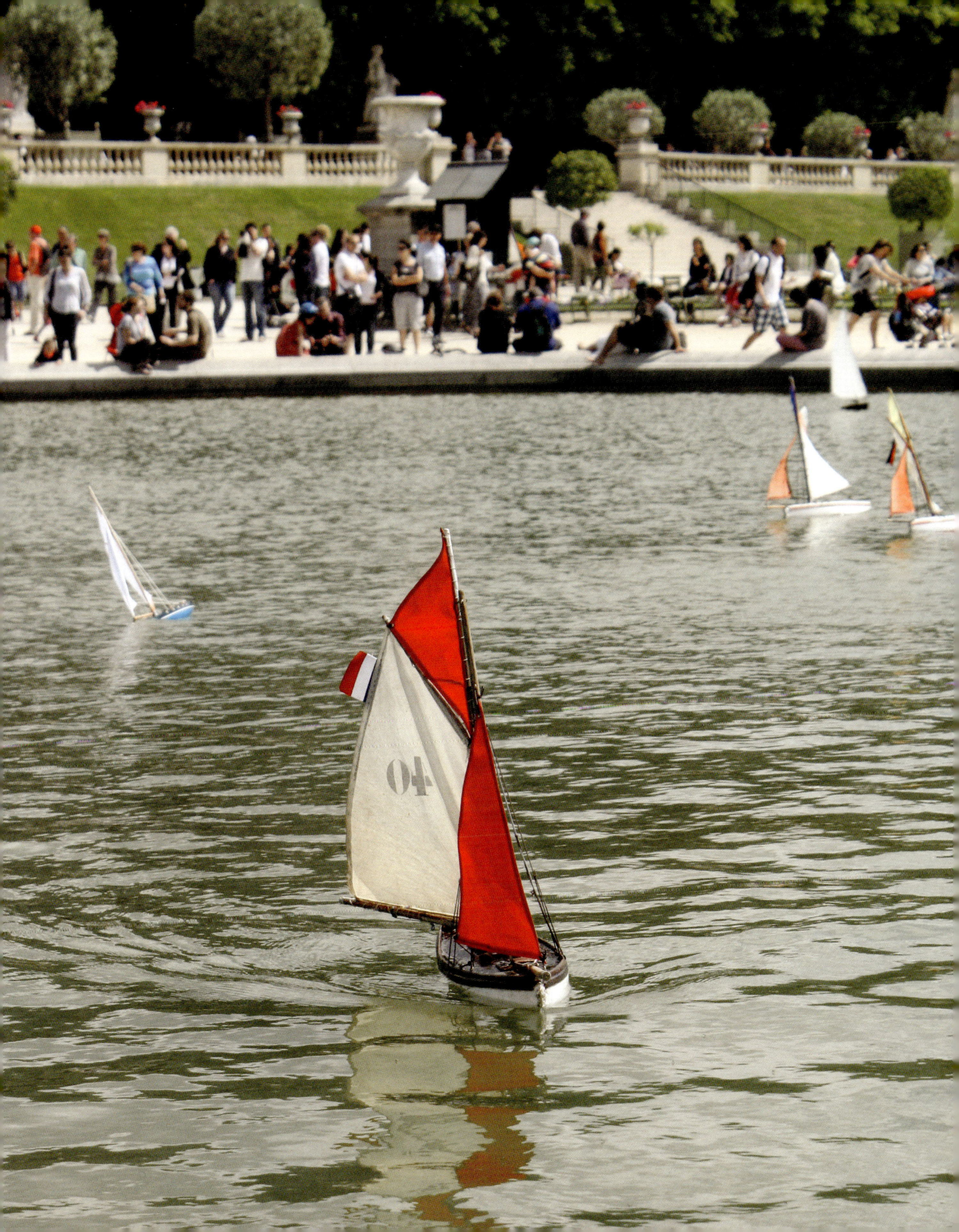
04

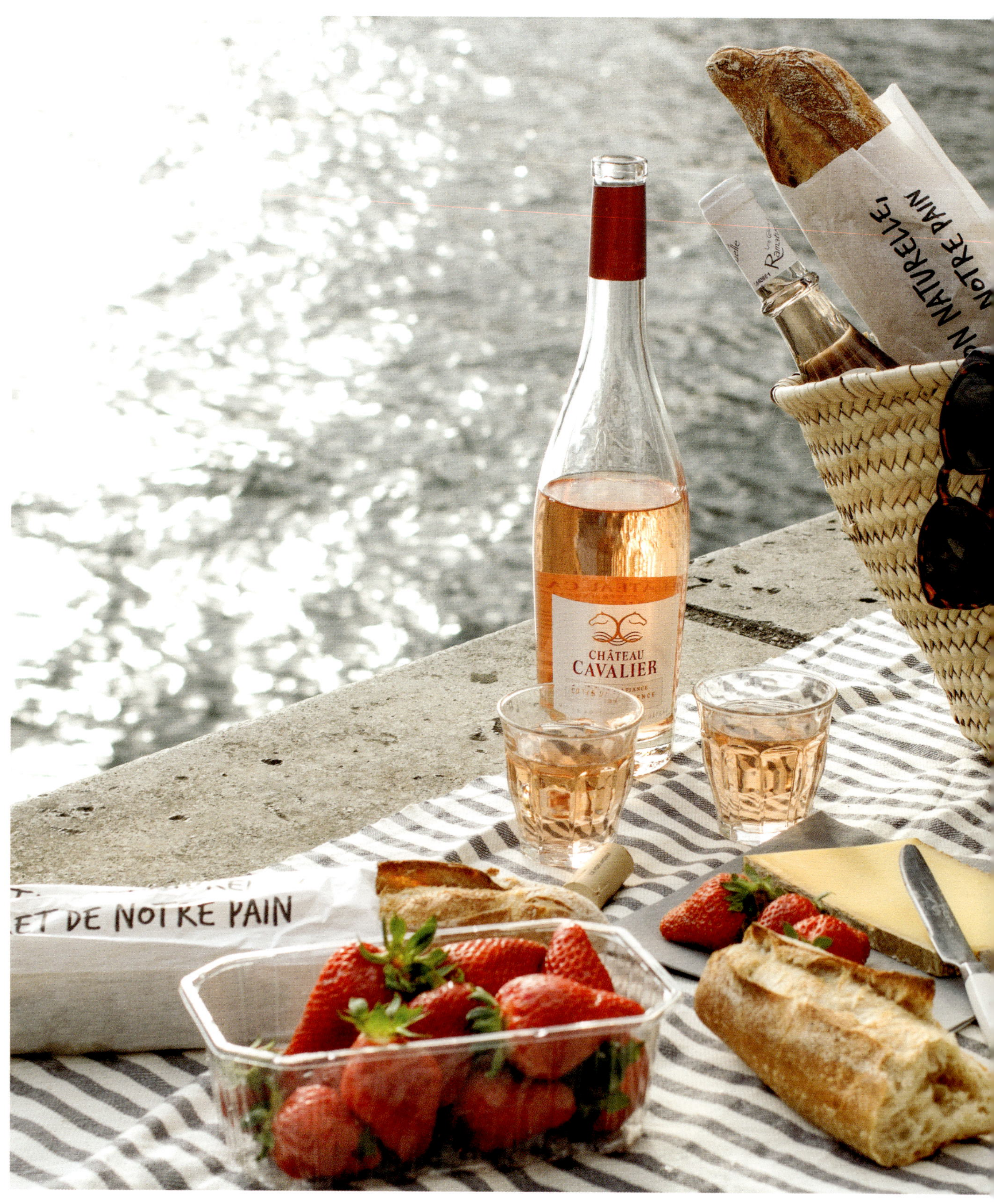
NOTRE PAIN
NATURELLE,
CHÂTEAU
CAVALIER
ET DE NOTRE PAIN

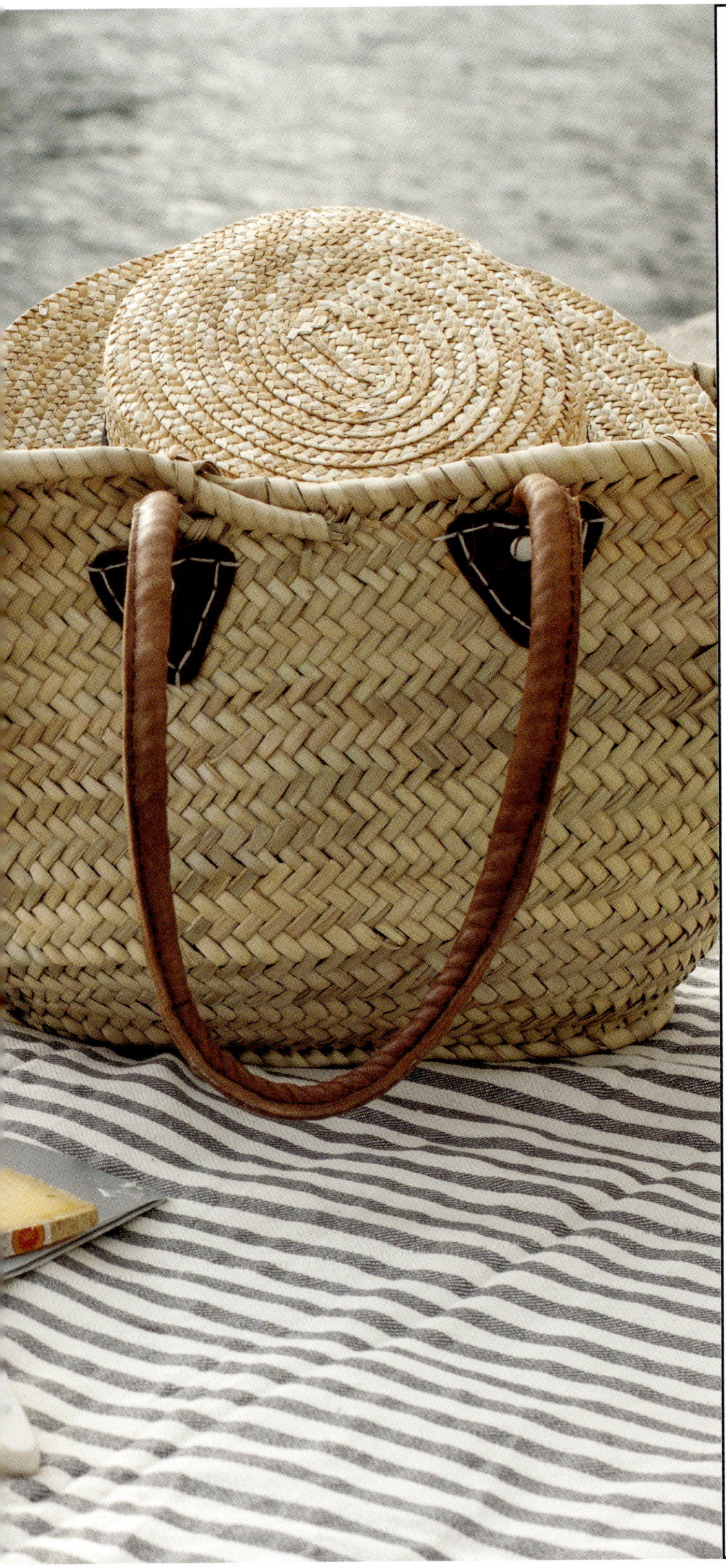

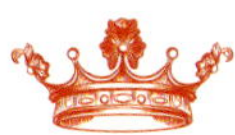

TIPS FOR PICNICKING IN PARIS

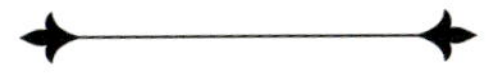

Picnic season begins as people congregate in the grassy parks throughout Paris. The banks of the Seine River are lined with locals sipping rosé, smoking cigarettes, and walking their dogs. Stroll a park or bike ride the trails along the Seine. Outdoor gatherings are a Parisian way of life. There are various places where you can purchase baguettes, cheese, wine, and charcuterie for your picnic.

- Visit a local market and collect everything at once. Stop at vendor stalls to buy cheese, fruit, and a baguette.

- Stop by a market street, such as Rue Cler on the Left Bank or Rue Montorgueil on the Right Bank, offering individual specialty shops.

- A boulangerie sells individual baguettes along with sandwiches on the crusty bread, salads, and quiches. You will want to order a *baguette tradition* with artisanal bread over a *baguette ordinaire*.

- Fromageries offer a wide variety of cheeses. The cheesemonger may make suggestions based on your preferences.

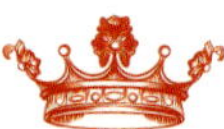

BOULANGERIES IN PARIS

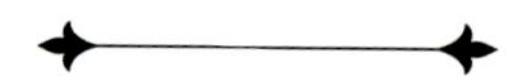

Baguettes in Paris

- Ordering a baguette in Paris is not always as simple as it sounds. There are typically two types of baguettes that are offered: *baguette tradition* and *baguette ordinaire*. The price for a *baguette tradition* may be a few centimes more, but it is worth it. This type of baguette is subject to strict government regulations and can only be made with water, flour, salt, and yeast. A *baguette ordinaire* may contain additives or be prebaked. I promise you can taste the difference.

- You can specify how you want your baguette cooked when you order it. "*Une baguette pas trop cuite, s'il vous plaît*" translates to "a baguette not too cooked, please." *Bien cuite* is well-cooked, and the baguette will be crisper on the outside. I always go for a baguette *pas trop cuite* while my husband prefers a *bien cuite* baguette. My rule is whoever orders gets to choose, and that is typically me.

- A demi-baguette is also an option if you're looking for just half a baguette. Select your demi-baguette the same way, with your preference on how it is cooked. Having euros on hand helps when purchasing this inexpensive bakery item.

- Arrive at the boulangerie early in the morning or before dinner to purchase a warm baguette fresh out of the oven. I promise; there is nothing like a warm baguette from your favorite boulangerie slathered with salted butter. My go-to boulangerie is Maison Landemaine, located at 28 Boulevard Beaumarchais.

Croissants in Paris

- There are also two types of croissants offered in Paris, aside from the almond and *pain au chocolat* variations. For a classic croissant made with butter, order a *croissant au beurre*. A *croissant ordinaire* is made with margarine or a butter/margarine mix, which is typically cheaper.

- You can spot the difference just by looking at the different croissants in the pastry case. A croissant au beurre is usually straight and golden brown with a shiny finish. Expect flakes and crumbs as you enjoy this croissant. I always say the more crumbs, the better. A croissant ordinaire is typically curved in the shape of a crescent; the color is paler, and the texture is drier with fewer flakes.

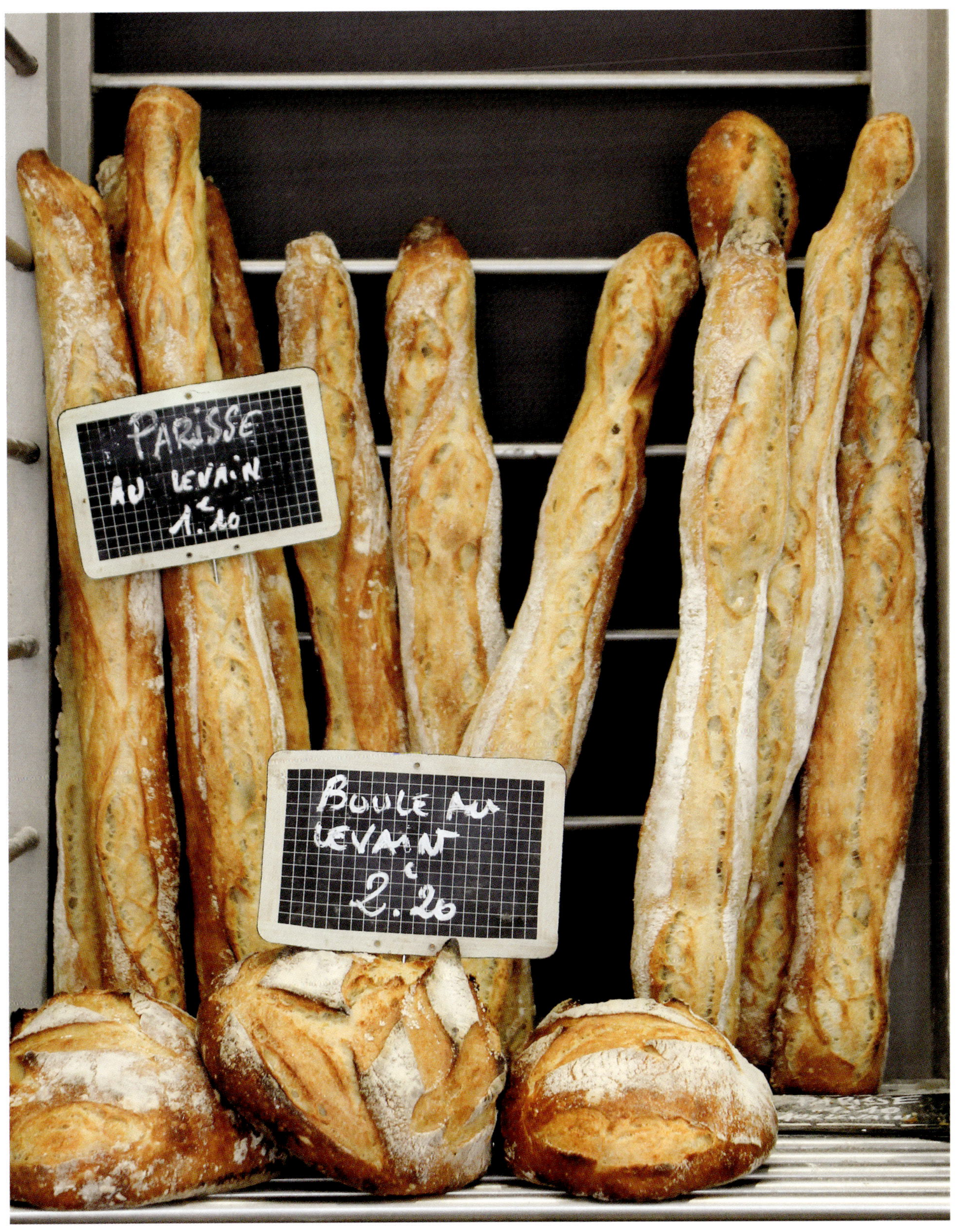
PARISSE
AU LEVAIN
1.10
BOULE AU
LEVAIN
2.20

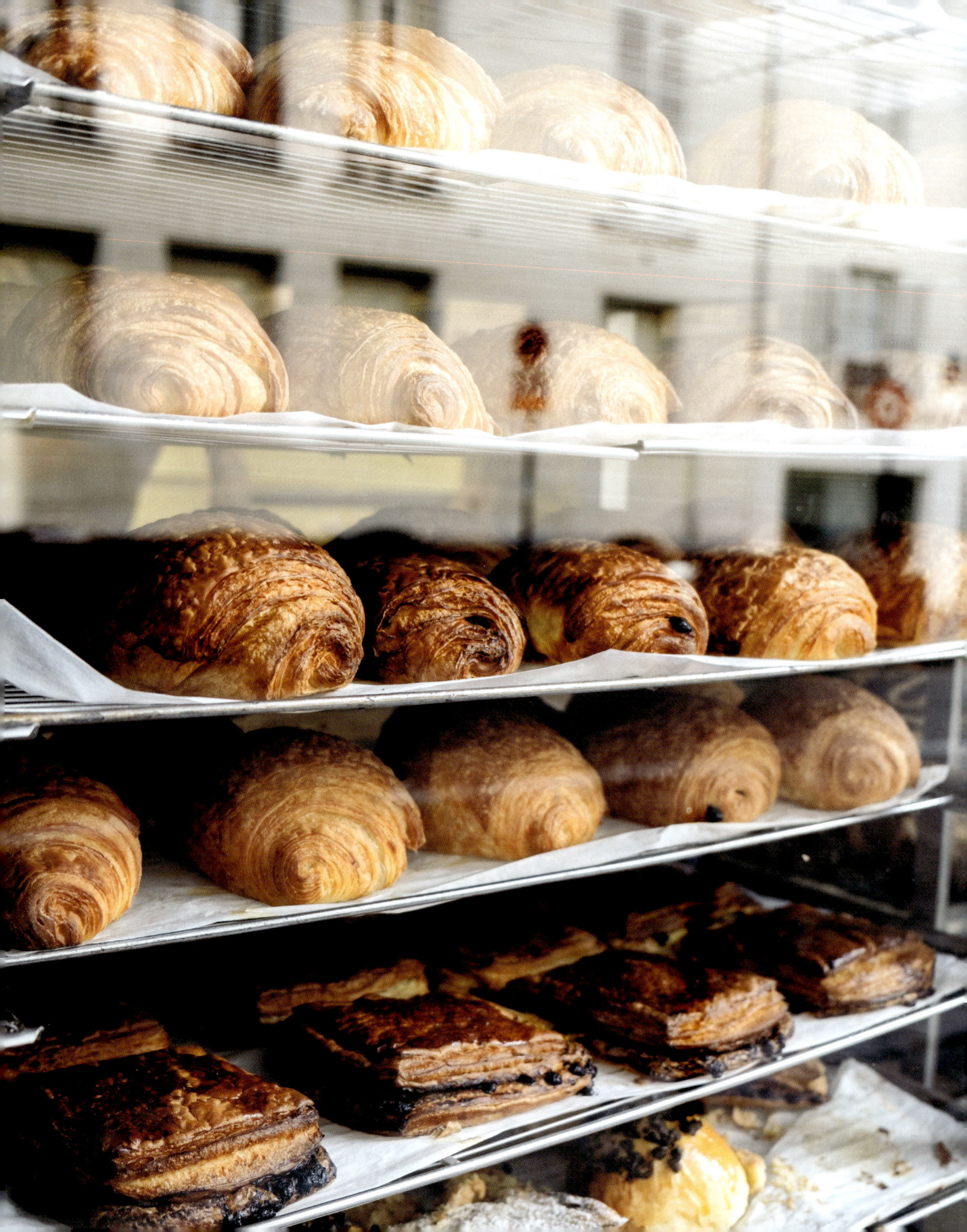

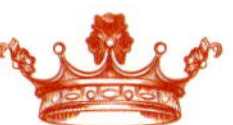

FAVORITE SPOTS FOR A CROISSANT

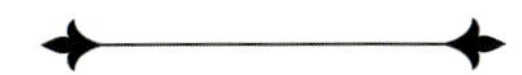

- **Boulangerie Utopie** (11th arrondissement) Opened in 2013, this sourdough-centric bakery has a wonderful assortment. You might also try the baguette.
- **Petite Île Boulangerie** (3rd arrondissement) With its cozy and inviting wooden façade, you'll find an Asian touch here and unique renditions of French classics.
- **Quignon** (9th arrondissement) A spot that offers both classic and artistic pastries.
- **Mamiche** (several locations in the 9th and 10th arrondissements) If a croissant isn't enough, and you want to go big, do it with their orange blossom brioche or chocolate marble babka.
- **Boulangerie-Pâtisserie Terroirs d'Avenir** (2nd arrondissement) Life-changing. Don't say I didn't warn you.
- **Poilâne** (6th arrondissement) In the heart of Saint-Germaine-des-Prés, this bakery founded in 1932 has its third generation of the Poilâne family at the helm.
- **Boulangerie du Musée** (7th arrondissement) These items are not to miss—the almond croissant and the chouquettes.
- **Le Grenier à Pain** (18th arrondissement) Located on Rue des Abbesses in Montmartre, it's also great place to also pick up a sandwich or a loaf of bread for a picnic.

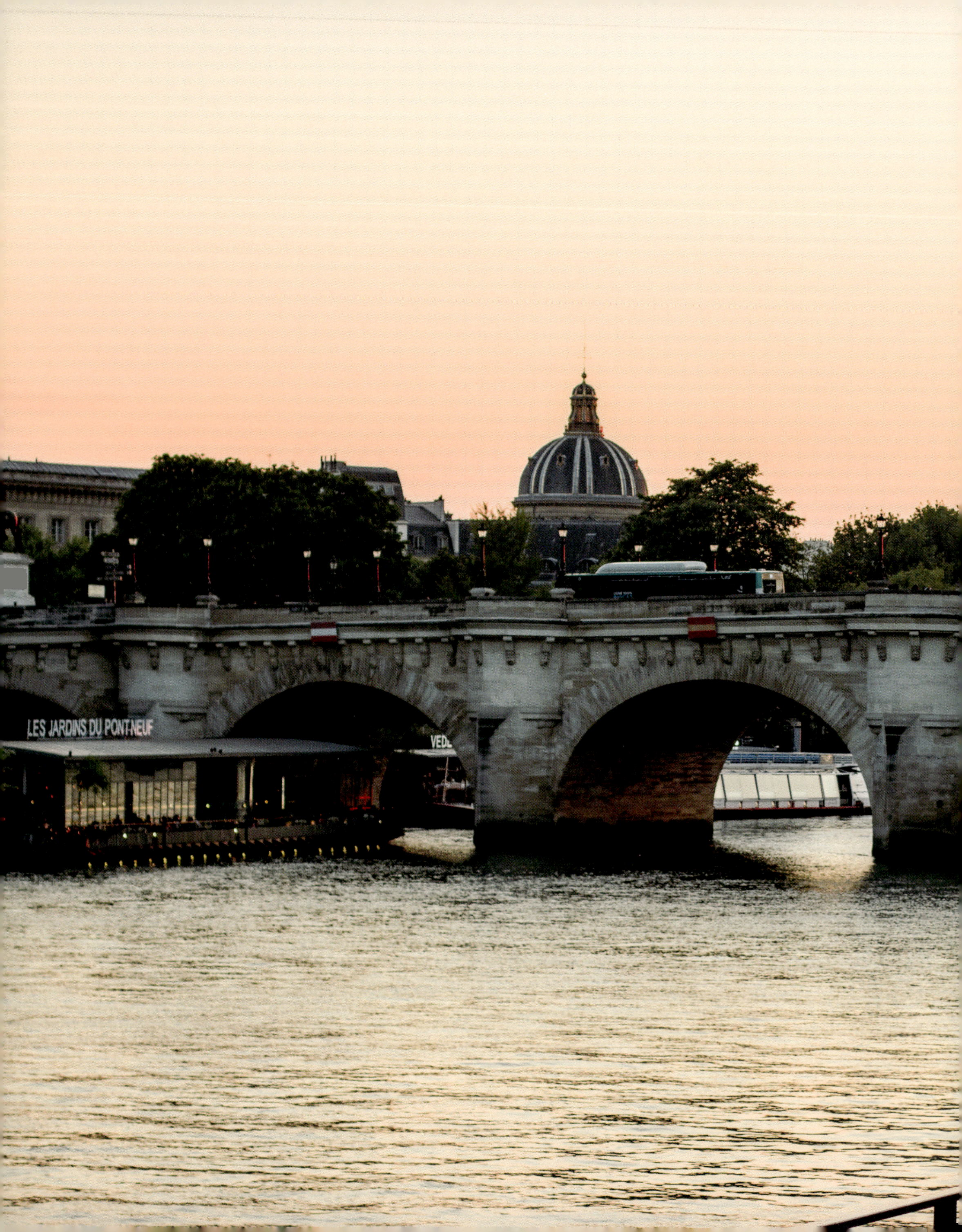
LES JARDINS DU PONT-NEUF

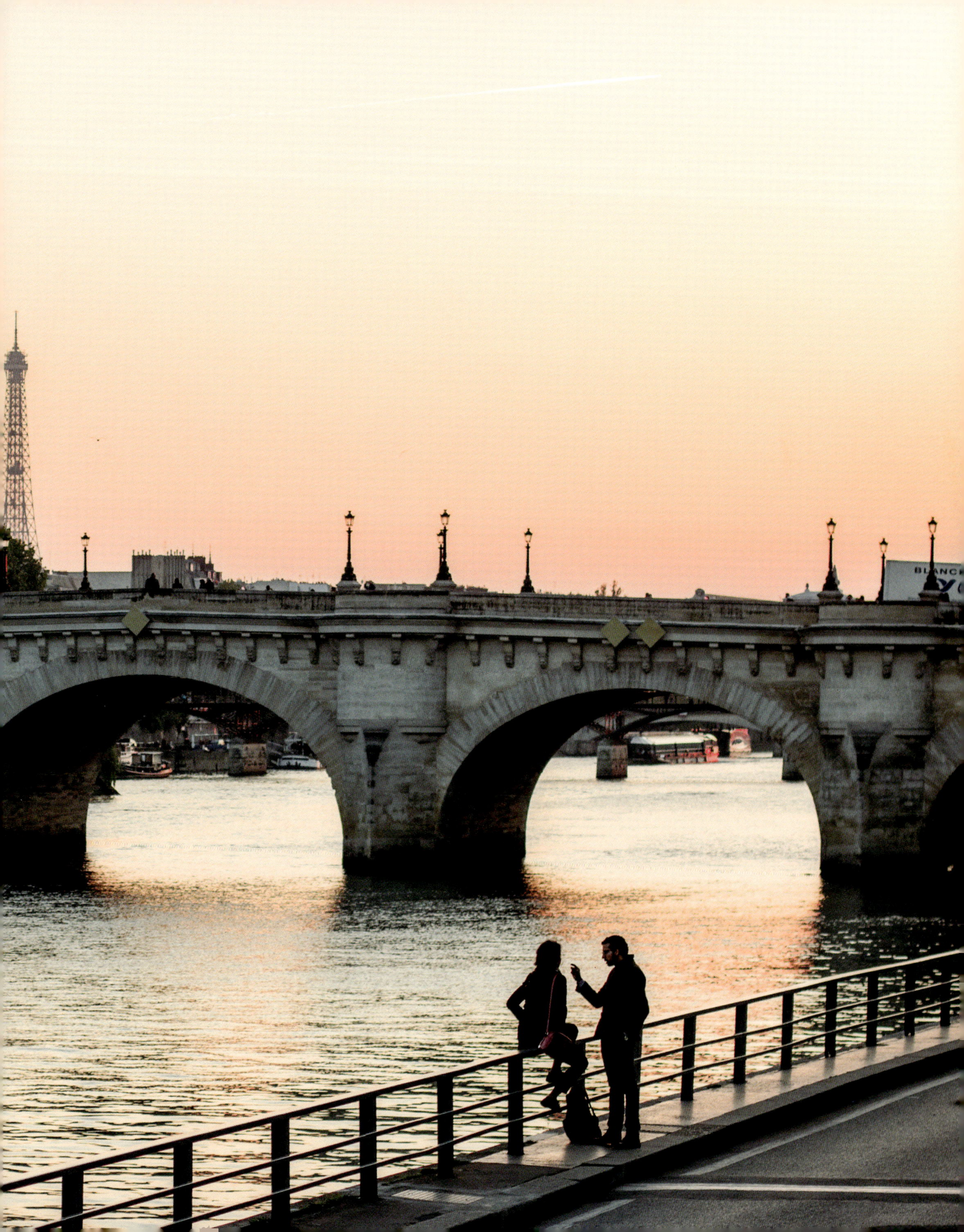

Each season reveals a new side of Paris, like seeing the city through a fresh lens.

With every shift in season, Paris transforms. The same terrace that was quieted by winter's chill in December is now bathed in the warmth of early summer light. Paris buzzes with activity on the streets. Cafés are alive with conversation and the sounds of laughter and clinking glasses. Parisians shed their layers for sundresses, sunglasses, and leather sandals.

Lush greenery fills every corner, from manicured parks to tree-lined boulevards. Jasmine vines begin to climb balconies and wrap around café terraces, their sweet scent blended with the warmth of the summer air. Afternoons call for a scoop of ice cream while evenings feature a crisp glass of rosé paired with creamy goat cheese. Summer days stretch on endlessly, with sunrises that wake the city early and golden sunsets that cast a warm glow over the Parisian rooftops.

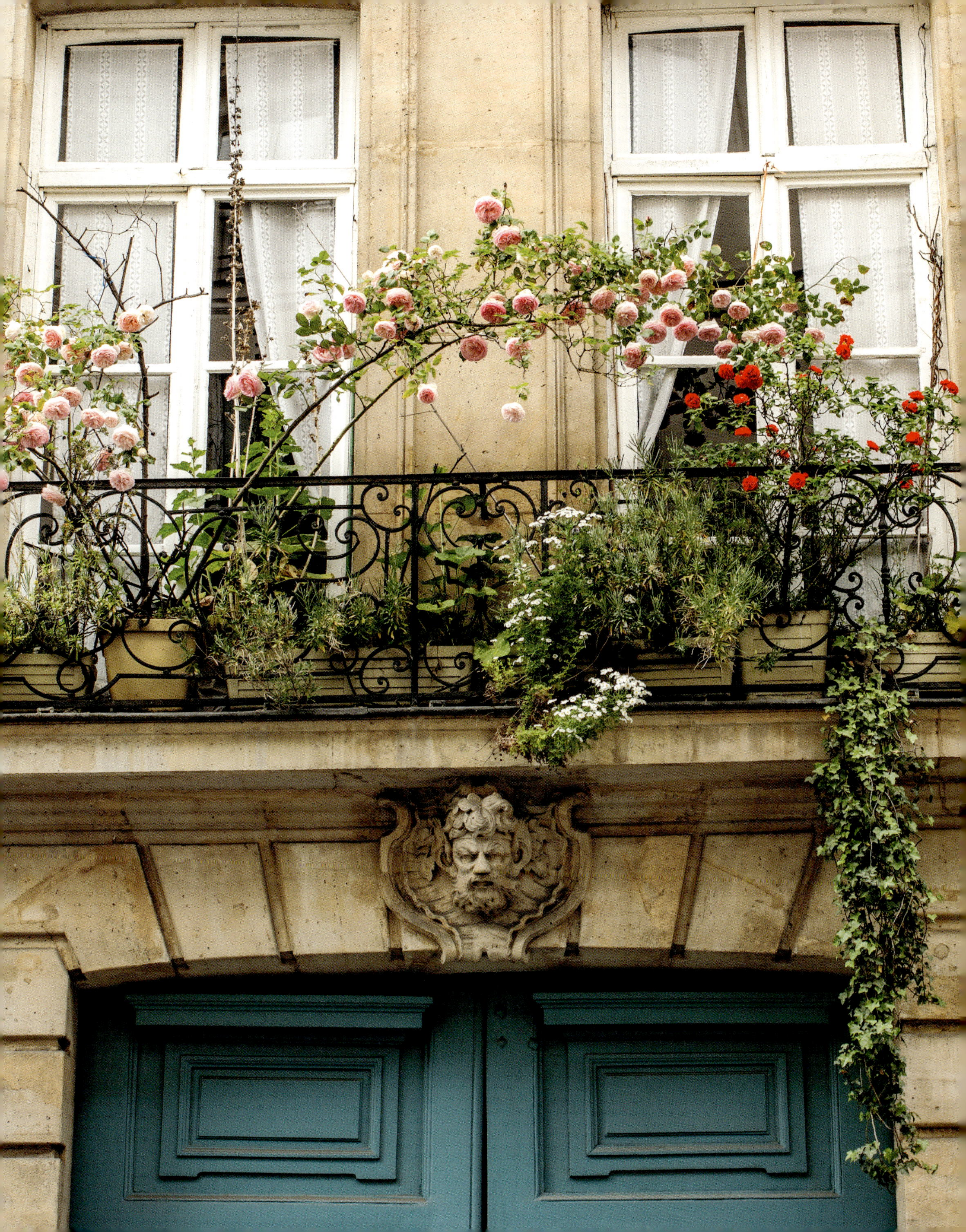

la rentrée

La Rentrée, a seasonal transition period, begins in early September as Parisians return home after vacation and start back to their routines. Kids begin school again, and friends reunite at terraces and parks around the city. The energy in Paris is high with the start of a new beginning.

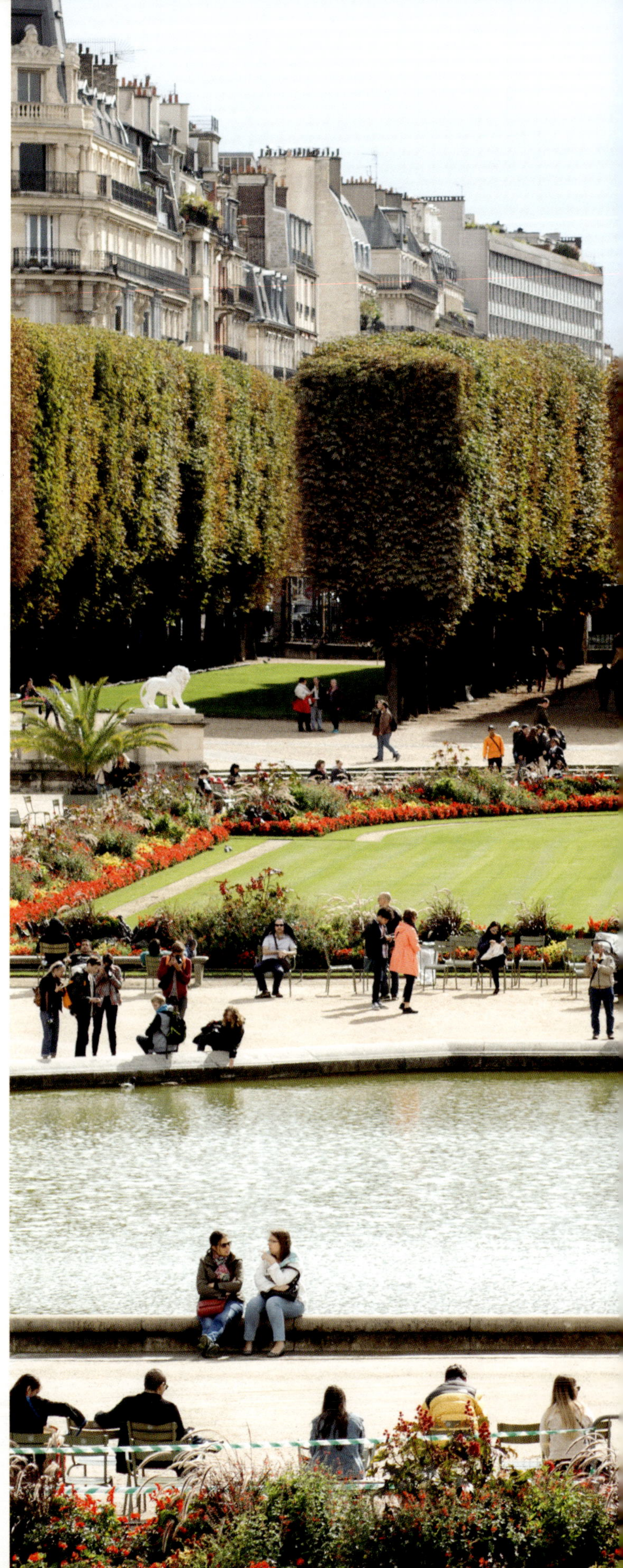

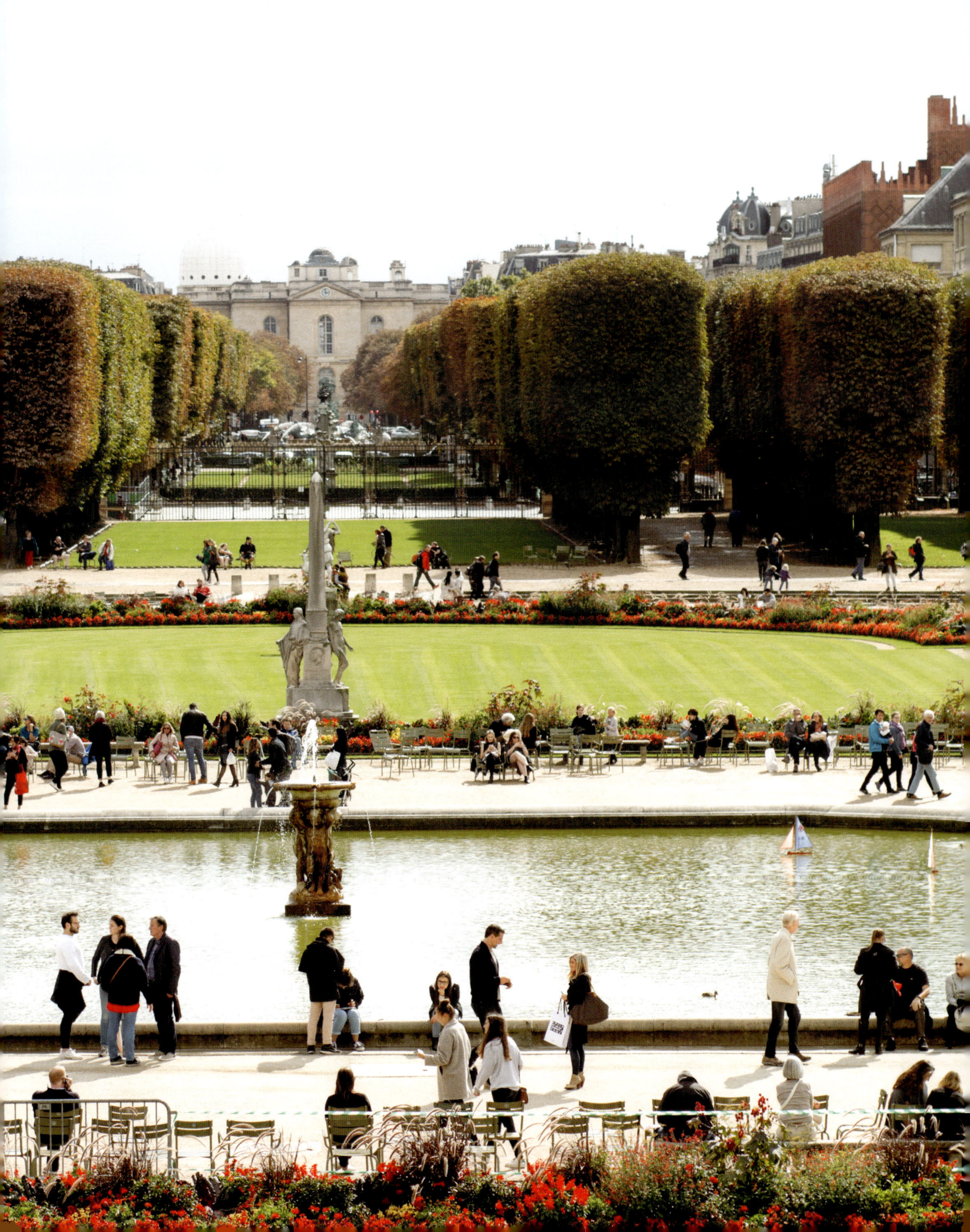

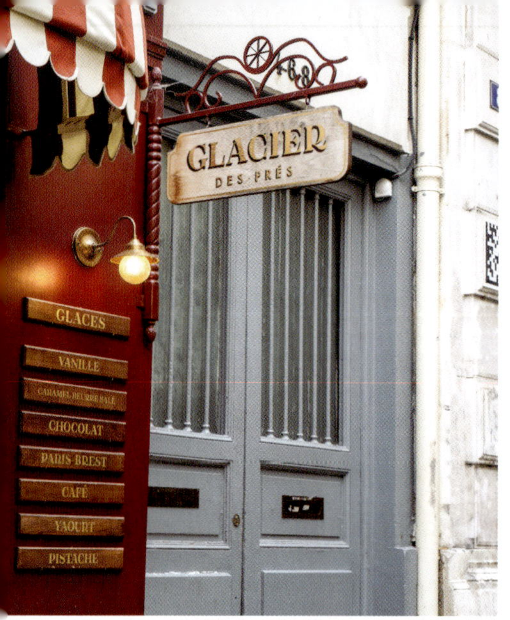

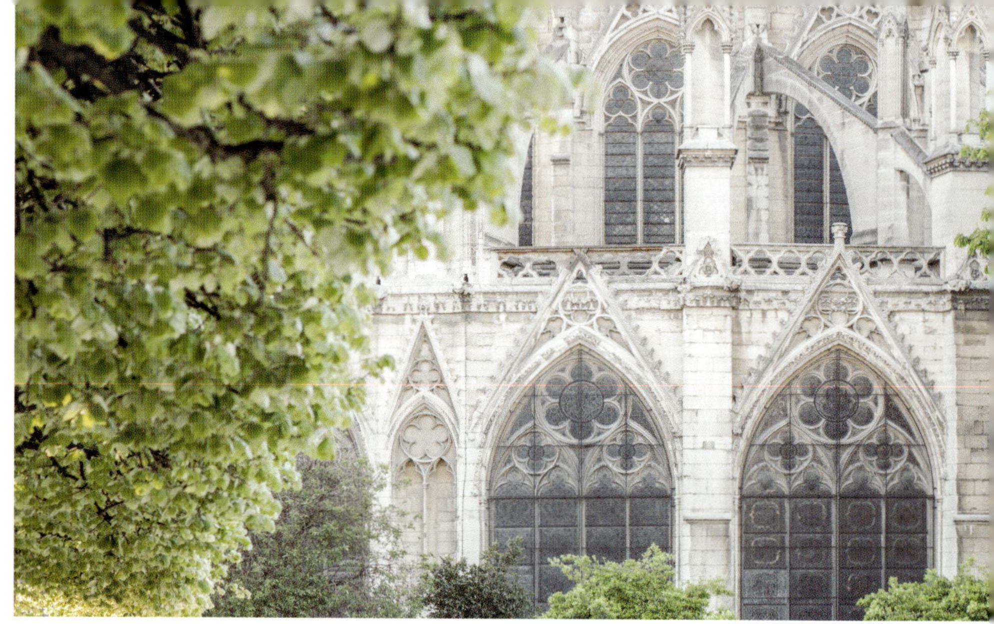

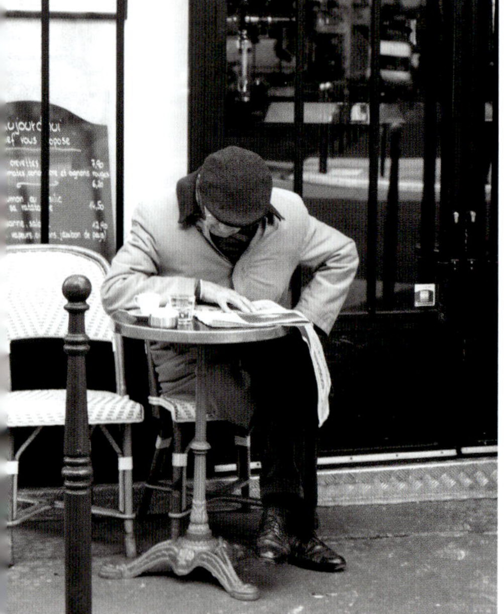

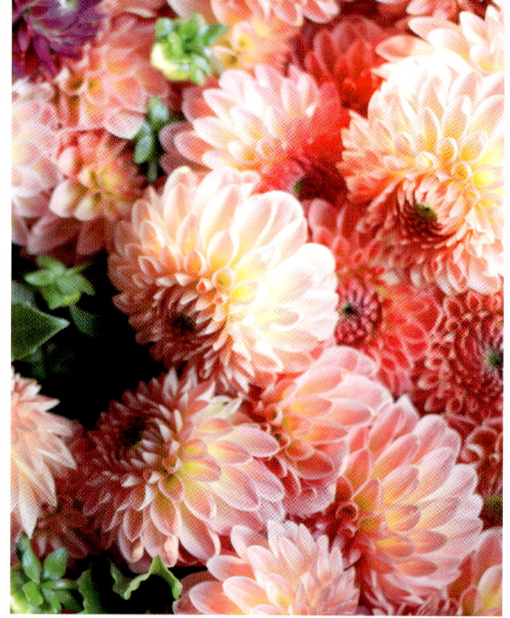

September weather can be a mix of rain and warm temps and sunny days, with summer weather stretching into the new season. But the mornings and evenings cool down from the summer sun, and a slight chill enters the air. The beginning of September is a great time to visit Paris and enjoy the city's buzz at this unique time of year.

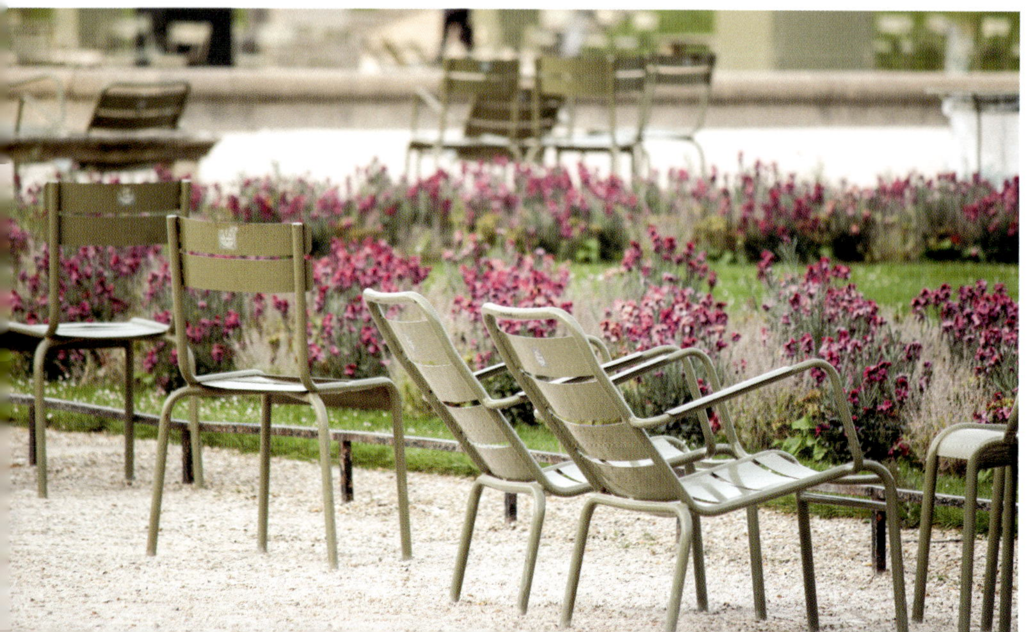

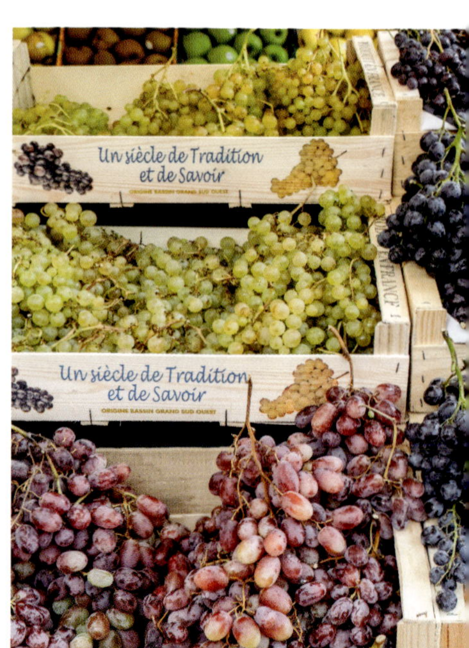

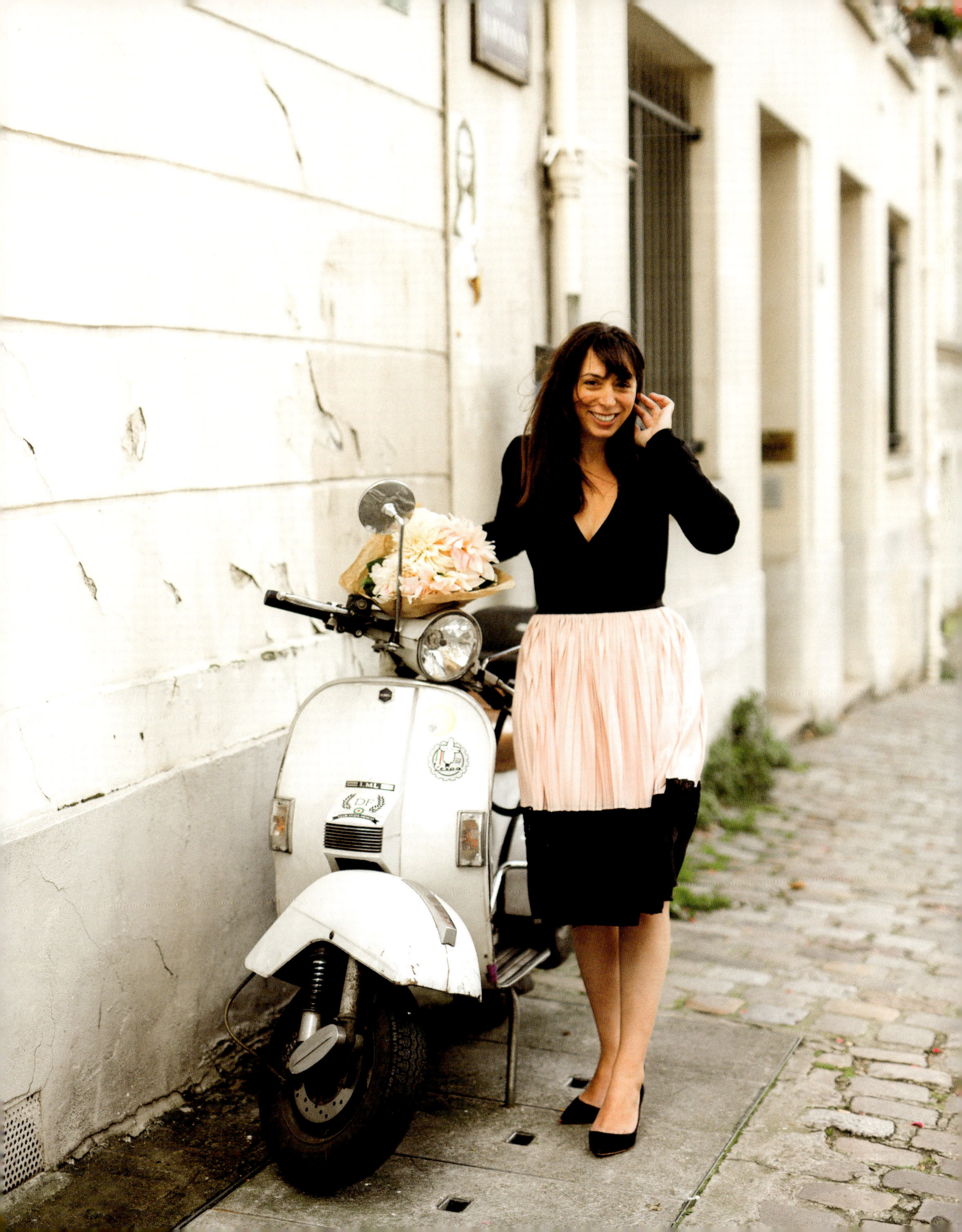

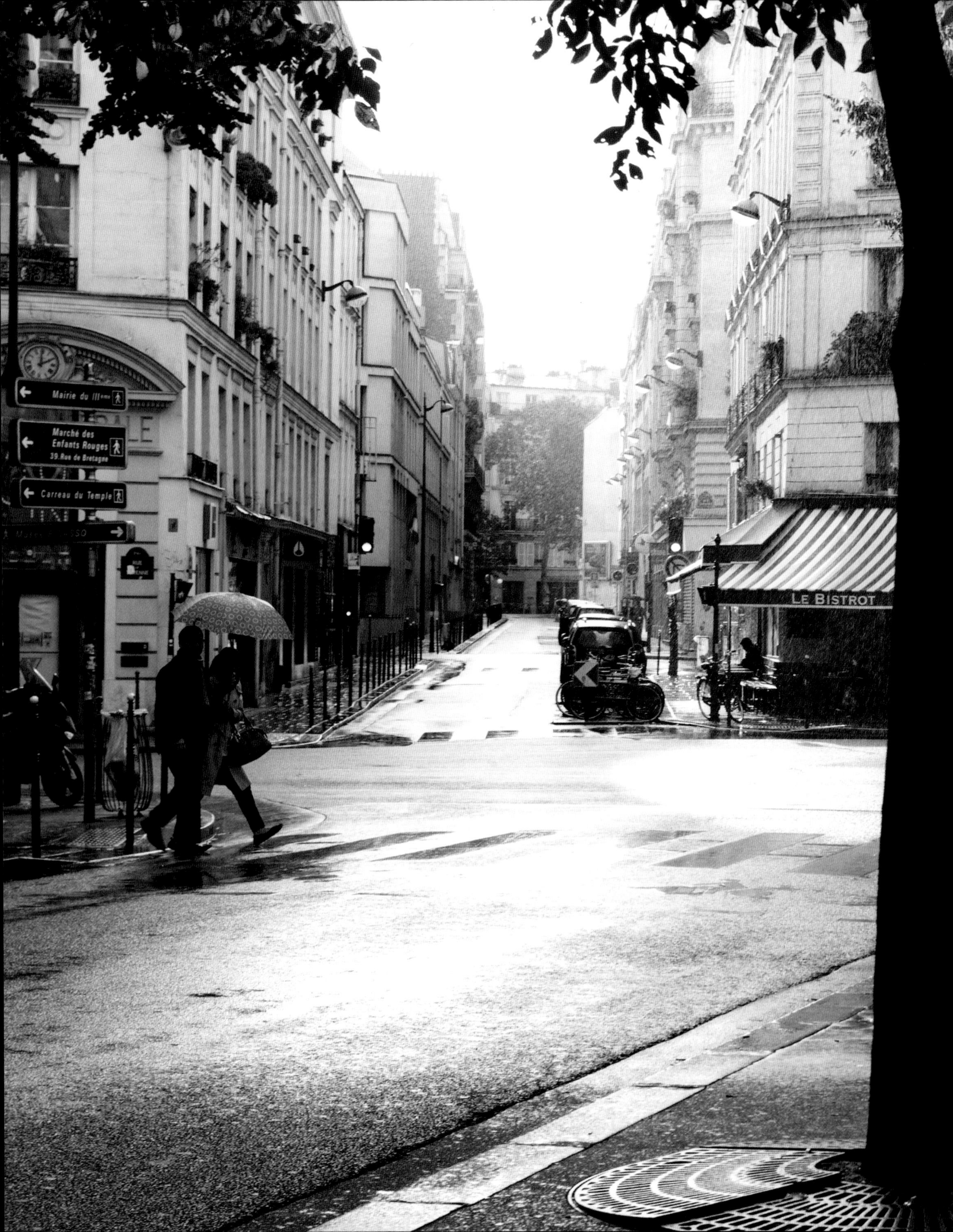
Mairie du IIIème
Marché des
Enfants Rouges
39.Rue de Bretagne
Carreau du Temple
LE BISTROT

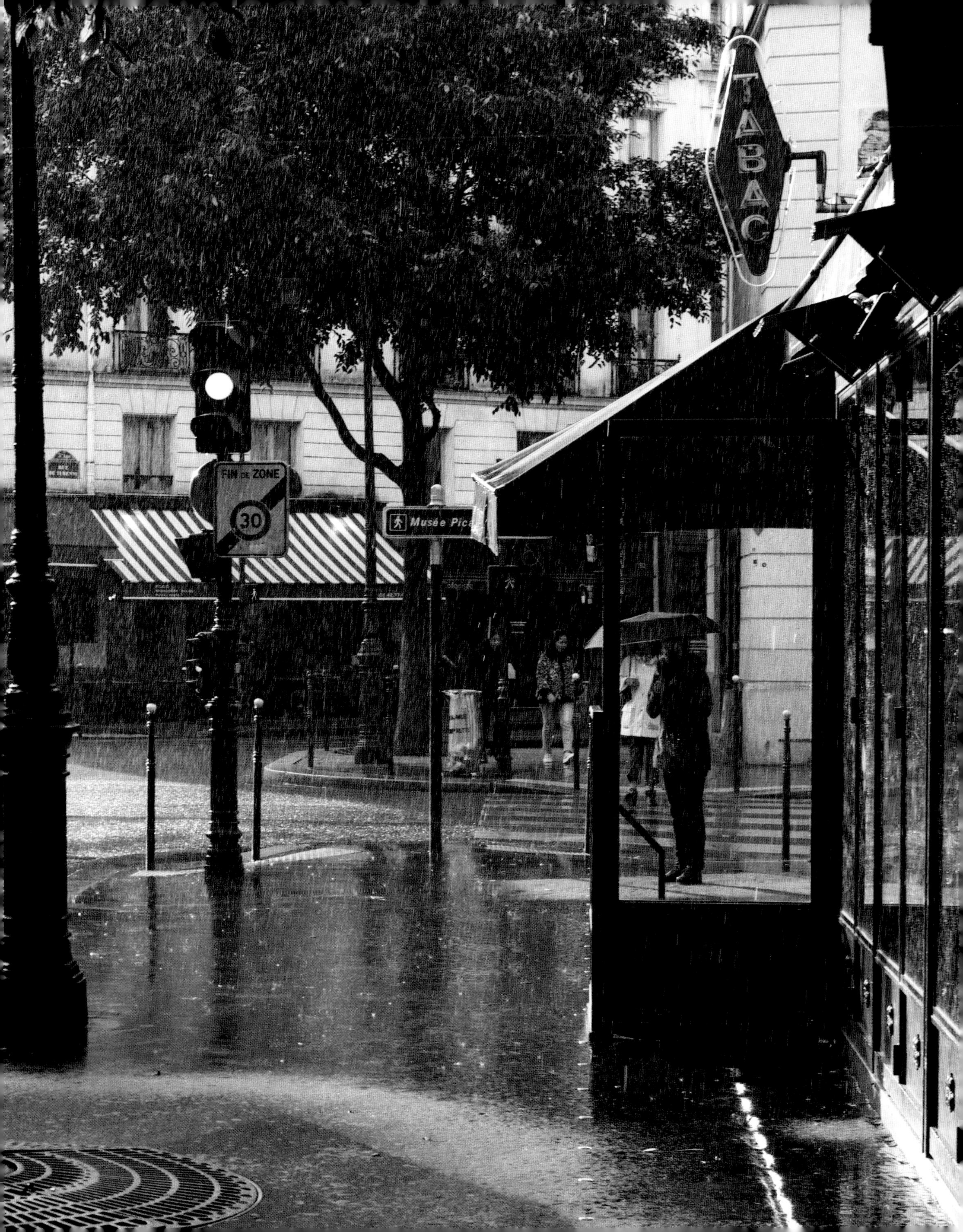
TABAC
FIN DE ZONE
30
Musée Pica

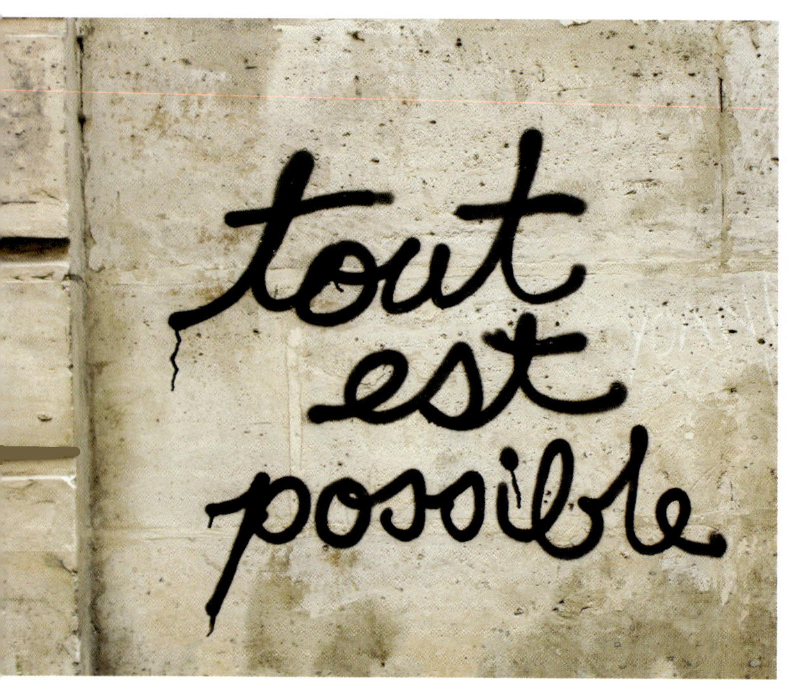

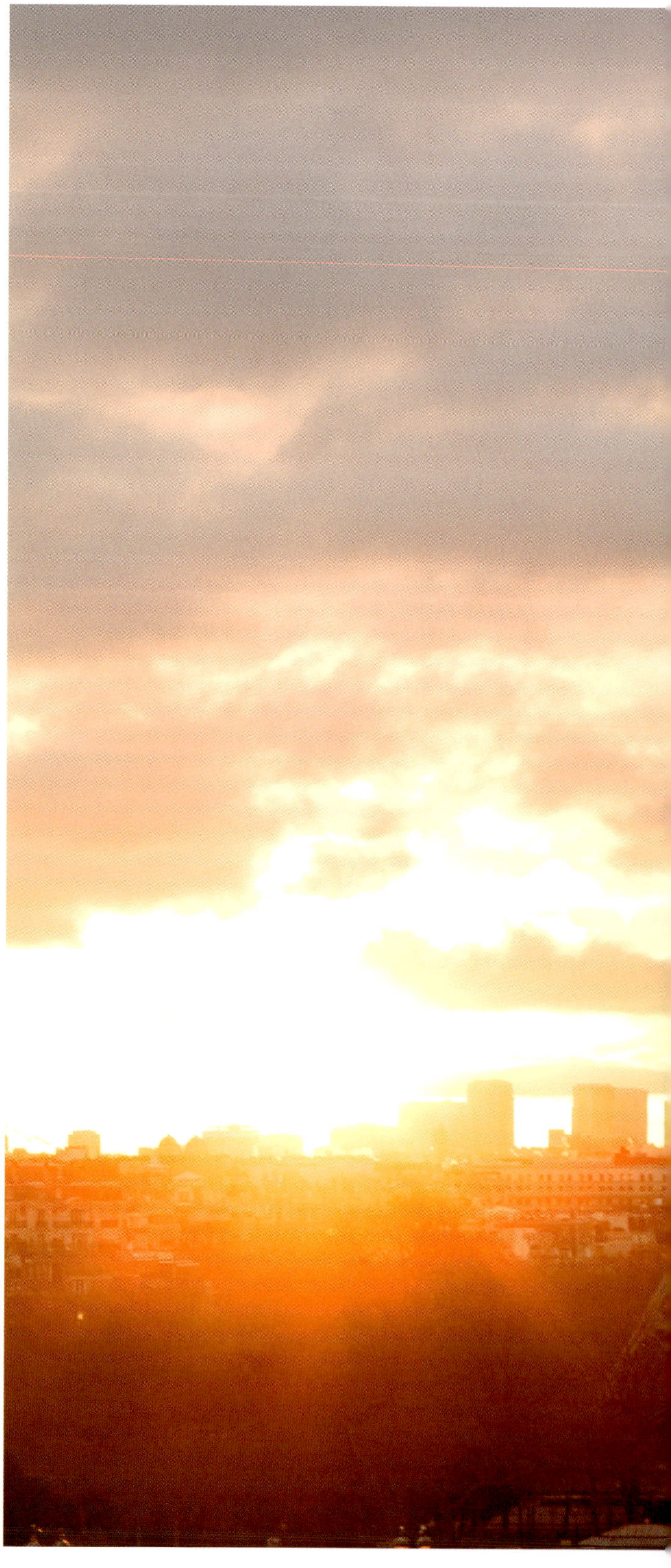

On a Sunday in autumn 2013, I walked the banks of the Seine River and strolled onto Île de la Cité near Notre-Dame. A majority of my photography is found by just such walking and by chance. I wandered down a tiny side street and saw graffiti on the side of one of the buildings: "tout est possible." In French, this means "all is possible." It brought me to tears, thinking about how hard I had worked to make my dream of living in Paris a reality. I looked up to see an older man standing on his balcony. We locked eyes, and he nodded when he saw my emotional connection to these words. I took a few shots of the wall with my camera and left to meet a friend. The next day, I returned, looking for the same small street to see if the words were still there. They were gone. This photograph continues to provide motivation not only for me but also for many community members over the years.

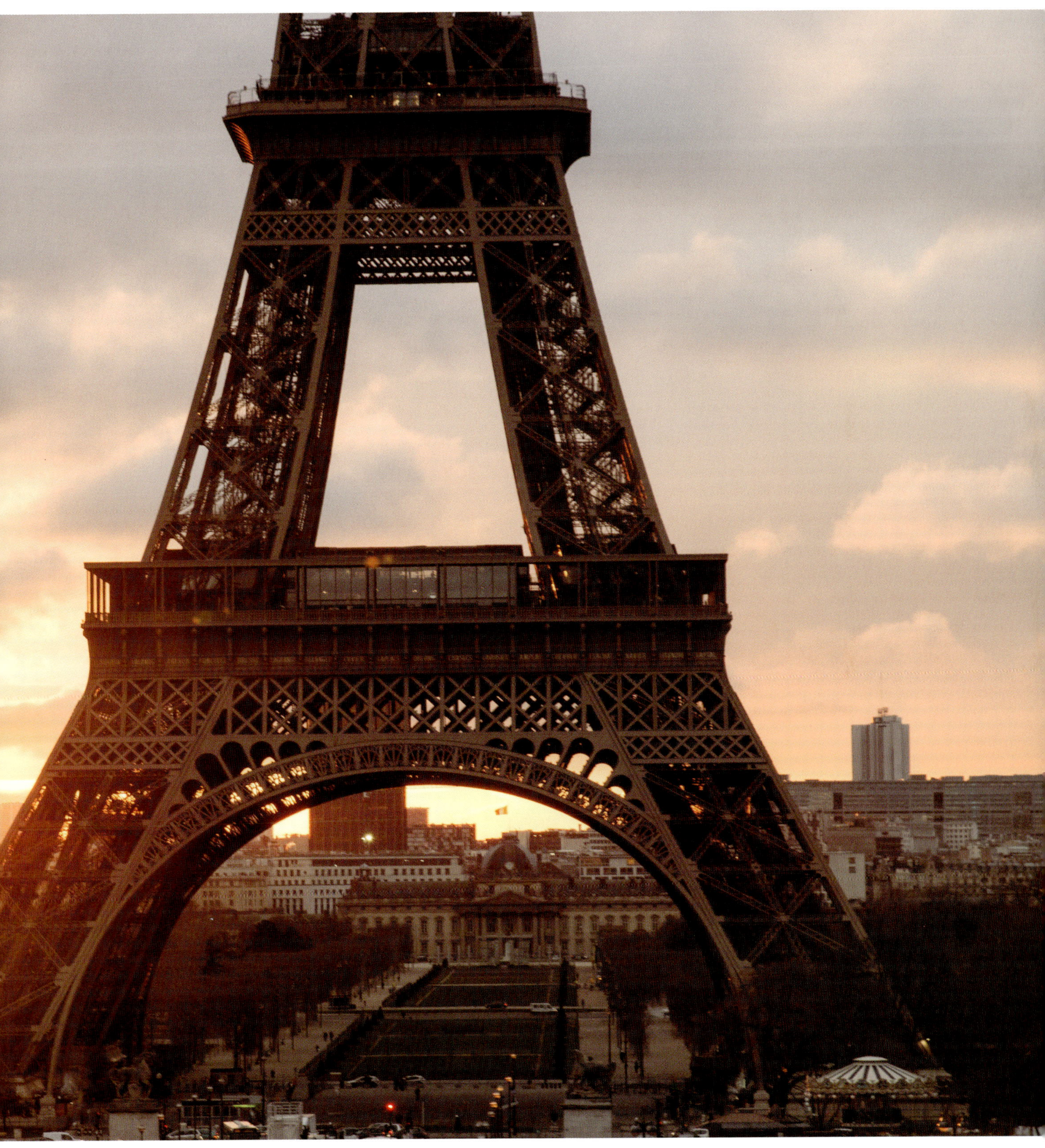

l'automne

{AUTUMN}

One of the things I love most about autumn in Paris is the ivy, which changes from green to shades of orange and vibrant red. Ivy covers the city's buildings, the walls along the Seine, and courtyards with pops of color. Parisian parks transition to fall early, as trees lose their leaves and cover the ground. Autumn in Paris may include crisp, cool temperatures with warm light, followed by rainy days with piles of leaves at your feet.

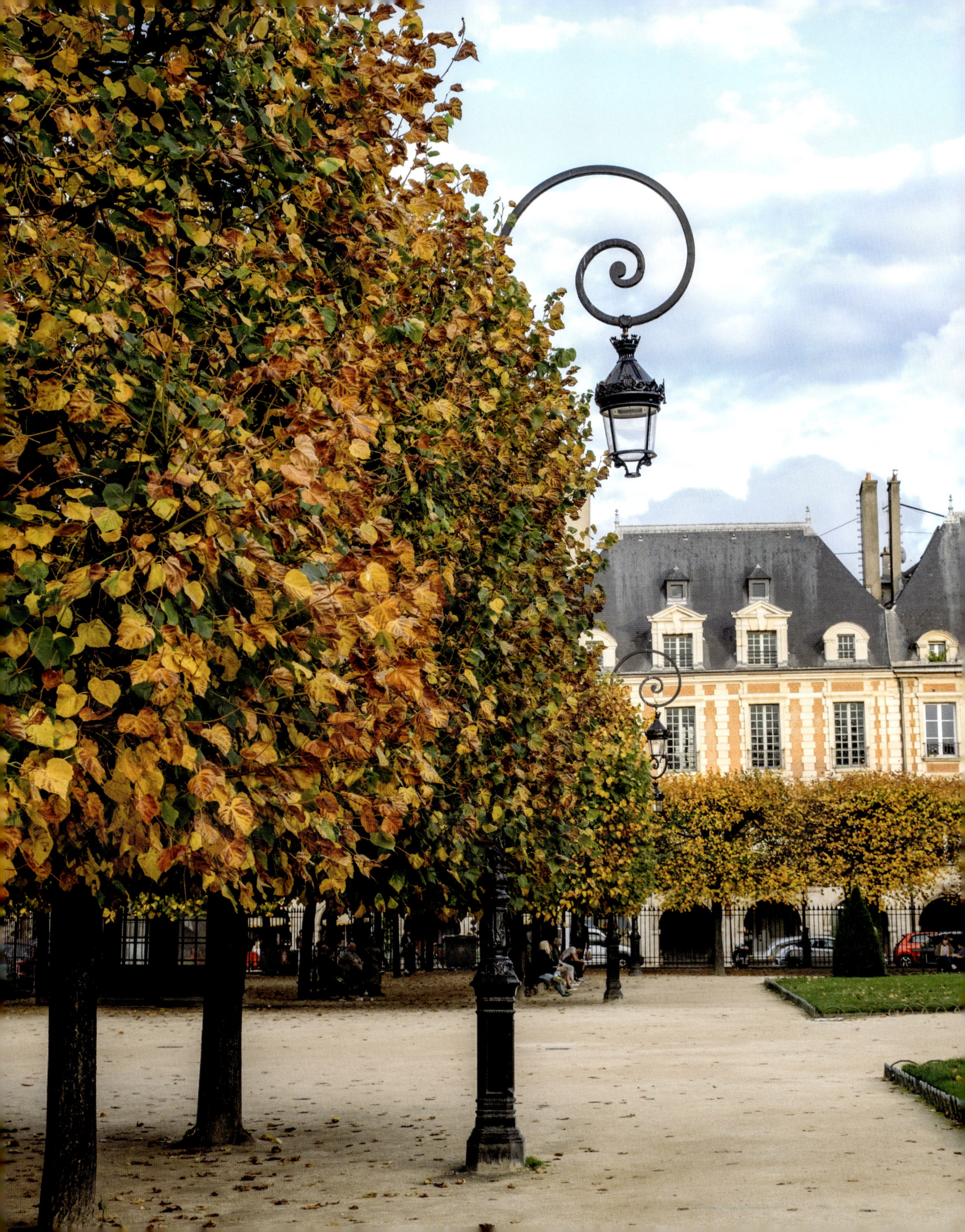

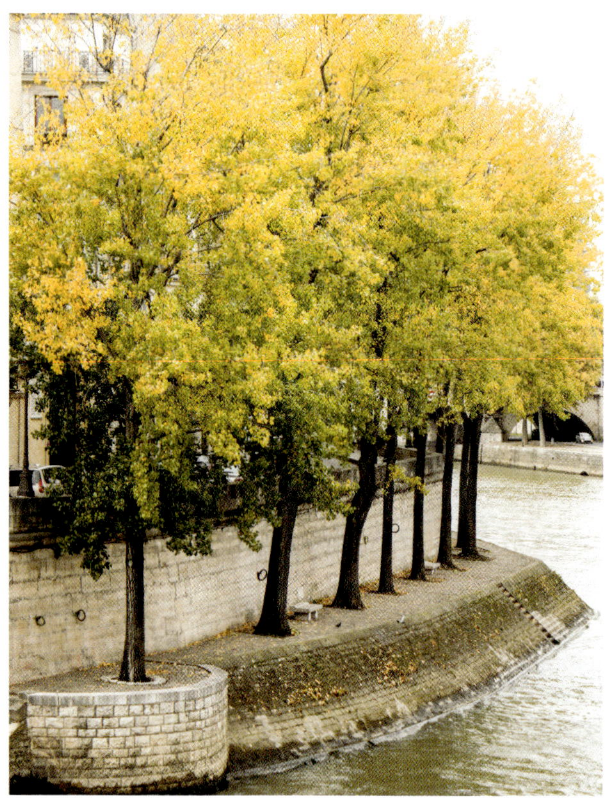

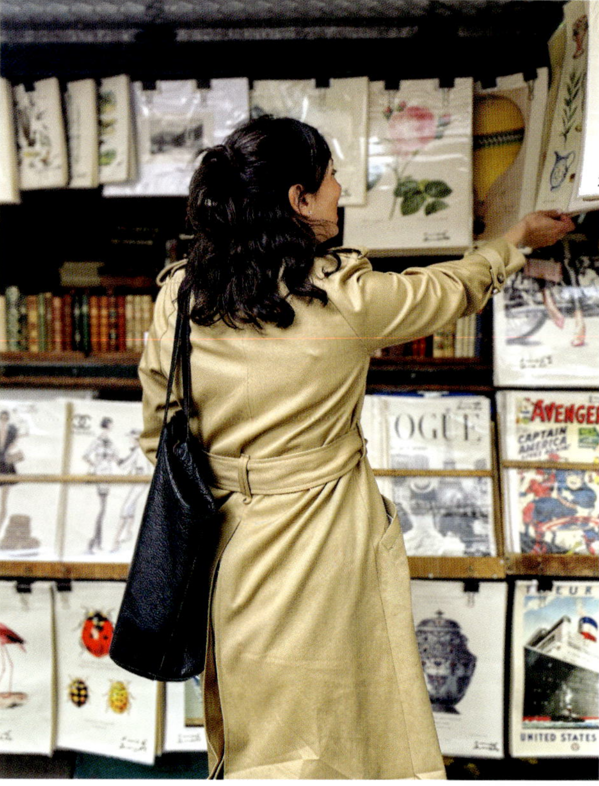

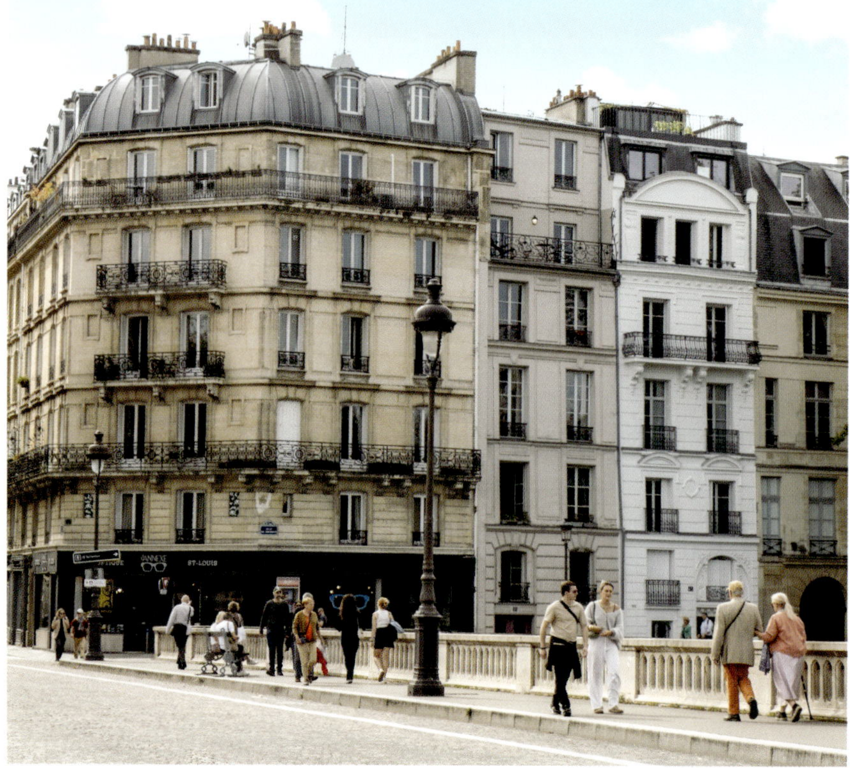

Get out and enjoy the weather and colors of fall. Book lunch at Anne, the restaurant at Le Pavillon de la Reine hotel, on the terrace surrounded by climbing red ivy. The hotel's floral balconies spill with pops of red. Tucked away on Rue des Francs-Bourgeois, a tiny courtyard awaits. It is filled with a rainbow of ivy, transitioning through the many colors of autumn. As the leaves change, walk along the Seine River to take in the vivid trees that line its banks.

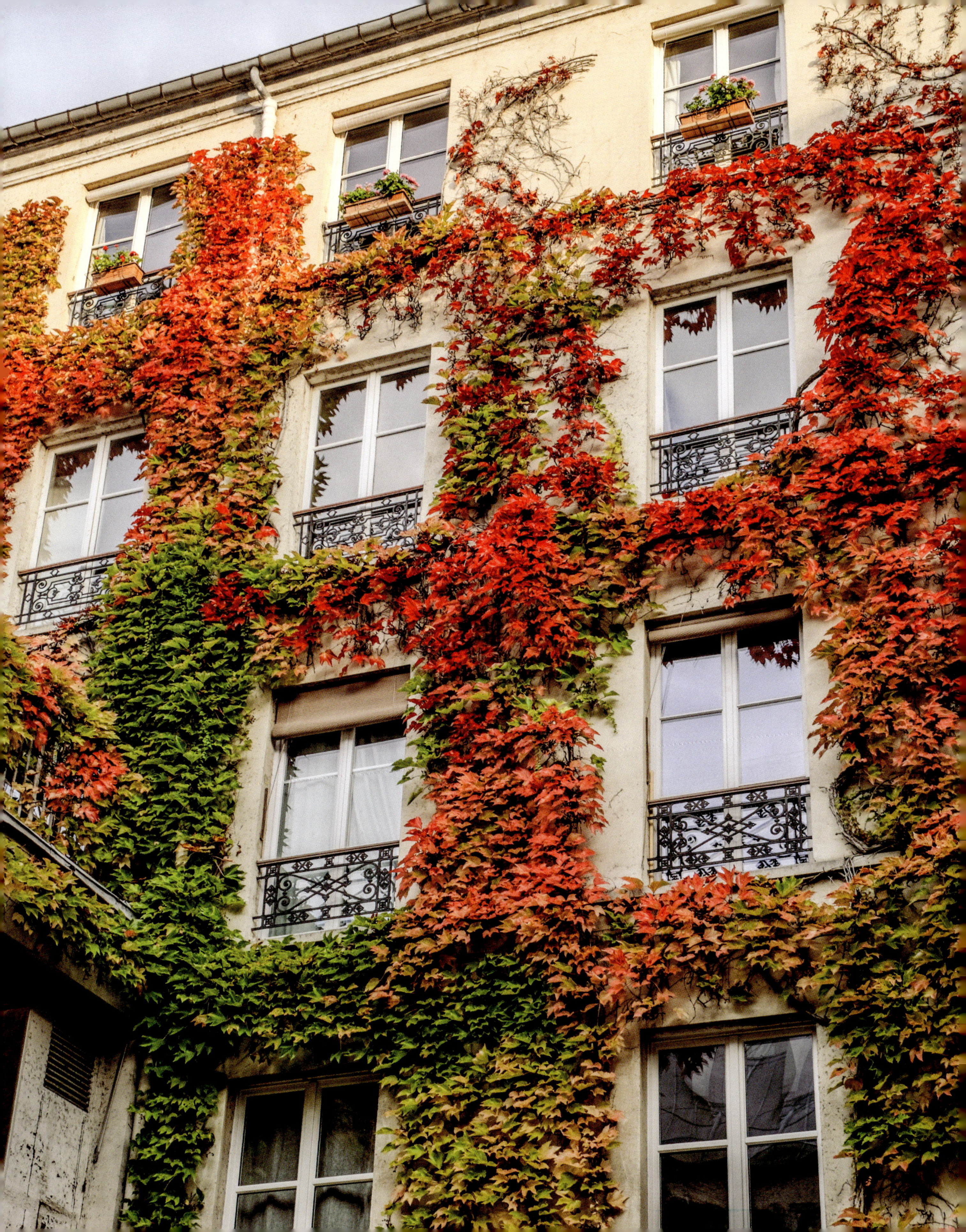

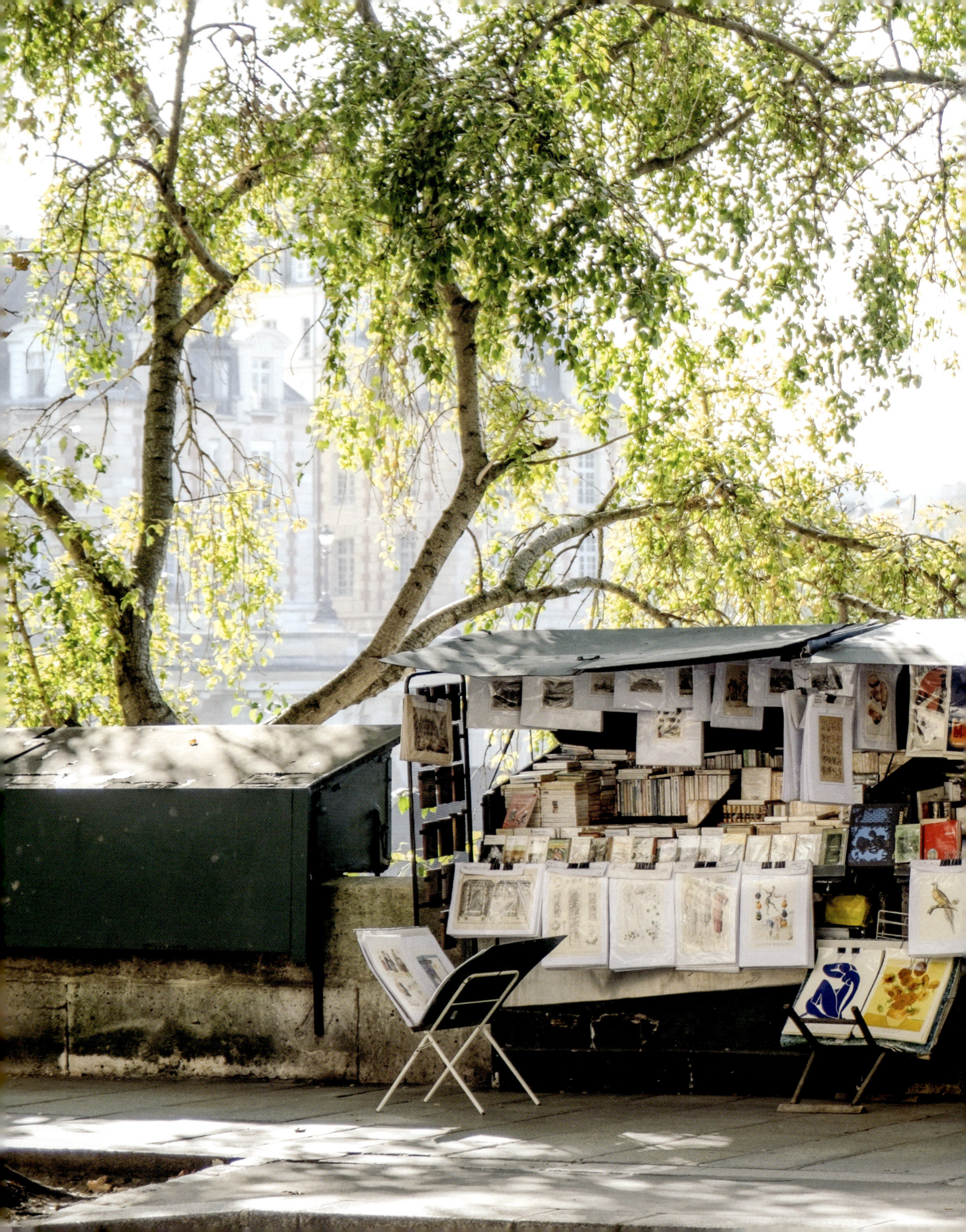

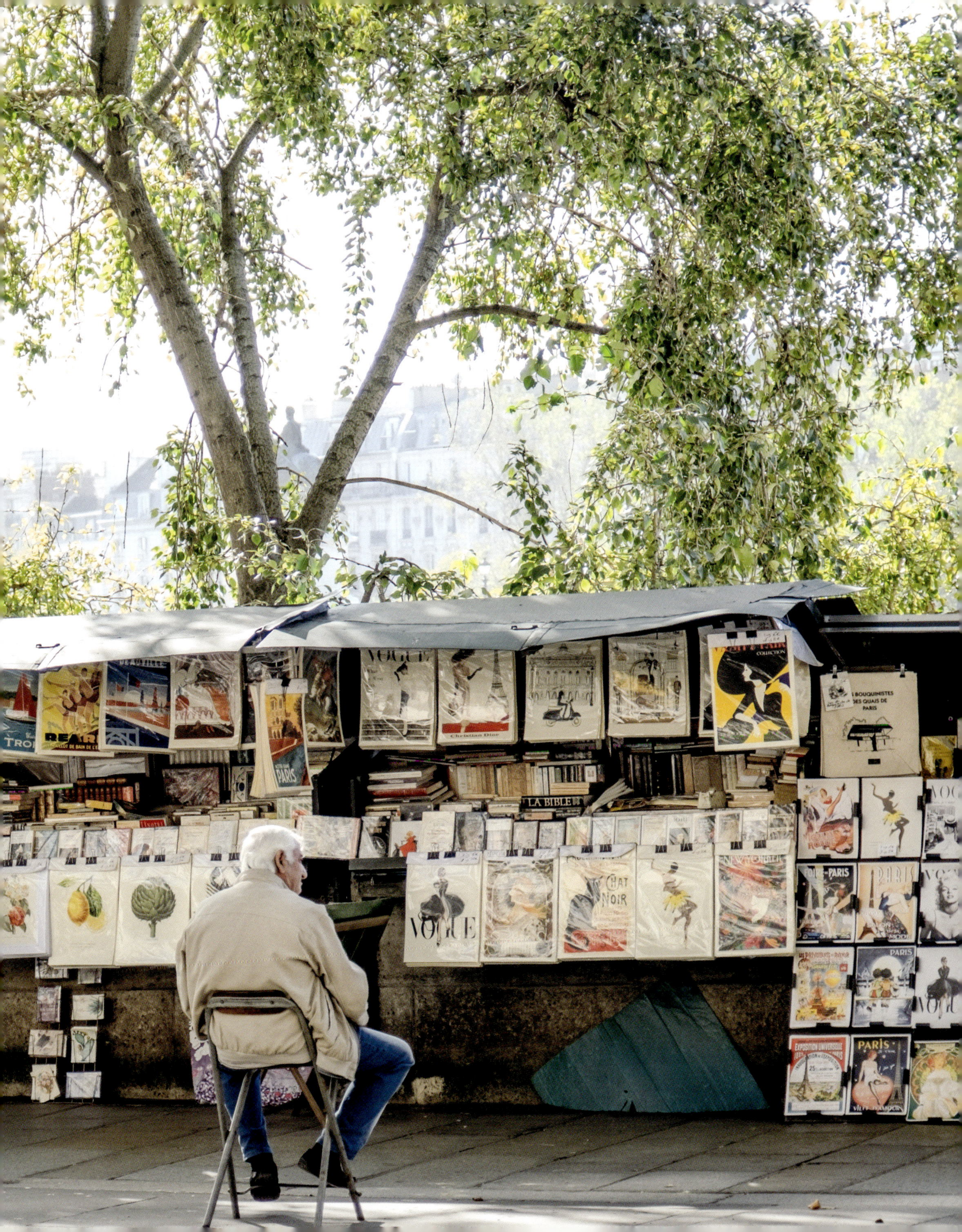
VOGUE
Christian Dior
LA BIBLE
VOGUE
CHAT NOIR
PARIS
PARIS

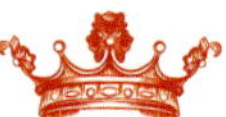

AUTUMN STYLES

Expect to wear transitional clothing as the season and weather change from warm to cold, clear days. Layers are key with scarves, jackets, and knits.

- **Coats:** For early in the season, choose a trench coat or a leather jacket; for later, a wool-tailored coat is ideal.

- **Shoes:** You'll find ankle boots, sneakers, ballet flats, and socks with loafers.

- **Skirts/Shorts:** Parisians will extend the skirt and shorts season, styling these pieces with black tights and boots. A monochromatic black look is popular.

- **Crossbody Bag:** You will see crossbody leather bags for day and night and canvas bags for books, work, and transporting other essentials.

- **Hats:** Baseball hats in seasonal autumn dark colors have become more regular and part of the culture, especially on weekends.

- **Accessories:** Sunglasses and an umbrella help you to be prepared for whatever the weather might bring.

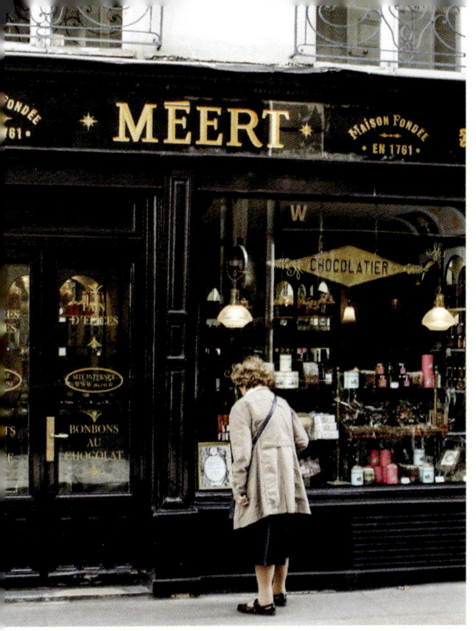
MEERT
Maison Fondée
EN 1761
CHOCOLATIER
BONBONS
AU
CHOCOLAT

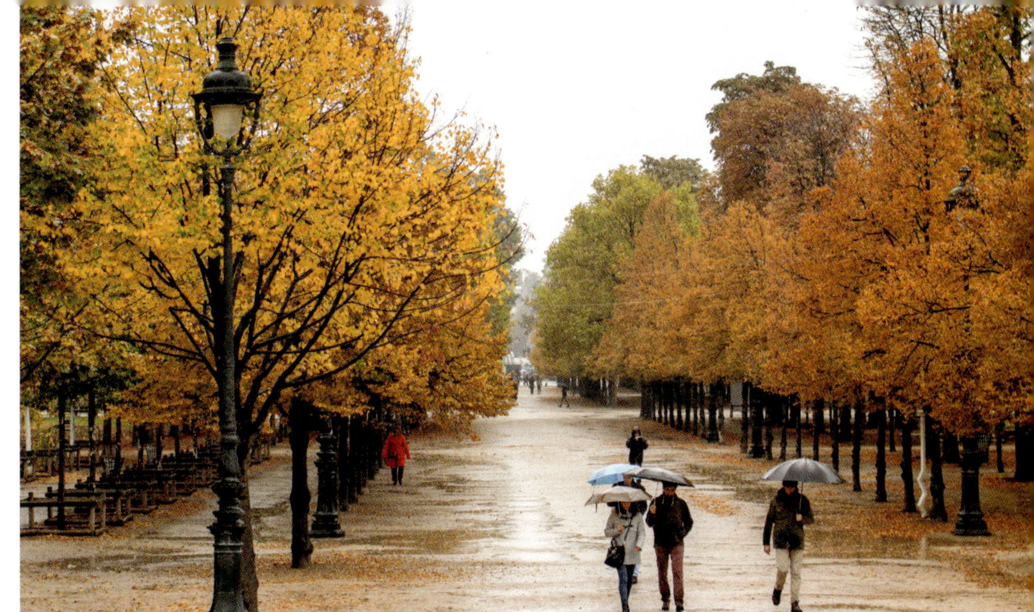

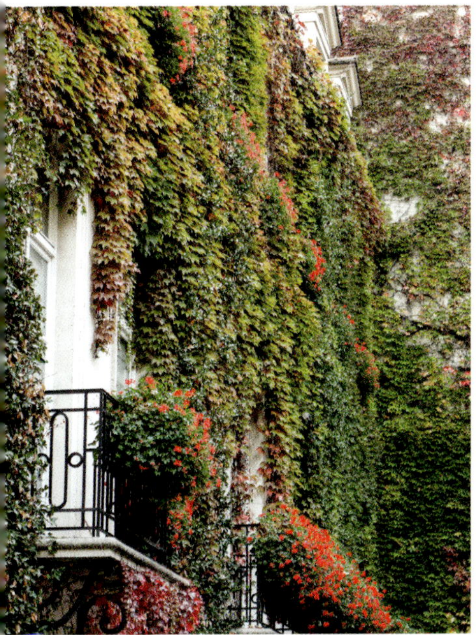

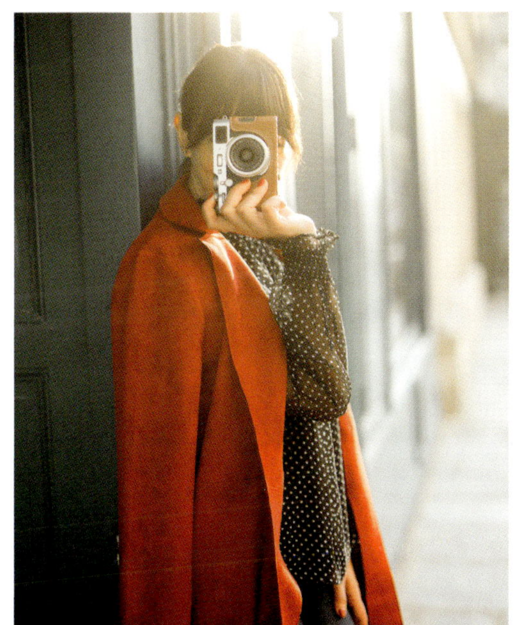

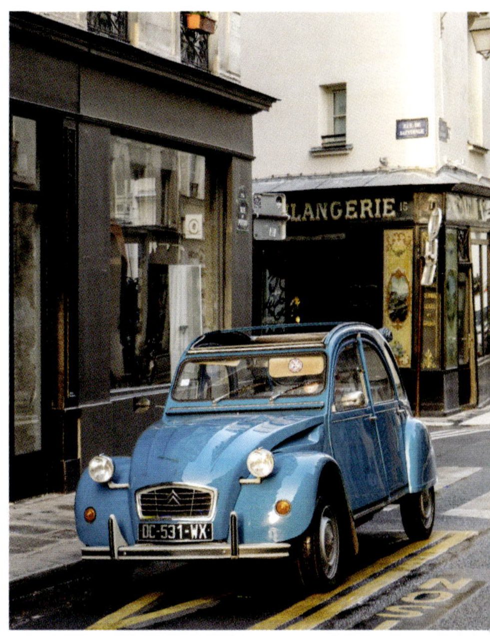
LANGERIE
DC-531-WX

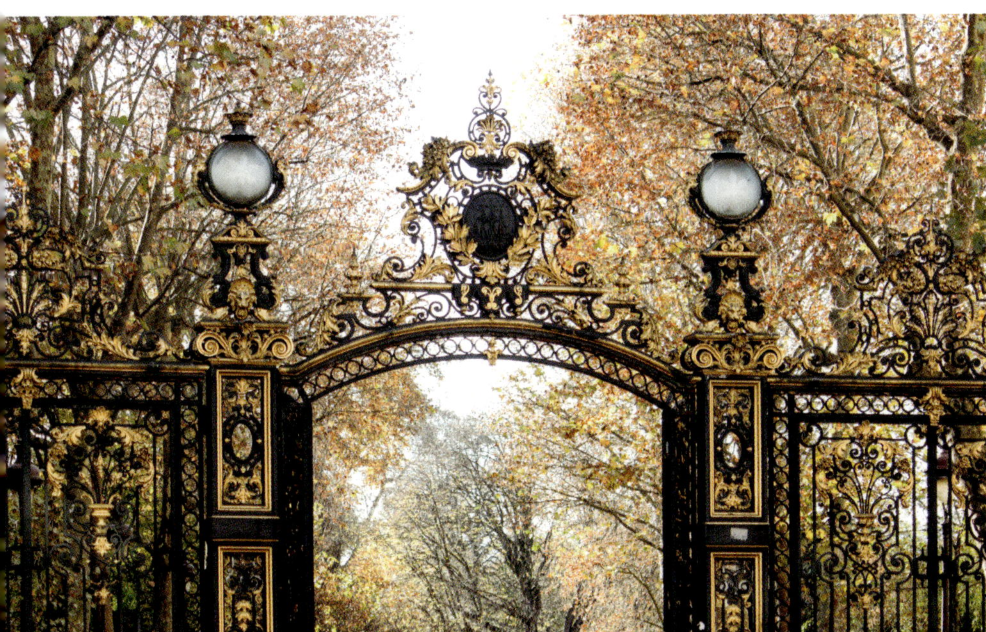

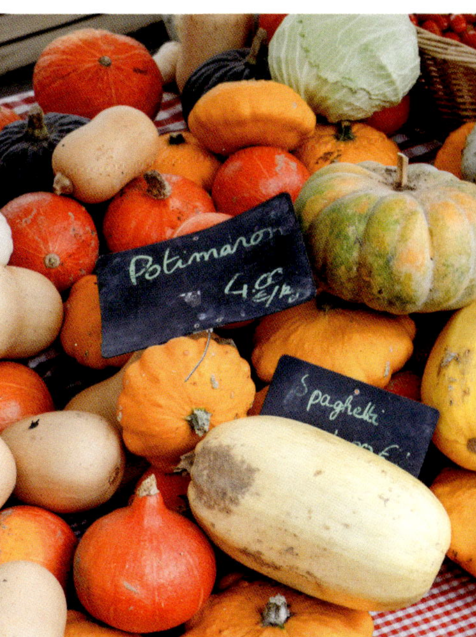
Potimarron

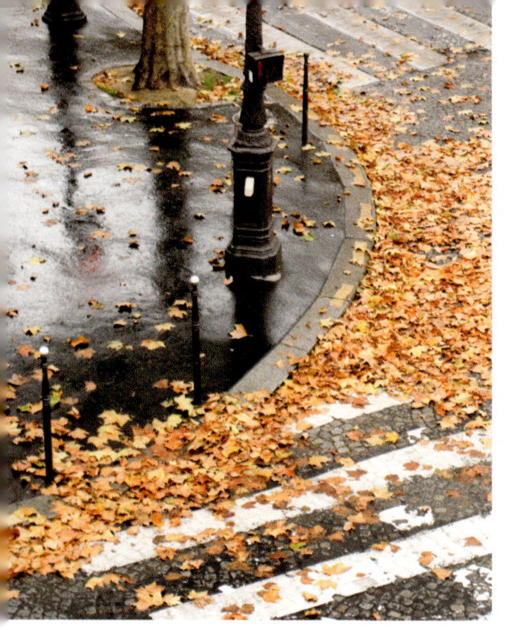

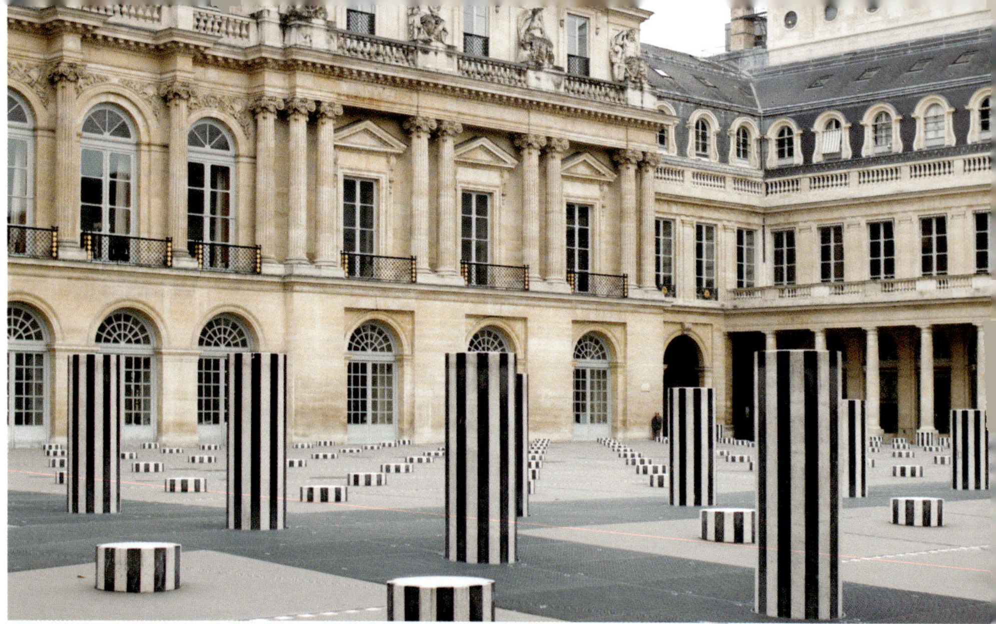

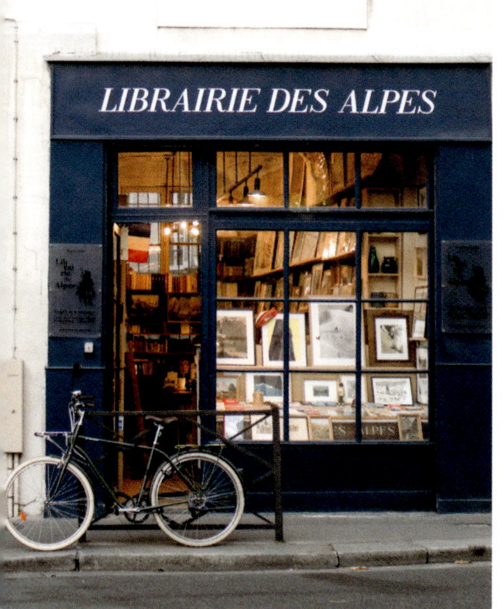

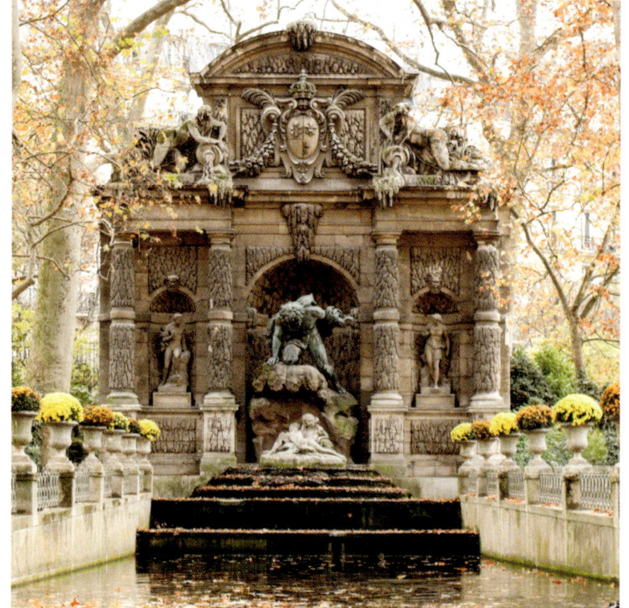

The weather fluctuates in the fall as temperatures drop. When venturing out, it is a good idea to wear layers. A trench coat is great for chilly mornings and evenings as well as for the unexpected downpour. A scarf works for layering over a light jacket or sweater when you are exploring the city.

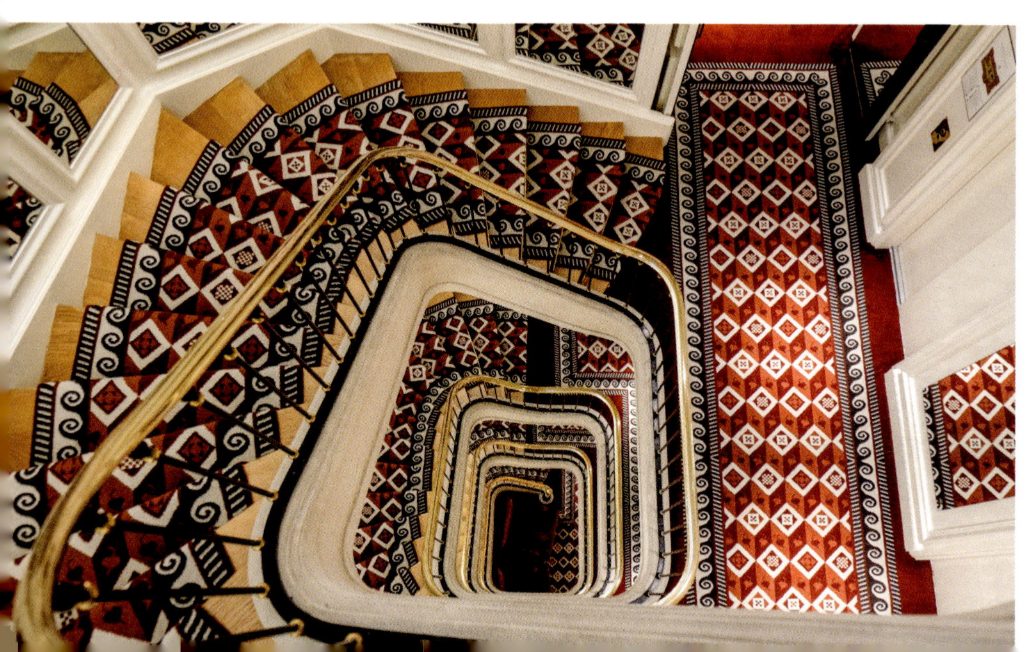

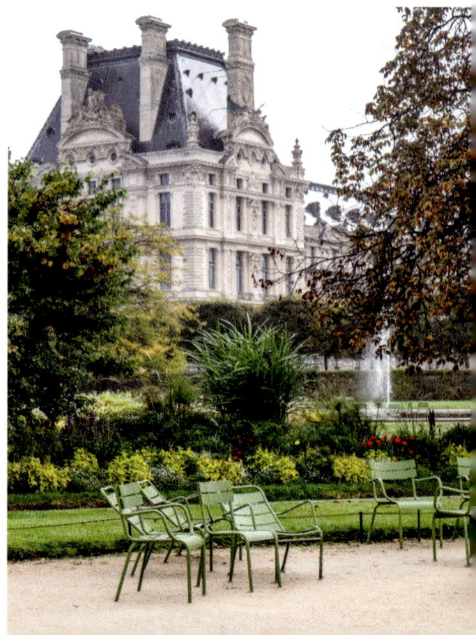

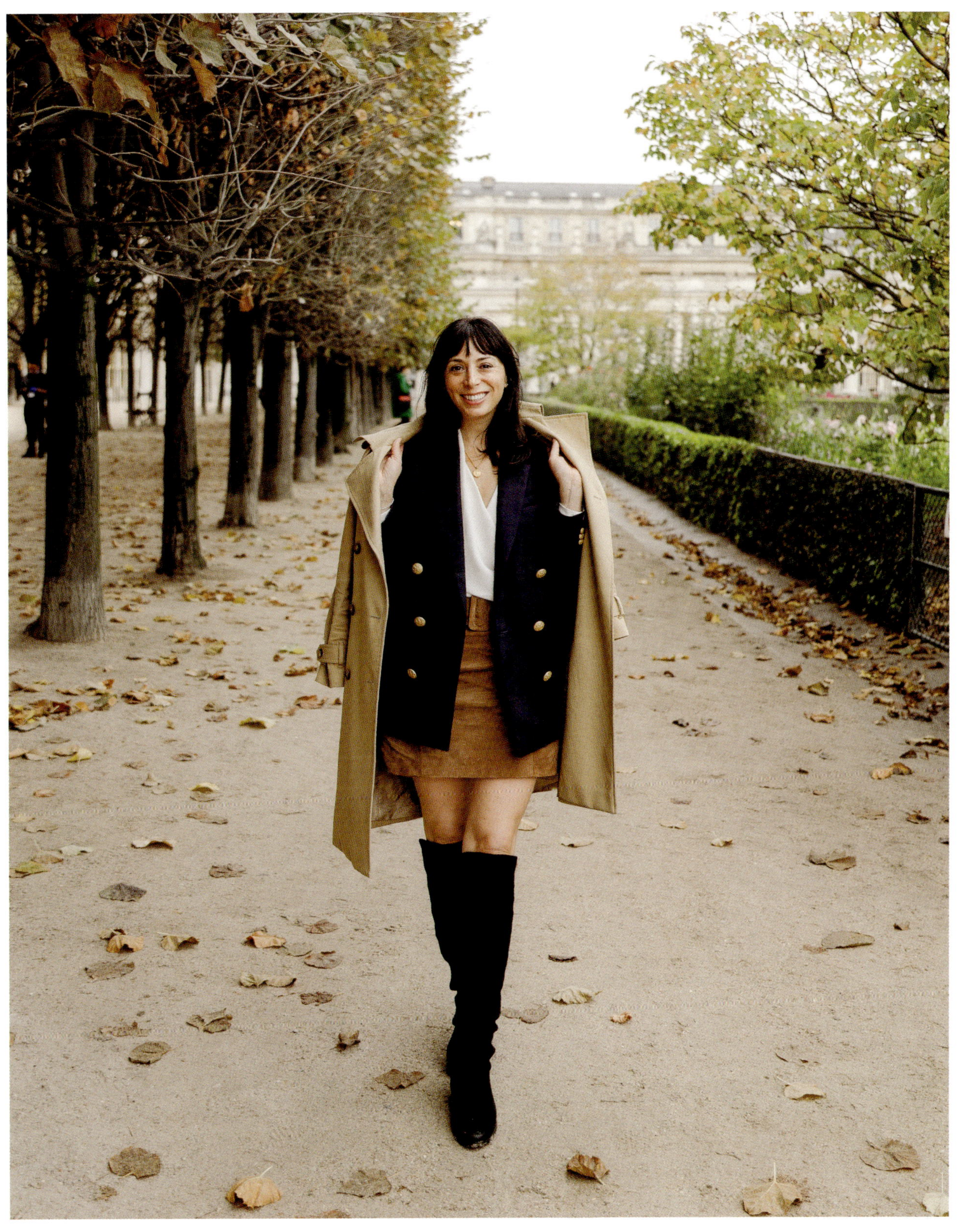

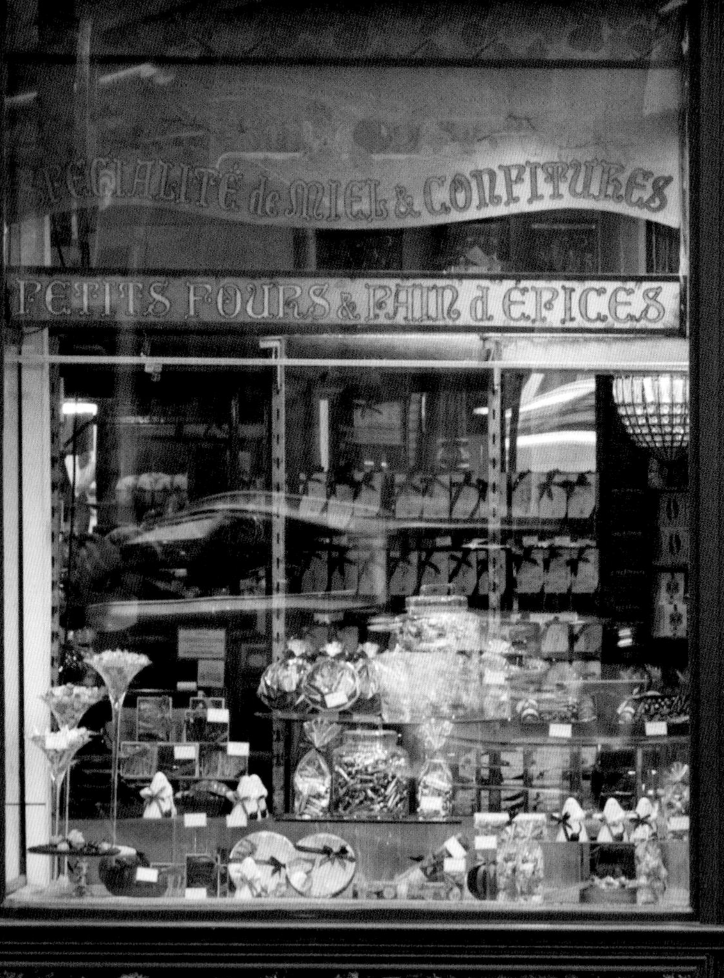
de MIEL & CONFITURES
PETITS FOURS & PAIN d'ÉPICES

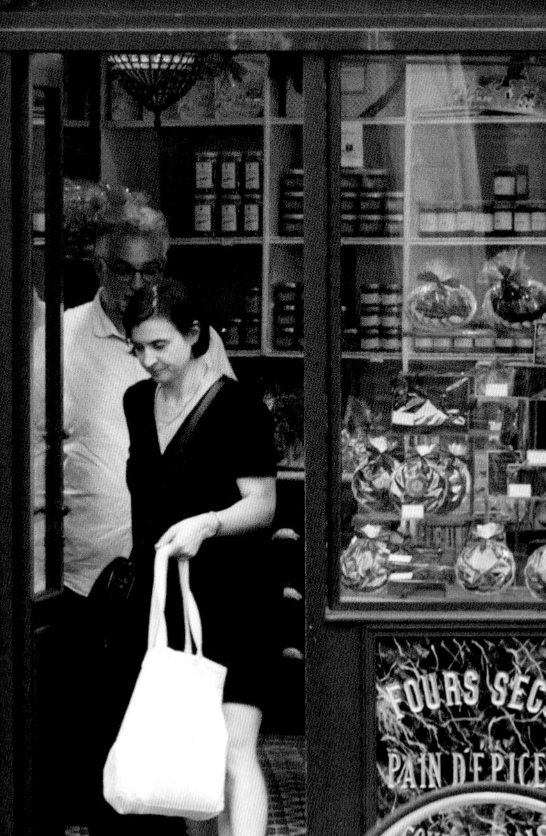
FOURS SECS
PAIN D'EPICE

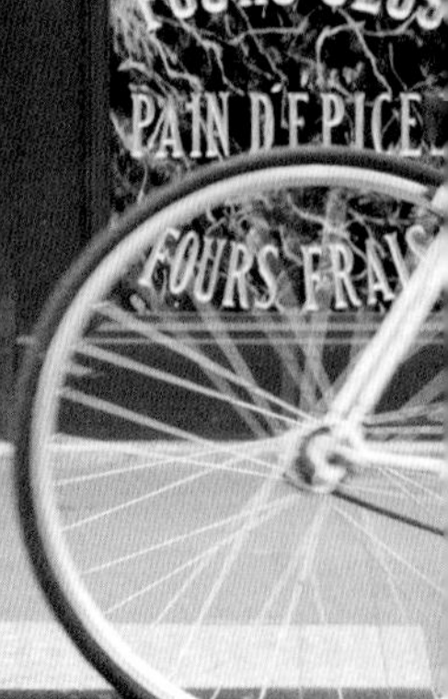

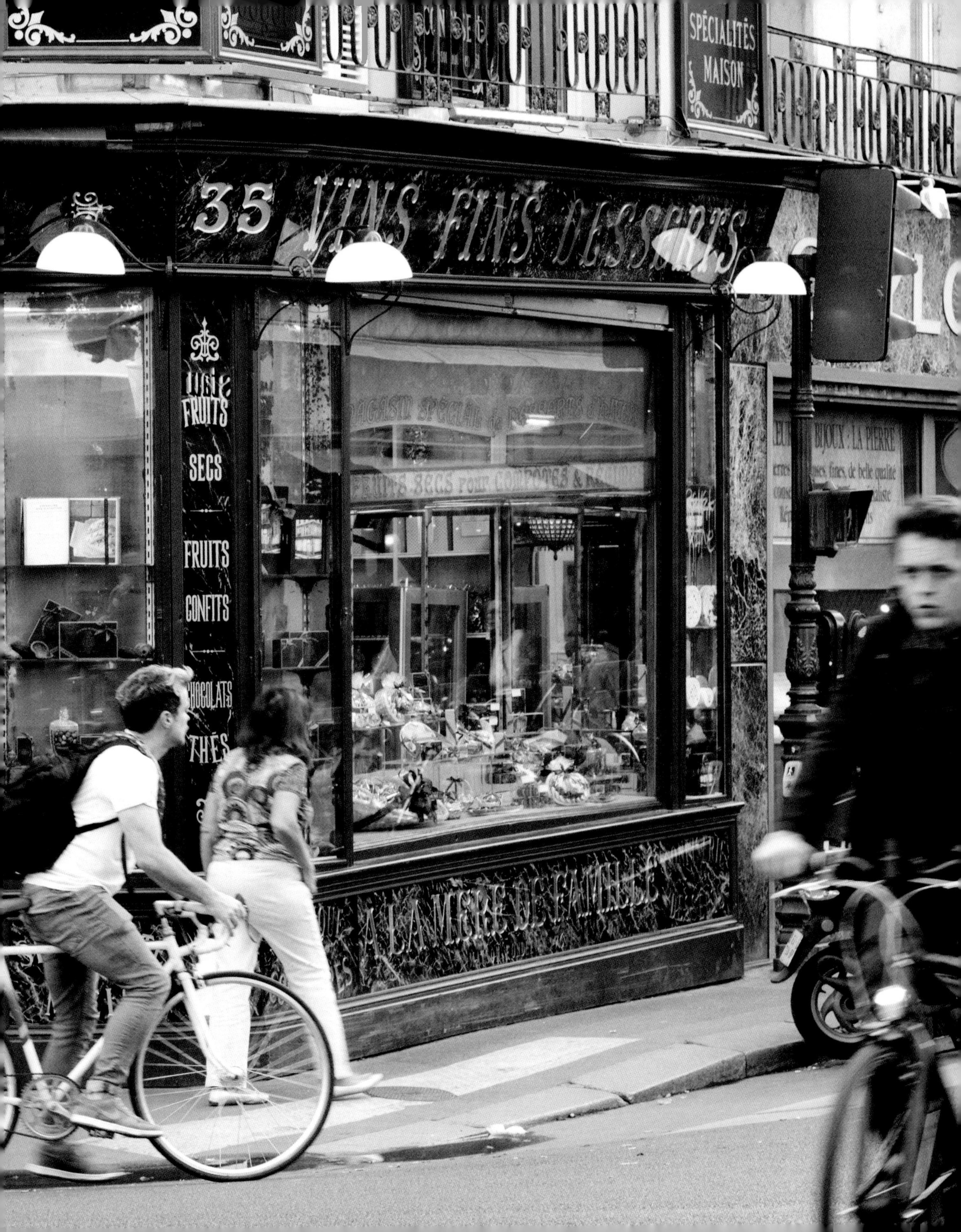
SPÉCIALITÉS
MAISON
35
VINS FINS DESSERTS
FRUITS
SECS
FRUITS
CONFITS
THÉS
A LA MERE DE FAMILLE

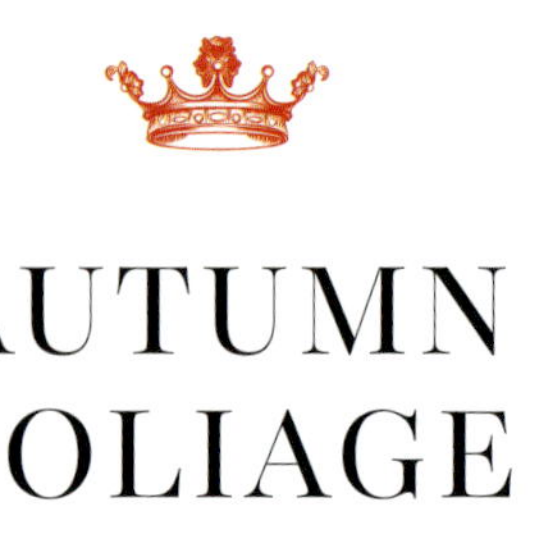

AUTUMN FOLIAGE

Where to see autumn foliage in Paris:

- **Jardin des Tuileries:** Not too far from the Palais-Royal, just in front of the Louvre, these gardens are perfectly manicured in every season, and the color scheme of the flowers changes yearly. Expect to find dahlias in bloom in early autumn. Don't just walk through—grab one of the iconic green chairs by the fountains and soak up the sunshine.

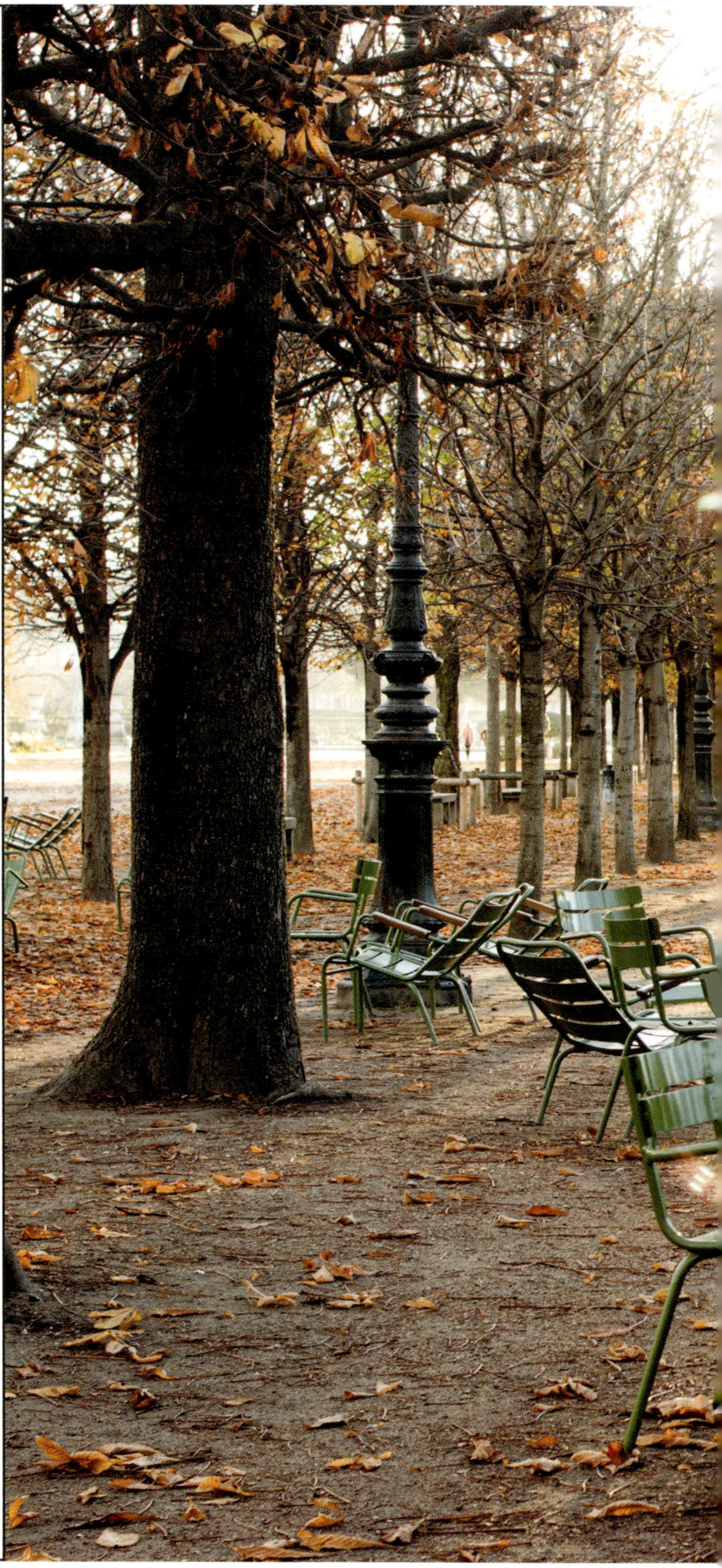

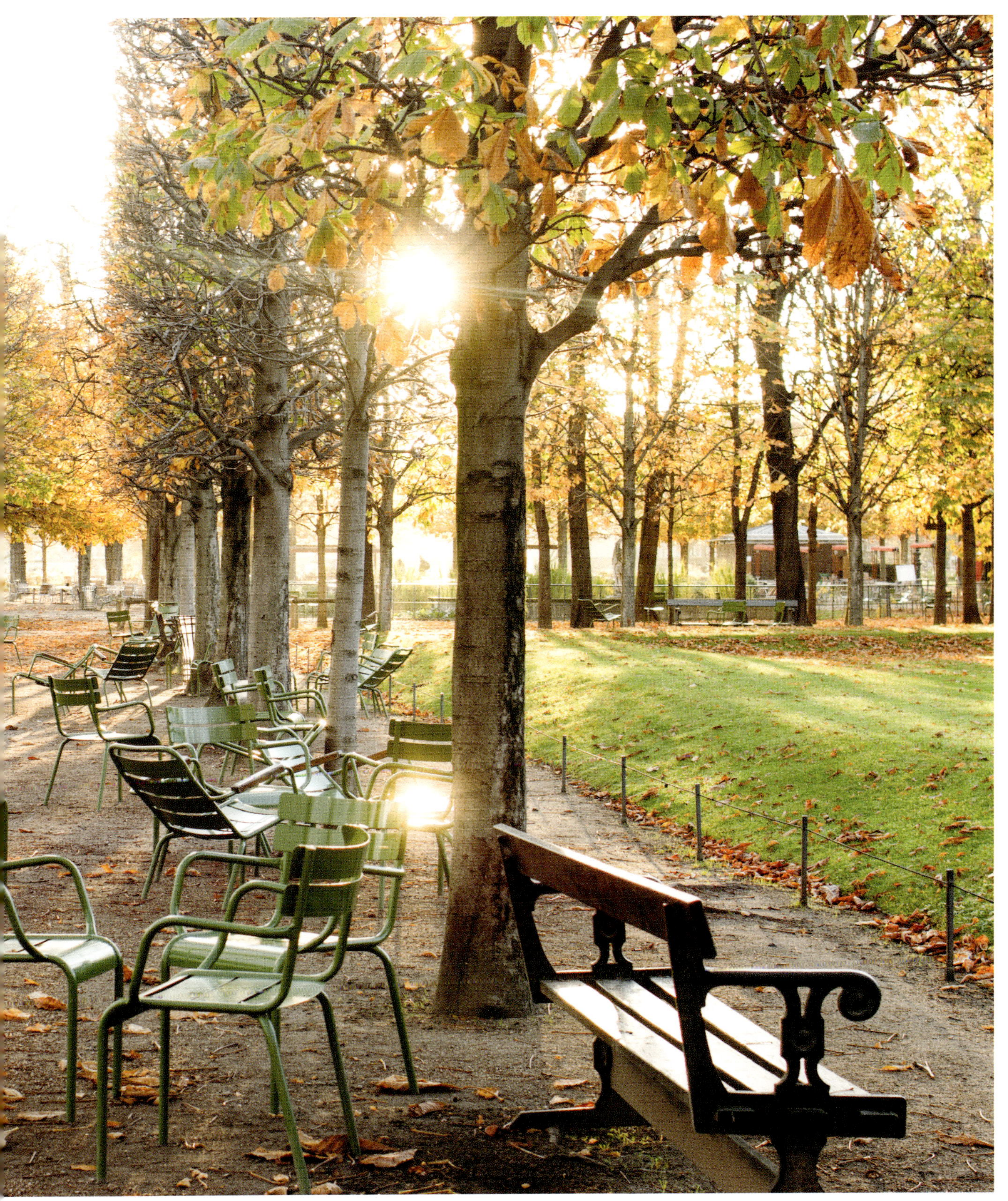

- **Palais-Royal:** Explore the Palais-Royal area in early autumn before the trees are bare. October is the prime time to soak up the warm weather and stroll through this unique part of Paris. My husband and I got engaged in mid-October at Palais-Royal. I can't miss a stroll through here with a cup of coffee on any visit to Paris. In the morning and afternoon, the arcades are illuminated by the light of a golden autumn sun with a warmth that's unique to this time of year.

- **Le Marais:** Place des Vosges, the oldest planned square in Paris, is beautiful in every season. In autumn, this historic square is a must for a stroll. People-watch here as Parisians of all ages gather to soak up the last light and warmth of the season.

- **Palace of Versailles:** The palace gardens are an excellent place to experience the autumn season. Visit the town market and pick up everything you need for a picnic in the garden on a warm afternoon. Stroll or bike through the gardens to find the perfect spot to have your meal—under a tree for shade on a sunny autumn day is ideal.

- **Jardin du Luxembourg:** Autumn is an ideal time to stroll through the gardens and spot the dahlias and the mums planted throughout. The flowers' colors pop against the gold and brown hues of the season. Visit the Médicis Fountain early in the morning for a quiet retreat in the city. The fountain area of the garden fills up quickly with visitors and locals looking for the perfect photo opportunity. Pack a picnic lunch or your favorite book to unplug on a warm morning or afternoon.

- **Parc Monceau:** Off the beaten path in the 8th arrondissement, you will find Parc Monceau. The autumn leaves frame the golden gates to the entrance. As the trees become bare, they reveal a stunning view of the Arc de Triomphe from the garden.

- **The Seine River:** Take a cruise on one of the open-air boats on the Seine to soak up the season's colors. The trees lining the Seine put on a show before the crisp days of November arrive. You can also stroll the Seine or picnic along the river's banks. An ideal spot is in front of the Louvre on the Left Bank of the river.

- **Montmartre:** Spend an afternoon in Montmartre strolling Rue Lepic and Avenue Junot. Let Paris lead you as you discover hidden courtyards and tiny streets filled with colorful ivy and flower boxes on their last blooms of the year.

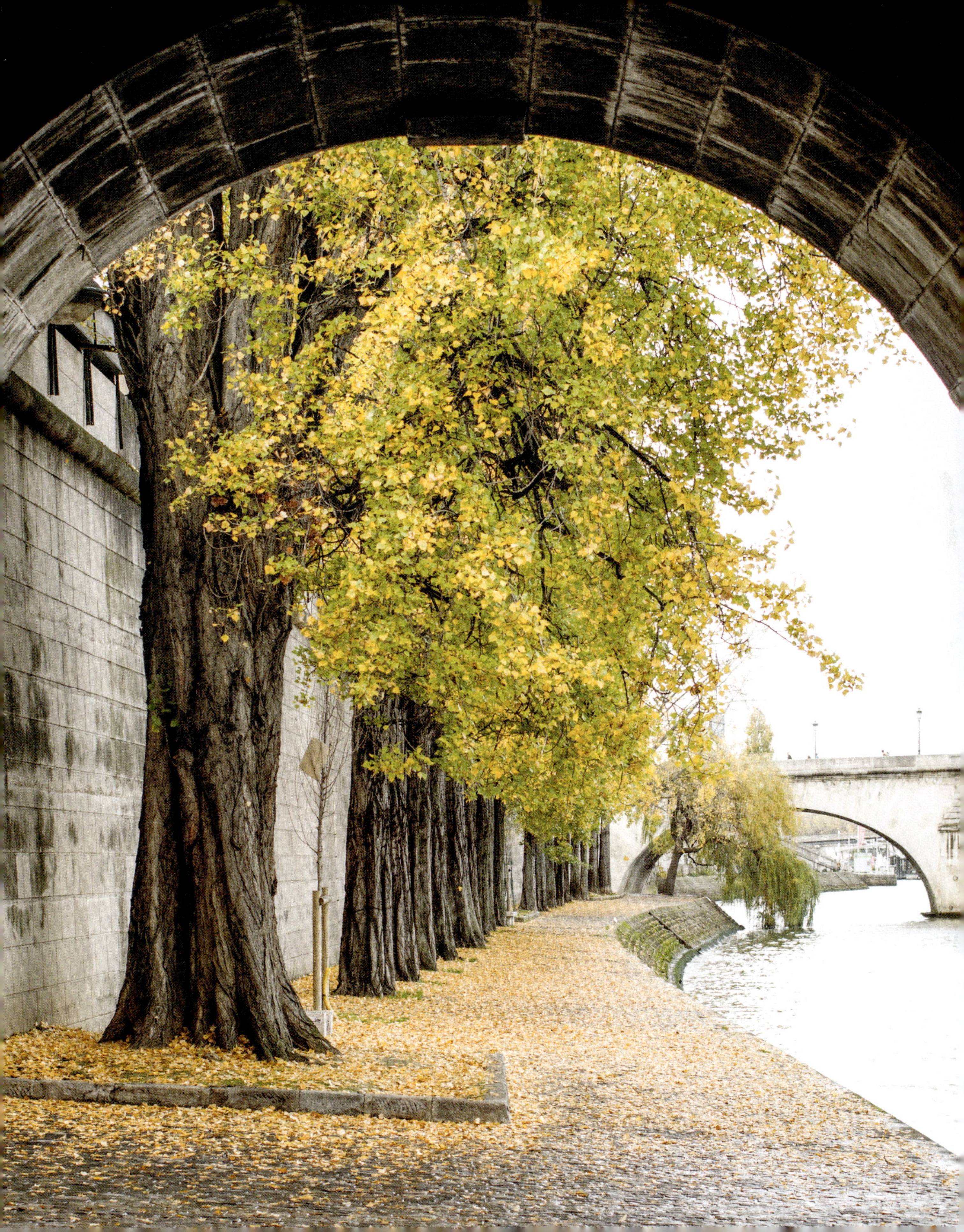

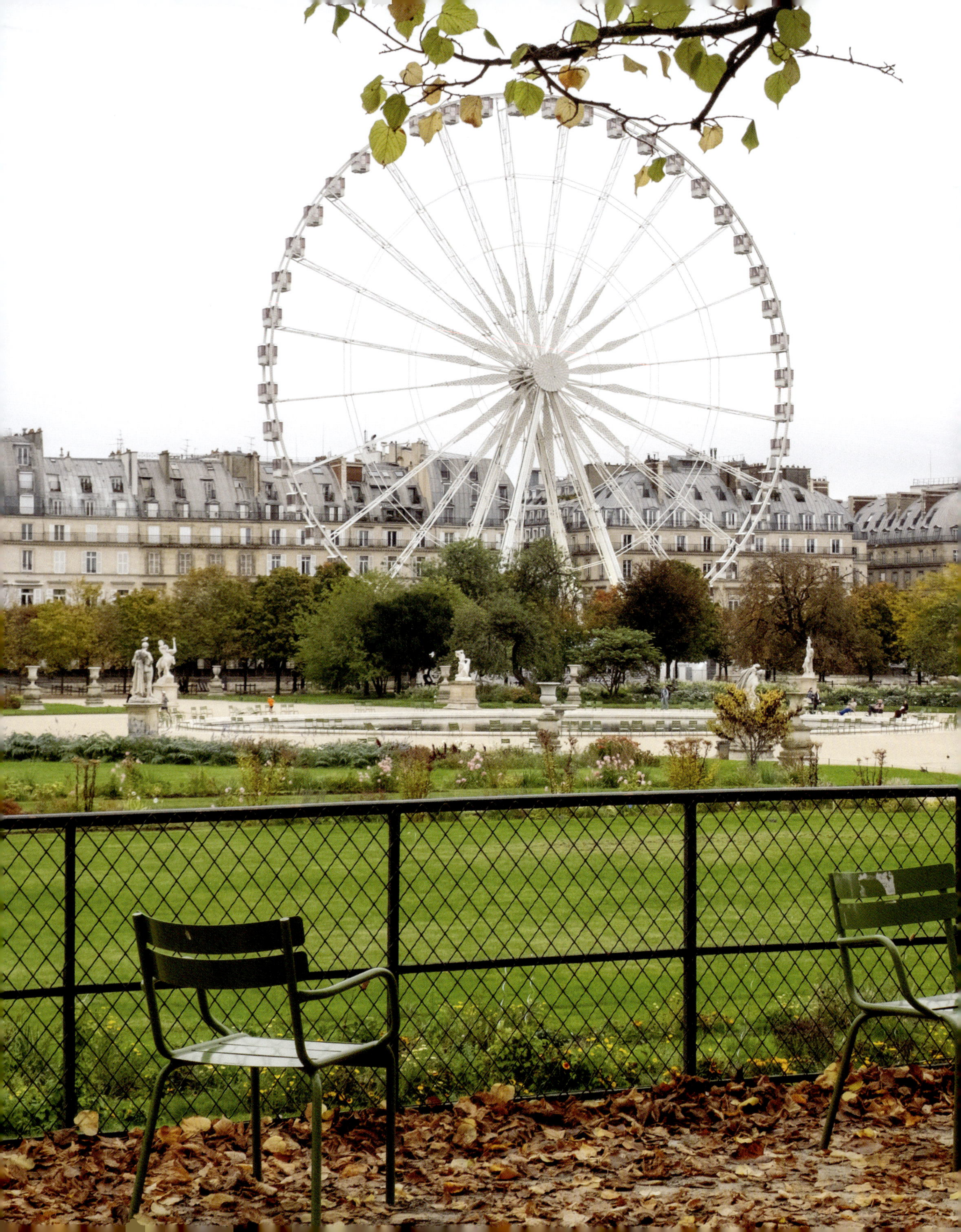

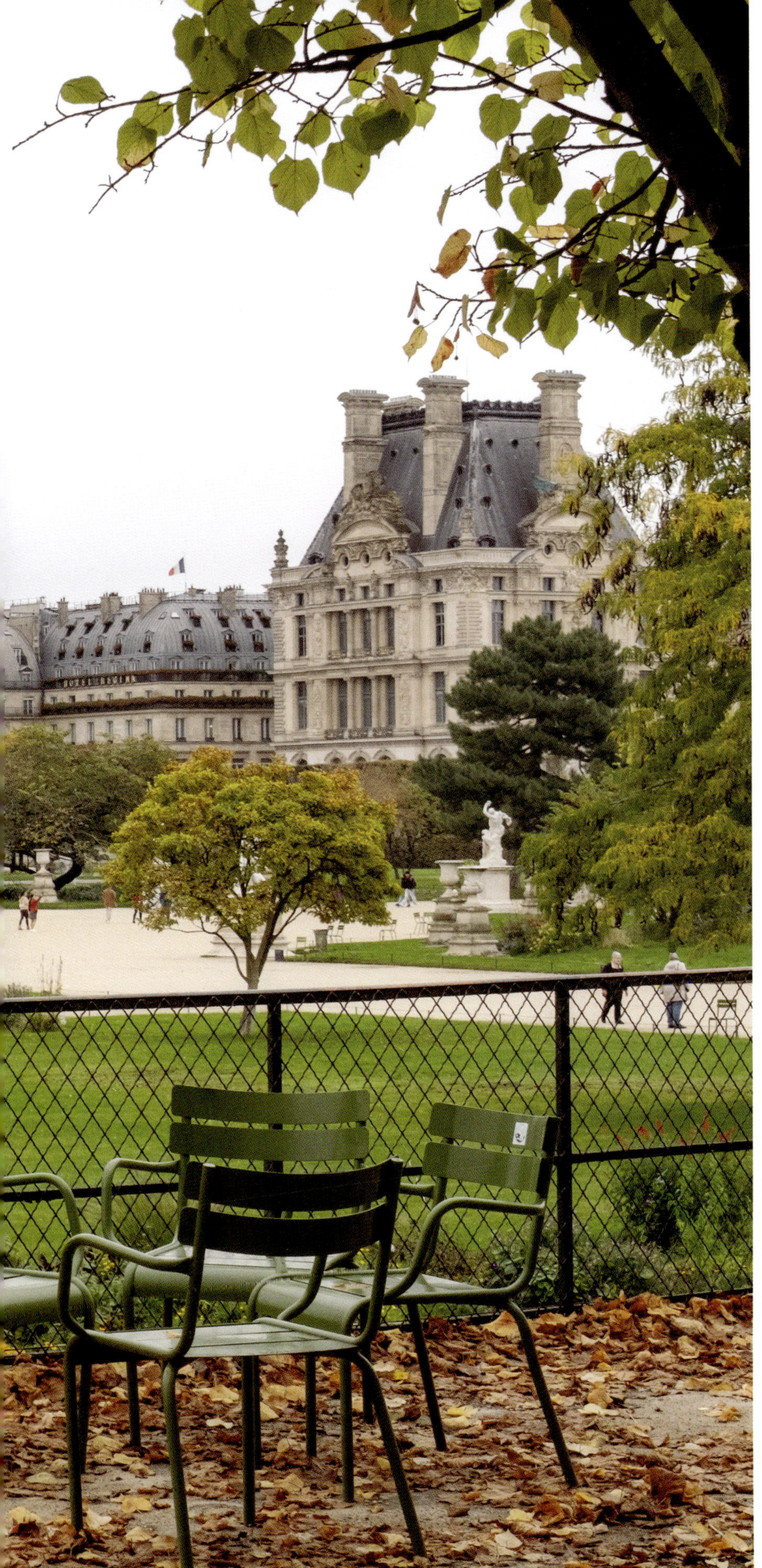

The Ferris wheel, typically a holiday staple in the Jardin des Tuileries, is set up in mid-October. For a few euros, you can take a ride to get a bird's-eye view of Paris from the Tuileries to Montmartre to the Eiffel Tower. Walk towards the Seine River, closest to the beginning of the garden, for a beautiful, classic view of the Louvre with the autumn foliage.

AUTUMN MENUS

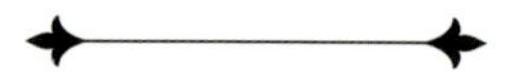

le menu

Magret de Canard
(a Moulard duck breast)

Gnocchi à la Parisian
(pillowy gnocchi with butter, sage, and pine nuts)

Poire à la Beaujolaise
(poached pears in red wine)

Mont Blanc
(sweetened chestnut purée topped with whipped cream)

- Apples, pears, figs, and chestnuts give galettes and tarts their pizzazz at this time of year.
- Root vegetables inspire stews and rich soups; popular cheeses include chèvre, Mont D'or, Brie, and blue cheeses like Roquefort and Bleu d'Auvergne.
- Beaujolais brings a light touch to fall beverage selections, which also include cider and cocktails with fruitful flavors like pear and apple.

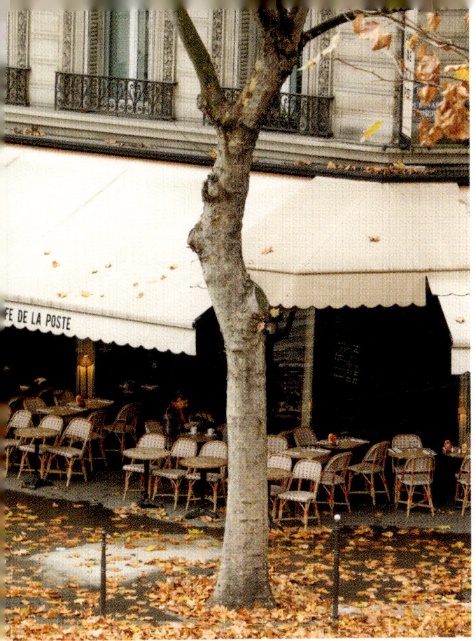
FE DE LA POSTE

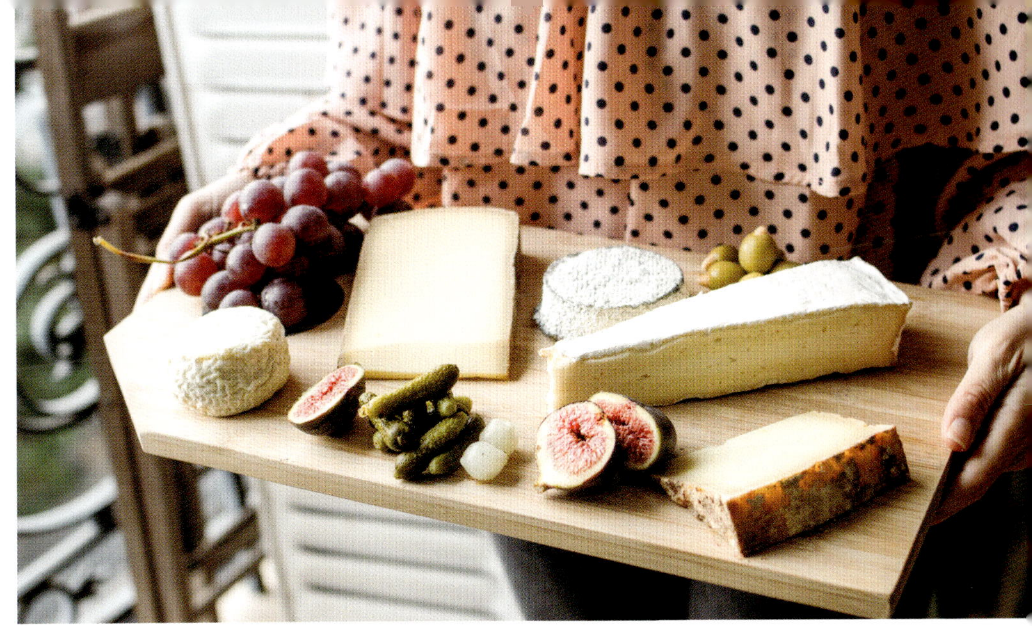

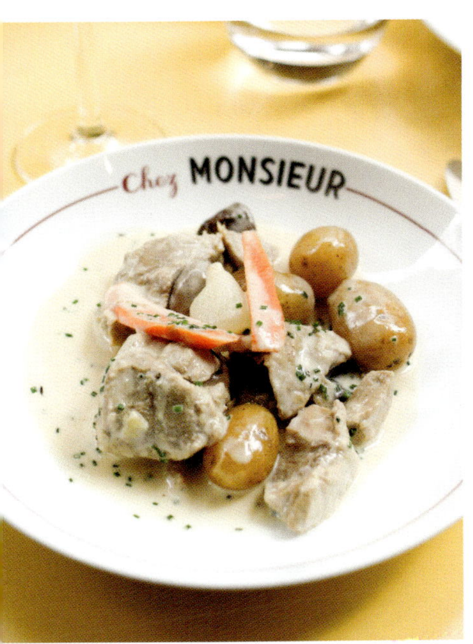
Chez MONSIEUR

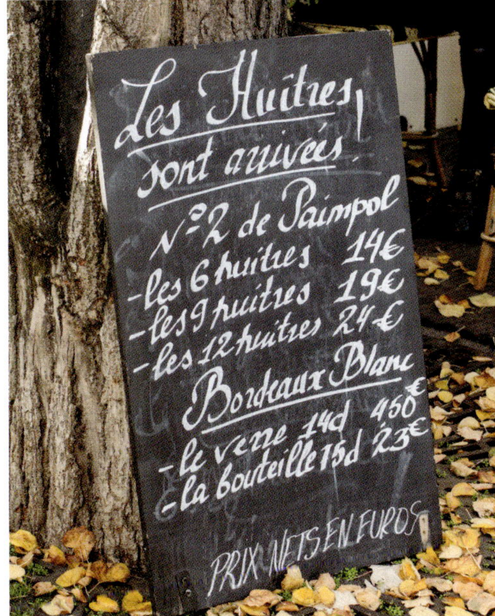
Les Huitres
sont arrivées!
N°2 de Paimpol
-les 6 huitres 14€
-les 9 huitres 19€
-les 12 huitres 24€
Bordeaux Blanc
-le verre 14cl 4,50€
-la bouteille 75cl 23€
PRIX NETS EN EUROS

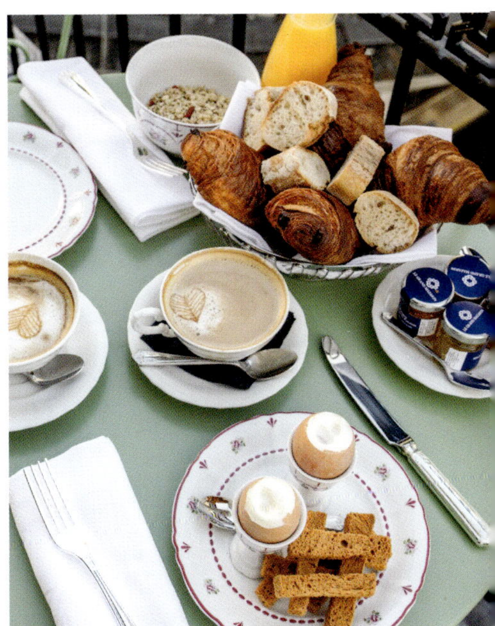

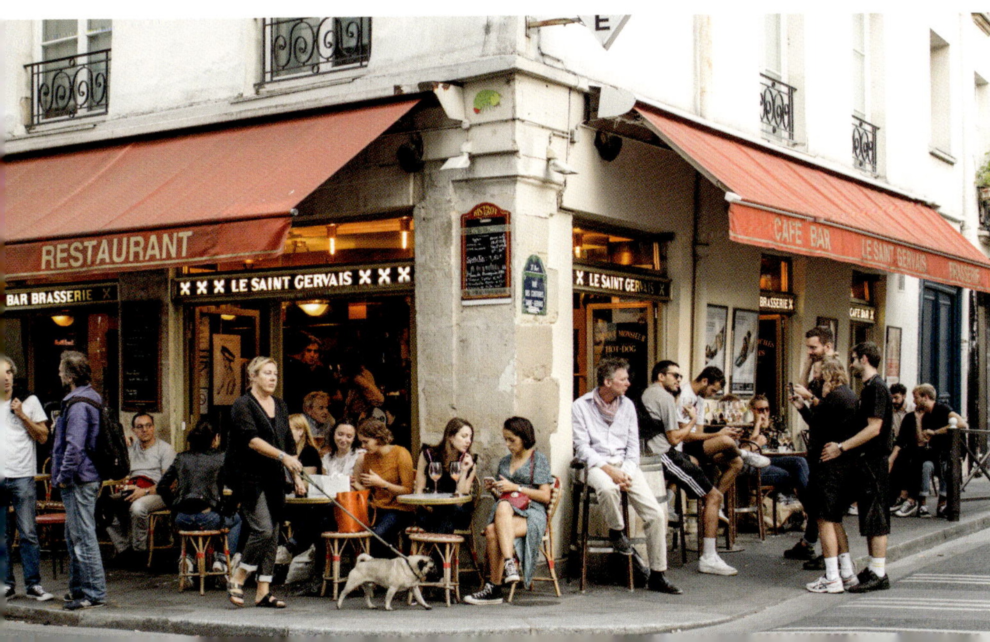
RESTAURANT
BAR BRASSERIE
LE SAINT GERVAIS
LE SAINT GERVAIS
CAFÉ BAR
LE SAINT GERVAIS
BRASSERIE

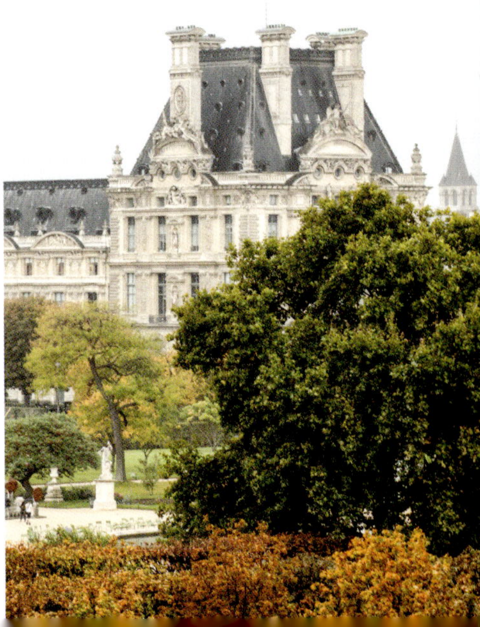

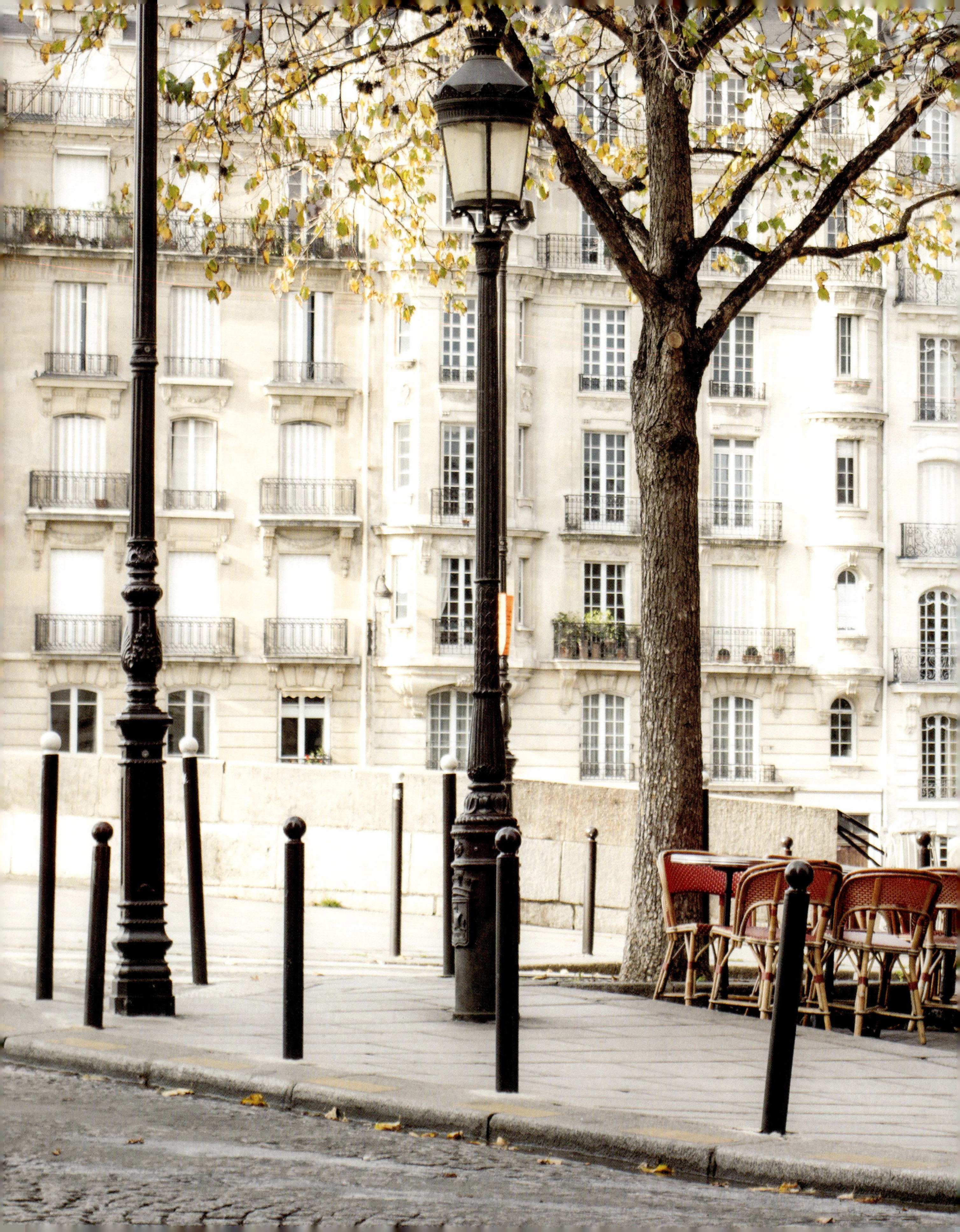

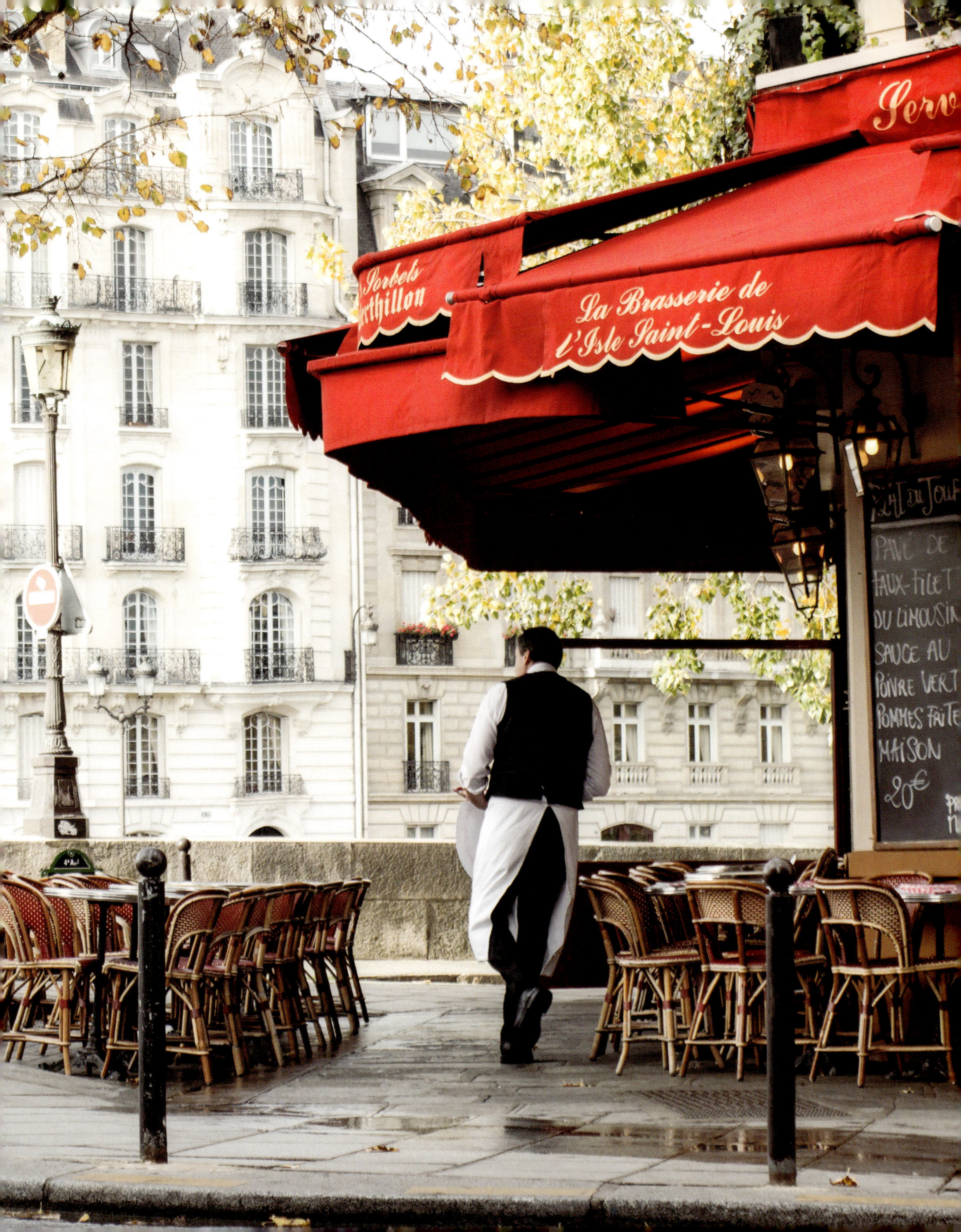
Sorbets
La Brasserie de
l'Isle Saint-Louis
PAVE DE
SAUCE AU
POIVRE VERT
MAISON
20€

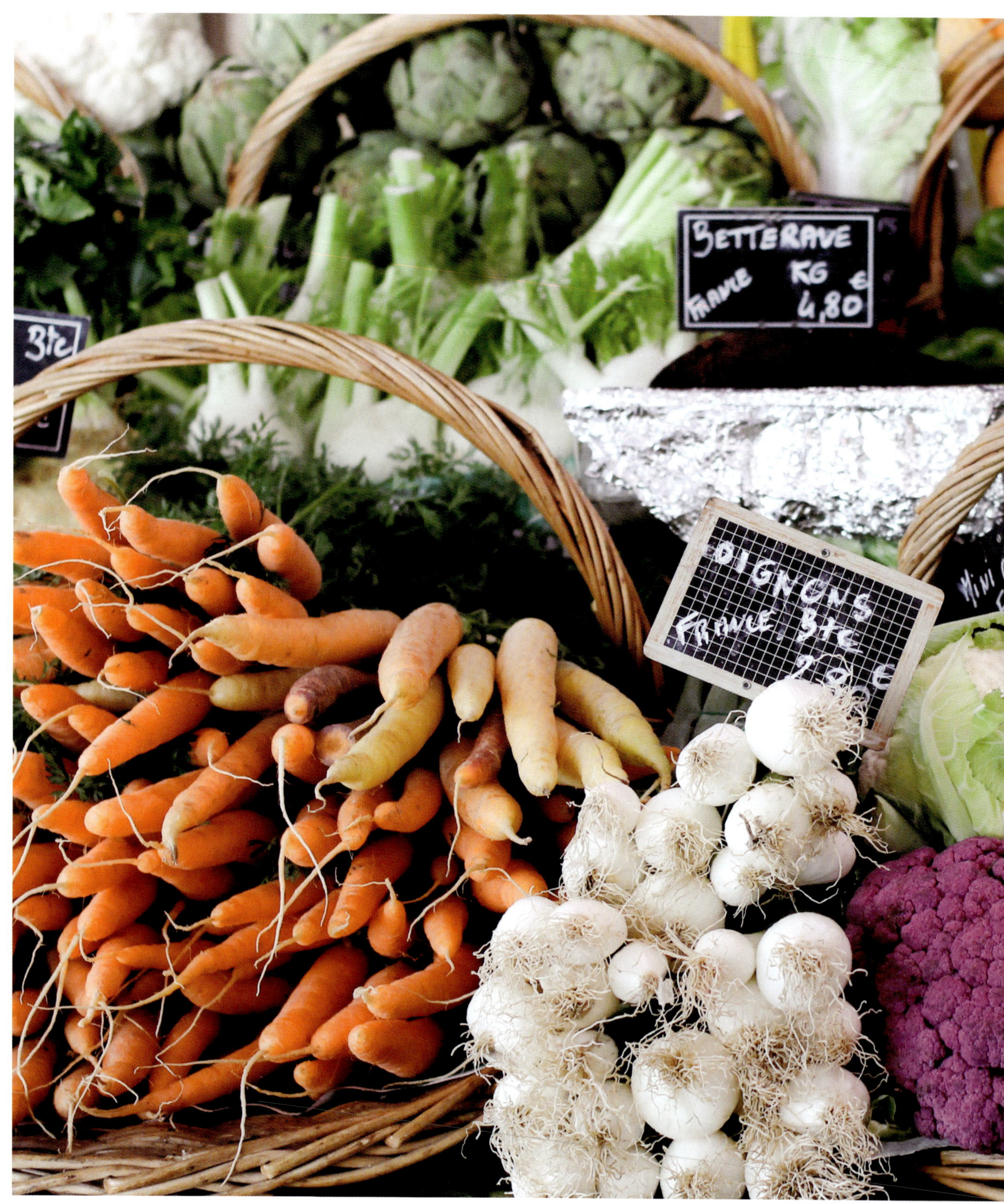
BETTERAVE
FRANCE KG €
4,80
3tc
OIGNONS
FRANCE 3tc

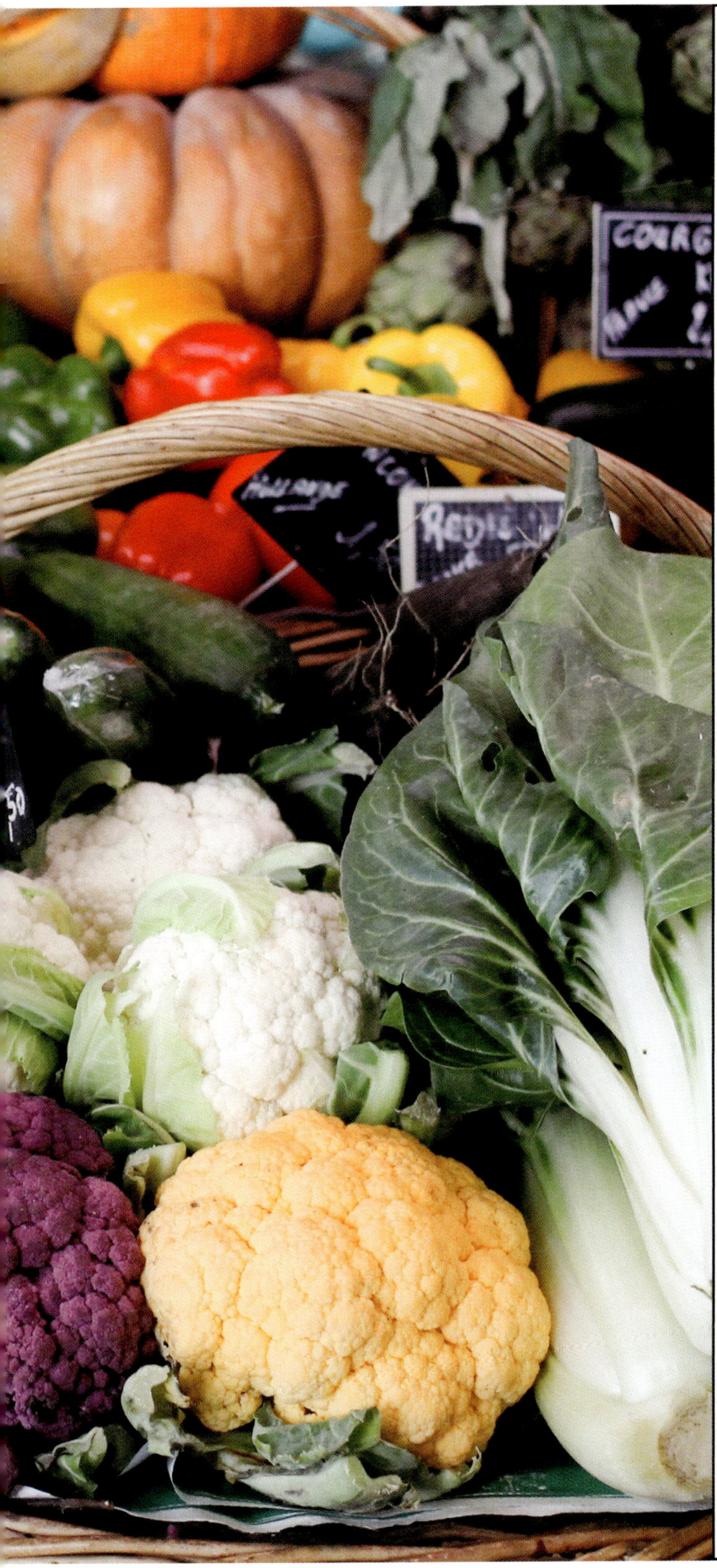

AUTUMN AT THE MARKET

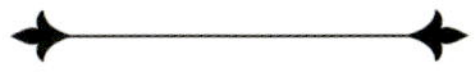

The brilliant colors of fall show off at the fresh-air markets around the city. Pumpkins, carrots, cabbages, and richly vibrant flowers beckon.

Fruits
- Grapes
- Apples
- Pears
- Plums
- Hazelnuts

Vegetables
- Pumpkin
- Squash
- Mushrooms (chanterelles)
- Endives

Cheeses
- Comté
- Roquefort

Flowers
- Dahlias
- Sunflowers
- Eucalyptus
- Hydrangeas

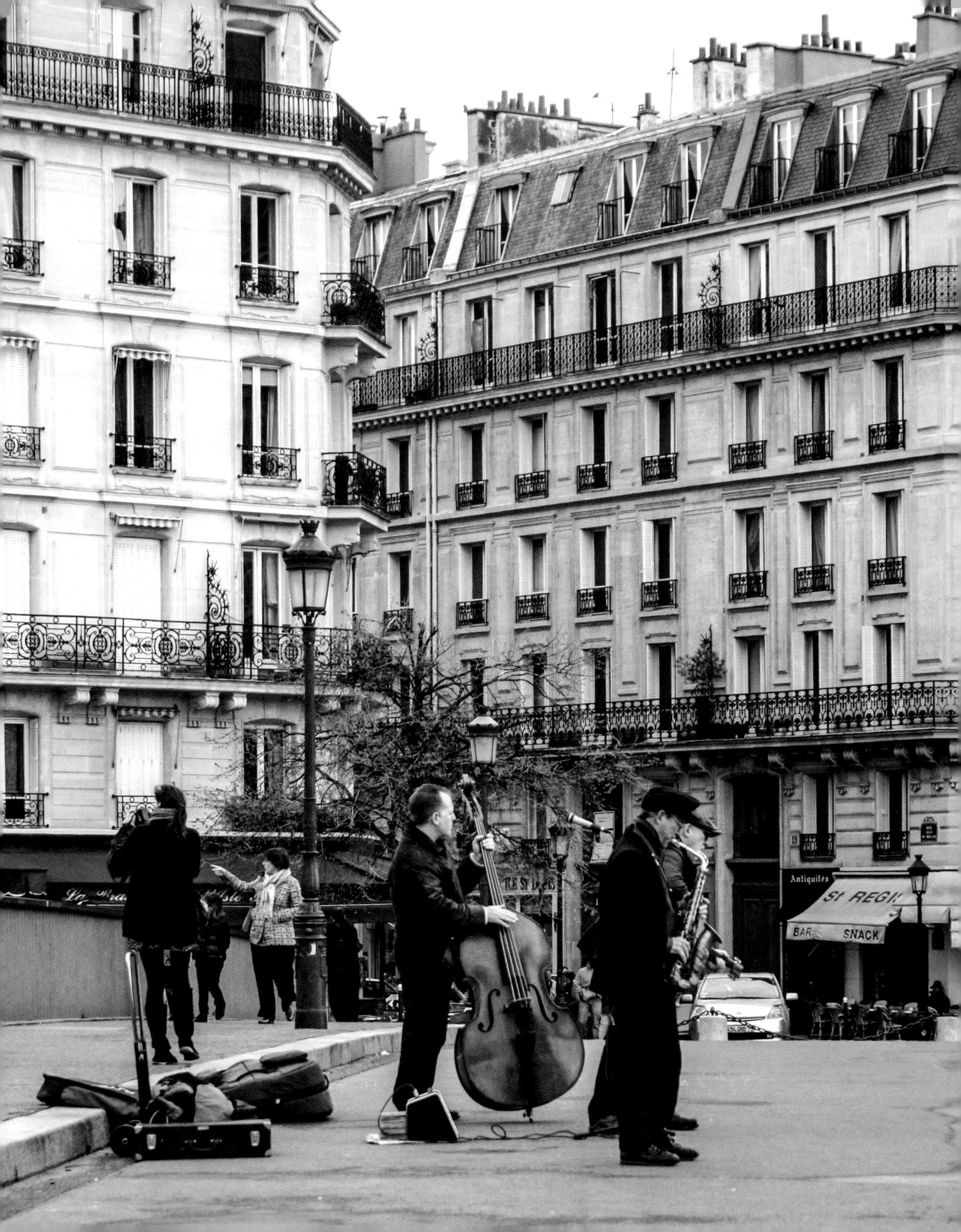
Antiquités
St REGI
BAR
SNACK

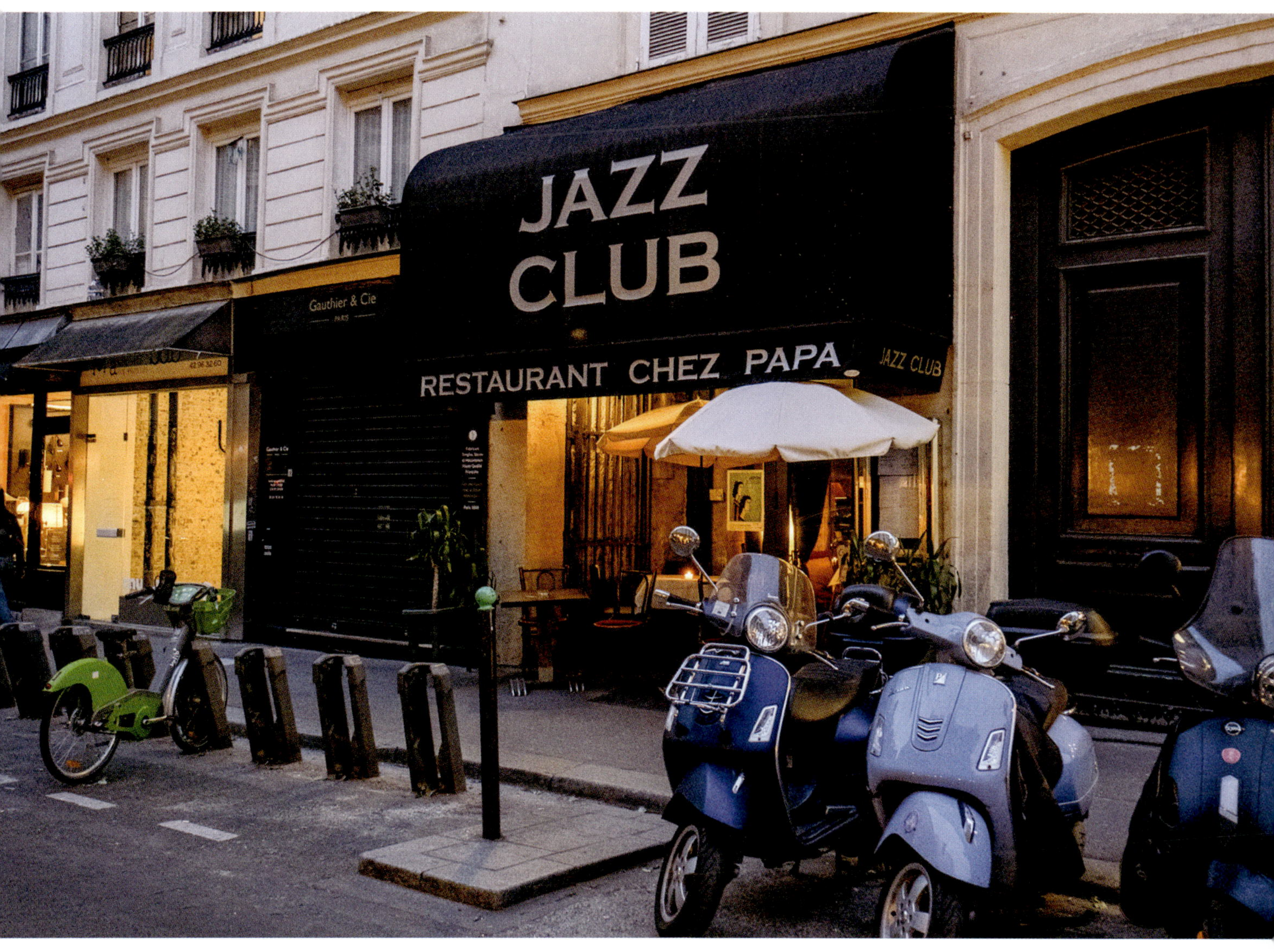

On Sundays, my husband and I love turning on a jazz playlist on Spotify while we read the paper, sit by the fire in the evening, or cook dinner.

I first fell in love with jazz in Paris at the French restaurant next to my hotel. They streamed TSF Jazz, which was the background music during dinner. The radio station, its letters standing for "télégraphie sans fils," broadcasts from the Île-de-France. Over the years, my uncle fueled my love of jazz, followed by my Paris family. My sister and brother-in-law play TSF Jazz in their kitchen when we cook.

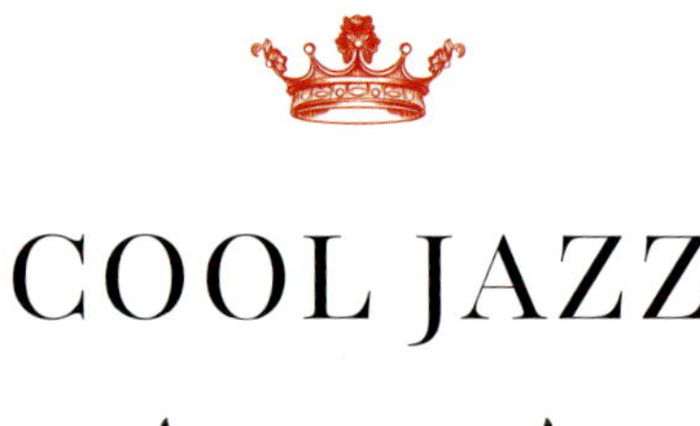

COOL JAZZ

Here are a few favorite spots to listen to jazz that I have found over the years in Paris:

- **Café Laurent in the Hôtel d'Aubusson on Rue Dauphine:** The only requirement is to purchase a cocktail or drink to enjoy the live music in the hotel bar. Enjoy a classic French meal at Chez Fernand on Rue Christine before or after.

- **Le Duc des Lombards in the Marais:** On some evenings, this is where TSF Jazz streams live artists. You can book tickets online to enjoy live music.

- **Pavillon Faubourg Saint-Germain:** The James Joyce bar in this hotel offers live music, often jazz, on the first Thursday of every month.

- **Bar 228 Le Meurice:** Enjoy nightly jazz and a cocktail in this classic hotel bar, which is located across from the Jardin des Tuileries.

- **Hôtel de Crillon Bar Les Ambassadeurs:** This spot offers creative seasonal cocktails by world-famous bartenders. Not feeling adventurous? They claim to make the best classic cocktails, too. From experience, the Negroni (my go-to) was fabulous. The bar does not offer reservations, but go ahead and test your luck on an evening in Paris.

- **Le Caveau de la Huchette:** This jazz and swing bar in the 5th arrondissement was made famous by the movie *La La Land*. Immerse yourself in a total jazz experience.

- **Chez Papa Jazz Club:** Located in Saint-Germain-des-Prés, stop in for an evening of live jazz.

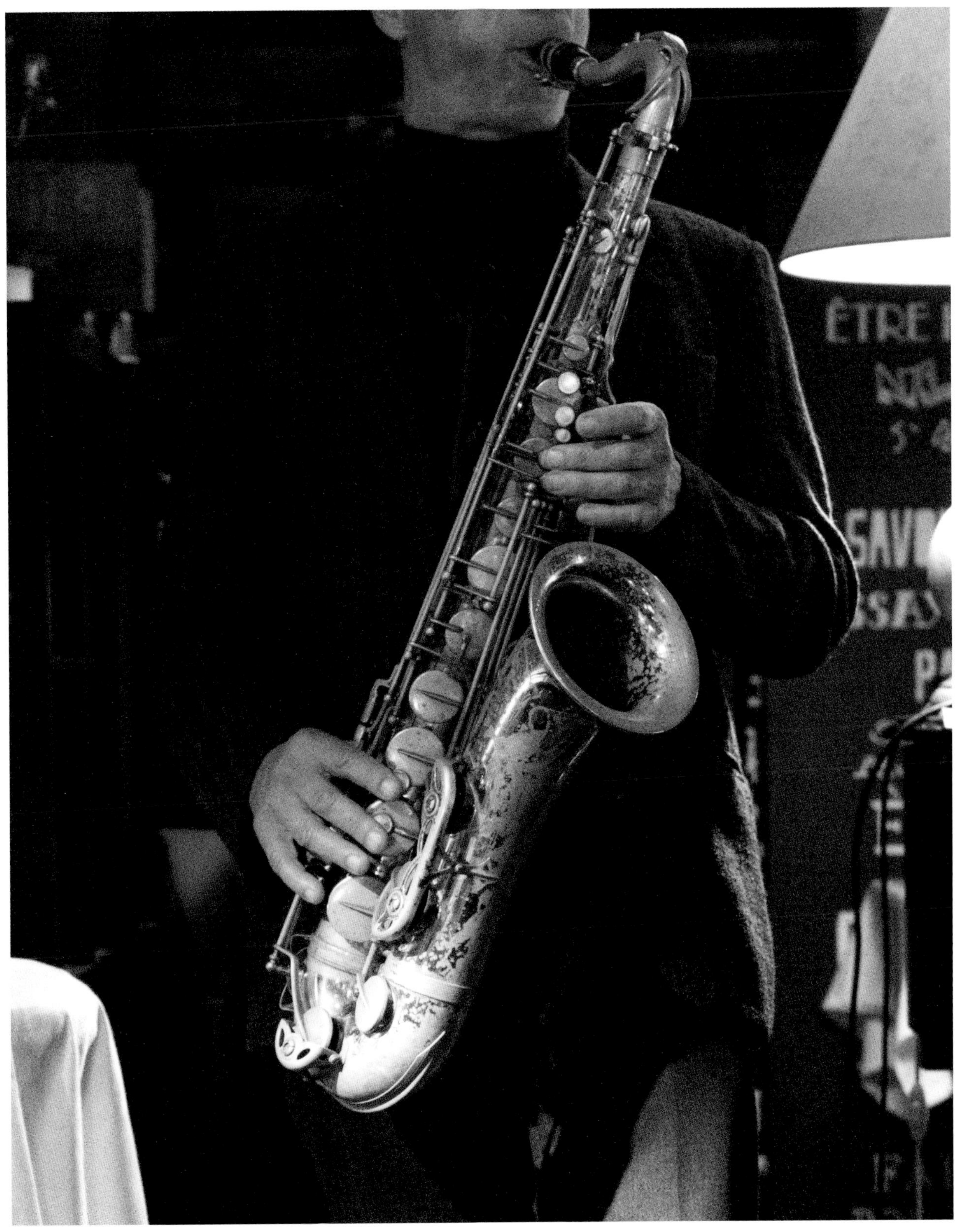

Take a cruise on one of the open-air boats on the Seine to soak up the season's colors. The trees lining the river put on a show before the crisp days of November arrive. You can also stroll the Seine or picnic along the river's banks. An ideal spot is in front of the Louvre on the Left Bank of the river.

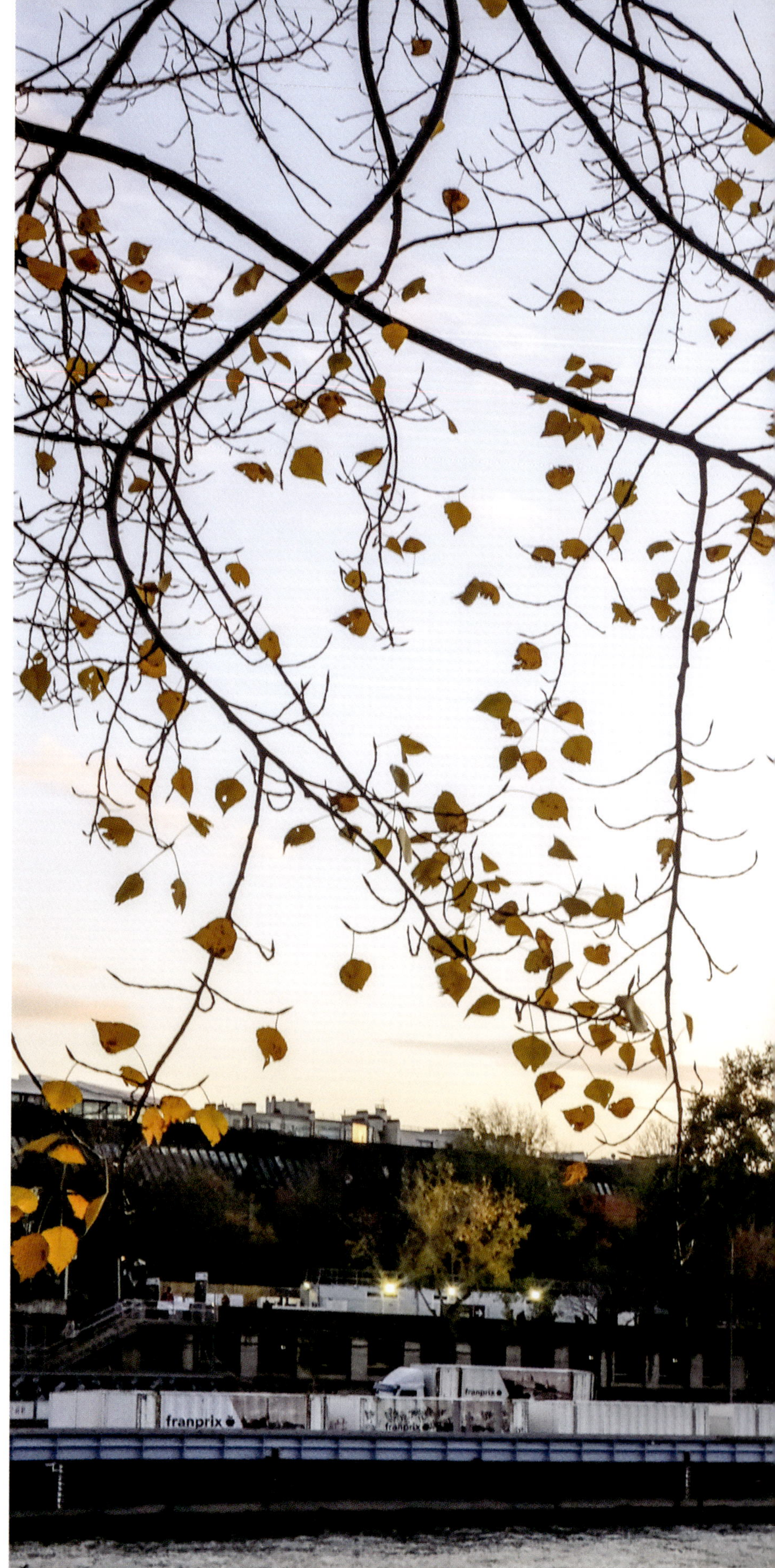

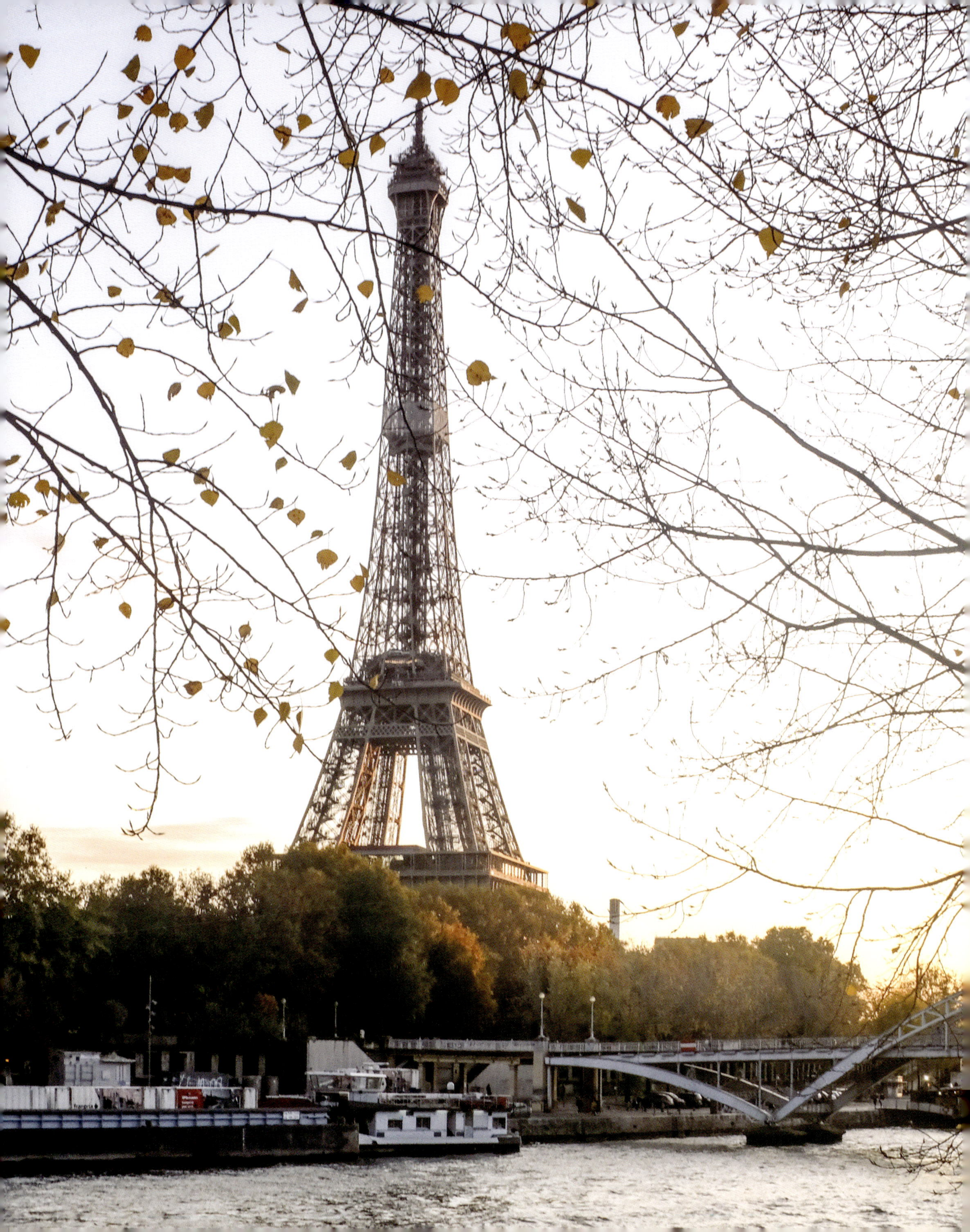

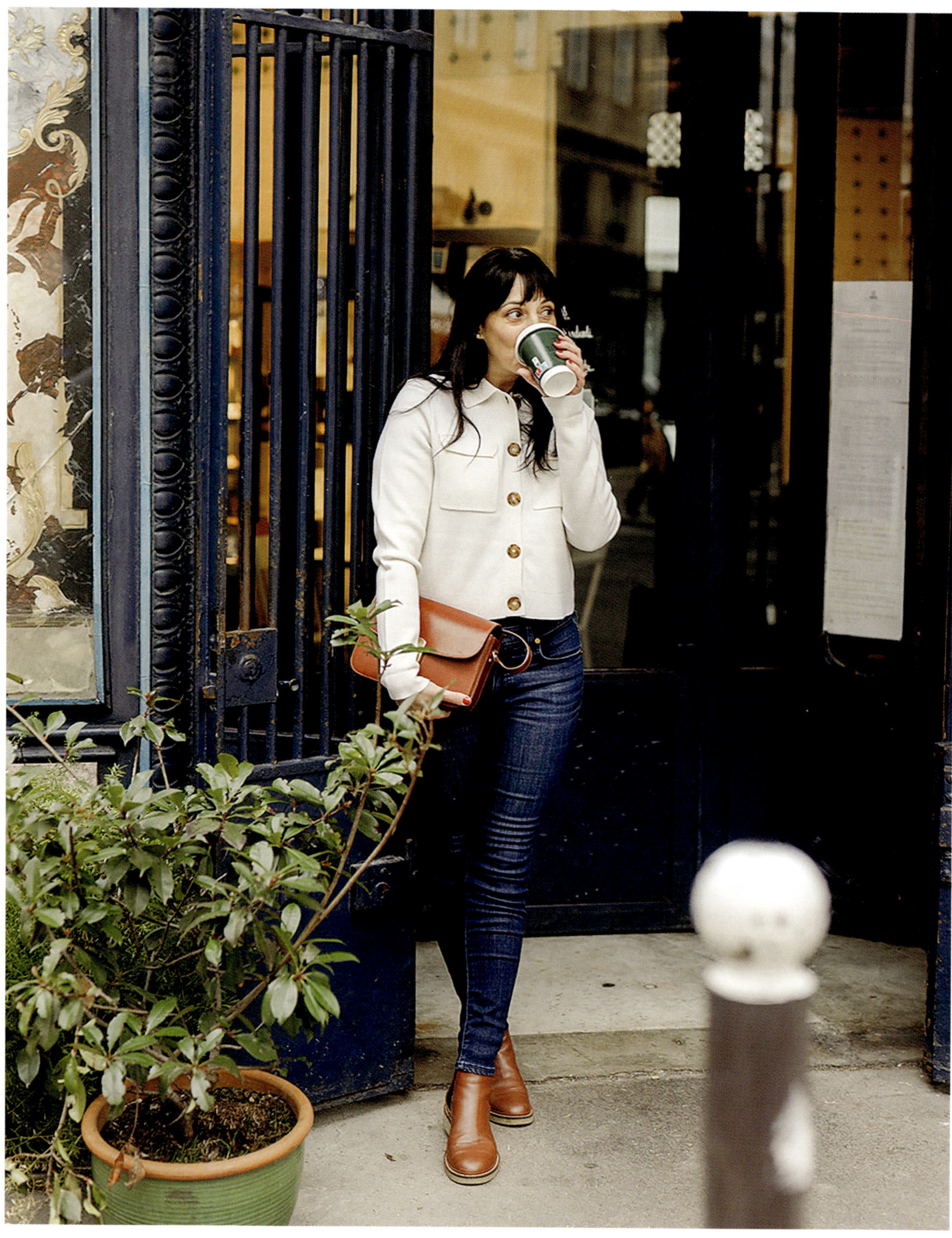

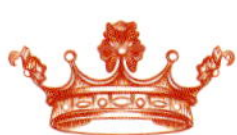

COFFEE IN PARIS

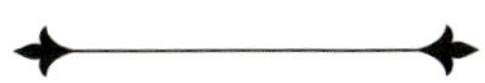

The coffee scene in Paris continues to explode, with various shops opening on every corner. You can enjoy a coffee *sur place* (at the shop) or *emporter* (for takeaway). Some shops are small enough to only offer takeaway coffee options in paper cups. Tap to pay is a common form of payment; don't expect to take out euros for your coffee. *Vache* (cow's milk) is the traditional milk offered with coffee drinks, but most places also offer oat or almond milk. They will typically ask now as you order, but if you have dietary restrictions, it is definitely best to confirm when ordering.

Some of the traditional coffee options you will see on the menu: Espresso, Macchiato, Americano, Latte, Cappuccino, Matcha, and my preferred coffee order, Flat White—two shots of espresso instead of one. In spring and summer, you might find on the menu Café Glacé, which is iced coffee. It may cost a minor upcharge.

- **L'Arbre à Café**—2nd arrondisement, Rue de Nil
- **Clove**—18th arrondisement, Rue Chappe in Montmartre
- **Coeur Coffee Roasters**—18th arrondisement, Rue Ravignan in Montmartre
- **Strada Café**—5th arrondissement, Rue Monge
- **Café Nuances**—6th arrondissement, Rue du Vieux Columbier in Saint-Germain-des-Prés (multiple locations)
- **Paolina Caffè (Italian coffee shop)**—2nd arrondissement, Rue d'Aboukir. This coffee shop will transport you to Italy with a cappuccino.
- **Noir**—9th arrondissement, Rue Richer (multiple locations)
- **Terres de Café**—6th arrondissement, Rue de Bourbon le Château in Saint-Germain-des-Prés (multiple locations)

I was invited to a Sunday lunch at my Paris family's apartment in early November while visiting the city.

It was one of the last warm, sunny days of the year, and the city was buzzing with everyone soaking up the beautiful day. Laughter echoed through the apartment as kids played tag. Dishes were cleared between courses, and the afternoon light poured in. The dining room was illuminated with a soft autumn glow. I asked if I could quickly grab my camera to capture the moment. This photo remains one of my favorites in my collection. It symbolizes love, laughter, and light.

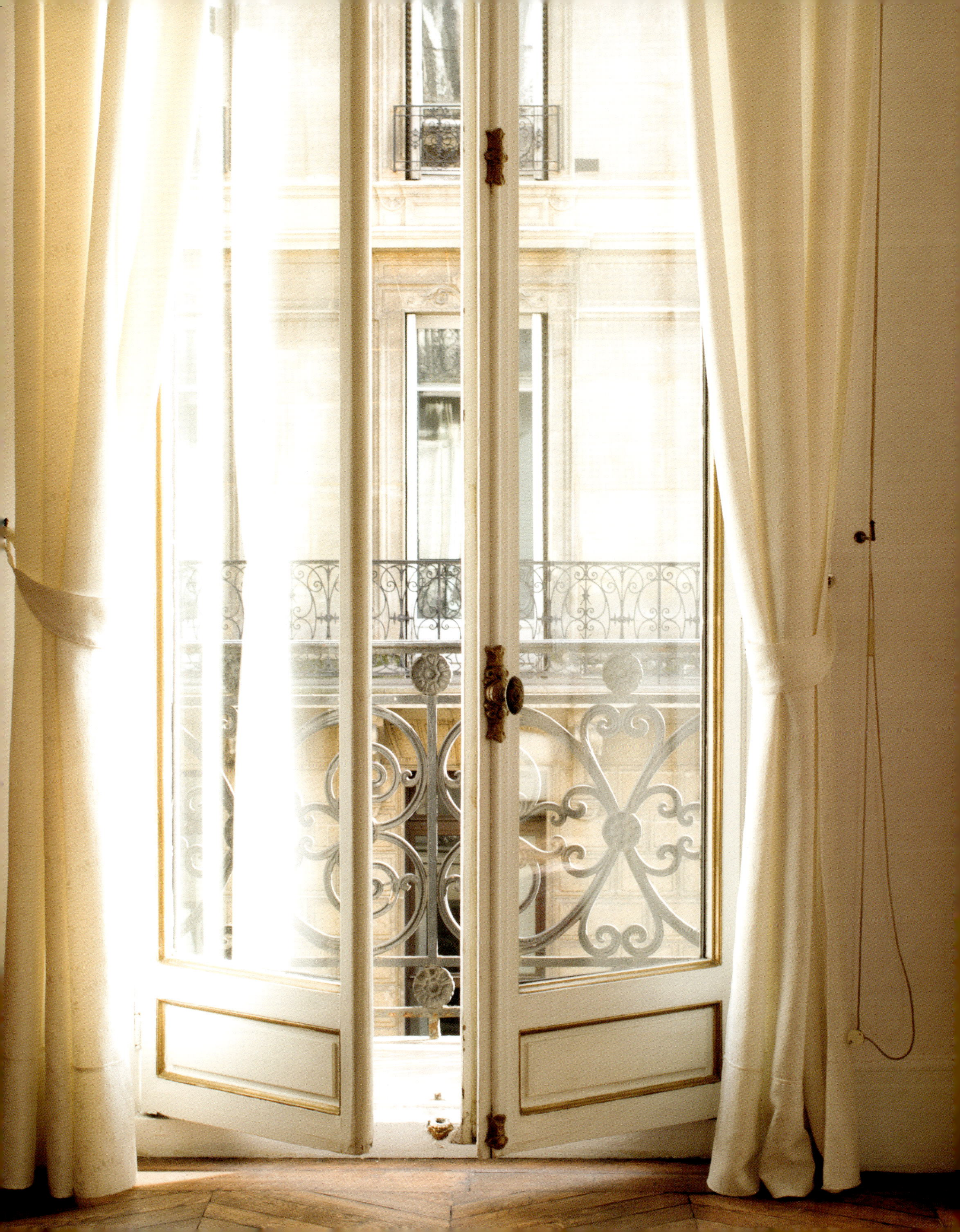

joyeuses fêtes

Christmas in Paris is magical. Festive markets and decorative streetlights appear earlier each year, as the holiday season starts in late October. Twinkle lights illuminate Paris evenings with greetings, such as *Joyeuses Fêtes* (Happy Holidays)! Visit the major department stores to see the enchanting interior décor and window displays. Galeries Lafayette and Le Bon Marché typically have elaborate scenes. During the holiday rush, visit the massive Christmas tree inside Galeries Lafayette. Each year, the tree has a different design, set against the backdrop of the iconic stained-glass ceiling in the flagship store.

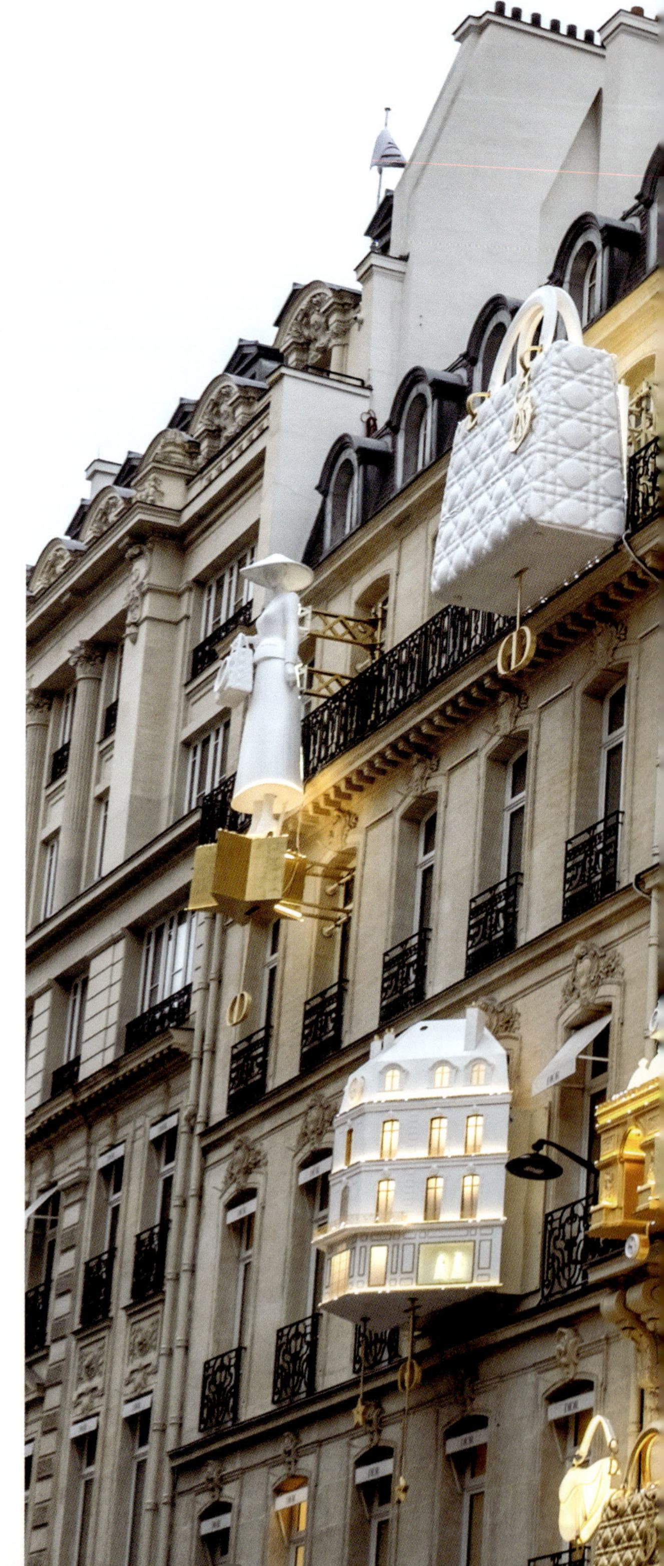

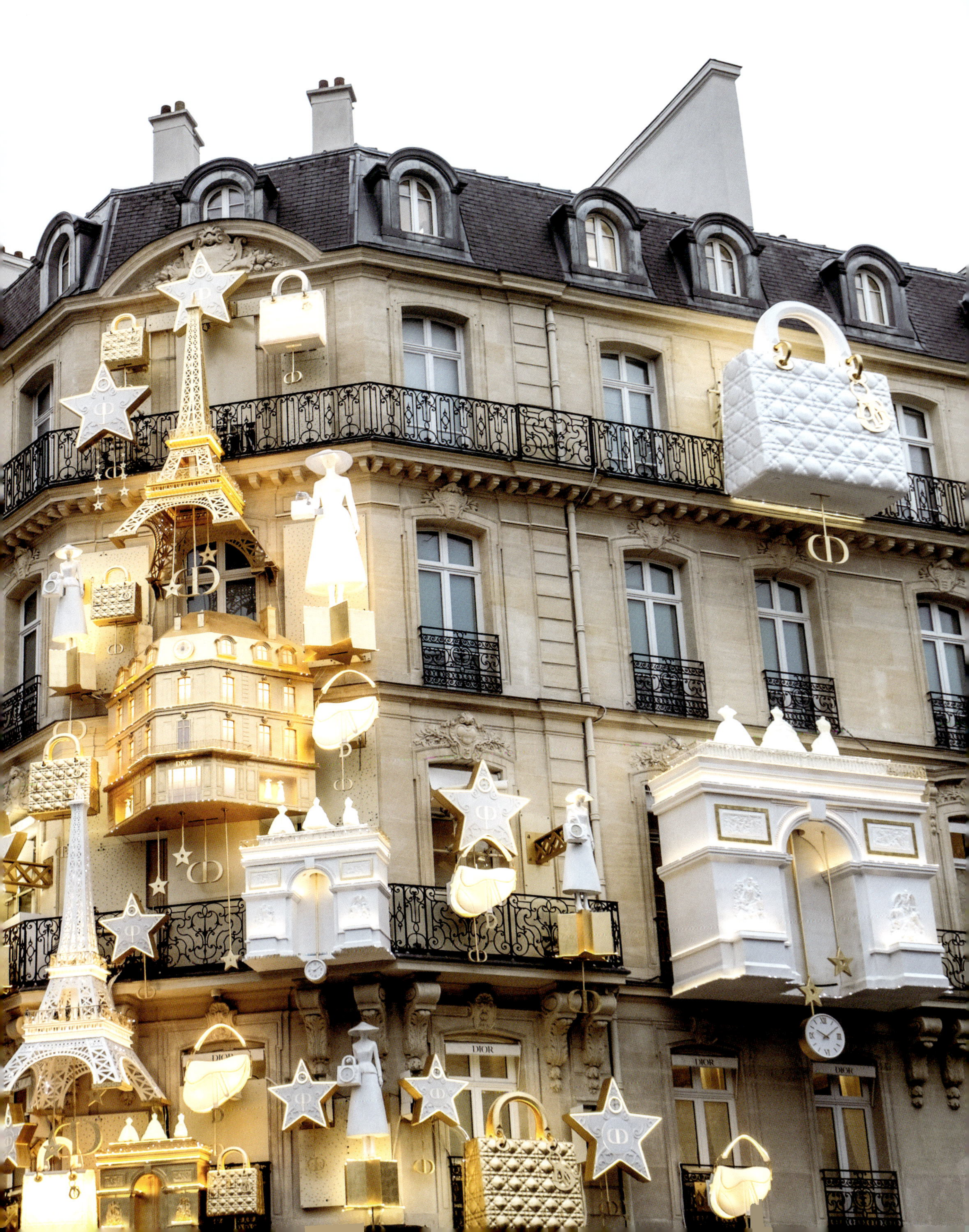
DIOR
DIOR
DIOR

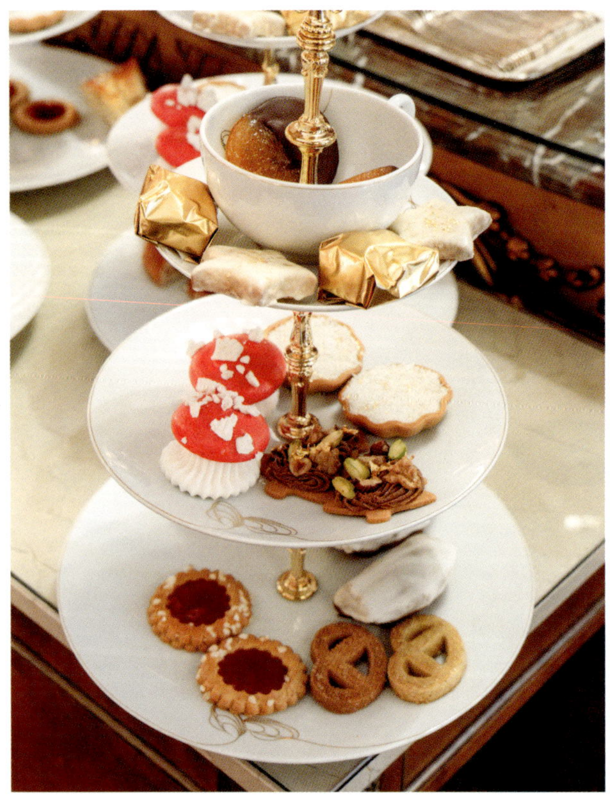

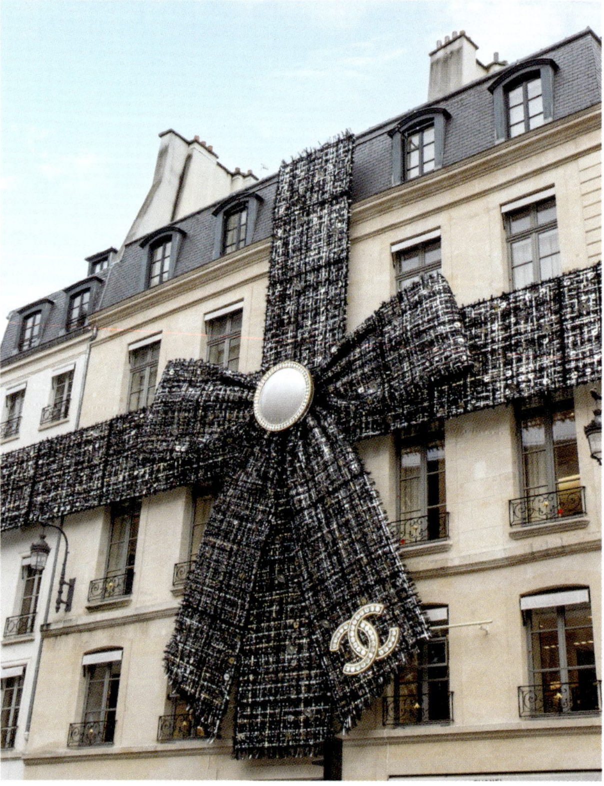

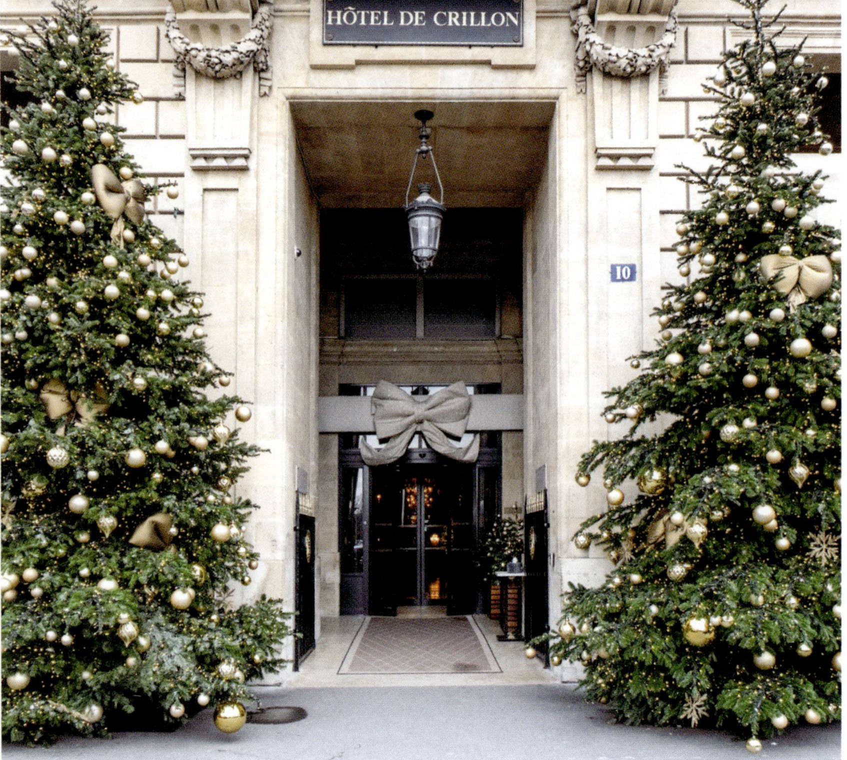

Book a Christmas teatime and dress up for an elevated afternoon experience. The Hôtel Plaza Athénée, the Ritz Paris, and Hôtel de Crillon all offer wonderful holiday teatime options, but they book early, so be sure to make your reservation well ahead of time. You can stroll through the lobbies and relish the holiday finery Parisian hotels have to offer.

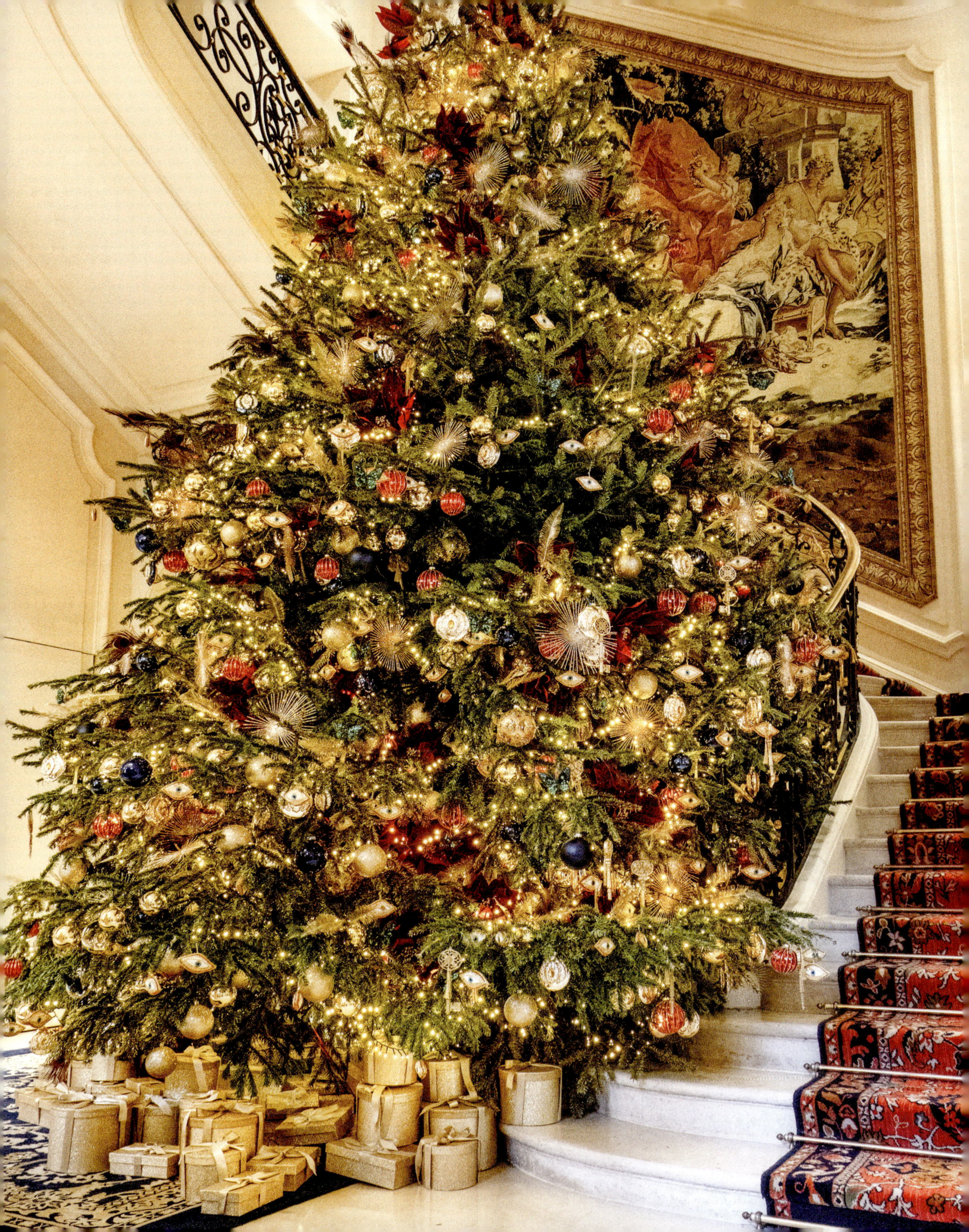

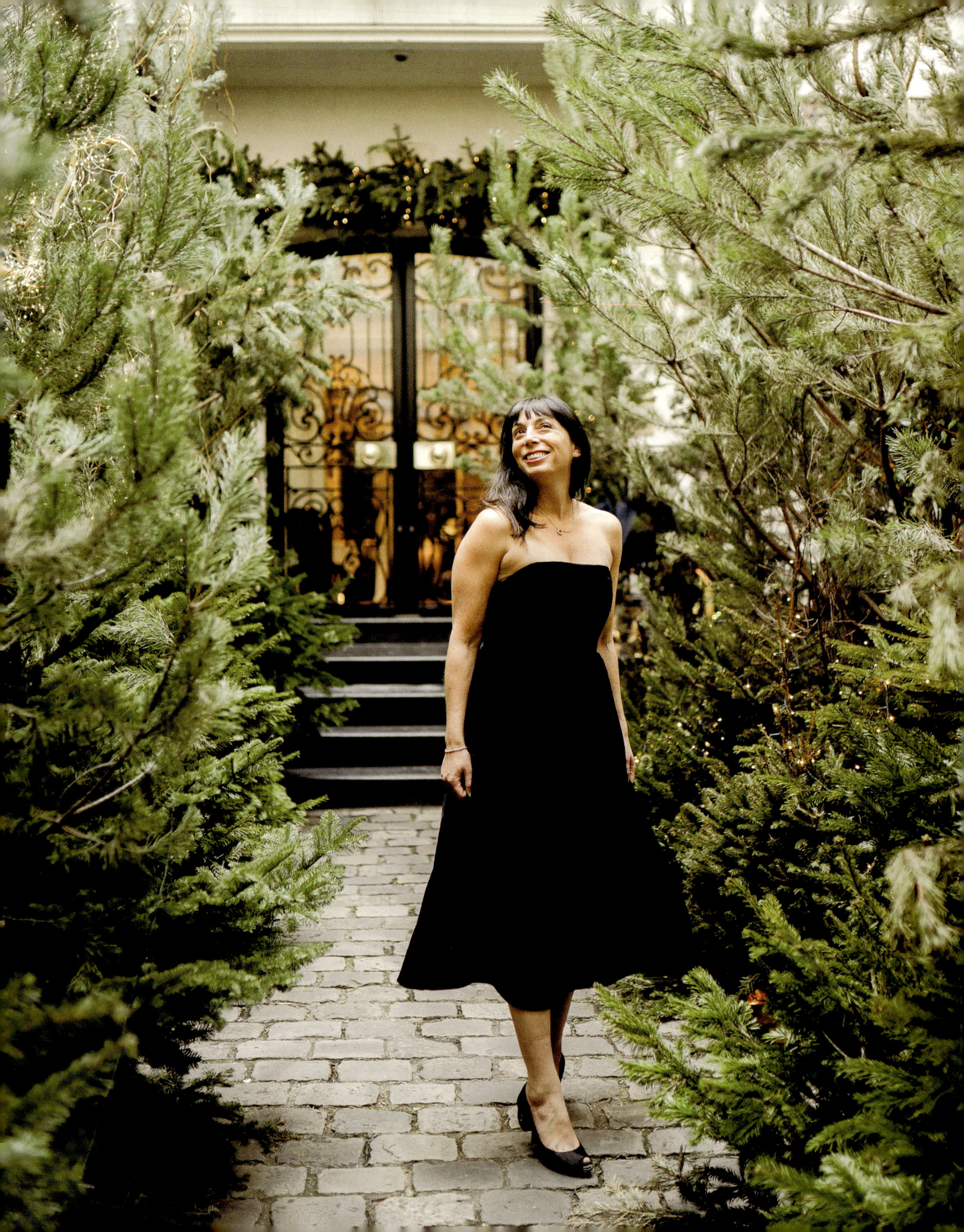

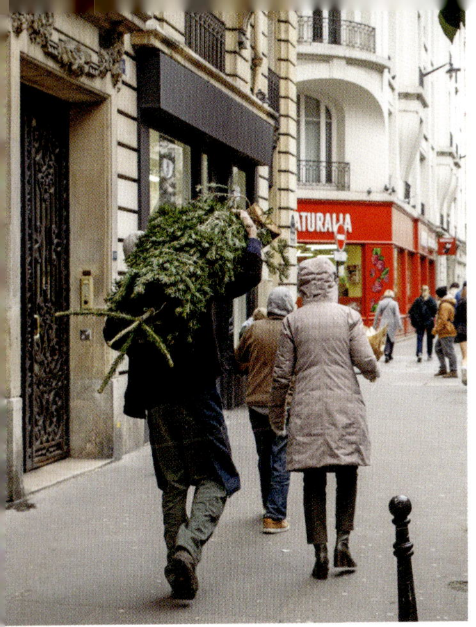

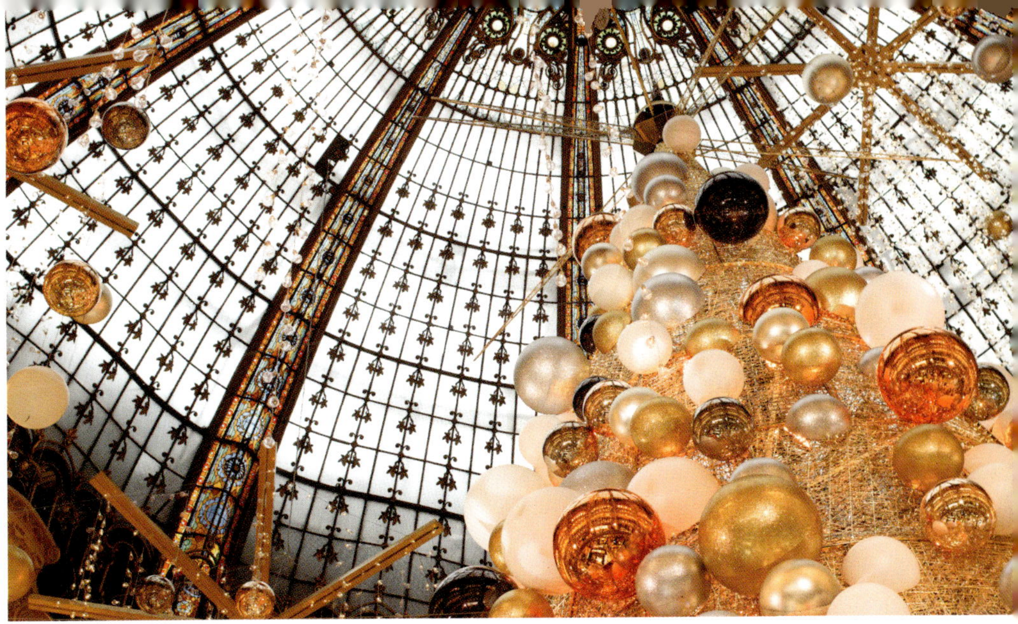

Hot chocolate is a great way to warm up in Paris on a cold winter day. Visit Carette or Angelina for a classic hot chocolate with whipped cream. PLAQ Chocolat on Rue du Nil is a boutique chocolatier offering hot chocolate and is one of my personal favorites.

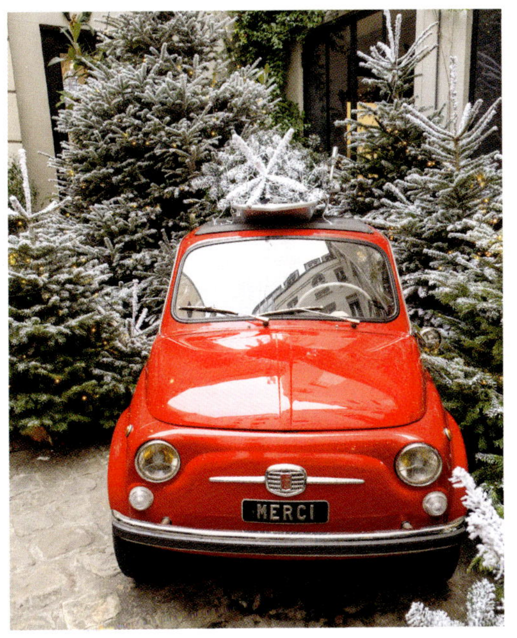

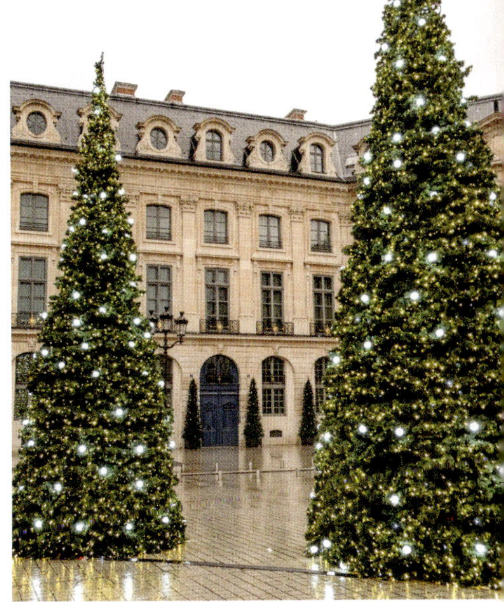

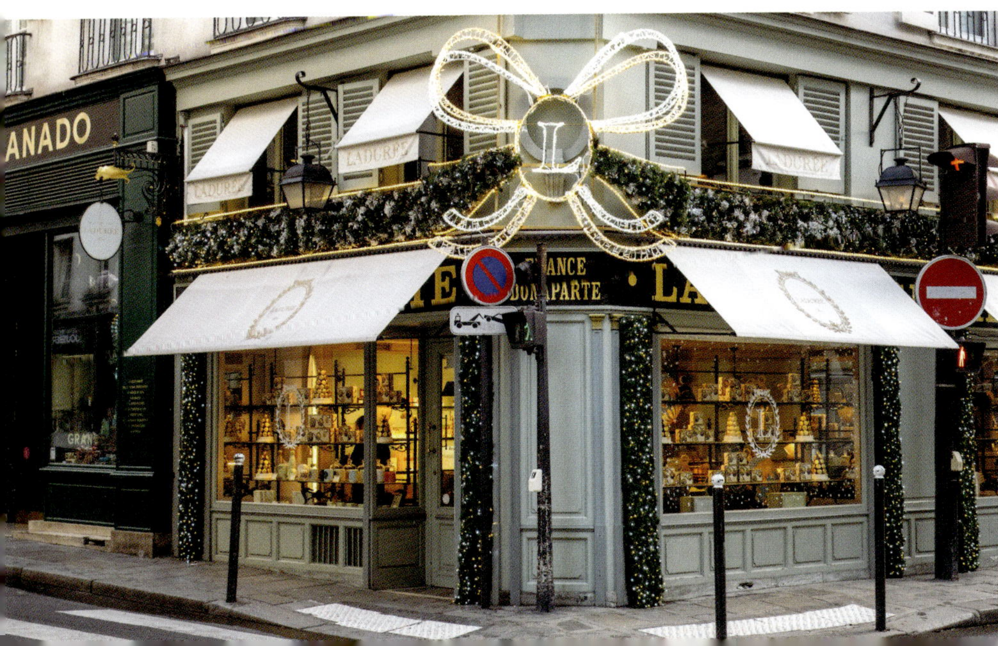

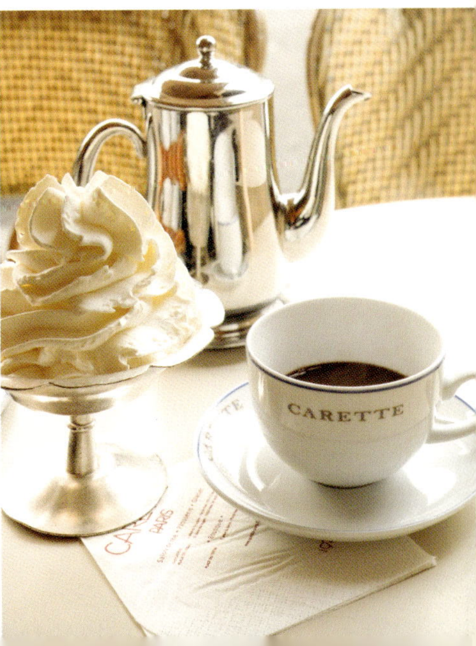

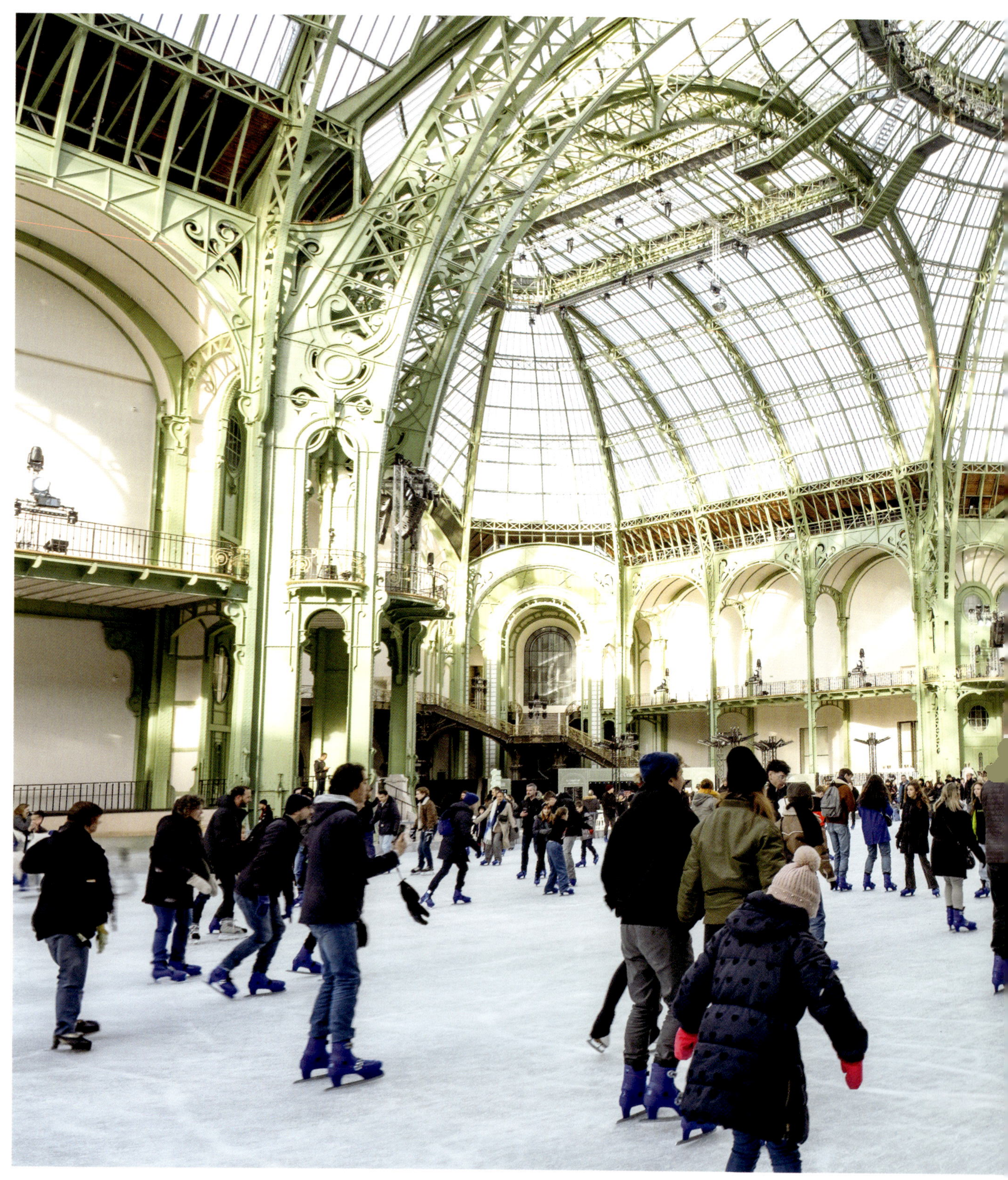

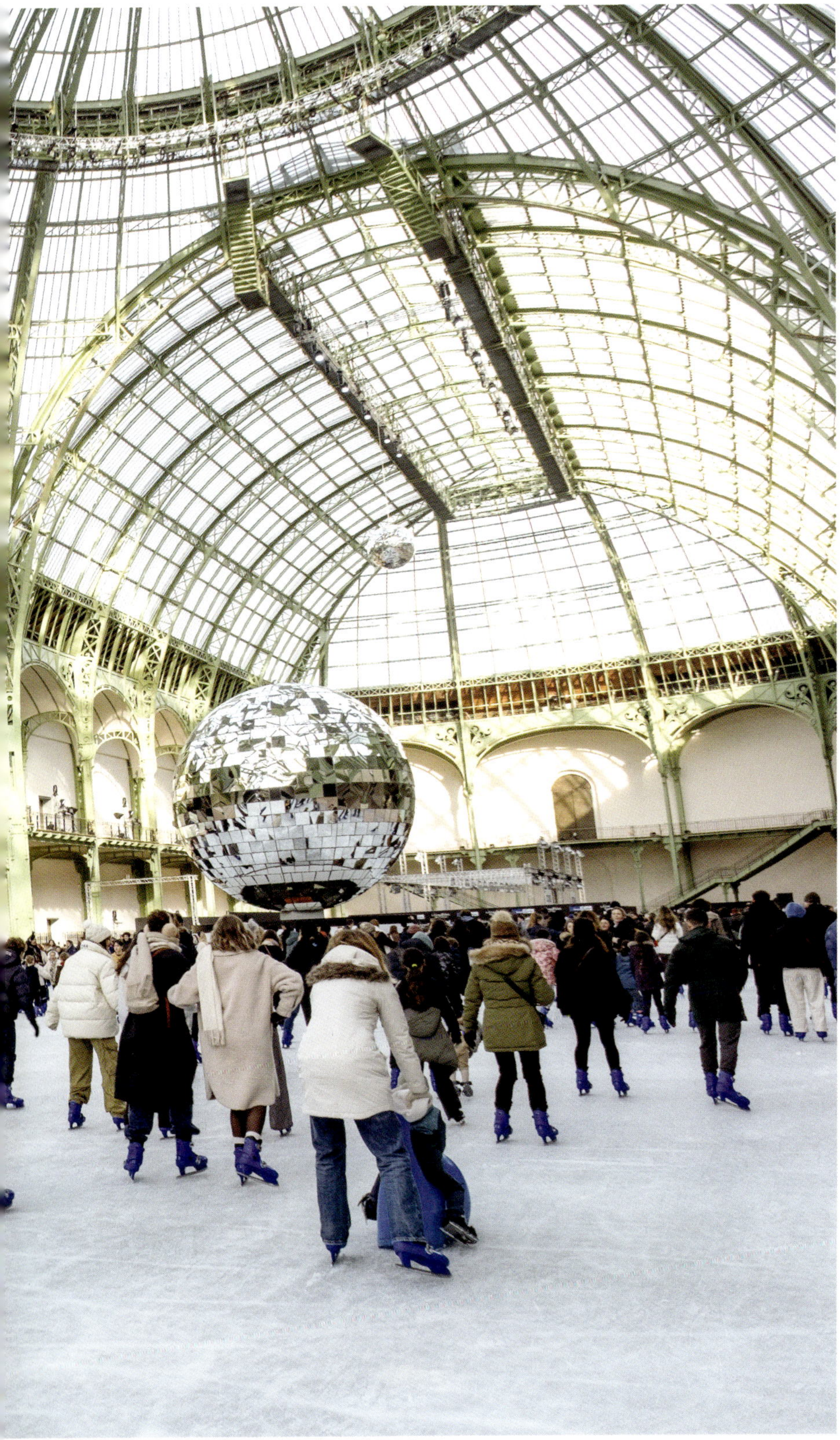

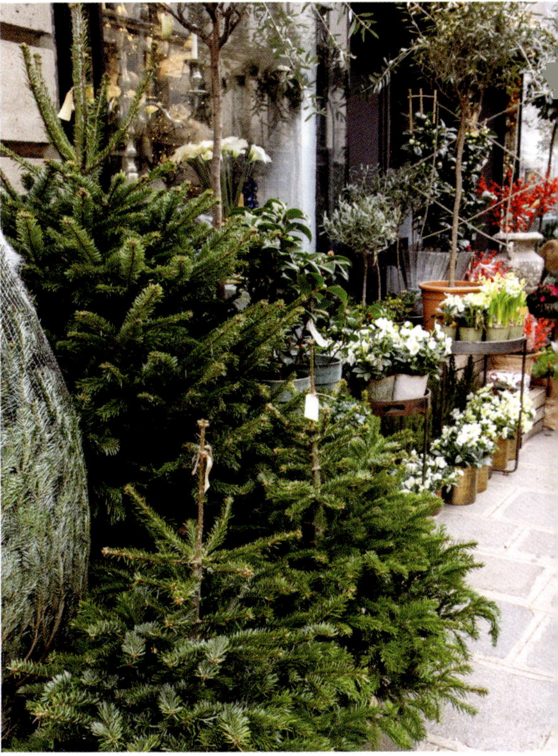

Don't miss ice-skating in Paris during the holidays. Grand Palais recently reopened and offers a family-friendly skating experience during the day and a lively disco vibe in the evening. Florists line the streets outside their shops with Christmas trees of various sizes, bringing the scent of pine to the city in December. Paris is filled with special scents. Nothing is more iconic than the aroma of a boulangerie baking fresh goods. Boulangeries pump out the air to entice customers. I wish I could bottle it up to share year-round.

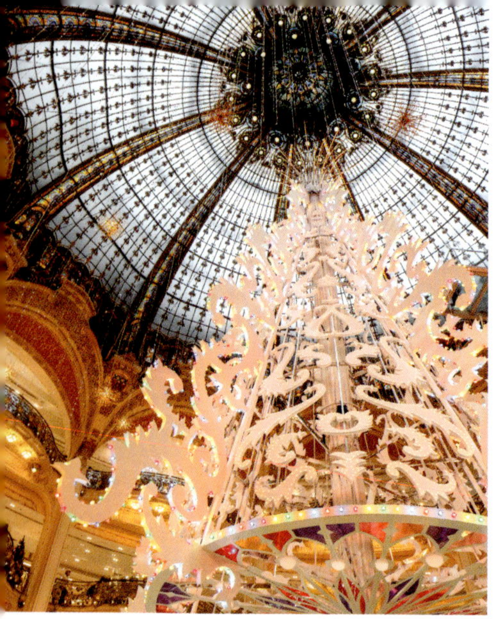

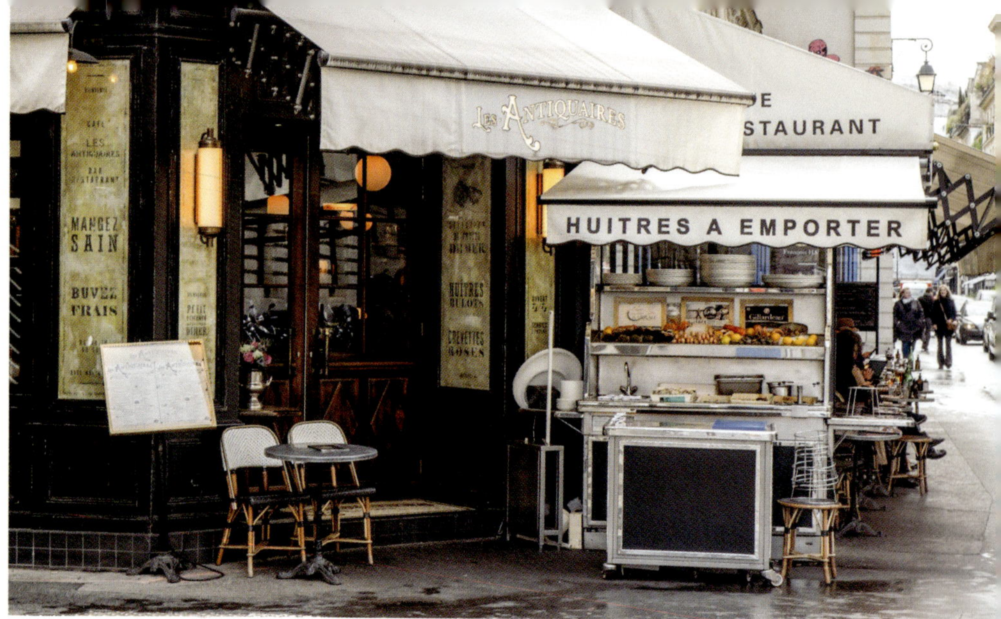

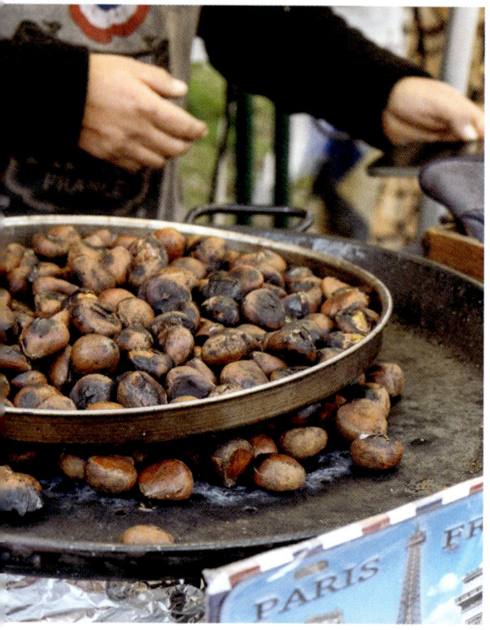

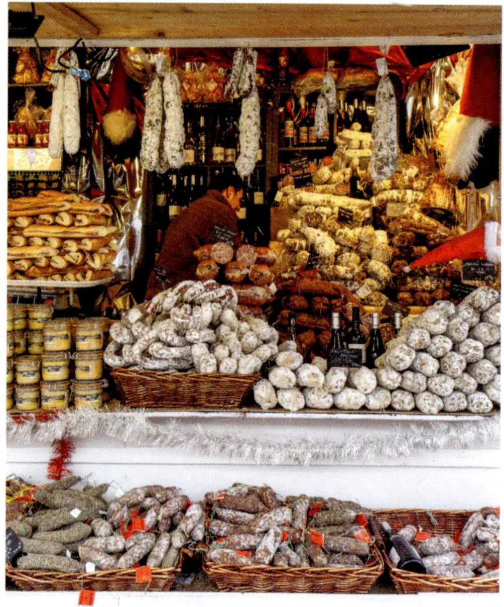

Enjoy the holiday markets set up around the city. In addition to small gifts and delightful crafts, you will find a variety of foods, including roasted chestnuts, truffled cheeses, foie gras, oysters, and wine. The classic Yule log cake, or Bûche de Noël, is served in various flavors and unique ways at pâtisseries. Buy Christmas chocolates from Pierre Hermé, La Maison du Chocolat, and À la Mère de Famille. These make great gift items and souvenirs. Chestnut is a popular dessert flavor, and you can find it offered at different pâtisseries. Traditional marrons glacés is a candied chestnut soaked in sugar and vanilla syrup and enrobed in a sugar glaze. Look for the small gold foil-wrapped candy.

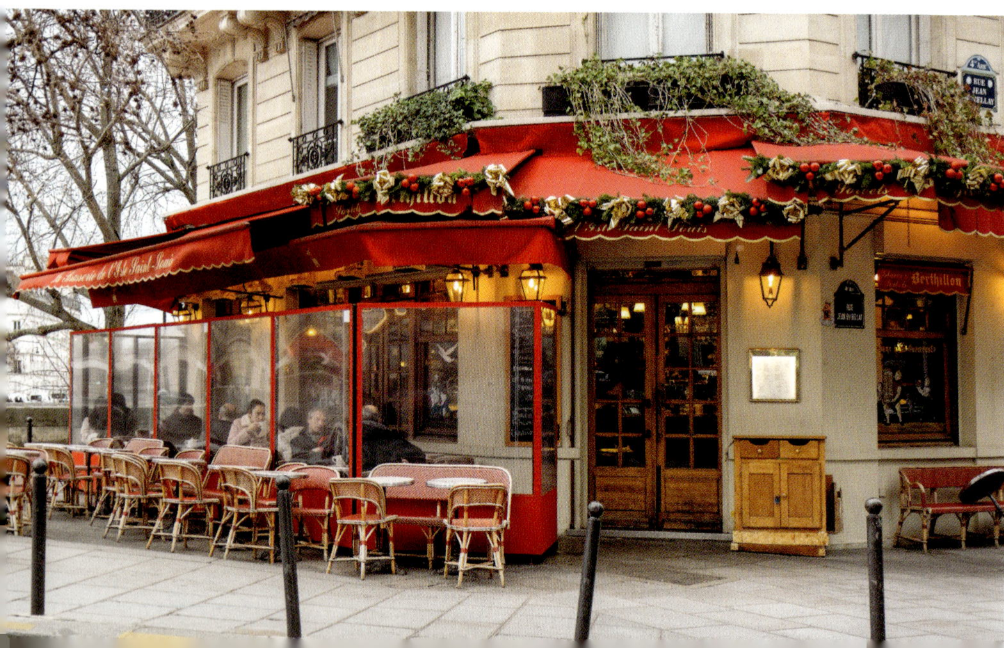

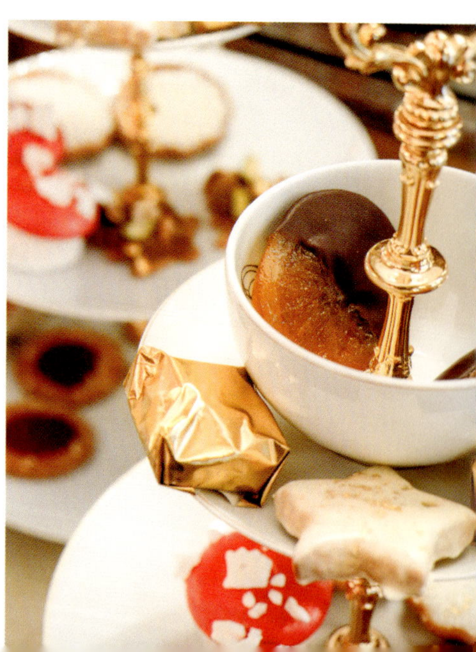

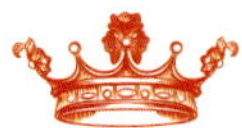

SCENTS BY THE SEASON

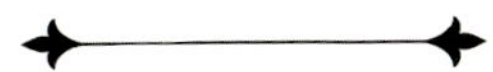

Paris has unique aromas throughout the year, often depending on what is in bloom. Scents spark memories and transport you back to a specific time and place. Think of your favorite time of year to visit Paris. What does it smell like? Often, a certain fragrance conjures up memories of holidays past or a special occasion.

Here are a few key scents to identify each season in Paris:

Winter
- Mimosa flowers at the market
- Mulled wine, crêpes, and the melted cheese of raclette
- Citrus fruits
- A wood-burning fireplace and spiced teas
- At Christmas, the scents of pine and cinnamon

Spring
- The fragrance of peonies, chestnut trees, and wisteria
- Ripening strawberries at the market
- Fresh spring rain on a warm day

Summer
- Roses in bloom
- Lavender and linden blossoms
- The clean floral smell of jasmine in courtyards, doorways, and terraces

Autumn
- Earth scents of oak and amber
- A wood fire burning outdoors
- Roasted chestnuts

Inevitable Change

The city has changed so much since my first trip to Paris in 2010. Classic French bistros have slowly faded, and some of my favorite small streets have been filled with chains that steal the charm. Craft coffee spots, once rare, now offer beans imported from around the world and include burgers on their menu. The city's food scene is constantly changing, and American influence is felt. Parisians are increasingly interested in American culture, just as Americans are in love with anything French. The cultures are sharing and blending.

Expats

A new wave of Americans will always move to Paris. This wave is very transient, with people coming and going every few years. The American expatriates develop a circle of adopted families, creating a special bond. During my two years of back-and-forth visits, I formed friendships that are still strong. Since those years, each return trip is filled with coffee dates, park visits, and extended terrace time catching up with friends. Over the last 15 years, I have been able to turn a passion for photography and my love for the city of Paris into something wonderful. I hope you enjoy seeing Paris through my lens season by season. Every person has their own unique experience and favorite memories of Paris. Use this book as a guide to make it your own.

Why Paris?

The common question I am asked is: "What makes you return to Paris year after year?"

Paris is a love affair. My time in Paris has always been long enough but not too long. My stays are short enough to miss Paris when I'm away. The city has fueled my creativity and business for the last 15 years. I dream of putting down roots in France with my husband and dog, Henri. I would like a place where we can live like locals, make long-term friendships, and practice speaking French daily.

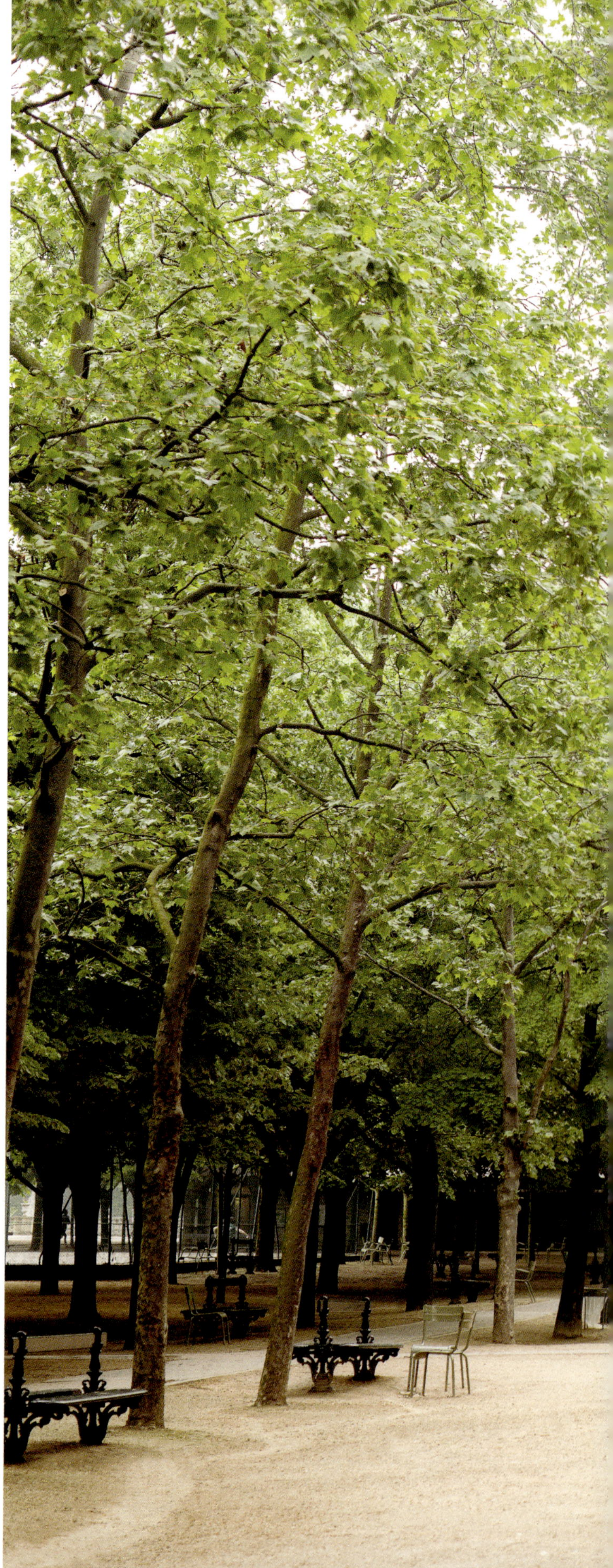

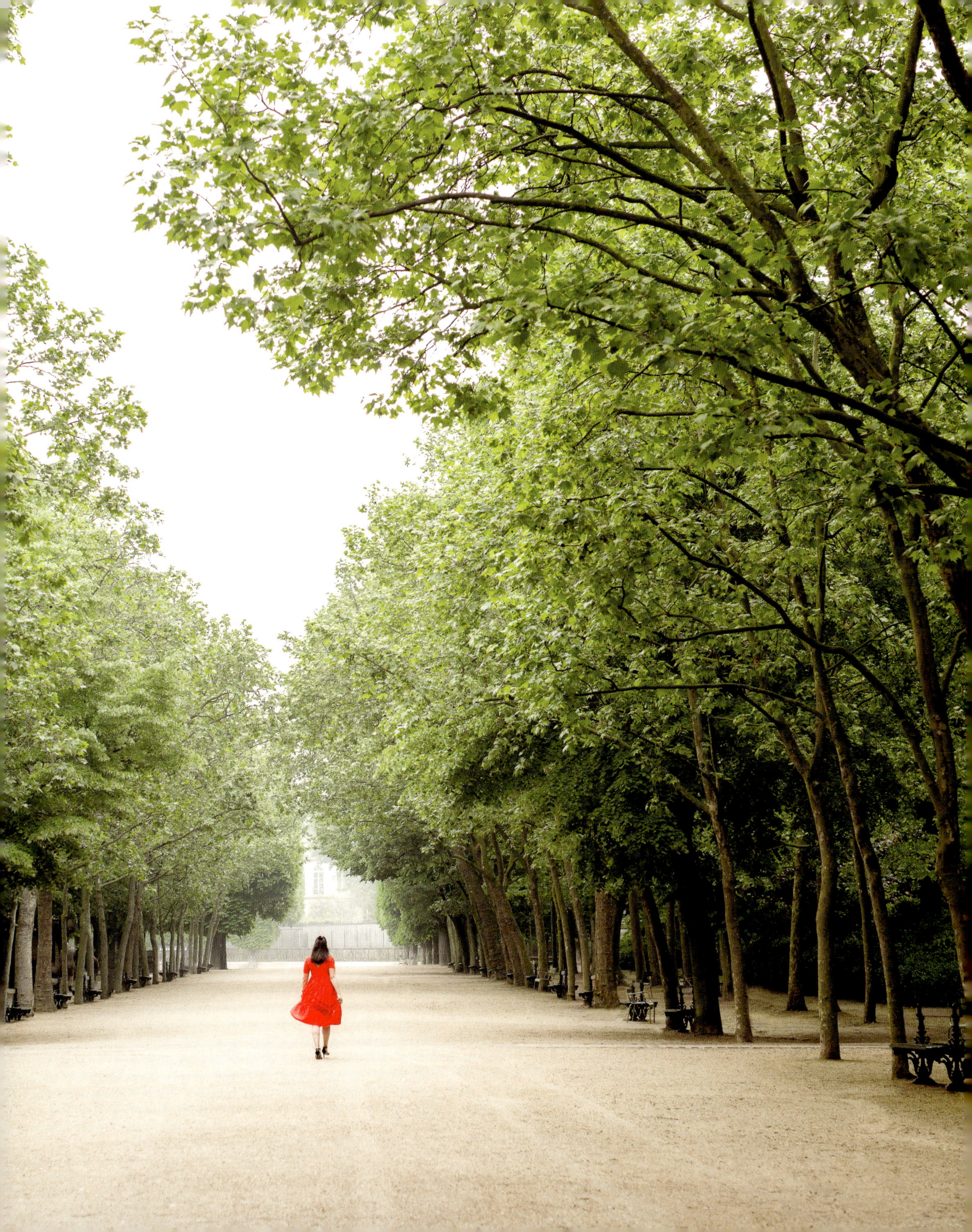

acknowledgments

Thank you to Katie Donnelly, my talented photographer and close friend. When we met 10 years ago, I was known for always being behind the camera and never in front. You offered to do a photo shoot with me, which sparked a friendship. I will always be grateful to you for capturing years of special memories in Paris. From my husband's proposal at Palais-Royal to the gorgeous photographs on the front and back cover of this book, *Paris Every Day*, you have been by my side, cheering me on in every chapter of life.

My wonderful parents have always supported my creativity, passion for travel, and stubbornness to go at my own pace and path through life. I love you both.

To my incredible sister and best friend, you have always been my rock and my first phone call to share news, including this book. I am grateful for your support, love, and enthusiasm for everything I do.

To my husband, thank you for encouraging me to chase my dreams. You push me to think bigger than I ever thought was possible. Our weekend coffee walks with Henri are my favorite and have sparked many creative ideas over the years.

Brooke Bell and Brian Hart Hoffman, you are the dream team. You took a big chance on me, and I am so grateful to both of you. Thanks to the two of you, the book I have always wanted to publish is better than I ever imagined it would be.

A special thank you to my incredible editor, Marie Baxley. It has been an absolute joy to work with you on this book. You polished my vision and words into a book that I am deeply proud of. I can't thank you enough, and I hope we can create another book together.

To Karissa Brown, Kristy Harrison, and the whole Hoffman Media team, thank you for your patience and passion in bringing this book to life.

Jane Bertch, thank you for your support and encouragement from the beginning. Our friendship has covered many life chapters, filled with much laughter. I can't thank you enough for introducing me to Brooke and Brian.

Allyssa Wallen, you have been an incredible addition to *Everyday Parisian* since day one. Your hard work, encouragement, creativity, and organizational skills have allowed my business to flourish during the pandemic and the years following. Thank you for "all things EDP" and beyond! Together, we wrote the best book outline that became the framework for *Paris Every Day*.

Kat Siegel, thank you for enthusiastically answering every late-night text and email. I met you at the beginning of *Every Day Parisian*, and you have cheered me on through every failure, roadblock, and win in business and life.

Tam Hennessy, you have known my dream of a book since we met. Thank you for your encouragement in every life chapter. Our holiday celebrations have always included a brainstorming session on a book title and ideas. She is finally here and well worth the wait! I can't wait to toast in December to our friendship and the extraordinary lives we have both built.

To my "Paris Family," I am happy our shared passion for Paris aligned with the first move many years ago. I will always cherish our long meals, neighborhood walks, and visits. Your support and encouragement have helped me flourish. We miss you in Chicago and always look forward to seeing you in Paris.

My sweet baby boy, Henri! Thank you for your unconditional love, companionship, and patience. Now that this book is complete, I owe you a walk, a Sunday nap, and a croissant. I am so happy you are a part of my life and bring me so much joy every day.

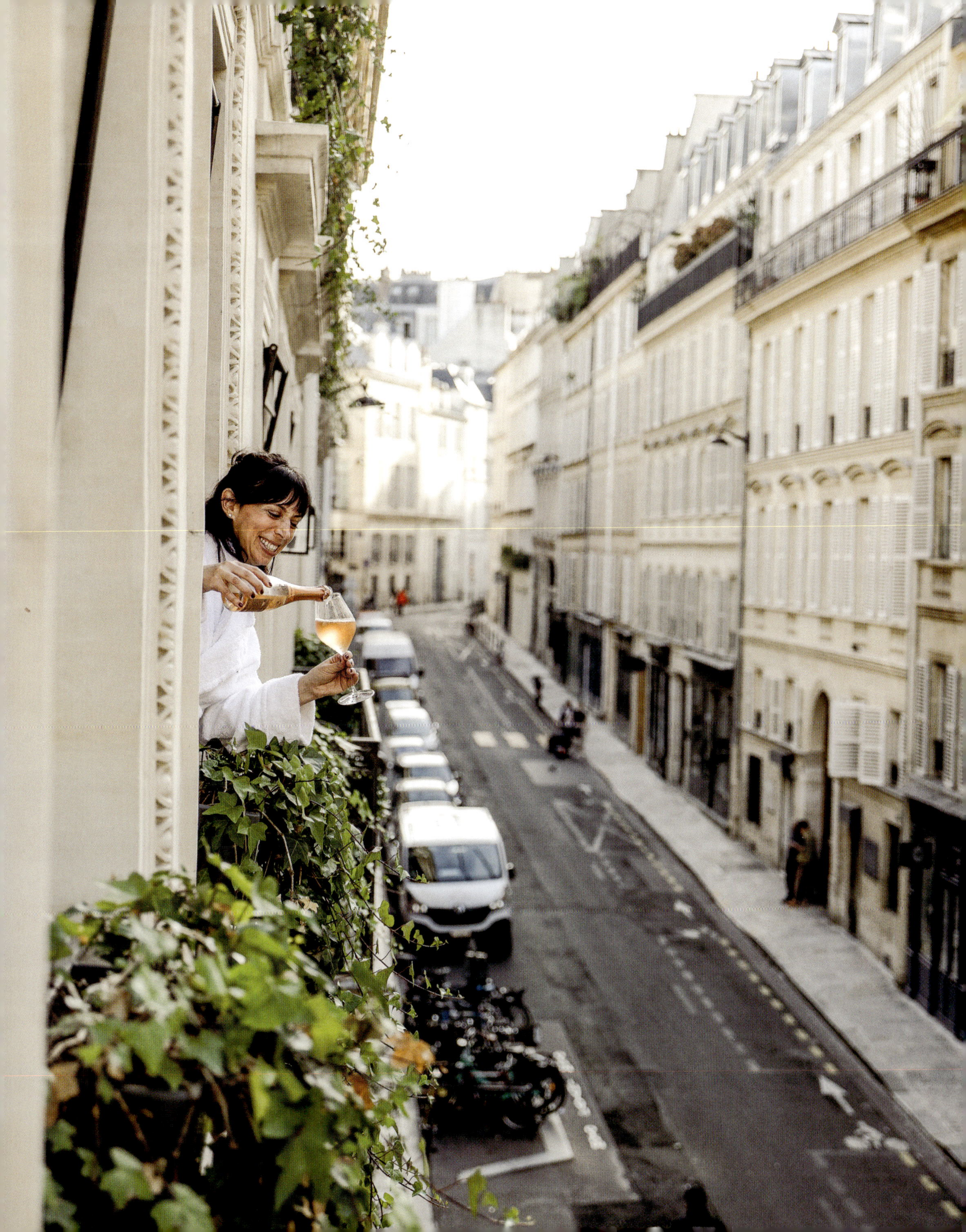

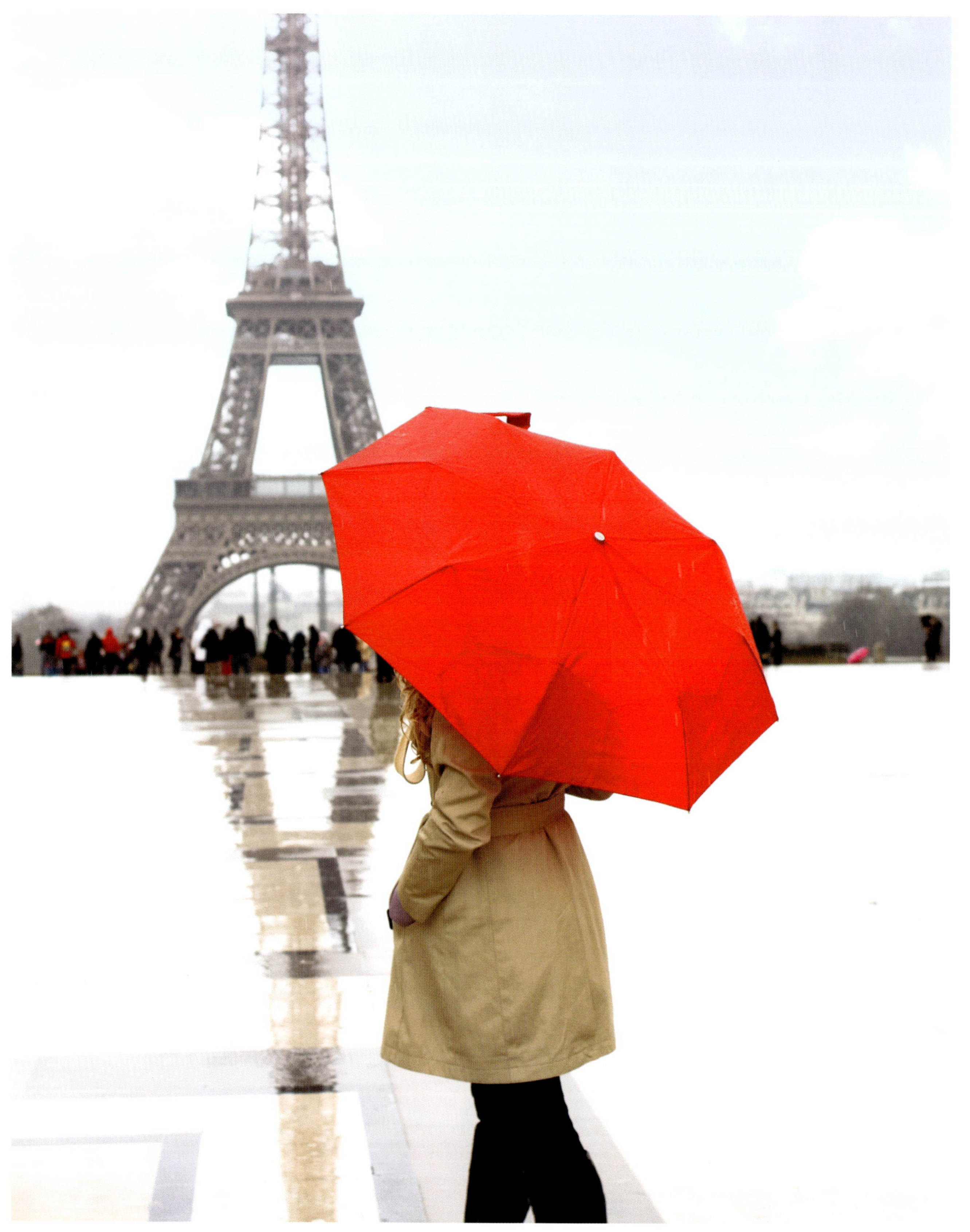